ALEX WESTWATER'S
LOCHGELLY

History, especially local history, can all too easily be lost if active steps are not taken to preserve it and pass it on. A community can lose its identity by losing sight of its origins and history. It was with these thoughts that the Alexander Westwater Memorial Trust was established in the summer of 1994. The aim of the Trust is to promote understanding of the heritage, history and culture of Lochgelly and the surrounding area, and by so doing, the Trust hopes both to commemorate and to carry on Alex Westwater's work.

The Trustees are pleased to bring out this book, which contains much of what Alex Westwater wrote about Lochgelly. The text of five booklets has been reproduced as originally published, save that the opportunity has been taken to correct some typographical errors. The same is true of the account of the Burgh of Lochgelly, which appeared in the Third Statistical Account of Scotland. The chapter "Danders around Lochgelly" has been compiled from the text of various talks given at different dates, and here some editing has been felt appropriate.

First published November 1994 by Alexander Westwater Memorial Trust
Designed, typeset, produced and printed by Barr Printers Glenrothes Limited.

ISBN 0 9524723 0 9

Price £7.95

CONTENTS

On the cover: Centre: Alex Westwater; Top Left: Co-operative Fleshing Department (Original Store); Top Right: Lochgelly Town House (Built May 1909); Bottom Left: Parish Church (St Andrews) in Bank Street, Lochgelly; Bottom Right: Lochgelly Public Park (circa 1924).

INTRODUCTION

"Mining communities are generally looked upon as of mushroom growth, but not so Lochgelly. As a settlement it has a long pedigree. It is a place with a history, a parochial history certainly, but it is through that mainly that traditions are formed.
It is a story of toil, progress, culture and character, and surely there can be no finer traditions than these."

Alexander Westwater, J.P., F.J.I., F.S.A.(Scot.), was born in Bank Street, Lochgelly, in 1875, and died in 1960. By profession he was a journalist, editor and publisher of the **Lochgelly Times** and **Cowdenbeath Advertiser**, carrying on the family business of John Westwater and Son, printers, publishers, and stationers, founded by his father. By enthusiasm, he was an antiquary and historian, poring over old records and walking the ground to learn more about his home town and its surrounding area; realising that he lived in a time of rapid social, economic, and cultural change, he knew that the past had to be captured and preserved before it was lost from memory. He was a keen sportsman, helping to establish or run golf, bowling, football, cricket, cycling, and curling clubs in the town. He was a committed church member. He gave "a lifetime of service, there being scarcely an association or organisation he had not been connected with at some time or other" – the Rotary Club, the Ex-Servicemen's Club, the British Legion , Lodge Minto 385, Benarty Antiquarian Club, the Musical Association, the Horticultural Society. He was appointed a Justice of the Peace in 1921, served on Lochgelly Town Council from 1929 to 1938, and was for twenty years a member of Fife County Council's Education Committee.

In September 1951, Alex Westwater was invested by Lochgelly Town Council as their first Honorary Burgess – this was believed to be a unique occasion, the first time such an honour had been conferred by a Police Burgh (as opposed to a Royal Burgh) in Scotland. Accepting the burgess ticket, he confessed that one of his early (but unfulfilled) ambitions had been to become Provost: but the distinction now bestowed on him far surpassed even the honour of being Provost. "Apart from the personal aspect of this honour, I have reason to be proud to belong to the town that has conferred it. I don't think

there is a purely mining community in Scotland with such long and honourable traditions, or a better community to live in."

Alex Westwater was born two years before Lochgelly became a Burgh, in
1877, and died fifteen years before that Burgh lost its independent
existence in the re-organisation of local government. His life, therefore, runs
parallel to the life of the Burgh he lived in, loved, and served. But, unlike
other mining communities, Lochgelly was much more than a "new town", an
instant creation of nineteenth-century industrialisation. The first mention of
Lochgelly itself dates back to 1485, and the original hamlet grew to a village,
then to a town: in 1790, the population was some 342 persons, mainly
engaged in farming and weaving: by 1845, it had risen to 612 – and by 1877,
when the Burgh was formed, to a little under 2,000 people. By the 1870s, the
Westwaters were already a long-established family in the town.

This rapid increase in population resulted from mid-Victorian industrial
growth – the more systematic and scientific exploitation of the local deposits
of ironstone and coal (the Jenny Gray pit started operations in 1854), the coming of the railway. Industrial changes were paralleled by social developments
– the provision of new housing; the formation of the Lochgelly Equitable Co-
operative Society in 1864, the building of churches – the two present Church
of Scotland congregations, St Andrews and Macainsh, both use buildings
erected in the 1850s, the first for the Established Church, the other for the Free
Church – and of schools; the organisation of clubs and associations, social and
benevolent, charitable, recreational and sporting.

Alex Westwater grew up to know older men and women, men and women
who had been in at the start of the industrial and social development, who
could describe the changes they had witnessed or helped bring about, who
knew themselves or had heard from their parents of the past Lochgelly, a village of weavers, surrounded by moors with permanent gypsy encampments.
His town, its history and traditions, and those of the surrounding area, became
his life's interest, and he started to research and record, and to pass on his
knowledge by way of articles and talks – and, when a Lochgelly institution
came to celebrate a centenary or other significant anniversary, who better to
describe its origins and progress than Alex Westwater?

<u>JENNY GRAY PIT – A HUNDRED YEARS' WORKING</u>

History of the Early Lochgelly Coalfield

Story of Lochgelly Village in 1854

with Maps

A MEMENTO OF A NOTABLE
MINING CENTENARY

LOCHGELLY 1954

Printed and Published by John Westwater & Son, "Lochgelly and District Times" Office

JENNY GRAY CENTENARY COMMITTEE
– 1954 –

President : Mr DEMPSTER SMITH
Vice President : Mr JAMES RAEBURN
Secretary : Mr JOHN MILNE
Treasurer : Mr WILLIAM KINNELL

Members of Committee:

Mr THOMAS NEALON
Mr PETER BAIRD
Mr JAMES JOHNSTONE
Mr MICHAEL COOK
Mr HENRY CONWAY
Mr PETER WEBSTER
Mr JAMES HUNTER
Mr JAMES STIVEN
Mr ANDREW HARROWER
Mr DANIEL BEATTON

FOREWORD

It was originally intended to issue a small Brochure to commemorate the Jenny Gray Centenary.

The occasion was, however, opportune for a broader story of the town in the most important period of its transition and development.

We hope our researches in local history in permanent form will be of present interest and future value.

The first part deals specially with its mining story, and the second part is memoranda of the village a hundred years ago.

PETER W. BROWN
ALEXANDER WESTWATER

PREFACE

This little booklet is intended to be a Souvenir of the Centenary of Jenny Gray Colliery. Its object is to make known, and place on record, some interesting facts and figures relating to the town of Lochgelly, and, in particular, to Jenny Gray Colliery.

The Centenary Committee are to be congratulated on the choice of authors – Mr A. Westwater, J.P., F.J.I., F.S.A.Scot., and Mr P. W. Brown, F.S.A.Scot. They have produced a wealth of information in brief form. They have traced the transition and development of Lochgelly from a small hamlet to a prosperous and progressive town. The industrial portion contains much information that will prove of great interest, not only to technical men, but also to the community as a whole.

We wish to record our grateful thanks to the authors for a job well done.

GEORGE MULLIN,
Area General Manager,
West Fife Area,
National Coal Board

Contents

ILLUSTRATIONS

Plan of Lochgelly early Pits

Plan of Lochgelly Village, 1854

Jenny Gray Pit, 1954

Andrew Landale, General Manager in 1854

Iron Company School

Coal Hutch or Tub

The Auld Stane Well

HISTORY OF COAL MINING IN LOCHGELLY

By PETER W. BROWN, F.S.A.SCOT., Area Chief Planner for N.C.B., West Fife Area.

It has afforded me much pleasure in preparing the following notes for the Jenny Gray "Centenary Book".

In addition to my local acquaintance with the coalfield, I have to acknowledge the help I got from old records, and from the Minute Books of Lochgelly Iron and Coal Company Ltd. The research has added to my personal knowledge; it has been interesting and informative. I now hope my research will interest the readers of this booklet, and be handed down as a brief record.

PETER W. BROWN

LOCHGELLY PITS IN 1854

The first Government Survey Map of Lochgelly district was printed in 1854 (exactly 100 years ago).

From this map a picture of the dwellings, coal shafts, and enclosures can be got and when compared with the present day position it is shown that considerable changes have taken place down the century which we are now celebrating.

Even in 1854 there was, relatively speaking, considerable industrial activity in the area.

Splashed across the map (herewith reproduced) there are the words:– LOCHGELLY COLLIERY, embracing all the then known working and abandoned shafts. A few of the old shafts indicated on the map are shown as working Ironstone.

As has been stated elsewhere in this brochure, there was a Lochgelly hamlet or village many centuries before the period of 1854 and where mining operations had been carried out, but there is very little written or plan records preserved. Such workings would, of course, be very limited in extent and of a primitive nature, and long before legislation made it necessary for mining plans and records to be preserved and the underground workings to be surveyed. The little that one can glean of the past is from searching of private papers and other archives.

JENNY GRAY 1854–1954.

Etymologists have long been puzzled by the name:– JENNY GRAY. The name of many collieries in this district commemorates one of the owners, their wives, or even a member of the landowner's family, such as Arthur, Nellie, Minto, Melgund, Dora, etc. It has been difficult to trace the reason for such a double name as Jenny Gray. The name, we think, is not derived from any former owner, nor it is connected with any member of the Minto family. A field nearby is known as Jenny Gray's Park, and we suggest that the Colliery has derived its name from an old lady who perhaps owned a croft hereabout.

On the map of 1854 some of the present shafts at Jenny Gray are shown and also the "Tram Road" connection to the main railway line. At the east end of Plantation Street, in what was known as Berry Plantation or Park (now Public Park), are the sites of two old shafts. One, the Bye Pit to Lochgelly Splint, was coupled to Jenny Gray by a surface tramway. Presumably the coal was screened from this Bye Pit at the Jenny Gray plant.

During the century under review there have been five shafts at the present Jenny Gray fitting as follows:– No. 1 Pit situated to east of Boilers still used as a ventilation and pumping shaft. No. 2 Pit presently in use and No. 3 Pit in use for winding coal. There were, in addition, other two shafts to the Little Splint seam. The winding shaft of the two to the Little Splint was situated between the present Nos. 1 and 2, while the other shaft was in front of the present manager's office. As stated, these shafts worked the Little Splint seam sometime about 1868.

THE EARLIEST WORKING

The earliest recorded working of coal at the Jenny Gray seems to have been in the Lochgelly Splint. As can be appreciated, only working to the "Rise" of the shaft was carried out. The workings in this seam extended round to the east of Lochgelly House and to the "Waste" of the Bye Pit at Plantation Street. The workings from the Bye Pit contacted still older workings, of which there were no records, and in which an old wooden shovel was found (now in Pittencrieff

Museum).

At various times the following coal seams have been operated:–

Little Splint

Seven Foot (Rough Coal)

Fourteen Foot (Top)

Fourteen Foot (Bottom)

Lochgelly Splint

Lochgelly Parrot

Glassee

Mynheer

Five Foot

Dunfermline Splint

The first working to the dip was in the Five Foot seam. A steam driven haulage engine was placed on the surface, the ropes passing down the shaft. A rather novel system of stopping this engine was devised: to do so, a wire was led from the engine, down the shaft and along the haulage way. This wire was connected to the throttle of the engine and, exerting a pull on the wire, the engine was stopped. The pulling of the wire also blew a whistle which drew the attention of a pithead worker to stand by for starting the engine when required. This saved the expense of an engine attendant.

METHODS OF WORKING

Previous to about 1880 the method of working a coal seam was the driving of roads of from six to ten feet wide, according to the nature of the overlying roof, and connecting these roads at intervals of from ten to twenty feet, thus forming small pillars of coal called "stoops". In course of time the small pillars were robbed and only sufficient left to support the roof.

It was somewhat after 1880 that the Longwall System was introduced, a system in which a long breast of coal is extracted at one operation. A further development of this system is in vogue right up to the present.

Electric coal cutters have replaced the arduous task of the collier undercutting the seam with a pick. The evolution of transporting the coal along the roadways was from coal-bearers who carried the output on their backs, followed by slipes or sledges on which the coal was placed, by hutches on wheels hand pushed, to haulage by ponies, by haulage rope or electric locomotives. From carrying the coal up the shaft by means of ladders to horse gins, "steam or electric power operated" winding engines. The earliest form of winding ropes were made of hemp pleated to form a band of a suitable width. Electrically operated conveyors take the coal now from the miner and deliver it into hutches at a suitable loading point.

Before the introduction of coal washing plant and separating screens, the small coal was originally left underground and only the larger coal brought by the various means to the surface. This small coal was separated underground by means of a "Riddle" or by using a "Harp", an open shovel similar to a Graip. In course of time this small coal was reckoned to have a value and was filled into the hutches separately from the large coal and for which the miner received a less "Ton Rate".

With the advent of screening and washing plant all the coal was filled as one, called "triping".

Originally, to reduce the amount of small coal, the miner exercised great care, especially in bringing down the coal by the use of explosives. The earliest explosive used in the district was loose gunpowder made up at home into suitable paper cartridges, which were exploded by "home made squibs". The squibs were straw or paper tubes containing powder, made up at home. The powder was generally purchased from the grocer or ironmonger. It was in the use of this explosive that many miners suffered from the "Black Spit", a disease common in the early days of mining.

At the Jenny Gray and other early coal pits, ventilation was caused by heating the air in the upcast or ventilation shaft by means of a "Fire Bucket" suspended a few yards down the shaft: a development of this system was to have a furnace built underground at the bottom of the upcast shaft. By these means the air was heated and travelled upwards, causing fresh air to descend the winding shaft.

During the century there has been very little change in the design of hutch or tub used at Jenny Gray. The wheels are still of the "Biscuit" type and used on angle iron rails: only the height has been increased since the original.

PUMPING PLANT

The earliest method that we can record of dealing with water met with underground was by means of a shaft Cornish Pump worked by a steam engine on the surface; remains of this gear are still to be seen in No. 1 shaft.

About the year 1904/5 an underground steam driven Riedler Pump was installed, which still exists. Some time afterwards an electric operated turbine pump was fitted up in the pit bottom, and this is in service today, with the steam pump as a "stand by".

RAILWAY CONNECTION

As the site of the Jenny Gray is much higher than the main line, a self-acting wheel brae delivers the coal from the pit to the sidings along the main line. Formerly the wagons were taken from the colliery to the top of the incline by horses.

ELECTRIC POWER

Under the management of Mr. Nisbet the first electric power system was introduced in Jenny Gray to drive a Dook Pump about the year 1901. A 50 h.p. generator was fitted up on the surface.

ROOF SUPPORTS

Steel props and girders are now used to support the roof at the face and on the roadway and packs built of roof stone are built at right angles to the conveyor face. Formerly wood props and bars and wood pillars were the usual form of support.

MANAGERS ASSOCIATED WITH JENNY GRAY

Mr Henry Chisholm,	Mining Manager of the Company
Mr Symington Macdonald	do. do. do. do.
Mr N. Stevenson	do. do. do. do.
Mr John Anderson	do. do. do. do.
Mr Andrew Nisbet	do. do. do. do.
Mr John Paul	Agent and afterwards General Manager
Mr A. Ramsay	Deceased (first Pit Manager)
Mr W. Barclay	Deceased
Mr R. Stewart	Retired, living at Charlestown
Mr P. Henderson	who became General Manager (now retired)
Mr. L.R. Milligan, O.B.E.	who succeeded Mr Henderson as general manager
Mr R. Park	Deceased
Mr G. Marshall	Agent with Coal Board
Mr Wm. Speirs	Agent with Coal Board
Mr D. Davis	Now at Kinglassie
Mr D. Smith	Present Manager

Previous to Mr. Paul's appointment there were no managers of the individual pits. In the early part of the list, Mr Landale was what we would now designate General Manager. Mr Peter Henderson became General Mining

Manager of the Company. On his retiral he was succeeded by Mr L. R. Milligan, O.B.E.

MINING IN LOCHGELLY

The early history of mining in and around Lochgelly is rather scanty and the only documentary evidence of any value in early nineteenth century is a report by Mr. John Geddes in 1825 on Lochgelly Colliery.

It would appear from the report that Lochgelly No. 1 Pit was then working Lochgelly Splint in a westerly direction, and a number of Pits were working on the Cartmore Coalfield, mainly in the Great Coal or Jersey Coal Seam. In 1836 the output of coal from Lochgelly Coalfield was reported to be slightly over 100 tons daily and there were some 50 persons employed. In those early years the pits were drained by a succession of Day Levels leading into the River Ore and the Beagle Burn and the Seams extracted were worked by means of shallow pits near the outcrop.

A lease of the minerals in Lochgelly Estate, belonging to the Earl of Minto, was granted to Mr. John Henderson some time previous to 1840 – then in 1841 Mr. John Henderson went into partnership with Messrs. Grainger and Millar, both Engineers in Edinburgh, and they obtained a lease, for 31 years from Martinmas 1841 of Coal, Ironstone, Limestone and Fireclay under the lands of Lochgelly and Cartmore, this partnership being known as John Henderson and Company. At some period between 1841 and 1848 the partnership changed its personnel, the parties to the Company then being John Henderson, Thomas Grainger, James Russell, Robert Kennard, Graham Hardie and Wm. Fraser. At this period the output of coal remained fairly static as the sale of coal was limited by the method of transport – Lochgelly not then having a railway – it being put through in 1851.

BLAST FURNACES

The mining of ironstone and the manufacture of iron was taken up between 1845 and 1850. This development can be traced to the demonstration about 1830 by one David Mushet, on the use of blackband ironstone, also the Hot Blast Furnace Invention of James Beaumont Neilson. Blast furnaces were built in 1847 to the east end of the present workshops and the output of Lochgelly Blackband Ironstone was gradually stepped up and a great number of shallow pits were sunk to this profitable deposit of ironstone between the years 1848 to 1865. In 1850 Mr. Henderson severed his connection with his original partners and confined his activities to Cuttlehill Colliery to the west of Cowdenbeath. In 1851 the Company took the name of The Lochgelly Iron Company.

COMPANY CHANGES ITS DESIGNATION AND INCREASES CAPITAL

In 1872 the Company took its present name, The Lochgelly Iron and Coal Company Ltd., as, by this time, efforts were more concentrated on the mining of coal rather than ironstone. In 1875 the furnaces were damped down – the iron could not be made at a profit, because of the low price of pig iron then prevailing. The sinking and manning of shafts to win coal went on continuously during the next period in the history of the Company. This is evident by the available data.

In 1896 the capital of The Lochgelly Iron and Coal Company Ltd. was increased and there was then launched a scheme of development. The collieries at that time producing coal were Mary, Melgund, Jenny Gray, Arthur, with Dora and Lady Pits on Little Raith leasehold, the annual output being nearly half a million tons. The development scheme included sinking of two pits at Brigghills–Minto Colliery, the re-opening and deepening of Nellie Pit and the sinking of Mary Pit to a lower level to enable a level Crosscut Mine to reach the lowest workable seams to the dip of the shaft. Dundonald Colliery was purchased as a going concern in 1910, and the widening of Lady Helen Shaft and West Mine transformed this colliery into a modern structure.

Within ten years the annual output of coal had doubled and by 1913 there was over $1\frac{1}{4}$ million tons of coal extracted from the collieries comprising Dundonald, Minto, Nellie, Mary, Jenny Gray, Arthur and Little Raith.

Coal cutting machines were introduced in 1905 and there was also one conveyor installed. By 1914 the percentage of coal cut by machines was 28, and this percentage increased until in 1939 the entire output was obtained from coal cut by machinery, and also all but a small fraction conveyed by conveyors of one kind or another.

HOUSING OF THE WORKERS

It was recognised very early in the history of the Company that it was necessary to provide the workers with good substantial houses. By 1876 the Company had 420 houses available for their workmen, 464 by 1900 and from that date up to 1910 a further 423 were built or bought. During the course of time a number of these houses were demolished owing to their condition and since the first World War it was recognised that it was a duty of the local authority to provide houses – and therefore the tempo of building houses by all Colliery Companies was considerably retarded, but, nevertheless, from 1910 up to the end of 1946 a further 143 houses were either built or purchased. At 31st December, 1946, the total number of houses owned by the Company or held under terms of the lease was 747.

PROGRESSIVE DEVELOPMENT

The undernoted table will give some indication of the development of mining during the past 100 years:–

Year	Output of Coal Tons.	Ironstone Tons.	No. of Persons Employed.
1841	30,000	–	119
1850	Not available	28,000	Figures
1860	100,000	20,000	not
1866	186,424	15,936	available
1870	189,746	5,485	
1875	165,982	6,187	
1880	275,000		
1890	325,000		
1896	469,423		1,361
1900	580,169		1,589
1905	767,732		2,261
1910	1,171,158		4,043
1915	978,851		3,139
1920	910,190		4,137
1925	816,414		2,381
1930	786,155		2,019
1935	884,704		2,075
1940	799,667		2,090
1946	714,832		1,912

From the records available it would seem that wages in the Mining Industry fluctuated in a seemingly erratic fashion but actually the rise and fall varied closely with prices obtained for coal.

COAL "TUB" AS USED IN JENNY GRAY COLLIERY

DETAILS OF LOCHGELLY PIT SHAFTS

Colliery	Depth in Fathoms	Period Working
Lochgelly No. 1	31	1820?–1864
No. 16 Pit (at East Colquhally)	17	1864–1877
Nellie	174	1880–1894
		1905 – still operating
Mary No. 1	89	1872–1877
No. 2	141	1886–1936
No. 4 Sawmill		1850
Nottingham No. 5	13	1848–1850
Eliza No. 11	11	1850
Eliza	94	1863–1884
Melgund	65	1886–1908
Ironstone Pits No. 3		1849–1850
No. 4		1848–1850
No. 5		1849
No. 6	15	1852–1854
No. 7		1849
No. 8	17	1852–1854
No. 10	13	1852–1866
No. 13	13	1860
No. 15	9	1855–1857
No. 18	13	1852–1858
No. 19		1868
Jenny Gray No. 1	82	1854–1866
		resumed and deepened
do. No. 2	83	1889–1942
do. No. 3	23	1927 – still operating
Blackdean Pit		1854–1858
Castle Pit		1859–1876
Arthur Pits	80	1892–1925
Foulford	71	1854–1880
Minto No. 1	101	1903 – still operating
do. No. 2	165	
Lady Helen	25	1892 – still operating
West Mine	–	1897–1928
Smithy	48	1840

No. 1 Engine	58	1849
No. 2 West Pit	53	1845
Little Raith John	44	1855–1874
Little Raith Lady	81	1855–1898
Dora	97	1875 – still operating
Lochhead	43	1897–1932
Gordon	106	1893–1939

MINING REGULATIONS

The following are the main regulations passed concerning Coal Mining:–

1842 Although Coal Mining has been carried on for many hundreds of years, it was only in the year 1842 that Regulations were framed by the Government under which Coal Mines would be operated. In 1842 the famous Lord Ashley's Act was passed, the main provisions of which prohibited the employment underground of females and all boys under ten years of age and established the principle of Government inspection of all mines.

1850 The actual practice of Government inspection of underground workings was firmly established by an Act passed in 1850 "For the Inspection of Mines in Great Britain". This Act also made it compulsory to keep plans of the workings.

1855/1860 Succeeding Acts were passed in 1855 and 1860.

1862 As a result of the Hartley disaster an Act was passed in the same year 1862, making it compulsory to have two shafts or outlets to every underground working.

1872 The Act of 1872 made compulsory the surveying of collieries (every six months) and the making and preservation of plans of underground operations. By this Act, no boy was allowed underground if under 12 years of age unless the seam worked was very thin and only then by the owner making application to the Home Secretary. Even then, part-time education of the boy was made compulsory. One of the most important requirements of the Act of 1872 was that every Mine was to be under the control and daily supervision of a certificated Manager.

1911 Finally the Coal Mines Act of 1911 brought the law closely into line with the advances made in the practice of the Science and Art of Mining.

EXCERPT FROM CHILDREN'S EMPLOYMENT
COMMISSION MINES, 1842
COLLECTED BY ROBERT HUGH FRANKS, ESQ.

LOCHGELLY, CATTLE-HILL and DEAN-PIT
COLLIERIES, parishes of BEATH and AUCHTERDERRAN,
County of Fife. – (JOHN HENDERSON, ESQ., Lessee)

Henry Chisholm, Manager of Lochgelly:

We have employed at present 94 males and 25 females, who are wrought below ground; 26 are under 18 years of age, and 10 under the age of 13. Our seams of coal being thick, five to eight feet, very young children are not needed – indeed they are never required; and no children ought to be employed under 12 years of age in any mines, as they lose both education and strength by being underground so early.

At some coal-workings, children commence as early as six years of age, and remain below as long as the adults.

The time in the Lochgelly Colliery is limited to nine hours, and no one is allowed to work at night except the engineman.

No accidents here have ever taken place of a fatal nature. Carbonic acid gas exists, but we drive it out by superior ventilation. In rainy weather we suffer by water in the pit.

Men are employed in our mines at the hewing only, and the females as putters; each are ranked distinct, and no married women now work in our mines. The mines at Dean-Pit and Cattle-hill are at present stopped from working.

Agnes Cook, 15 years old, putter:

Has wrought at Lochgelly 12 months; worked in the fields prior to coal-work; has four brothers at coal-work; father is a collier; mother was a farm servant. Can read (reads well; intelligent); never was at writing; makes own clothes and stockings.

Eliza Dixon, 17 years old, putter:

Began work below five years since; worked nine hours every day; never been off work; was in fields before at the coals; left there, as more money is to be had than field-labour: could never earn more than 8d a day above, now gets 15d when working in the wet roads. Never got hurt; was below when a young man (Joseph Harrower) was crushed to death by a fall of roof three years ago and remembers one, Andrew Beveridge, being killed in same manner two years since. Reads; was a wee while at the writing, but not since down.

(Reads badly; ignorant, but has a knowledge of the verses of many Psalms, which she learned at Sabbath-School).

Alexander Gillespie, 12 years old, hewer:

Began work at eight years old; was born at Polmont, in Stirlingshire. Father dead eight years – died from dropsy, brought on by sitting in damp work: he was 28 years old. Can read a little, and am learning to write at night-school.

(Dejected and ill informed).

COAL MINING IN FIFE
HISTORICAL BACKGROUND

Coal has been worked in and around the Lochgelly Area for many centuries. As early as 1643 the Earl David of Wemyss has the following entry in his diary–

"John, Earle of Wemyss, 1643, did work a levell of four colles in his lands of Louchhead, nier Lochgellie, as the mind ther lyes still wrought, first meeting in ye mind with a good colle of 3 fitts thick, 3 with a colle of five fitts thick, 4 and last with a colle of eight fitts, all good burning colles."

The Earl of Wemyss saw that if operations were to be continued at Lochhead, the "in-going-eye" system must be abandoned, and he went on to say:–

"To mine ther colles cause doune sinks (pits) on them, and so work them, for they are standing drye ther unwrought, only my father levelled them".

In 1631, the land of Lochgelly were included in the barony.

ACTS RELATING TO COLLIERS (AND OTHERS)
1579

Scots Poor Law in 1579 ordained that a convicted vagrant might have his usual sentence of stripes or ear-burning commuted to a year's service to any private employer who would take him.

1597

The administration of the foregoing Act of 1579 was handed over to the Kirk Sessions, and in the town to the Magistrates. Convicted tramps and their children were increased to their life-times.

1600

Calls upon the Presbyteries to compel the Kirk Sessions to fulfil the letter of the law.

1605

Employers of labour were empowered to pick their own employees from the highways with the Sheriff's sanction.

1606

Coalmasters, etc., are given powers to lift what labourers they choose from the highways without bringing them before a Magistrate.

1607

The foregoing power is extended to include workers in metal works.

1617

The children of the indigent were legislated for as in the enactment already in force for dealing with the children of tramps.

1621

Extends the privilege already granted to mine-owners to apprehend labour wherever they chose, to all other employers.

1641

Parliament ordains that "masterless men" must labour at "reasonable rates".

1698

Coal-owners empowered to retain the "child slave" perpetually.

Note:

5th December, 1701.

The Commissions of Justiciary handed over a convicted thief to Sir John Erskine of Alva as his perpetual and unrestricted slave and to have a metal collar riveted round his neck.

Sir John Erskine's slave had the following inscribed on his collar–"Alexander Stewart found guilty of death at Perth for theft the 5th of December, 1701 and gifted as a perpetual servant to Sir John Erskine of Alva." This collar which was dragged up in a fishing net afterwards in the Firth of Forth now lies in the Scottish Antiquarian Museum, Edinburgh.

EMANCIPATION ACT

1775

An act which freed the colliers from serfdom was passed on 23rd May,

1775, which was titled "An Act for altering, explaining and amending several Acts of Parliament of Scotland respecting colliers, coal-bearers and salters, etc." The preamble of this Act reads as follows– "whereas many colliers, coal-bearers, and salters in Scotland are in a state of slavery or bondage, bound to the collieries and salt works, where they work for life, and are sold with the mines be it enacted that–

"1. No person shall be bound to work in them in any way different from common labourers.

2. It shall be lawful for the owners and lessees of collieries and salt works to take apprentices for the legal term in Scotland.

3. All persons under a given age, now employed in them to be free after a given day.

4. Others of a given age not to be free till they have instructed an apprentice."

1799

Under the 1775 Act colliers under the age of 21 were liberated in seven years; those between 21 and 35 in two years. It was only after another Act had been passed in 1799 that all colliers in Scotland were freed and the last relic of this barbarism was removed.

TRUCK SYSTEM

1831

The word TRUCK is from the French TROQUER "to barter." This name is applied to a practice of paying workmen in goods in lieu of money. Employers established stores at which the workmen were supplied with food, clothing, etc., to the value of their labour, or, if money was paid in wages, they were compelled to purchase at these stores. Several such stores were run by colliery-owners. As the miners were only paid fortnightly or in some cases, monthly, they were compelled to get their supplies from the "Store". Several collieries had their own coins minted and these could only be used at the "Colliery Store". The Truck system was abolished by the Act of 1831 which provided that payment of wages was to be made only in the current coin of the realm.

1887

The Truck Act continued to be evaded and another Act was passed in 1887 to supplement that of 1831.

LOCHGELLY COLLIERIES
SOME EVENTS BEFORE 1854

1825   No. 1 Pit working. Probably the shaft at foot of "Wheel Brae."

1836   Output 100 tons per day. 50 persons employed.

1840   Mention of Lease of coal to Mr. Henderson.

1841   Henderson in partnership with Grainger and Millar.

1842   In the Commission Report of 1842 Henderson was owner and Mr Chisholm manager.

1844   Partners – Henderson, Grainger, Russell, Kennard, Hardie and Fraser.

1847   Blast Furnaces built.

1848   Mining of Ironstone commenced.

1850   Henderson severs his connection with the Company. The Company takes the name Lochgelly Iron Company. Mr Landale is manager. Dunfermline – Thornton Railway is constructed through Lochgelly about this time.

1853   Mr Connel is a Clerk.

JENNY GRAY

SOME EVENTS DURING THE CENTURY 1854 – 1954

1854   Jenny Gray No. 1 Shaft working Lochgelly Splint seam at a depth of 50 fathoms and only to the rise of Pit bottom.

1863   Mr Connel is Shipping Agent.

1866   Mr Connel is assistant manager. Working of Lochgelly Splint to rise of No. 1 Pit stopped. At this date the Jenny Gray stopped operations.

1868   Two old shafts at Jenny Gray (now filled in) working a small area of Little Splint at a depth of 6 fathoms.

1872   Name changed to Lochgelly Iron and Coal Company. Mr Landale, Managing Director.

1873   Estimate made for resinking and fitting No. 2 Shaft.

1875   Blast Furnaces damped down. Mr Connel appointed assistant to Mr Landale.

1877   Mr Thomson resigns. Mr Symington Macdonald appointed mining manager.

1882   Mr Stevenson appointed mining manager.

1884   Sinking of Melgund commenced.

1885   Unwatering Jenny Gray Shafts.
       Wire rope guides installed in shaft.

1886   Connection made from Melgund to Jenny Gray in Lochgelly Splint.

1887 Railway to Melgund completed.

1889 Jenny Gray resumes working of Lochgelly Parrot to rise of shaft.

1890 Working Five Foot coal from No. 2 shaft at a depth of 83 fathoms. Mr Connel is managing director.

1893 Mr Anderson resigns and Mr Nisbet is appointed mining manager of the Company.

1896 The Company carry out large developments.

1903 Mr Landale dies.

1904 New Lancashire boilers installed and about this time Riedler Pump installed.

1905 Mr Connel dies.

1923 Working Fourteen Foot seam from mid bottom in No. 2 shaft.

1927 No. 3 shaft sunk to wind Fourteen Foot coal.

1936 Chimney damaged by lightning. Pit idle only 3 days.

THE JENNY GRAY COLLIERY FROM THE PUBLIC PARK, 1954.

LOCHGELLY VILLAGE A HUNDRED YEARS AGO

By ALEXANDER WESTWATER

This article is written at the request of the "Jenny Gray" Centenary Committee. The Colliery, started in 1854, is the oldest still in production in the district with a current output of between 400 and 500 tons a day. Situated adjacent to the burgh's eastern boundary, the pit has generally been manned by the descendants of the old mining stock.

Our immediate purpose is to pinpoint a description of the village a hundred years ago.

The notes are drawn from various sources—old records; the files of the two oldest Fife newspapers (at Cupar and Kirkcaldy) kindly put at my disposal; references found in the Register House and National and Fife Libraries; tradition; and from contact in my youth with men who lived in that period.

L ochgelly's general story is solely parochial notwithstanding that within a few miles of its four sides gay cavalcades passed and events occurred that take a notable place in Scottish history.

Lochgelly by 1854, had grown from a hamlet with records back to 1485, to a village of just under 1,000 inhabitants, having turned the century with a population of 600. It was built on a hill facing north, with its highest point nearly 600 feet above sea level.

In the decade of the Fifties it was suddenly transformed from a village of weavers and husbandmen and a score of miners, to become the largest coal and iron producing centre in Fife. The change was brought about by the exploitation of its mineral wealth and the smelting of iron, all of which followed the development of steam power, plus the opening of the Thornton-Stirling railway, and the branch line from Lumphinnans to Kinross.

SHAPE OF THE VILLAGE

A plan of the village as it was in 1854 is given in the attached map. It was in the form of a rough square and covered an area of 350 acres, with South Street on the extreme south, on the ridge of the hill. No further extension has taken place in that direction where lie the policies of Lochgelly House. From the ridge at right angles ran High Street (then "The Wynd"), Well Road and Church Street, Mid Street, East and West Park Street (Johnnie Trotter's Lane), Gardiner Street ("The Rotten Row"). Plantation Street, where the eminent geologist, Professor Page, was born, was colloquially known as "Knowledge Street". Main Street at the north end of the square had a few houses, stretching on one side westwards to where the Free Kirk was built in 1857, and on the opposite side of Cartmore Road, then known as the Coal Road. Bank Street, which was to become its principal throughfare, had been opened up for feuing as was also the land of the Berry Trust – Francis Street, Berry Street and North Street.

There was an almost entire blank from North Street to old Launcherhead, a distance from the village of about three quarters of a mile. No building existed between North Street and Launcherhead except the Iron Company School, and not long after, Dr Nelson's Braehead Cottage. A year or so later the Parish Church Manse was built there. Almost a decade after the railway was opened a deep cutting was made in the road to the Railway Station. The gradient to the village was found unsuitable for horse drawn traffic; so much so that goods for Lochgelly Station were directed westwards to Cowdenbeath Station and transferred back to Lochgelly by the level road joining the two places. The cutting necessitated building a retaining wall underneath the one at the Manse; an instance, as a native pointed out, of an upper half of a wall being built before the lower.

THE OLD MINERS' ROW

Houses existed north-east of the village at Couperhall and Launcherhead. They provided the living accommodation for the score or so of colliers who worked in the early shallow surface mines – "water levels" and "ingaunees" which preceded the sunk shaft and mechanical winding gear adopted when the Jenny Gray pit was sunk. These houses had walls three feet thick, single-ends with a small window and no sanitary conveniences, and earthen floors. When

a number of years ago this row was demolished to become a site for modern Council houses, an inmate transferred to one of the latter, remarked to the writer that she would rather have been left in her old house, it was so warm and couthy.

LOCHGELLY MUIR – VILLAGE LOSES ITS COMMON

Adjoining Haggishall was a Muir regarded by the villagers as a Common. At the period under review the influx of miners occasioned the erection of a large number of workmen's houses and the Coal Company feued that ground from the Superior. The loss of the common land was a blow to the villagers.

The Superior was the Earl of Minto. Lochgelly Estate came into possession of the border Elliot family about the middle of the Eighteenth Century through marriage with an heiress, Agnes Murray Kinninmonth of that ilk and Melgund. Her husband, Sir Gilbert Elliot, was the grandfather of the first Earl of Minto. They built the old Lochgelly mansion house which had a thatched roof. Demolished a hundred years ago, it was replaced by the present house.

THE VILLAGE COMMON – MARKETS AND FAIRS

The Muir was the site of Lochgelly Markets and Fairs and had always been looked upon as a Village Common, of which public use was made. The feuars took from it turf and water and it was used for grazing. The weavers had their lint holes there and it was the village play park. Ord, Scotland's greatest equestrian, came regularly and set up his circus on the Muir. His visits were events. On the occasion of his last visit to the Muir, he found his usual site fenced off and a padlocked gate which the coal owners had put to emphasise their right to the ground. To the delight of the villagers, Ord yoked a couple of horses and demolished the gate. He was not further interfered with but when he came back to Lochgelly he set up his establishment at the Birnie Braes. Ord was very popular with the villagers who have told how he regularly attended church and "never missed putting a golden sovereign in the plate."

LOCHGELLIE GYPSIES

The Muir had also been back beyond memory the encampment of Lochgellie Gypsies, a notorious band known and feared over the East of Scotland to the Moray Firth . The Lochgellie settlement was one of the three gypsy headquarters in Scotland, the others being at Yetholm in Roxburghshire, and Patiesmuir, south of Dunfermline. All three tribes were closely connected and intermarried. The Lochgellie Band was of sufficient importance to attract a visit to the village by Sir Walter Scott in search of information.

The loss of the Muir led to the break-up of the Band. They found a site for their encampment at the south end of the village on the "Drum", the old disused road to Cowdenbeath, but they gradually dispersed. Some degenerated into tinkers but other took work in the pits and settled down to citizenship. Several prominent Lochgelly families are descended from the original tribe.

COURT OF SESSION ACTION

Incensed by the loss of the Common, which they held had been illegally taken from them, the villagers resolved on action. A fund was raised and at the instance of the Feuars, the matter was taken to the Court of Session.

The plea was decided against them and they had to pay expenses. The Court maintained that the landlord had never relinquished his right to the ground and was, therefore, entitled to feu it, and further, that the feuars not being a corporate body were not entitled to sue. After a lapse of a hundred years the loss of the Common still ranks as an injustice. It may, therefore, be appropriate as of local interest, to relate the history of the case.

ACT OF PARLIAMENT

The story starts with an Act of Parliament passed in 1705, in the reign of Queen Anne, by the Scots Parliament, which had only two years to run before the Union. The Act was as follows:–

"Act of Parliament 1705 – Queen Anne :– In favour of Mrs Grizel Kinninmonth of that Ilk (it was through this family that the Elliots came to acquire Lochgelly Estate) and the Estates of Parliament considering that Fairs and Markets in convenient places tend to the good and advantage of the inhabitants thereof, and of Her Majesty's other lieges dwelling near thereto, and authorises Two Fairs yearly on the days following at the toun of Lochgellie in the Shire of Fife, and belonging to Mistress Grizel Kinninmonth of that Ilk.

"Do therefore by these presents appoint two Fairs, one on the third Tuesday of May, and the other upon the second Tuesday of September, to be kept yearly in all time coming at the said toun of Lochgellie.

"And have given and grant thereby to the said Mistress Grizel Kinninmonth , her heirs and successors, and to Sir Alexander of

Melgund, her husband, for his interest, the right and privilege of keeping the said Fairs yearly for all kinds of merchandise, with all the Tolls, Customs and Casualties thereof, and all other liberties, privileges and advantages, used and wont to belong to any having the privilege of keeping Fairs or Markets within this Kingdom."

It will be noted that the land had been assigned to the Superior for the specific purpose of holding Fairs and Markets with the right to charge Tolls and Dues. That right had never been relinquished but logically it seemed to have gone by default.

The Feuars considered the matter of an appeal against the Court's finding but dropped the idea on legal advice, plus the additional costs that would have been involved had the appeal not succeeded. Their presumptive claim had failed.

The weavers lost their lint holes on the Muir but by that time that industry, as far as Lochgelly was concerned, was fading out. Most of the weavers took to working in the pits.

FAIRS AND MARKETS

Fairs continued on another site for a time on the usual Fair dates. Circuses and "shows" set up, first at the square adjoining the Feuars School (site of the present Town House) and later at the Birnie Braes. The usual stalls with household goods and confectionery continued for a decade or so. The last to come regularly was a Kirkcaldy baker named Robbie Salmond, whose ginger-bread was a special attraction as a "Market Fare".

The Markets and Fairs had been extended from two to four yearly and they ceased at the period under review.

The Markets were mainly sales of the Fife breed of cattle – a big boned black animal said to have been in demand at Smithfield. The breed has long been extinct. The last to keep the Fife breed in Lochgelly was the father of Professors Andrew and Thomas Gray, distinguished scientists in the last century. The father worked on the land and owned a house and byre in South Street, still standing but condemned for habitation.

In the stopping of the Markets, after running 150 years, Lochgelly lost some of its importance as a centre. It had been an important epoch in the life of the village.

Like the Parliament that passed the Act which had established them, they faded out – "the end o' an auld sang".

THE AULD STANE WELL

Before Lochgelly became a burgh, and a gravitation supply was introduced, the inhabitants had to depend on wells for their water.

The one illustrated, situated at the junction of Well Road, Mid Street and the Birnie Braes, was the principal spring for the early hamlet. It continued as a village well till condemned as unfit for domestic use about eighty years ago.

Elsewhere we quote the last verse of a poem by the late Alexander Brown, a member of the Lochhead farming family , who was born early in the last century. The first stanza runs:–

> When summer blinks on flowery braes,
>   And whins in bloom are gay;
> Where labour rests at golden eve,
>   And rosy children play;
> How sweet to hear when evening's glow
>   Is fading in the dell,
> The lisping murmur of the spring
>   That fills the village well.

THE VILLAGE EXPANDS

A short distance from Launcherhead and near the railway station is Stationhead with houses of fixed dates. The earlier ones were built to house the workers engaged in making the railway. Further north was Grainger Square, named after one of the colliery owners. It was the settlement of the workers at the Iron Works. That site is now completely cleared. Nearby, the Colliery office and works occupy their original sites and further east is the site where the blast furnaces stood.

In 1854 the foundations were being laid for two of the three now existing Presbyterian Churches and it was the eve of other developments. In the decade the Minto Masonic Lodge 385 was instituted; the first move in Co-operative trading was made with the start of the Co-op. Baking Society (later to develop into one of the largest Co-operative Societies in Fife); the first Bank (the Union) was opened. A "Temperance" Flute Band and also a Brass Band were formed and the first railway opened for traffic; the Iron Company School (now developed into a Junior Secondary) was built; the first steps taken (1859) demonstrated the patriotism of the villagers in the formation of Lochgelly Company of the Fife Volunteer Battalion; a Sick and Funeral Benefit Society operated at Hall Street. This, the "Societies" hall, has a date mark 1839.

THE BREWERY CLOSED

In addition to weaving and mining, the village had another industry, a large brewery situated in High Street, in process in 1854 of closing down. It was turned into tenements known as the Brewery Court with an entrance called "The Pend". The water for making Lochgelly beer was obtained from a well in the Court worked by a windlass, and also from wells at the Birnie Braes carried a few hundred yards in barrels through "The Tent Park", a rough piece of ground on which the U.P. Kirk manse was later built. The Tent Park got its name from the box from which the preachers conducted the open air Communion Services (known as "The Occasions"). These services were the mecca of the Seceders from a large area, for the Lochgelly Burgher Kirk was the only Secession Kirk within a radius of eight miles. Worshippers, men and women from the landward generally, walked barefoot putting on their boots and shoes as they approached the village. It was a modified version of Burns' "The Holy Fair."

The services were protracted and refreshments were got at the Change House nearby, later known as "Castle Rags" when it degenerated into a

common lodging house. The Burgher Kirk and manse, by 1854 United
Presbyterian, was situated in Mid Street. After the new U.P. Kirk was built the
old kirk became a hall, known as the Music Hall, and the manse was let. The
older kirk was opened in 1766. The eccentric Rev. Mr Shirra was closely
associated with it. The Music Hall became the principal centre for political
meetings and the headquarters of the Volunteer Company and for dancing and
balls. It continued as such till the Drill Hall (now the Town Hall) was erected
in Bank Street in 1892.

LOCHGELLY AN IMPORTANT CENTRE

Lochgelly village had an added importance through its geographical situation. Sited on a hill, it was "the toon" for four large parishes. Distant round a
perimeter of almost exactly eight miles are the towns of Kirkcaldy,
Dunfermline, Kinross, Burntisland, Leslie, Inverkeithing and Thornton. At the
period of which we write there was no other village of importance between.
Its markets and fairs, its games, its shops, its social events and its industry
combined to give it importance.

BECOMES A FOCAL POINT IN MINING

As the growing centre of the mining industry in the mid century,
Lochgelly, 100 years ago , became the focal point of agitation by the miners
for better and safer working conditions. Much was then afoot organising for
what was to follow in industrial action and legislation. A break had already
been made in the feudal tradition of miners but only partially had their rights
to a place in the sun been won. The Government, influenced by the
disclosures made by several Commissions, passed legislation which was progressive but slow, and the miners were getting impatient, influenced in their
minds by the Chartist Movement of a little earlier and the demand for the
Franchise. Up till the Reform Act of 1884 scarcely any miners had a vote on
account of the low rental of their houses.

A notable figure in the forward movement, who strengthened the agitation
at that period, was Alex. Macdonald. I reckon he was one of the greatest
miners' leaders of all time. He belonged to the west country, born in 1821, the
son of a miner and entered the pits at eight years of age. Later he was the first
member of the working class to enter Parliament and was President of the
British Miners' Association. He worked through Committees consisting of the
bolder spirits and for obvious reasons they worked quietly. There was always
the risk of "victimisation". Macdonald came to Lochgelly frequently and

stayed in the home of one of his miner sympathisers. One of his principal henchmen in Fife was a Lochgelly man, Henry Cook, descendant of one of the oldest Lochgelly mining families. When the triumph of the eight hours day and the formation of the Fife Miners' Union was celebrated by the first miners' gala at Kirkcaldy in 1871, Henry Cook was one of the principal speakers. He is reported to have been "very eloquent". He was first secretary of Fife Miners' Union.

The lot of the miners has shown a gradual improvement but the memory of these pioneers is not forgotten. The sordid conditions of earlier times still influence their outlook. We knew men in our youth who have told us they never saw the sun in winter unless on Sundays; men who went to work below ground at nine years of age as half-timers – morning in the pit, afternoon in the school. I knew in my youth women who had worked in the pits previous to the Act of 1842 which prohibited female labour underground. They generally lived to a great age, well into the eighties; one was a nonagenarian and all were active in mind and body. Previous to 1842 men and women miners worked twelve to fourteen hours a day. The women's job was to draw the loads in hutches from the coal face and then carry them up a stairway to the surface. This point of view is dealt with in the other article in this booklet and I need not enlarge on it. I have, however, added an addendum to this article; a touching story written over sixty years ago by Archibald ("Bauldie") Cook, brother of Henry Cook, already mentioned. But certain it is that the native miners' outlook is still influenced by the conditions of those early times creating a psychology that persists to this day.

VILLAGE LIFE IN 1854

The village was administered by Auchterderran Parochial Board and later had a special committee. It did not have amenities sufficient for what was a growing urban community. Drainage, however, was not a problem. The altitude of the village was such that drainage had a steep direct flow to the River Ore. Sewage was carried off in this way by open ditches, one on the west side from the Birnie Braes area, crossing Main Street by a culvert and thence by ditch along the Loan (or "land") to Lumphinnans Junction where it entered a tributary of the River Ore. The other ditch on the east side found its way through the Jenny Gray Plantin' (later called the Berry Plantin') and now the Public Park, via the Black Ditch to the River Ore.

A gravitation water supply was still in the distant future (1881) five years after the burgh was formed. For water they had to rely on wells. There were numerous wells, four public and the others private. It was the practice for house owners in the village (and many then owned their "but and ben") to sink a well in the garden. The public wells had pumps.

The public wells were the auld Stane Well adjoining the Birnie Braes, the Mine Well in Main Street, one in Auchterderran Road and another at Launcherhead. In the intervening years till the gravitation supply was laid on the position became acute. Nearly all the wells had been condemned by the analysts as unfit for human use. This offset the advantage of drainage, but does not seem to have affected the general health.

The Stane Well referred to dates back to the early hamlet, and it certainly served Lochgelly for hundreds of years. It still stands, the oldest structural relic in the town. Situated next the Birnie Braes at the bottom of Well Road, the village well is extolled in a poem by Alexander Brown, one of the minor poets of Scotland. He passed it daily on his way from his home, Lochhead Farm, to the village school fully a century ago. The closing verse runs:-

> Long be the Braes with gowans bright,
> The whins with blossom gay;
> Long village sons thy memory keep,
> Though far from thee they stray;
> And long by thee may peaceful age,
> With kindling glances tell
> Of boyhood's days and boyhood's ways,
> Around the village well.

At the Birnie Braes the whins and the gowans have gone. Now covered with corporation houses, it was, like the Muir, long looked upon and used as common ground. From the Braes there is a beautiful expansive view across the valley to the Cleish hills and the Ochil Range; in front the big hulk of Benarty; and eastwards to the Lomonds and Largo Ward.

The advantage of altitude for drainage became a disadvantage for water supply. The problem was to find a head giving sufficient pressure to supply the higher part of the village, commensurate with the financial aspect.

A HEALTHY PLACE

Notwithstanding these deterrents, Lochgelly, exposed on three sides, continued to be a healthy place. A writer records that when the great cholera epidemic swept West Fife in 1850 not a single case occurred in the town of Lochgelly. In that connection it may be further stated that another epidemic occurred in the sixties. As a precaution, a temporary hospital was set up in Grainger Street. It proved redundant; it didn't have a patient.

HOUSES AND TRADES

A perusal of the Fife Valuation Roll of 1855 emphasises the changes that have taken place. Houses, which were of low rent, mostly white washed and covered with a thatched roof, have gone as well as the Crafts of those who occupied them. Mass production has taken their place. Tailors, shoemakers, joiners and bakers were relatively numerous; masons and carters, fencers and labourers ; houses with byres attached (the village had 20 of these). The house rentals ranged from £3 to £7. The two doctor's houses (Drs Nelson and Gellatly) had valued rents of £10 and £4 15s respectively. The Brewery was valued in rent at £34. The one policeman in the parish lived in a house owned by the Coal Coy. and rented at £4; the U.P. manse and offices, £14; the Village School (Johnstone's) £7.

Colliery houses occupied by the miners are not given in detail nor are the occupiers'names. Slumped together for rating their total rental was £456 which works out at a rental of £3 to £4 a house. Rents were deducted from pay lines. For education at the Iron Company School 2d a fortnight was charged.

The Blast Furnaces and connections are entered at £400. The four public houses in the village were rented at £10, £14, £15 and £22. The licence holders were James Hugh, John Morris, James Cook and Henry Chisholm. There was no hotel.

Chisholm was at one time manager of the Colliery. He built what was first known as Chisholm's Hall. The name of this hall followed the respective owners – Littlejohn and Henderson. Behind it was a quoiting ground. The hall was much in demand for dancing. Chisholm's family, by the way, emigrated to Pittsburg, U.S.A., started manufacturing kitchen ware and are reputed to have become very wealthy. A sum of money left by Henry Chisholm is administered as the Chisholm Trust by the Session of Lochgelly (St. Andrew's) Parish Church.

The total number of entries on that valuation roll is 269 for the parish of Auchterderran. 161 of that number were in the village of Lochgelly.

THE VILLAGE LIGHTS AND SHADOWS

It is an axiom everywhere that life today is very different from that of 1854.

The cultural tone of the village was relatively high. The Scots traditional urge for learning was clearly apparent in looking through the records of the time.

On the elementary side of Education it had three schools – the oldest, a voluntary school maintained by the Feuars; the Iron Company School, controlled by the coal owners; and Ewings School, kept by an itinerant teacher, probably, as was common then, a "stickit" minister. In addition, there were the Parish School at Auchterderran and a Dames (girls) school in that vicinity.

Evening classes were started by Andrew Landale, governor of the Iron Coy's School. This gentleman, manager of the Coal Coy., and later managing director and the Burgh's first Provost, incidentally, was a great force for good in the growing community. He had great power: was dictatorial but of a benevolent type. Indeed, he laid the tradition of a mining community of a superior standard.

The Evening School was available for Coal Coy. employees only, but exceptions were made. One of these exceptions, within our personal knowledge, may be instanced. This lad was working in the adjacent Lumphinnans Colliery and therefore not eligible for enrolment. Anxious to improve his elementary studies which had been gained as a miner half-timer, he walked to East Colquhally where Mr Landale resided and in fear and trembling, as he told us, put forward his request. To his delight, Mr Landale, after a few questions, said he could enrol. That lad, by the way, was able to matriculate and become a graduate of Edinburgh University with a Divinity course and proceed to "wag his pow in a pu'pit." He attained that ambition by working in the pits during the summer recess and saving sufficient to support himself in Edinburgh. He has told me that some days his entire food consisted of courses of porridge, milk and bread.

That is only one of the many such instances of Lochgelly miner lads or the sons of miners and labourers making their way from poverty background into the professions – teaching, the church, medicine, mining and law.

In 1854, as shown by newspaper paragraphs, Lochgelly had two Literary Societies, as well as a Scientific Society and a Library. Three men seem to have been the leaders in that direction – Mr Ogilvie, who was headmaster of the Iron Company School, Mr Landale, and the U.P. Minister, the Rev. William Reid.

Lectures were given on intellectual subjects and essays were read by members on Education, Mechanics, Geology, Theology, Temperance, History and Science. One of these Societies stated as its purpose "the necessity of making still greater exertions for intellectual improvement and advancement in knowledge."

Geology, allied to mining, was a popular study. The Library included all the publications of Professor Page, native of Lochgelly, eminent in that science in the early part of the 19th century. This, doubtless, gave an added stimulus.

Discussions on the more elevated subjects often took place in the village inn where groups met on the Saturday evenings. At one of these, a heated argument took place in which the protagonists were two men who later became Provosts of the burgh. One was a nephew of Professor Page. The other sought to squash his opponent (both had the reputation of being very dogmatic) with the remark – "Man, Johnnie, what I said was a quotation from your uncle's book." – "A weel," was the rejoinder, "my uncle maun be wrang."

SPORT AND PASTIME – THE GYMNASTIC GAMES

Sport was distinctive in several ways as compared with today. The youth found outlet in games for their surplus energy; not as so pertains in this commercialised age of watching others play. Sport then gave scope for initiative; "make and make do" provided the means and gave a better sense of the fitness of things rather than spectacle and displays. Football, which was later to become the main sport, by then had not reached the village.

One big event in the year which gave scope for both athletic prowess of local youth and athletes from all over Fife and at the same time provided at least one spectacle for all ages, was the annual Gymnastic Games and Horse Races. In 1854 they are reported to have attracted 3,000 spectators, at a time when the total population of the village was one third of that number. The main forms of exercise were field sports, running, jumping and vaulting. Vaulting was much practised and in this Lochgelly youths were noted for their dexterity all over Fife. A damper was put on this game by a serious accident when a Lochgelly man was competing at Dunfermline. In taking the vault he fell on an onlooker who was dangerously hurt.

Ordinarily, quoiting was the main game. The quoiting ground was at Haggishall and later a good enclosure was made at the rear of Chisholm's Hall. Many exciting matches took place there. Lochgelly quoiters became noted exponents all over the country and, in a later generation, two, Gillespie and Watters, became Scottish champions. Many other skilled players figured prominently in Fife competitions. In quoiting matches there was always a money stake and side betting took place on the "ends." Lochgelly was the leading club in the country both in membership and playing strength.

Another game played for stakes was wall ball. The ball was hit against a wall. This pastime took place against the west gable of the two storey Friendly Society Hall.

Cricket came to the village at the period under review. It was introduced by a Northern Irishman named Michael Vail and continued in popularity for two generations till supplanted by football. At one time there were three clubs, the Senior, the Zetland Juniors and a School Club. The former had engagements with the leading Fife clubs – Cupar , Dunfermline, Kirkcaldy and Burntisland. Vail had the reputation of a tremendous slogger. He once drove a ball from the centre of Cooperha' field on to Station Road, reckoned a phenomenal feat.

Poaching and cock fighting figured in the excitement of these days. The gatherings, at which there was much gambling, were, of course, held covertly. Places of seclusion for the "sport" were at Cluny Woods, Denend, Spittal and Shirram Brae. There were other rendezvous further afield and matches called "mains" took place with other Fife clubs.

The Loch, when "bearing" in winter, was a seasonal lido, a mecca for curlers and skaters and sliders. Curlers were numerous (the club was formed in 1831). People came from all around the countryside. On a Saturday afternoon it took on the form of a carnival. Whetted appetites were catered for by pies and ale supplied at the edge of the loch. Curling stones then were not of the fine polished variety; it was a more strenuous game. Skaters played a form of hockey. The skates were home made – a wood sole and an iron keel attached to the boot by a screw to the heel and a strap over the instep. The privilege was given of a short cut to the loch through the private policies when the loch was "bearing".

Draughts was the popular indoor game.

The four public houses were well patronised on Saturday evenings. There the miner contractor in the pit paid out the wages to his men. A common practice for customers was to leave a shilling with the publican and at the low price of liquor this served to provide a nightly refreshment throughout the week.

POST OFFICE AND TELEGRAMS

Lochgelly was early established as the post town for a large district embracing Cowdenbeath, and the parishes of Auchterderran and Ballingry. In the former case a postman travelled from Cowdenbeath to Lochgelly, collected the mails in bulk and delivered them at Cowdenbeath, and a rural postman carried the deliveries to Lochore and Auchterderran districts. The Telegraph was added. It was operated on a circular instrument with the letters of the alphabet tapped as on a typewriter. Apparently the morse code had not reached Lochgelly.

FERRIES

Four ferries were in use in 1854 for south-going passengers and goods – Kirkcaldy, Burntisland, Pettycur and Queensferry.

Regular sailings across the Forth also took place from Leven, Anstruther, Kirkcaldy, St. Andrews and Inverkeithing.

Two "packets" left Kirkcaldy regularly for Glasgow and there was a fortnightly service from that port to London.

PARLIAMENTARY ELECTORS

The M.P. for Fife in 1854 was John Fergus of Strathore. He defeated Lord Loughborough, eldest son of the Earl of Rosslyn. (Lord Loughborough was the first R.W.M. of Minto Masonic Lodge.)

It was not till 1884 that the working classes in the counties secured a Parliamentary Vote. Citizens in the burghs got it in 1867. In 1854 there were therefore no miners' votes in the village of Lochgelly.

In the forepart of the century the voters' roll of Fife numbered less than 200. It was still based on the feudal land system. The Royal Burghs in combination had three members. Local landowners entitled to the franchise then were:– Sir Gilbert Elliot of Lochgelly; John Syme of Cartmore; Alexander Park of Lochore; Sir Michael Malcolm of Balbedie; Robert Ayton of Inchdairnie. The bigger land owners had a "packet" of votes.

Nominations were made at the Hustings at Cupar and voting, which lasted over a period of days, was open. (Secret vote by ballot did not become law till 1870.) Bulletins were issued daily as to the progress of the poll. One of these I have in my possession.

Agitation for reform of the Franchise went on throughout the country and culminated in the Reform Act of 1884. Gladstone in his Midlothian campaign, strongly backed by "The Scotsman", raised the tempo of the country to fever heat. While the Reform Bill was in session mass demonstrations took place in many parts of the country. West Fife concentrated on Dunfermline. At this Lochgelly provided the largest contingent. They carried two large banners and tableaux depicting miners working at the coal face.

A Redistribution Act followed. This divided Fife into two constituencies, East and West Fife.

THE FAST DAY–"LOVE OF MONEY "

"It is surprising," writes a Lochgelly correspondent in a Fife newspaper of that year, "what schemes individuals and companies will fall out about to make a shilling or two. All kinds of nets are spread.

"On Market and Fair Days every kind of invention is set forth – Shows, Stage Dancing, Punch's Opera and Merry-go-rounds. But if set near a church door on a Fast Day or a Sunday there is a great probability no one would look near it."

The Railway Company is condemned for advertising cheap travelling on Fast Days and succeeding in getting numbers, most of whom would be horrified to go on a Merry-go-round on Sunday. The object was the same–"a trial trip to popularise the railways".

Another note– "Last Thursday being Auchterderran Fast Day the parishioners were favoured with the means of escaping out of the parish to any other station on the line".

LOCHGELLY "RIOT"

In July, 1854, the inhabitants of Lochgelly were thrown into a state of great alarm. A report which carries the above heading stated–"The rumour went that a number of Irish labourers were knocking down and killing all and sundry that came within their reach." The reporter apparently applied a good deal of imagination to the incident for the report continued–"Our very active policeman was instantly on the spot and succeeded in restoring peace, but not till four or five peaceful inhabitants were more or less injured. Had it not been for the dauntless exertions of Constable McGregor the offenders might have escaped justice. He apprehended nine and took them to Cupar for trial. 'We may add,' states the report, 'that John Barleycorn was the cause of the brawl!'."

A SCHOOL EXAMINATION

The Earl of Minto and his Commissioner, Mr. Tod, and the clergymen of five parishes attended with parents at the inspection of the Iron Coy.'s School in July, 1854. Mr Andrew Landale, the governor, was also present. Much

ANDREW LANDALE

Manager of Lochgelly Colliery
when Jenny Gray Pit was sunk.
Later Managing Director;
Lochgelly Iron & Coal Company,
Limited. He died in 1903

satisfaction was expressed as to the Scriptural Knowledge of the pupils. "In the Shorter Catechism they showed great facility. The general education imparted was such as to prepare the pupils for perceiving sufficiently the pleasure afforded by acquiring knowledge. The Iron Coy. was congratulated on the material supplied such as maps and diagrams. Prizes were awarded and each child got an abundant supply of confectionery. Then they were given a few weeks relaxation."

THE KIRKS

Kirkcaldy Presbytery decided to build a Chapel of Ease at Lochgelly in 1854 and the foundation stone was laid of what was to become Lochgelly Parish Church (now St. Andrews) in the following year.

The Free Presbytery of Kirkcaldy gave assent to a requisition from the congregation at Lochgelly praying that they appoint the Rev. Peter Macainsh, missionary at Methil, to take charge of the congregation at Lochgelly. The foundation stone of this church was laid in 1856.

The Burgher Kirk (U.P. now Churchmount) has already been referred to.

RAILWAY INCIDENTS

The novelty of the railway had not worn off by 1854 as evidenced by references to it then.

A young Lochgelly miner, who had been drinking at Dunfermline, was in a train which passed at a rapid rate to Cowdenbeath Station. He was seen to put his head and shoulders out of a carriage window. Then he suddenly opened the carriage door and stepped out leaving his fellow passengers in a state of great alarm. The communication cord had not yet arrived and there was no way of stopping the train till it reached the next station. On arrival there, a number of passengers and officials rushed back along the line expecting to find him killed or badly injured. Judge their relief when they saw him walking round a bend in the line, seemingly unconcerned and uninjured. On being asked why he made such a sudden exit, he explained that the wind had carried off his bonnet and he had just stepped out to pick it up but, having had a fall of which he was none the worse, "the ruddy thing (the train) was out of sight and he could not catch it up!"

Another incident later concerned Miss Fenton, a female teacher at Flockhouse School. Then, Lochgelly platform was short on the east side where the line crosses the main road to Ballingry. A low fence had been put up. On a dark night the train in which she was travelling overran the platform. Assuming the carriage was opposite the platform she stepped out. The floor of the carriage was above the low railing and she stepped into space. It was the period of the crinolines and as she fell her skirt bellowed out and she floated down, parachute fashion. The wide skirt broke the fall and she landed on her feet. Beyond a bit of a shock and a sore ankle she miraculously escaped injury. Later this low railing was heightened and was bound by a close wooden fence.

MINER WHO DIDN'T GIVE NOTICE

A miner named Walter Skinner sued the Iron Coy. for wages. The Company refused to pay on the ground that he left work without a fortnight's warning notice. The Sheriff decided that Skinner was in the wrong and fined him 10/- and 4/- expenses.

MINING RULES – STRIKE AVERTED

Disagreement which arose consequent on the introduction of new mining rules led to a suspension of work ("not a strike"), states a report. A conference was held and things looked ominous at first over objectionable clauses but "by mutual forbearance and kindly feeling an amicable settlement was reached." Wm. Hunter, Lochgelly, acted as Clerk for the miners.

THE ANNUAL GAMES

The Games were held on 31st August in 1854 and a report says– "We were glad to see so few cases of intoxication, and harmony prevailed." There were two classes for quoiters and the following names of winners are given – James Campbell, Robert Gillespie, David Paton and Robert McLean. In other sports, winners were Wm. Stuart, Alex. Paton, Henry Cook, John Henderson, George Miller and Wm. Tevendale.

HORSE RACING

What were termed "Lochgelly Subscription Horse Races" took place in a "pretty field" at the east end of the burgh.

One of the horses threw its rider. The little fellow, the report continues, got up and ran after it for a short distance, but seeing he was no match, gave up the chase. The animal continued the course and came in first amidst a good deal of cheering. The proceedings went off quietly without incident.

NO POLICEMAN AT COWDENBEATH

A correspondent wrote that Cowdenbeath locality stood greatly in need of a policeman who could act along with the one at Lochgelly. "Cowdenbeath has now," he stated, "a growing mining population and the constable at Crossgates is not able to visit it often enough."

TOLL HOUSES

The village had no tolls adjacent. There was one in Auchterderran Parish at Cluny.

The tolls were farmed out by Road Trustees for turnpike roads in the Kirkcaldy district. They were advertised to be sold by public roup and were let for £1171, plus Cluny Bar Gate which fetched £752.

Other adverts of 1854 include the sale by public roup of a large quantity of wood on Lochgelly Estate comprising ash, elm, beech and larch. A roup of parks included the East Bank Park and a further sale of wood at Launcherhead.

PRICE OF COAL

Dundonald Coal Coy. announced the opening of a new seam of splint which for house use could not be surpassed. The Company firmly "adhered to their rule of just weight and no excess" and intimated the following prices–Hard Great Splint 4s 7d per ton; Household Great Splint, 4s 2d per ton, and Chew, 3s 4d per ton.

PLEASURE TRIP GIVEN TO LOCHGELLY WORKMEN

Workmen employed by the Lochgelly Iron Company enjoyed an excursion by rail to Perth. Also included were the workmen of Dundonald and Cardenden Collieries. At Perth the crowd proceeded by procession, headed by two bands, to the South Inch.

Lochgelly workmen were regaled with pies, bread and beers. They engaged in dancing and later separated to see the town.

The report stated that "Lochgelly Iron Coy. deserve great credit for thus giving their workmen the opportunity of enjoying such a gala day and likewise for paying one-third of the railway expenses and providing refreshments. Great praise is due to their spirited manager, Mr Andrew Landale, who took upon himself the whole arrangements. We were delighted to see him passing through the groups to see that all were enjoying themselves . Such kindly feeling between master and servant cannot but be highly prized." (The outing may have given the cue to the annual Gala which came later but under different circumstances.)

J.P.'s

There were no Justices of the Peace in Lochgelly in 1854. Two served the parishes of Auchterderran and Ballingry:- L. Ayton, described as of Capledrae and residing at Balgreggie, and R. Henderson of Glencraig.

DATES OF LOCHGELLY FAIRS

The dates of the four Lochgelly Fairs were:–

First Monday of April (old style)	(cattle)
Third Wednesday of July	(cattle)
Third Wednesday of September	(cattle)
First Monday of November	(general)

RAILWAY PROJECTS – MADE AND ABANDONED

The Fifties was a time of much railway activity. Their revolutionary influence on industry was realised. Speculators joined in schemes all over the country and not least in Fife. Much of the capital raised went in land way-leaves to the landlords. The land was a monopoly and the main winners were the lairds. Much money was lost as well as gained in early railway enterprises.

By the middle of the Fifties two main lines were operated in Fife – one from Burntisland to Tayport and the other from Thornton to Dunfermline and then to Stirling. Mineral traffic was the main objective of the speculators here-abouts.

A mineral line was projected from Dunfermline, via Steelend, Lassodie, Kelty to Kinross. This was abandoned.

Another railway, however, was in course of making in mid-century. It was the line from Lumphinnans to Kinross, a single line which was diverted from the Thornton – Stirling line by a junction a mile west of Lochgelly. Passengers to Kinross changed at Cowdenbeath station. Part of that line is now used for mineral traffic for North Lumphinnans Colliery ("The Peeweep".)

Earlier there was a project to lay a railway from Lochgelly to Kirkcaldy. The promoters' intention to "make a railroad of the simplest construction and intended solely for the transport of coals and such like minerals." Kirkcaldy harbour had been improved and then functioned as one of the Fife ferries to the other side of the Forth. The project states:-

"Commencing in the heart of the Lochgelly coalfield and sweeping through that of Dundonald, Cluny, Dunnikier by Dothan and Easter Bogie it will terminate at the harbour of Kirkcaldy. It is physically impossible to construct a railway from Lochgelly to any other port on the Forth nearer than Aberdour or St. Davids and the latter could only be done by excessive outlay. Although the Lochgelly field has been won for two centuries it can scarcely be said to be touched beyond the meanest cropping, and fair working has not yet been attempted. We look upon Lochgelly, Lumphinnans and Dundonald as the three great coalfields which would supply the projected railway, a supply not to be equalled by any other coalfield in Fife."

"There are patches of coalfield such as Cowdenbeath, Lochore and Capledrae which have not been taken into the estimate for they are not adjacent to the line as to calculate the revenue to the latter."

It was also pointed out that "skirting the limits of the foregoing coalfield is limestone, 11 to 50 feet thick from Lochhead, Little Raith, Glenniston, Shawsmill, Foulford, Chapel and Bogie. At present limestone is extensively worked at Glenniston and Chapel and sells from 2s 2d to 2s 6d per boll."

"Ironstone, too, is associated with the Lochgelly coal measures both in the form of bands and bell and nearly allied in character to the black band of Airdrie."

"The construction of the railway would be of the easiest description. Comparatively in its course, or rather one long gentle decline to the sea, there is no rock cutting to be met with, no serious bridges would be required save at Cardenden."

A year later it is recorded that Mr Grainger's engineers were surveying the area and that a Bill would be brought into Parliament. About half of the sum required was already subscribed. But the project did not mature.

Many years later a mineral railway was laid from the west of Lochgelly to Seafield, near Kirkcaldy, through the Bogs of Lochhead, via Auchtertool.

OTTERS IN THE LOCH

Otters were reported as fairly numerous in the loch. One shot by a servant at Little Raith farm was four feet long, said to be the largest seen there. The same man also shot "a very large swan."

PRICE OF BREAD

A newspaper report states that "Lochgelly has to pay the highest price for all the necessities of life. This is mainly attributed to the Store or Truck System as it is called. Along with our neighbours at Dundonald where there is also a Store we are paying 8½ d for the 4 lb. loaf, while our neighbours at Cluny, a place where no Store exists, are paying just 8d. The quality is the same, served by the same carts from Leslie and Kirkcaldy. It is too heavy a tax to be quietly borne." The Stores referred to were run by the Coal Coy., who deducted the cost of groceries, etc., by agreement from the pay packet.

STAGE COACH

The usual Stage Coach was running in 1854 from Queensferry to Perth. Horses were changed at Kinross. They passed the west end of Lochgelly Road.

HOME LIFE

The houses in the village consisted almost entirely of one or two ends without sculleries. The earliest houses in the miners' rows had earthen floors or were laid with flat bricks. The garden ground contained communal dry privies and middens. Gardens were attached to all houses and were well cultivated, mostly with vegetables for the kail pot.

Large families were normal and accommodation and sanitation must have presented a problem for the housewife. Nevertheless strong and healthy men and women were reared in these houses.

Kitchen furnishings consisted of a couple of beds in a recess; the older houses had the "box bed"; a "dresser" which was the repository for the delf, cutlery, and all sorts of odds and ends; stout handmade table and chairs with an extra chair with arms for the guidman. Ornaments were few and consisted mostly of china dogs and other china figures and generally a "purley pig." Fireplaces were primitive – a grating and ribs, and sometimes a "swey" on which hung the big pot for boiling the water for the wash and the meat for the pigs and the kye. A barrel of oatmeal stood by the fireside.

The duties of the miners' housewives were hard and continuous; their work was never done. In the very early morning they had to see their men out with breakfast and a "piece" and flask, the latter containing tea but often water. Then the bairns had to be fed and got ready for school, followed by the household chores and shopping for the "messages"; children back for dinner and the men from the pit following later. Water had to be drawn and carried from the well. Then came the wash or bath for the men folk. For this a tub was stood on the floor-head filled with hot water, already prepared in a boiler or on the fire and carried from the well often some distance away. If the miner had a few sons working, as was then normal, it is easy to visualise the state of the kitchen floor. In warm weather the pit bath was often outside the back door. Wet and dirty clothes had to be scraped and washed. After the wash and dinner the men folk generally rested in bed or sat round the fire in their thick hand-knitted worsted drawers, recuperating from their toil. The kitchen was cleaned up and the bairns attended to on their return from school.

But there was no leisure for the women folk. In the evening they were busy mending and drying the pit clothes, or knitting the heavy woollen underwear and socks that were universally worn.

Pit accidents were frequent then and there was constant anxiety whether their men would come home unscathed or on a springless cart lying on a bed of straw. No ambulance or hospital was then available. Illness and lying-in intensified the internal conditions. Kindly neighbourliness, however, was a feature of the miners' rows. Some women had a flair for nursing, and sympathy and help were never lacking. The miners' wives of that age were unsung heroines.

As the girls in the family grew up they found employment on the pithead and in domestic service. Later they went in large numbers to work in the Dunfermline Linen Factories as these developed. They travelled by special "Factory Trains," leaving home between five and six in the morning and did not get back till seven at night.

PAROCHIAL BOARD

Assessments collected by Auchterderran Parochial Board (including Lochgelly) in 1854 amounted to £118 14s 7d and from other sources there was a revenue of £82.

Ballingry Parish had an income of £102 14s and from other sources £13 13s 6d. The cost of Poor Relief was £30 14s 2d; Medical Relief £7 18s 6d; and Management, £23 1s 7½d.

Parish Clerk and Inspector of Poor for Auchterderran was Mr W. B. Low, and for Ballingry, Andrew Lawrence. Dr Nelson was the Parish Doctor.

NEWSPAPERS

Newspapers were still subject to tax which at one time made their price 10d per copy. By 1853 the tax had gradually been reduced to 1d. But the impost on paper continued till 1861 in which year Gladstone entirely removed "the shackles of the press." Working men could not yet afford the luxury of a daily, so clubs were formed and the copy passed round. This system was mostly adopted by the weavers and by mid-century had extended to the miners.

Two Fife newspapers were published weekly – The "Fife Herald", and the "Fifeshire Advertiser." (The first named is the oldest, 1822.) It was from the files of these papers that I gathered a number of notes for this article. They had a bigger, though still limited, circulation than the dailies. Generally when the paper reached the house, the news was read out to the family.

District news of the village at that period was very scanty. There were no accredited local correspondents, and such as is recorded was sent in by persons specially interested in something being published. It involved considerable time in research. When my father started the local paper in 1892 some of the public men resented the presence of a reporter at the public boards. I recall some cold receptions when I attended as a cub reporter. Provost Landale and the Laird of Glencraig, Geo. W. Constable, described the local paper as "a nuisance."

The news of general interest in 1854 was the Crimean War in which several Lochgelly Men took part. I recall two – Sergeants Hunter and Bain. The former was in the "Thin Red Line." Parliamentary news, then of vital interest, was intently followed.

Our soldier poet, John Leslie (Pindar), was still attending the evening school. He did not become a soldier till the close of the Indian Mutiny.

Mr Landale started a library at the Company School. It was highly beneficial.

MINERS' MEETING ON SHORTER HOURS

Miners' delegates met at Dunfermline to deliver opinions of their dissents with regard to a reduction of the hours of labour. All the collieries in West Fife were represented except Lochgelly, and the absence of Robert Gillespie was especially noted.

The general opinion was for shorter hours and a Bill to this effect was advocated. One delegate proposed a petition to Parliament for acceleration of the matter. A Shorter Hours Bill had been passed for factory workers but the error in it was that shorter hours were only made for young people.

Some delegates did not want to restrict wages, like hours, to the same standard "and thus reduce skill, strength and industry to the same level into weakness, laziness and incompetence."

THE IRON COMPANY SCHOOL

The Iron Company's School which is a little older than the Jenny Gray Pit is referred to in the text of this book. It was built by the Lochgelly Iron Company, which later became Lochgelly Iron and Coal Company, Limited, for the children of their workmen.

The building is shown as it was in 1854. On the north side of the block is the headmaster's house, long ago turned into a classroom. The school was referred to at an early period by an Examiner as one of the best seminaries in Fife. Greatly extended, it is now a Junior Secondary.

WEDDINGS

Weddings were generally held at Hogmanay, taking the place of "Auld Hansel Monday," which came about a fortnight after Hogmanay. Penny Weddings were still common. At these the guests made contributions of money (2s 6d or 3s 6d) or goods to help the newly weds in furnishing their house.

Entertainment was provided by dancing to a fiddle and the inner man was provided for by oatmeal cakes and bannocks with ample whisky to wash it all down.

SHEEBEENING

The Act of Parliament, known as the Forbes Mackenzie Act, restricting the hours for the sale of excisable liquor, led to publicans breaking the new law.

Several charges were heard against Lochgelly publicans for keeping their house open in excess of the new hours.

In the village and district it also led to more sheebeening. A common practice to indicate a place of illicit sale was to put two church warden pipes crossed in the window. This practice was more common in the landward part than in the village.

AT THE "LOMOND GOLD DIGGINGS"

A number of Lochgelly men set out with pick and shovel in 1852, for the "gold diggings" on the north flank of the Bishop Hill, some five miles from the village.

The rumour of gold there originated in a letter from a Kinnesswood man to his mother. He had taken part in the first rush to the Australian diggings. He said the deposits in Australia were similar to what he had seen on his native hill and he thought that gold ought to be found there. The rumour spread and Fife was all agog. The view from the village was of a hillside of active movement, prospectors eagerly searching and staking their claims – a picture of the early mining camps. I knew one of these prospectors, a well known tradesman, who on setting out in high hope, observed to his wife, "Marget, ye can throw oot my workin' tools. I'll hae nae mair need o' them, for I'm off to mak my fortune".

After fully a week of feverish excitement, the camp broke up. The gold miners returned crestfallen and subject to much chaff.

Geologists, who had been called in, provided the anticlimax. They issued an analysis of the metal. It was published in "The Scotsman" along with the story of the gold diggings.

PRICES OF CLOTHING

Advertisements of clothing etc., show the following prices current in 1854 – Linen Sheeting, 7d to 1/- per yd.; Cotton Sheeting, 5½d to 7½d per yd.; Table Linens, 1/5½ per yd.; Lace Window Curtains, 5/- to 16/6 per pair; Corded Skirts, 1/- to 5/9 each; Plain Silks 1/10 to 3/10 per yd.; Silk Velvets, 7/- to 12/- per yd.; Printed Dresses, 1/10 to 4/- each; Worsted Polka Jackets, 11½d to 7/6; Cloths for Men's Suits, 5/- up per yd.; Satin Hats 4/-; Cloth Caps, 8½d; Corduroy and Moleskins, 11d to 2/- per yard.

A hundred years ago! What a change in the pattern of life.

ADDENDUM

A HUMAN DOCUMENT

TOUCHING STORY OF EARLY LOCHGELLY PITS
FROM 1777

The following narrative was written by Archibald (Bauldie) Cook, who was born in 1837. His grandfather and grandmother were two of the earliest Lochgelly miners. Both worked below ground when the industry was started by Sir Gilbert Elliot shortly after acquiring Lochgelly estate by succession after the middle of the 18th century. "Bauldie's" brother, Henry, was the first secretary of the Fife Miners' Union, formed in 1870. The Cook family has always held a high position in character and ability in the town. A great-great-grand-son of the first mentioned in this article is at present a member of Lochgelly Town Council and of the Fife Miners' Union Executive.

The family was prototype of the old Fife mining stock – muscular, accustomed to danger, intelligent, dogmatic and radical in political outlook.

The story is so quaintly written that I have not presumed to edit it. The document was given to Andrew Nisbet, my father-in-law, who came to Lochgelly in 1893 to be general mining manager to Lochgelly Iron and Coal Company, Ltd. Shortly before he died in 1903, he handed it to me. It has not hitherto been published. I consider this a fitting opportunity. A few friends have had a read of it and one of these, an elderly cousin, now dead, wrote in returning it, "The Cooks were rather remarkable men. I knew "Bauldie" and his brother, Henry, the latter I often talked to. I question if any other miner could have written such an account as "Bauldie" has given. And I don't know of anything in literature more pathetic than the story of his granny putting her two infants in a coal creel, taking them down the pit with her, and depositing them at the stoop side. What a picture that is – these two little mites lying in the dark; the mother meanwhile toiling for her children's bread or "stoved" potatoes and oatmeal; going at times to give the younger the breast."

Bauldie starts off with references to his own time and then proceeds to delve into the past. As far as possible I have retained his own phraseology.

"I can give you," he says, "the number of miners employed in Lochgelly in 1777 and their wives along with them. First, Henry Chisholm, Robert Chisholm, James Chisholm, Charles Baxter, Henry Baxter, Hannah Hodge, James Hunter, George Erskine. Their daily output of coal was ten tons – not a great output but when it is considered that the women carried the coal in baskets along the workings a good number of fathoms and up a long stair, ten tons was a fair output. It was a pretty hard day's work with scanty food and clothing.

WOMEN CARRIERS' FEAT

"The regular burden they carried on their back was twenty-one stone Dutch, equal to a hundredweight.

"There was a trial of strength between Janet Erskine and Hannah Hodge and they each carried four hundredweight. Their wage was six shillings per week. Miners' wages were set down at nine shillings per week.

"Working hours were from twelve to fourteen per day. Each one had their own bit of ground for laying the coals.

"The laird kept a man for selling them. He was known as a Coal Grieve. He advanced the workers money on their each little bing of coals, and, as the stock was sold off, he cleared them both up.

"In the winter season they never saw daylight but only on Sundays.

"I can give here an abstract of a week's profit at Lochgelly Coal Works. In the year 1777 from February 9 to the 20th, after paying wages and all oncosts the owner had £3 14/- to himself. He considered that awful good. For a number of weeks previous to then, in the same year, after paying all expenses he had only 4/6 to himself – a very small sum compared with the revenues the coalmasters receive at this time.

"It was a hard life of slavery and serfdom. But as they knew no better they were quite happy with their situation.

"With the advance of education, progress was made. In Lochgelly, we could look back to the time when a miner's wife had to take her six months' old child in her coal creel below ground and lie at the stoop side until she wrought her day's work, giving it a drink as she had time.

"Miners' sons and daughters nowadays are equal with any class of Society. We have miners' sons and daughters, teachers, ministers and business men of all kinds, fitted to fill any situation in the country.

"I am among the oldest miners belonging to Lochgelly and belong to the oldest race of miners born on the Earl of Minto's estate.

WORK AND LIFE OF A FEMALE COLLIER

"I can give some particulars of the system of working and their mode of living of my ancestors. If anything went wrong with the man such as sickness or death the women had to be both miner and bearer. Such was the case with my grandmother. She was left a widow with five young children and no way of supporting them, only by her own hand. My father was only 4 months old and my uncle

'Bauldy' was two years. Her three girls were older.

"There was nothing for her but to go and dig her coals. She carried the infant children down the pit, laid them at the stoop side until she dug her coals and carried it to the pit bank. When she rested she gave my father a drink and my uncle a few spoonfuls of cold stoved potatoes. Oatmeal and potatoes provided all their living in those days.

"Their provisions were all prepared at night before they went to bed. She wrought on till her family was able to help her.

"Sir Gilbert Elliot declared that she brought more coals to the bank than any miner at his works.

"She was a general miner for she drove off the Day Level, leading from the River Ore. She wrought where no light would burn, breathing the foulest air the mineral world could blow out upon her.

LIGHT FROM FISH HEADS

"The only light she had was the reflection from fish heads.

"As they grew up her family carried the coals and redd. My father started at eight years of age.

"After Henry Chisholm's two sons reached manhood they improved the system a little. They had a windlass which did away with carrying the coals up the stair and thus raised the output to fifteen tons a day.

"But there was little ease for the women for they had to work the windlass.

"Then they introduced a 'gin' which brought the output up to twenty-five tons. The 'gin' was wrought with horses.

"The Chisholms, after holding the contract of Lochgelly Colliery for a hundred years, finished up in the Muirhead fields, Ballingry, and Cartmore farm. William Chisholm, a son, acted as clerk and timekeeper.

"They recommended him to Mr John Henderson when he took over the coalfield. He made him manager, knowing as he did the nature of the rule of working as an underground manager.

"David Chisholm's father lived all his time in a little old thatched house which stood in the Muir by itself. Stewart built the block of houses where John Henderson's public house is but died before they were finished. He left one to his mother, Betsy Cook, and sons.

"It was about 1827 that John Henderson took a lease of the minerals and fitted up machinery in the pits. This made the work more comfortable. He was always very kind to his workmen.

"The first pit Mr Henderson put down was called "Little Crafty." It was only a few fathoms. The Lochgelly Iron Company's School is built right on the top of it.

"The next pit he put down was the Lochhead Pit on the side of the Kirkcaldy Road.

"In about the year 1837, they started to put the pits down as near the public roads as possible as their sales were all land sales. At that time the daily output of coal was in about thirty five tons.

"Then he put down another two pits. One was the "Little Dean," and the "West Pit," now the Newton. That was in 1839. It was not well situated for sales for the want of a good road. But the Earl of Minto made a road to the Dean Pit and Mr Henderson made a railway from the Dean Pit to Cowdenbeath, which suited both pits. He started a Coal Reave at Cowdenbeath, and the coals were carted to Burntisland and shipped there. The output of Lochgelly pits had risen to fifty tons a day.

"I have seen as high as thirty carts standing on the pithead at four o'clock in the morning, at the pit bank to get coals, all the way from Perth and north of that. A man named Henry Mitchell was the coal grieve at that time and a man complained to him about the charge. Henry replied "Mind coals is coals now." "Well," replied the man, "I am glad, for the last I got was stones."

"Henry was always very clever. I heard them talk of James Hunter who, with his wife, went out to get coal. Henry met him and asked the reason why he was stealing the coals. James replied "Because we have not enough to put on the fire." Henry said "That's not enough." And then James said, "Oh, but the wife's coming with more."

"At one time Lochgelly coal could command a sale for its cleanness and quality throughout the whole country.

"My father finished his mining career about 1846, in the Nottingham Pit. It was in this pit, as I have already stated, that he was carried down the stair in his mother's coal creel at the age of six months, in the year 1778. He died in 1848 in the same house where he was born in old Launcherhead. Three generations of us were born there.

"I myself began as a miner in 1843, at the age of ten. Being a "quarter man" and as the miners' wage was then 2/-, I got sixpence a day.

"I wrought steady up till 1869 when I had a serious accident. I was told by the highest medical authority in Edinburgh that I would not work any more.

But I had the hope I would. I began again in 1873, and decided to keep a record from then on. I wrought very steady up till 1896 when I was fairly beat off. My average working during that time after I was told I would work no more, was four and a half days per week, and my average per year was 660 tons of coal and 108 of small coal. But I had always a boy for filling and drawing. The price I got per ton varied from 1/- to 3/4. My average price during those 23 years after I resumed was about 1/8 per ton of 22½ cwt.

"Taking the average for my fifty three years working including after the time when I was told I would work no more, my output, boy and self, would be round about 32,980 tons coal and 5,724 small coal, giving a grand total of 38,704 tons at 22½ cwts per ton. I believe this to be a steady miner's production.

"When we look back on the generations of slavery and serfdom that existed among the miners, we wonder how they lived compared with the pleasures and comforts they have now. And still there is great room and need for improvement, and I believe, will be till the end of time.

"I might mention the names of men who fought their lifetime for the freedom and comfort of the miners, urged on Acts of Parliament for the safety of the miner in the pit, for better ventilation, for his working day to be eight hours instead of twelve, all through the force of legislation.

"Such men were Normandhill, Pickard, Halliday and Alexander MacDonald. The last named laboured hard for the miners right up to his last hour. The miners of Fife ought to have a memorial of Alexander MacDonald placed in West Fife which he visited so often, perhaps placed at Dunfermline.

"He gave valuable instructions as to how miners should act. That memorial should be unveiled every year in order to show the young of the present day, and coming generations, what would have been for them, and by whom it was done.

"From the introduction of the eight hours day in the year 1870, we have always had leading Secretaries of Boards of Management – all men from our own ranks, able and well qualified to fulfil their duties.

"I mind the time since 1837, when there were only scattered houses in Lochgelly, mostly all thatched. When walking through it, you would only hear the clatter of a hand loom; now you will hear no such thing. All round the Cross where all the fine buildings now are, was only waste and garden ground.

"There was but one house on the Muir which belonged to David Chisholm.

The Muir was Lochgelly Play Park. Now every bit of ground suitable for building has been taken up. To the north, there was not a house on the road-side from Knockhill till you came to the Spail Inn, and now they are nearly all the way."

Bauldie concludes "I will now state the number of days I have wrought with an average of 4½ per week for 53 years – 12,402 days. And I wrought on the pithead for eight years, with an average of five days per week, a total of 2,080 days. And the grand total from 1843 to 1904, is to be seen in Lochgelly Office books, for I have wrought all the time in their works. I have travelled nearly as many miles in the bowels of the earth belonging to the Rt. Hon. the Earl of Minto (he was Viceroy of India) as what his trip is from London to Bombay."

(signed) ARCHIBALD COOK

1857 - 1957

LOCHGELLY MACAINSH
CHURCH OF SCOTLAND

CENTENARY BOOK

By ALEXANDER WESTWATER, J.P., F.J.I., F.S.A. Scot.

Printed and Published by
John Westwater & Son, Bank Street, Lochgelly

FOREWORD

It is a privilege to be allowed to write a few words of introduction to this history of Macainsh Church of Scotland, Lochgelly. The work entailed in producing such a book is great and all of us in the congregation are deeply indebted to Mr Alexander Westwater for so willingly undertaking the task. He has been untiring in his efforts to track down every possible source of information about the congregation and its Ministers, and, to this end, has consulted many files, records and people. Only one who loved greatly the Church of his Fathers would expend himself so selflessly on its behalf.

This is not his only publication, however, as he is keenly interested in the history of his native town and has written much about it. Some years ago he was honoured by the Town Council by being enrolled the first Honorary Burgess of Lochgelly.

The finished history is now in your hands and I believe it is a credit to all those ministers, office-bearers and members who have laboured faithfully during the past century to make known the Name of Christ in Lochgelly.

May we all resolve as we read it to enter into the work of the Kingdom with new determination and zeal, that in some small way we might be worthy of those who have gone before and of the great cause we represent.

GERALD B. MACALLAN.

PREFACE

Up to the publication of the First Scottish Statistical Account and the works of John Galt, parochial history was much neglected. Since then the value of it, which need not be stressed, has been recognised and the default is being made good.

This booklet records the story in brief of a Free Church congregation in a mining town in Fife, which stemmed from the Disruption.

It has been compiled from the records of the Free Presbytery of Kirkcaldy now in the church library at Castlehill; the minutes of the Session and Deacons' Court of the Macainsh Church; from the files of the oldest Fife newspapers (the "Fife Herald" and the "Fifeshire Advertiser") which I had the privilege of scanning, and the files of my own local paper since 1892. I had tradition to aid me. I was born 19 years after the kirk was opened and my family have been connected with it since. My grandfather, Alexander Westwater (he was born in 1795), had belonged to a Relief Kirk on the riggin o' Fife and was an active helper to Mr Macainsh when he was building the congregation by cottage meetings. He was a member of the first Session and first representative to the Presbytery.

I wish further to express my thanks to the present incumbent Mr Macallan. He provided me with the roll of Elders and Deacons throughout the 100 years, and showed an encouraging interest in the work.

The booklet will mainly be of interest to the Macainsh congregation. It contains, however, some relevant general matter.

A.W.

(From a line drawing by Rev. J. S. Sievwright, M.A., Ballingry)

LOCHGELLY MACAINSH CHURCH OF SCOTLAND

(Started as a Free Church Congregation in 1856)

THE Lochgelly Macainsh (Free) Church congregation was sanctioned by the General Assembly of 1856. The Rev. Peter Macainsh, probationer, was ordained on 12th October of that year and the church was opened on 19th July, 1857.

As early as 1849, however, a start was made by the Free Presbytery of Kirkcaldy by holding Sunday evening services in the village school. These were taken by ministers of the Presbytery. Later a probationer was appointed to attend the spiritual needs of the district which covered the parishes of Auchterderran, Ballingry and part of Beath.

The congregation stemmed, of course, from the Disruption of 1843.

LEADING UP TO THE DISRUPTION

It may be opportune to briefly recall the chequered story of the Church of Scotland from the Revolution Settlement in 1678 when Presbyterianism was restored as the national religion of Scotland. In the forepart of the succeeding century, it had to stand the strain of secession. The first break was the founding in 1734 of the Associate Synod at nearby Gairney Bridge and the setting up of a Divinity Hall at Milnathort. That body, the original Secession Church, split into several groups—the Burghers and the anti-Burghers, the Auld Lichts, and the New Lichts, and the Relief Kirk. The bodies were endemic to Fife and Kinross from which emanated other splinters. In course of time they composed their differences and in 1820, the earlier Secession Communions united at a General Assembly at which the Moderator was the Rev. D. Greig of Lochgelly Burgher Kirk, a notable divine. Later the Relief Kirk joined that Union and brought about the United Presbyterian Church which increased in size and influence.

PATRONAGE

In the Established Church of Scotland in the forepart of last century various differences again became acute. The cleavage was between Moderates and Evangelicals, the latter holding more to the basic doctrines of the

Reformation Church. But it was Patronage which brought about the crisis of
1843. This was the legal right of the patron, the principal heritor, to appoint a
minister without consultation with the congregation, and often in spite of their
wishes. This was held to be an intrusion on the right of the individual to exercise his spiritual independence and not be subject to either king or prelate, a
principle inherent in the Scot. It had been a bone of contention and was the
fundamental cause of all the Secessions. Patronage had been abolished with
the change-over from Episcopalianism but was restored in 1721. Efforts to
repeal that legislation had always failed and when the civil courts refused as
late as 1838 it led to the crisis. It became obvious that only a voluntary
church, independent in spiritual matters of the State, could solve the matter.
Bitter controversy ensued. The Government had rejected a measure, another
"Claim of Right." When the Assembly met on 18th May, 1843, a protest was
handed to the Royal Commissioner. The protesters walked out of the
Established Assembly and through crowded streets and amid suppressed
excitement, marched to Canonmills, and there constituted the Free Church of
Scotland. Dr Thomas Chalmers, a native of Anstruther, one of the greatest
Scotsmen of his age, and the spearhead of the movement, was unanimously
elected Moderator.

THE DISRUPTION

Over 400 ministers by that Act forfeited their churches, manses and
stipends and, strengthened by an abounding faith, walked out into the
unknown. The bulk of the Divinity students lessened their prospects by going
over to the new church.

It was a sacrificial act for a principle that thrilled not only Scotland, but
the Christian world. One effect was the expansion of evangelical preaching.
Scotland experienced a religious revival.

It is timely to recall that the Macainsh Church is in that tradition and that
its first minister was one of those who followed Chalmers; and that in his
enthusiasm in 1843, he placed a notice on the door of his parish kirk with the
word "Ichabod" (The glory is departed).

At the time it did seem as if the glory had indeed departed from the Auld
Kirk, bereft of nearly all its leading ministers and tens of thousands of laymen.
But in point of fact, it made a quick recovery and rallied to again become the
powerful Church of Scotland.

There is irony in the fact that 31 years later (1874) the British Parliament
removed the main cause of the dissensions of two centuries by repealing the
Patronage Act of 1712. Obviously had they been wiser in their generation the

story of the Kirk in Scotland would have been different.

By this time the ill-feeling engendered by the split had lost some of its intensity, if not its rivalry. Time is a great healer. The thoughts of earnest men began to turn towards unity. Increasing education and enlightenment bring a better perspective.

> Through the ages an increasing purpose runs,
> And the thoughts of men are widened with the process of the suns.

A further step towards unity in ecclesiastical affairs was the joining of the Secession and Relief Churches in 1852 to form the important United Presbyterian Church (the U.P.).

UNION OF THE U.P. AND THE FREE CHURCHES

Towards the end of last century, a larger union was envisaged. Deliberations were slow but this was accomplished in 1900 when the U.P. and Free became one under the title of "The United Free Church of Scotland." The decision of the former was unanimous, but there was considerable dissension in the Free Church. The minority, who refused to join the Union, carried on as the Free Church. By that Union, Lochgelly Free Church was named "Macainsh" and transferred from Kirkcaldy Presbytery to that of Dunfermline. Lochgelly U.P., which had always been in Dunfermline Presbytery, was renamed "Churchmount."

That union also amalgamated the Kinross-shire Presbytery into the Dunfermline Presbytery. The first united meeting took place at Dunfermline on 19th November, 1900.

The Rev. James Brown, Lochgelly, was elected Moderator, and also Convener of the Business Committee.

THE FINAL UNION

In 1929, came the bigger Union ratified at a memorable gathering in Edinburgh. The two Assemblies (Established and U.F.) met in the morning in their respective assembly halls nearby in Castle Terrace. By a synchronised arrangement as they emerged they joined up and marched in a long procession to a large hall in Allendale Street, near Leith Walk.

That day witnessed the consummation of a Union which brought Presbyterian Scotland under the auld roof tree and thereby restored the Kirk of the Reformation.

The Union brought about changes in the presbyteries and in ecclesiastical boundaries. The Lochgelly churches were transferred from Kirkcaldy to

Dunfermline Presbytery and districts and parishes allotted to the respective congregations. Lochgelly Parish Church was renamed "St. Andrew's."

GROWTH OF LOCHGELLY VILLAGE

In 1857, Lochgelly was still a village sited in the parish of Auchterderran. It became a Police Burgh in 1877, and its extended boundaries overlapped into the parish of Ballingry. The Macainsh Kirk, standing on the boundary line of the two parishes, is on the Ballingry side.

The mid-century was a period of great industrial activity and the population rapidly increased. It grew from a hamlet in the 15th century, and up to the turn of the 18th-19th century, its inhabitants were engaged in husbandry and weaving. In the first Statistical Account (1801) the population of the whole parish of Auchterderran was 1,200, including 342 in the village of Lochgelly; in the second official census (1811) the village had increased to 612; in 1821 to 786; 1850 to 870, and in the following decade it had nearly trebled. A notorious tribe of gypsies known as the "Lochgellie Band" dispersed early in the century, and the cattle markets ceased with the loss of a Common known as Lochgellie Muir.

The reason for the great increase was the development of the coalfield. The score or so of colliers had given place to several hundreds and the shallow surface mines were succeeded by sunk shafts. The discovery of ironstone led to the erection of extensive blast furnaces north of Lochgelly railway station, and for nearly three decades these flourished. Bituminous coal was subsidiary and the operators were known as Lochgelly Iron Coy. Later Lochgelly became the principal coal mining centre in Fife.

The spiritual needs of the villagers had been supplied by the Parish Kirk at Auchterderran (which is 2 - 3 miles distant) and the Burgher Kirk in Mid Street, later the U.P. and now Churchmount. The latter congregation was formed in 1761 and was the only Secession Church within an eight miles radius. Its second minister, the Rev. David Greig (from Kinross-shire) was a well known Scottish divine.

In 1855 a Chapel of Ease (Established) was erected in Bank Street, an offshoot from Auchterderran Parish Church. Its second minister, the Rev. Wm. Mair, D.D., was later a Moderator of the Established Assembly. A Quoad sacra parish of Lochgelly was formed in 1868. This parish extended partly into the landward districts of Auchterderran and Ballingry and included the mining villages of Lumphinnans and South Glencraig.

In the seventeenth century, Kirkcaldy Presbytery and Auchterderran Kirk held occasional services in the village of Lochgelly.

THE START OF LOCHGELLY FREE CONGREGATION

At the Disruption it generally followed that when a minister "came out," many of the congregation followed him. In our own district the incumbents of the parish Kirks all remained in the Establishment. Auchterderran parish minister was the Rev. Andrew Murray, D.D., then in his 95th year. He died the year following. Incidentally, he wrote the articles for the first Statistical Account and lived to write the second. He attained much publicity by a controversy with Malthus over the latter's publication on "Population."

In Ballingry Parish, the minister, the Rev. Mr Greig, was also an old man. It is recorded that in the great turmoil of 1843, Mr Greig wavered, but his brother Christopher, minister of St Ninian's, who often assisted him in Communion, was more precipitate. "He cam' oot and rued it" was the assessment of the villagers. At Auchtertool, the Rev. Walter Welsh had just been elected and stayed in. He was cousin to Jane Welsh, wife of Thomas Carlyle, who frequently visited the manse at Auchtertool. In the other neighbouring parish of Beath, the Rev. Dr. Thomson remained in the Establishment.

The First Free Kirk in this area was at Kinglassie. It was started in 1846. The first minister was the Rev. John Spears. 115 people took part in the first communion. The church, opened in 1847, seated 300 and it "was quite full" at the opening. It was one of the congregations which continued in the Free Communion after the House of Lords decision in 1903 when a crisis arose. A Free Church was formed early at Kelty.

ADHERENTS INCREASE

Such a promising district as Lochgelly was not overlooked by the Free Presbytery of Kirkcaldy, and at the first meeting of the newly constituted Presbytery (7th June, 1843), Lochgelly was mentioned as a suitable centre for starting a preaching station. It was not, however, till 1849 that action was taken to enquire into the condition of the district which was stated to be "in a state of great spiritual destitution."

The Free Presbytery Committee, reporting on Lochgelly, stated that the manager of the Subscription School had kindly consented to allow the Presbytery the use of their schoolroom for sermons on Sabbath evenings on payment of 1/- per Sabbath. This school stood on the site of the present Town House. It was maintained by the feuars in the village. It had been started in the middle of the 1700's and was closed on the passing of the Scottish Education Act in 1872, and the consequent set-up of a School Board.

The first Free Church Service was conducted in 1849 by the Rev. Harry Laird of Leslie, and Sunday services continued weekly, conducted by the ministers of Kirkcaldy Presbytery till the year following when the Home Mission Committee of the Church agreed to a Probationer being appointed. Towards the cost of this, the Presbytery contributed £20 for one year. The Assembly offered a donation of £40 for six months, conditional on a local contribution of £20 for the maintenance of the Probationer. Mr David Page (a relative of Professor Page, one of the leading geologists of his age), who represented the Lochgelly adherents at the Presbytery meeting, guaranteed £5 per quarter towards the Probationer's salary.

The Probationer appointed was Mr W. Ferguson who was then stationed at Gauldry in Cupar Presbytery. He remained at Lochgelly for three years and was able, when he left, to give an encouraging account regarding the prosperity of Lochgelly Station. Attendances at services had ranged from 50 to 90. So promising indeed was the situation that in 1851 at the request of the Lochgelly people, the Presbytery Clerk was instructed to approach the Home Mission for a Church. This was proposed but was not then entertained.

When Mr Ferguson was on duty at Lochgelly he was put under the charge of Mr Spears and the Kirk Session of Kinglassie for the dispensation of ordinances, and Mr Ferguson was instructed to apply to Mr Spears for Baptism ordinances and for administration and discipline.

At a subsequent meeting of the Presbytery, a Committee was appointed to consider the whole matter connected with Lochgelly Station and report. A student, Mr Grant, acted for a short time and was followed by a minister, the Rev. J. K. McLean. This gentleman seems to have been of a versatile turn, finding scope for his abilities in a dual occupation. During the week he was absorbed in literary matters as editor of a Fife paper while on Sunday he ministered to the needs of the Lochgelly folks. Such methods did not succeed and he resigned in the spring of 1854.

A year later, Mr Forman, Leven, reported to the Presbytery that Mr Peter Macainsh had commenced his labours at Methil Station, and on application from Lochgelly, it was agreed to transfer him to Lochgelly Station. He came to Lochgelly on 15th July, 1855, and lodged in High Street.

A FULL CHARGE

The advent of Mr Macainsh gave a great impetus to the movement, and in January, 1856, there appeared before the Presbytery the Rev. Peter Macainsh,

Messrs. Alexander Westwater and Thomas Thomson, a deputation from Lochgelly Station, who presented a memorial requesting the Presbytery to agree to support their application to the next General Assembly to have Lochgelly sanctioned as a ministerial charge. The Presbytery agreed to the request.

The following is a relevant extract from the Minutes of the General Assembly of 3rd June, 1856, from the Presbytery of Kirkcaldy — "A Minute was laid before the Presbytery by a deputation from Lochgelly (Alexander Westwater and Thomas Thomson), craving the Presbytery to proceed to moderate a call to Lochgelly. The Presbytery gave the assurance that in their opinion, a congregation at Lochgelly would implement all the conditions required by the General Assembly. The General Assembly of the Free Church of Scotland resolve to sanction, and hereby duly sanction the Station at Lochgelly as a full ministerial charge provided the congregation satisfy the Presbytery and the Sustentation Fund Committee that their contributions to the Sustentation Fund will not be under £100 a year, and in the meantime to be assisted by the Home Mission Committee."

[The conditions referred to, in order to allow the congregation to consolidate, were that the Home Mission Committee would continue their grant of £30 for three years, the fourth year it would be reduced to £25, the fifth year to £20, and so on, decreasing by £5 every year till the whole grants were exhausted.]

In March following, Mr Macainsh laid before the Presbytery, plans for a new Church.

The services were by then held in the Societies Hall. A date stone over the door indicated it was built in 1829. A Mutual Aid and Funeral Society was in existence in the village years before Friendly Societies were established by Act of Parliament. The Hall, on the upper flat, was the headquarters of the Lochgelly Company of Fife Volunteers embodied in 1859, and it was also the centre then of social gatherings. The building was demolished in 1955 to provide a site for Town Council houses.

Lochgelly congregation had by now determined to erect a church and the Presbytery was informed to that effect. Plans were submitted showing a building in the Gothic style, and a newspaper report stated "when finished, it will have a most elegant appearance. It is calculated to provide accommodation for a congregation of 500." A gallery was shown in the plans but this was deleted to keep down the cost. Contracts were accepted for the mason work by James Robertson, builder, and the joiner work by David and John Wilson, both of Lochgelly. The architect, Mr Dowie, Kirkcaldy, prepared the plans.

MR MACAINSH ORDAINED

The ordination of the Rev. Peter Macainsh took place in the Iron Company's School which was built and run by the Iron Company for the benefit of the children of their workmen, on 12th October, 1856. He was introduced to the congregation by the Rev. Wm. Omand of Monzie (Mr Macainsh's native parish) who, says a local newspaper report, preached "a singularly able and eloquent discourse from John XVI—"Ask and ye shall receive that your joy may be full." In introducing the new minister, Mr Omand said he had known him as a Sabbath School teacher, and as a student. The knowledge he had, warranted him to speak with confidence. Mr Macainsh duly passed his "trials." The success that Mr Macainsh met with increased encouragement, and the need for a church became clamant.

On the same day as the induction, the memorial stone of the new church was laid. A large crowd gathered to witness the ceremony by Patrick Don Swan, Esq., Provost of Kirkcaldy. He was a warm supporter of the Free Kirk, and had been active in the erection of St Brycedale's, Kirkcaldy. The first precentor was James Kinnell. He continued to serve under Mr Macainsh till 1886, without salary.

The Church is on the Lumphinnans estate of the Earl of Zetland on the extreme east boundary of Ballingry Parish. A ditch, now filled in, was the boundary line. The feu extended to three roods and 20 poles (approx. 7/8 of an acre), at a feu duty of £2 1s 6d. Part of the ground has since been sub-let for dwelling-houses. The church was insured for £800. In 1893, the insurance was £1,800, and in 1916, the church, manse and hall increased the insurance to £3,060.

OPENING OF THE CHURCH

The Church was opened for public worship on 19th July, 1857, by Dr. Hetherington, Professor of Church History, who preached in the forenoon, from Ps. 122. Mr Macainsh preached in the afternoon. The plate collection amounted to £22 14/-, "a handsome sum when it is considered that the people had subscribed within a few weeks past £40 for the purpose of clearing the debt to date of the Church."

A handsome service of Communion plate was presented to the congregation by Mrs Goodall of Craigderran House, Auchterderran, wife of the coal-master there. Presentation of Communion cups and two servers was also made by Mrs Macainsh in 1901.

Already there was a good sum in hand through contributions as a result of an appeal made by the Presbytery to Lochgelly Iron and Coal Company and the other coal and iron masters, whose workmen it was designed to help. Interest had been created by a circular "on behalf of the congregation among the wealthier Free Churchmen in the district."

The Presbytery, on the proposal of Mr Forman, however, agreed to memorialize the General Assembly and give a liberal grant to the Lochgelly Church from the General Funds. Messrs. Knight and Macainsh were appointed to support the prayer at the next General Assembly.

Mr Macainsh's first duty as a member of Presbytery was to preach at the trials of Mr George MacAuley on his ordination to Inverteil Kirk, Kirkcaldy.

The work under Mr Macainsh's guidance went steadily forward and, as the population increased, with greater impetus.

The various associations in connection with the church steadily developed. They comprised the Sabbath School, Bible Class, Prayer Meeting, Morning Fellowship and a Literary Society (the latter was a feature of Lochgelly life in the last century). All the churches had Mutual Improvement Societies and the village one in addition which met in the Iron Company's School. The latter Society held many lectures on scientific and cultural subjects.

The minister's time was fully occupied in addition to Sunday preparation. He continued the outdoor work he had started as a missionary and his visits round the district were keenly looked forward to.

APPEAL FOR A FREE KIRK AT COWDENBEATH

The Kirkcaldy Presbytery, on 24th September, 1858, had a letter from James Swanton, Portmoak, notifying them that Kinross Presbytery had taken steps to form a Preaching Station at the village of Cowdenbeath. The letter stated—"That village was on the outskirts of three Presbyteries—Kirkcaldy, Kinross and Dunfermline, all of which might be expected to take a deep interest in its spiritual welfare and contribute proportionately to its evangelisation. He described it as a mining village in the Parish of Beath containing 500 heads of families and increasing. Every house was occupied and there are lodgers who would rather be tenants. 33 new houses are in course of construction. The manager of one of the Coal Companies in the neighbourhood informed Mr Macainsh of Lochgelly, that his Company alone would ultimately employ 1,000 of the population. That was exclusive of Lumphinnans, a village adjoining Cowdenbeath on the Lochgelly road."

The letter continues, "There is no place of worship in Cowdenbeath and the Parish Church of Beath is upwards of a mile distant. Of the church-going population, the majority attend the Establishment, some attend the U.P. Churches at Lochgelly and Crossgates, and others who are comparatively few, attend the Free Church congregations at Lochgelly or Kelty. The mass of people will never go out of the village to any church; the Gospel must be carried to them. The distance to Lochgelly is two miles, not too far to walk, but it far exceeds a Sabbath day journey to such a population as is found at Cowdenbeath. Besides, Mr Macainsh at Lochgelly is set down in the midst of 3,000 people and has a large enough field for one man." "Cowdenbeath," the letter concludes, "is four miles from Kelty, a distance which precludes it uniting with the Free Church there. It is proposed by the Presbytery of Kinross that £30 should be raised by the three Presbyteries mentioned, of which Cowdenbeath is on the outskirts."

The reply of Kirkcaldy Presbytery was that they declined to undertake any pecuniary obligations as proposed.

In 1862, Mr Macainsh informed his Presbytery that measures had been adopted for erecting a Free Church at Cowdenbeath, and submitted his view that it could not fail to have injurious influences on his own charge. He agreed with a resolution that a searching investigation should be made into the spiritual needs of the district, including both Cowdenbeath and Lochgelly, and it was decided to hold a conference with Kinross Presbytery on the matter.

A Probationer was sent to Cowdenbeath, a congregation formed, and a small church erected in 1862 in what is now Factory road. A manse was later built in Broad Street. During the incumbency of the late Rev. James Muir (a former assistant to Mr Macainsh), the Free Church, now Guthrie Church, was built in High Street in 1892.

PROPOSED NEW PRESBYTERY

A petition for a new Presbytery from ministers in all the parishes in and adjoining Kinross-shire to be formed by that county had been before the General Assembly in 1855. The churches involved were Arngask (then in Perth Presbytery); Ballingry and Portmoak (Kirkcaldy); Fossoway and Muckhart (Auchterarder) and Cleish, Kinross and Orwell (Dunfermline).

The Kirkcaldy commissioners were instructed to oppose the proposal by all legitimate means and prepared a memorial setting out that where it is not necessary, it is an administrative evil. In the case of Kinross County of six charges, most of them small, none self sustaining, and erected subsequent to the Disruption, it was uncalled for. It was better that they be associated with stronger adjacent Presbyteries.

Subsequently the Presbytery of Kinross was formed.

In 1863, the Presbytery of Kinross petitioned the General Assembly to disjoin Lochgelly from Kirkcaldy and asked that a committee should consider the position at Lochgelly and Cowdenbeath.

Later the General Assembly declined to adopt any resolution with respect to the Presbyterial arrangements referred to.

The Assembly suggested to Kinross Presbytery that they should join the Kirkcaldy Presbytery.

NOTES FROM CONGREGATIONAL MINUTES

The first Session comprised Thomas Dick, Alexander Westwater, George Dowie, Andrew Beveridge and John Hunter.

First Deacons' Court—John Williamson, John Hodge, Thomas McKee, Walter Dryburgh, Robert Turner, Alexander Naysmith. William Small cashier to Lochgelly Iron Company, was co-opted to the Court and later elected a Deacon.

Communion seasons comprised meetings on Thursday, on Saturday afternoon, two diets on Sunday, and another on Monday.

Additional elders were elected in 1869 — Robert Fairfoul and John White; and the following deacons—William Small, Alexander Mailer, John Harrower, David Henderson, James Arnott, John Dryburgh, Thomas Ness and William Clark. The last-mentioned two refused to accept office.

William Small resigned on leaving the district, and James Arnott, Registrar, was appointed Clerk to the Court.

A manse was built in 1860—a substantial stone villa with an avenue approach.

THE FIRST BREAK

The first break in the office-bearers of the congregation occurred in 1865 with the death of Alexander Westwater, aged 70 years. He joined Mr Macainsh when he came to Lochgelly and assisted him in his numerous cottage meetings. Mr Macainsh, in a tribute, spoke of his warm interest in the congregation and said they had lost a valuable friend. He had been the first representative to the Presbytery, and Thomas Dick was appointed to take his place.

GALLERY ADDED

The need for more seating accommodation led to the erection in 1880 of a gallery (which had been in the original plan). The contractor was David Henderson, joiner, an elder. It cost £250. Mr Henderson presented the table and chair for the precentor. It was opened on 18th January, 1881, by the Rev. N. L. Walker, Dysart, and celebrated by a social on the Monday evening. Among those present were the Revs. Stalker, Kirkcaldy; Henderson, Crieff; W. Craig, Kettle (a former assistant); James Brown, Lochgelly U.P.; the Hon. Hugh Elliott, Lochgelly House; Provost Swan, Kirkcaldy, and R. Nairn, Kirkcaldy. Mr Nairn presented the linoleum for the lobbies and platform.

Said to be the worst storm of last century occurred in 1879 at a Communion season. The Rev. A. D. Paterson arrived as arranged for the Friday service, according to the Minute, "at a risk of his life." Communion service was postponed till the following Sabbath. This storm was often spoken of. It was dated by the villagers as starting "on the nicht o' the Gardeners' Ball."

A letter from an elder confessed "with deep sorrow and great heaviness of heart of being intoxicated with drink and so near the sacrament as he felt he could not take his place at the plate." The Session expressed deep sorrow at the sad event and suspended him from the office of eldership.

Mr Macainsh intimated the formation of a library for members and adherents.

What seems to have been the last Fast Day service was held in 1886. (The writer remembers attending it with his father and mother).

In 1886, James Kinnell, who had acted as Precentor since the formation of the congregation, intimated his resignation. For 36 years he did the duties voluntarily but later a collection was taken annually for a salary. From applications received for a successor, the late David S. Low, teacher, was appointed at a salary of £12 per annum. His duties were—to lead the psalmody at all church services; at the weekly prayer meeting, at Sabbath School; teach and train the adult and juvenile choirs; lead the praise at all socials in the Church and in the hall.

MISSIONS

By 1890, Missions were carried on by church office-bearers at Lumphinnans and the Muir district, Lochgelly. The former was held in a hall (two houses converted) which was given by Henry Mungall, coalmaster, who also contributed £5 to the Mission and promised more. In the Muir, Lochgelly Iron and Coal Company granted a dwelling house in Grainger Street, which was converted into a small hall.

Communion Cards were substituted for tokens in 1892.

MR MACAINSH'S RETIRAL — COLLEAGUE AND SUCCESSOR APPOINTED

In December, 1891, Mr Macainsh applied for a colleague and successor. He wished that the whole grants from the Sustenation Fund and surplus fund, with any supplements, and the manse and its pertinents should go to his colleague and successor. The annual payments to the fund would be paid by himself.

The congregation, as can be readily understood, paid sincere tributes to his great work in Lochgelly. David Philp was appointed to report Mr Macainsh's resignation to the Presbytery.

The Rev. Duncan Brown, M.A., who had previously been an assistant to Mr Macainsh, and who was then serving at Clackmannan, was the unanimous choice of the congregation.

On 18th August, 1892, the Free Presbytery of Kirkcaldy met in the Church and inducted the Rev. D. Brown. The Rev. G. C. Dalziel, Kinglassie preached and the Rev. A. B. Campbell, Markinch, ordained and addressed the new minister. The Rev. Professor A. B. Bruce, D.D., Glasgow, preached on the Sunday following.

THE UNION OF 1900—CHURCHES' NEW NAMES

The congregation was unanimously in favour of Union with the U.P. Church. A distinctive name was necessary in view of the three congregations in the town. The decision to call it the Macainsh United Free Church of Lochgelly was unanimous. David Philp, Lochgelly, was representative of the Presbytery at the Union consummation at Edinburgh. Mr Philp, who was a son-in-law of Mr Dick, played a big part in congregational work. His daughter, Mrs May Clark, presented two memorial windows in the south wall of the Church, in memory of her father and grandfather.

INSTRUMENTAL MUSIC

In 1901, the question of introducing instrumental music to the church service was suggested by John Rolland at a Session meeting. The Deacons' Court was consulted and it was decided to have a vote of the congregation. 122 were in favour, 46 against.

The Precentor, David Low, resigned, but was asked to continue for another year. He agreed to continue till a successor was appointed.

A year later, it was decided to advertise for an organist and choirmaster at a salary of £15 per annum. Nine applications were received and three were asked to lead the praise on successive Sundays, the congregation to choose by vote. Thomas Watson was the choice. He resigned a year later and a successor was again chosen by the congregation. Alexander Patrick, Leslie, received the majority of votes.

THE HOUSE OF LORDS DECISION

A crisis in the affairs of the United Free Church occurred in 1904, consequent on the decision of the House of Lords affecting the property of the former Free Church where congregations remained out of the Union of 1900 and continued as the Free Church. They were awarded much property. The Macainsh Session passed a resolution, "while deploring the decision of the Lords based on a misapprehension of factors, expressed their loyal adhesion to the Union, as well as the principle of spiritual independence according to which Christ was the Church's only Head, and His word the supreme standard." The senior minister, Mr Macainsh, associated himself with the resolution, testifying to the Church's freedom in 1904 as he had done in 1843. A communication was read from Professor Rainy and the Rev. D. Brown, and Mr D. Philp was appointed to represent the congregation at a Convocation at Edinburgh to consider the position. (In the neighbouring parish of Kinglassie, a majority adhered to the Free Church and claimed and got both the Kirk and the Manse. The change took place on a Sunday when two ministers occupied the pulpit. The writer was present at a very unseemly scene on that occasion.)

THE JUBILEE

The year 1906 was the Golden Jubilee of the congregation and of the ministry of Mr Macainsh, and the occasion was celebrated by a special service on Sunday, 22nd June and a social later. The Rev. Professor Stalker, D.D., conducted the Sunday service. Guests at the social included the Rev. A. Henderson, D.D., Crieff, principal clerk of the General Assembly; Rev. W.

Milne, M.A., Kirkcaldy (brother-in-law of Mr Macainsh); Revs. Hugh Elder (son-in-law); James Muir, B.D., Glasgow (a former assistant); G. Dalziel, Kinglassie; Charles Mason, Portmoak and Lochcraig; J. D. Dawson Scott, M.A., Cowdenbeath, and A. MacDonald, Lumphinnans.

Great interest was taken in the social held on the Tuesday night, when 14 ministerial friends were present, along with two previous members who signed the call to Mr Macainsh — Mrs Nelson, widow of Dr Nelson; and John Westwater, printer and publisher. Mrs Dick, widow of Thomas Dick, was not able to attend owing to illness.

A telegram was sent to Mr and Mrs Macainsh then living in retirement in Crieff, and Mr Brown read a letter from Mr Macainsh recalling his ordination and the meeting they held in 1863 to celebrate the extinction of debt on the church. Illuminated addresses were presented from the Presbytery of Kirkcaldy in which Mr Macainsh spent the active years of his ministry; from his native congregation at Monzie; the Presbytery of Dunfermline, and the Lochgelly congregation. Rev. Hugh Elder replied on behalf of his father-in-law.

The Session petitioned the House of Lords in favour of the Government's Licensing Bill and asked the local member, J. D. Hope, M.P., to support it.

The Lochgelly Friendly Societies asked and were granted a special Sunday service.

The spiritual condition of the part of Lochgelly known as the Muir (houses belonging to Lochgelly Iron and Coal Company) was raised by Mr Sam Stewart. He said there was a neglect of religious ordinances and much need for Mission work.

The Moderator made reference to the death the previous day of the Rev. James Brown, Churchmount, on the eve of his ministerial Jubilee. He said Mr Brown had made great efforts to elevate the life of the people and co-operate with their own church.

Special Bible classes and clubs were urged in a circular from the Presbytery. They also called attention to the amount of Sunday trading and labour which existed. Mr Brown pointed out that they already had Bible Classes but he would like to start a club for young men.

Reference was also made to the prevalence of gambling in the town and the existence of a club where betting was regularly carried on. It was decided to enquire into the law on the matter.

THE MUIR MISSION

A joint meeting was held in Churchmount Hall to consider Mission work in the Muir district, occupied by workers of Lochgelly Coal Company. The Rev. D. Brown presided. Both a Missionary and a meeting place were needed to keep in touch with the non-churchgoing people. Both sides agreed to further consider probable financial support to maintain a Missionary's salary. Intimation was made in June, 1911, of the appointment by the Presbytery of Mr Ralston, one of the Church's evangelists to work for the two congregations in the Muir district. A joint committee was formed.

In February, 1911, the Session discussed the Sunday evening entertainments carried on in one of the public halls. They agreed to consider means of putting a stop to what was felt to be a real evil in its effect on young people.

It was hoped to have a hall soon in the Muir, to be erected by the Presbytery's Home Mission Committee. S. Stewart and D. Moyes were appointed to represent the Session on the Muir Committee.

Mr Macainsh died on 17th February, 1913, at his residence, Knockearn, Crieff, at the age of 89. The Minute includes a long eulogy.

Miss Paris, a church sister, was appointed by the Home Mission in October, 1913, and was assisted by Miss Lamont, trained at the Women's Missionary College, Edinburgh.

An appeal was made by the Session to the Town Council against the constant and un-necessary shouting of newsboys on Sunday. It disturbed worship. The Council replied that they had asked the Magistrates to take steps to have it restricted, and if possible, stopped altogether. The Magistrates gave effect to the appeal.

A service of praise was held in the Public Park on behalf of the War Fund. The other churches were asked to join them and suggested that one of the local ministers should preside in turn. These continued to be well attended.

Collections were made on behalf of the Soldiers' and Sailor's Fund.

The roll of members in 1915 was reported to number 586.

The effect of the Liquor Control regulations in the war years, and so many men being called to the services, was reported as being the reason that drinking and crime had been greatly reduced.

Regarding Sunday observance, the Session noted the number of people travelling on tram-cars on Sundays; and the regular opening of the Picture Houses on Sunday evenings.

The second minister of the Church, the Rev. Duncan Brown, M.A., died in May, 1916. It was unexpected and caused much grief to the congregation. He was buried in the Kirkyard of Killin, his native parish. The Rev. Charles Mason conducted a funeral service in the church. Local clergy were present, and on the following Sunday, the pulpit was occupied by the Rev. J. Macainsh, Strathbran, a close friend of Mr Brown, and a frequent visitor to Lochgelly. Eloquent tributes were paid to his devotion to duty; his eagerness to spend and be spent in his Master's service.

On 21st May, the Vacancy Committee had seven applications and from a leet, the Rev. D. Davidson was chosen but later declined. A new leet was selected but none was chosen. A suggestion was made to write the Rev. Wm. McLeod, Whiting Bay, Arran, to preach. On 26th September, from the names submitted, Mr McLeod was chosen by a large majority. He was inducted on 16th November, 1916. After about two years, he was invited by the Foreign Mission to go to the Gold Coast for one year. The Court decided against the proposal, but later he was given leave to go to France (February, 1919) on Y.M.C.A. work. The Rev. Alex. Duncan of Haddington officiated in Mr McLeod's absence. He returned in September of the same year.

On 23rd February, 1920, a call to Mr McLeod was presented from another congregation.

The congregation met and appointed a deputation to Mr McLeod to convey to him the earnest desire that he should remain their minister. After the service on Sunday, he intimated his intention to remain and was warmly thanked.

It was intimated that the late Andrew Malcolm, solicitor, Lochgelly, had left a legacy of £100, the annual proceeds to be paid to the minister of the Macainsh Church for the time being as an addition to his stipend.

The Court decided to introduce individual Communion Cups.

On 29th January, 1922, Mr McLeod said goodbye to the congregation, having accepted a call to Fort William. He was a Gaelic speaker and accepted the post at the urgent request of the General Assembly.

A Vacancy Committee met and accepted the suggestion to write the Rev. Harry Law, M.A., Monifieth, to preach. On his name being put to the congregation, he was chosen by a unanimous vote and he was inducted on 17th May, 1922.

Various suggestions were made for a memorial to commemorate the loss of members and adherents of the congregation in the late war. The decision was to erect a new oak pulpit and have panels for names. It is of chaste design and holds the 59 names. The opportunity was taken to reconstruct the choir range and floor and put the pulpit on a sound foundation. The cost of the pulpit was £105.

After the second World War, a second memorial was erected—a plaque on the south wall of the Church, commemorating the members and adherents of the congregation who fell in that war. This memorial contains 12 names.

On the request of William Ritchie, the Court approved the formation of a football club for the youth of the congregation. Mr Ritchie asked the use of the hall for a social and dance to help the funds. The Court turned this down but agreed to pay 36/- entrance fees to the Churches League.

A SECOND HALL NEEDED

A move was made early in 1903 to erect a new and larger hall. Mr Birrell, architect, Kirkcaldy, was consulted about a building to accommodate 200 - 300 people. The smaller hall, which had been built in 1884, had become too small. The need for more accommodation was becoming clamant, partly due to a large attendance at Mr Brown's Bible Class on Sunday evenings and to the increasing congregational activities. The plan was adopted and an appeal made from the pulpit to finance the scheme. An appeal was at the same time made for financial support for a new church at Glencraig.

A grant for the new hall of £100 was promised from the Miners' Fund. Estimates for the work amounted to £599 11/-.

GIFTS OF £500

The gift of £500 was intimated by the Rev. P. Macainsh, senior minister. It was to be sent to the treasurer of the United Free Church of Scotland on behoof of the Sustentation Fund of the Macainsh Church. On the suggestion of the general treasurer of the church (A. Ellison Ross), it was agreed to give it to the General Trustees to invest in the General Investments Account. He had pointed out that the interest would be three per cent, free of income tax, which it would earn from the date of receipt. Each half-year it would be credited as a congregation donation to the Sustentation Fund of the Macainsh Church.

A further letter dated 2nd July, 1906, from the General Church treasurer intimated a donation of £500 from Mr Macainsh on behalf of the fund for aged and infirm ministers (Free Church Section) under the condition that if a colleague be required for the Macainsh Church, Lochgelly, the interest accruing should be given to the senior colleague for the time being, in addition to the general allowance from the church.

Mr Macainsh was thanked for this renewed manifestation of the warm and practical interest in his congregation.

In connection with the Kay Bequest, A. & J. Innes, Kirkcaldy, asked a report on the state of the Church and manse property in accordance with the terms of the Kay Bequest. The amount due the Macainsh Church was £13 5/11. It was agreed to forward a report as requested.

A large part of the feu, known as the Paddock, was opened for feuing subject to Lord Zetland's consent. With the latter's approval the ground was divided into six lots and soon was taken up for miners' cottages.

PIPE ORGAN

A new organ was needed and after discussion whether it should be a pipe organ, it was decided to purchase the latter. It was built by a Glasgow firm and cost fully £180. Several structural alterations were necessary to provide a suitable site.

Special services were held in connection with the inauguration of the organ, and it was agreed to ask Mr Gray, conductor of the Lochgelly Choral Union, to play it on the opening day. A boy was engaged as organ blower at

38/- per annum. The organist, Mr Patrick, asked for an increase of salary. £2 was offered, whereupon, Mr Patrick resigned. Several applications were received.

LARGER HALL OPENED

The larger hall was opened on 7th November, 1906. The need for this was primarily to accommodate the large attendance at Mr Brown's popular Bible Class meetings. The old hall (which had been built 20 years earlier) was crowded out at these gatherings. Until it was ready, the Church had to be used. At the opening social, Mr Williamson, convener of the Hall Building Committee (who was a great asset to the Church), was able to report that it was free of debt. A bazaar had realised the sum of £268; the Woman's Work Party, £67; and the Bible Class, £40. Mr Macainsh sent a cheque for £100; the Miners' Mission contributed £100 and with the donations and collections, the total amount raised was £733. The cost of its erection, with extras, was £729, leaving a credit balance of £4 13/8. The Rev. Duncan Brown, who presided, read a letter of congratulation from the senior minister, Rev. P. Macainsh, Crieff, who hoped the new hall would prove a boon and the means of yet further extending the work of the congregation.

In 1910, the Deacons' Court had an application from Lochgelly Co-op. Society for the use of the Church Hall for the quarterly meeting. After various opinions had been expressed it was deemed advisable, under the circumstances, to decline letting the hall. (The Society's own hall had been burned down).

In May, 1911, it was intimated that the Presbytery had agreed to place an Evangelist in the Muir district and they were making endeavours to secure a hall.

DEATH OF MR MACAINSH

The Rev. Peter Macainsh, first minister of the congregation, died at his residence, Knockearn, Crieff, on 17th February, 1913, at the age of 89. The Courts of the Church put on record their deep sense of the great loss which had befallen the congregation and the whole Free Church. A brief extract from a Minute says "He was not only senior pastor but the real founder of the congregation. He came to Lochgelly in 1855, when there was but a small meeting, and worked to such purpose that the General Assembly of 1856 sanctioned this as a full charge. In 1857 the present church was opened.

"For many years his sphere of labour extended from Dundonald and

Cardenden on the east, and Cowdenbeath and Lumphinnans on the west, and to Flockhouse School, Ballingry, and Lochore on the north. His efforts for the good of Lochgelly were unlimited. He did much in the cause of Education and Temperance. It may be said that in Home Mission efforts in the whole mining districts in Fife, he did more than any other man in his day. Numerous congregations were set up by the Free Church, from Leven to Dunfermline in which he took a leading part."

The whole community grieved at his death.

Memorial services were held on the following Sunday. A Memorial Tablet was later placed on the wall of the vestibule.

DIVISION OVER UNION IN 1929

There was an acute division in the congregation over the Union with the Established Church in 1929 and it was obvious that unanimity could not be secured in the Macainsh Church. The other Presbyterian Churches in Lochgelly, the Established and Churchmount, offered no opposition.

A long controversy had taken place in the year previous in the columns of the local paper, which, while arousing interest, showed a distinct cleavage.

The cleavage came to a head at a meeting of the congregation on 18th February, 1929, when in a crowded church, the matter came up for a decision. The Rev. J. D. Brown, who presided, explained the basis and plan of Union.

A motion in favour of the Union was proposed by Mr John Gray and seconded by Dr D. E. Dickson. To this, an amendment was put by Mr David Moyes, and seconded by Mr Sam. Stewart. Most of the congregation did not take part in the vote which was 34 for the motion and 22 for the amendment.

A number of the dissentients left the church and joined continuing congregations at Cowdenbeath and Cardenden.

Among them were the mover and seconder of the amendment. Both were elders and very active and keen churchmen, taking a special interest in evangelistic work. Mr Moyes had been acting for some time as Scottish Organising Agent for the minority party. He was later ordained as a minister in the Continuing Church and held appointments in Orkney, Stanley and Colmonell in Ayrshire. Another loss was Alexander Kerr, an elder and devoted member.

AT THE PRESBYTERY

When the Union question came up at Presbytery, Mr Moyes seconded a motion of disapproval to the Union plan. In referring to a statement made by

Lord Sands, he made a remark to which objection was taken by a member as being irrelevant. The protest was upheld by the Moderator who pointed out that he had to intervene when irrelevant matter was introduced.

The vote in Presbytery was — For the Plan of Union, 26; Against, 10.

PRESENTS

Two memorial windows, the gift of Mrs John Clark (nee May Philp), were unveiled on 4th November, 1945, by the Rev. John D. McLennan, a former minister of the church. The donor is a grand-daughter of the late Mr Thomas Dick, and daughter of the late Mr David Philp, both of whom played a big part in the history of the Macainsh Church. The first named was a member of the first Session in 1856, signed the call, and acted as treasurer for many years. He was succeeded in these offices by his son-in-law, the late Mr David Philp. For many years, the latter was representative to the Presbytery, and along with Rev. Duncan Brown took part in the culmination of Union negotiations in 1900. Assisting at the unveiling was Mr Alfred W. Philp, who, while resident in Lochgelly, took a keen interest in the welfare of the church and the town.

On Sunday, 14th October, 1956, which marked the exact date of the founding of the congregation, Communion Chairs were dedicated by the minister, Rev. G. B. Macallan.

These were the gift of Mr Peter Williamson, Belfast, son of the late Mr James Williamson, one of the most kenspeckle figures connected with the Church. He was for many years an elder and Session Clerk; took a great interest in the psalmody, and in numerous ways gave splendid service. The special occasion was taken by the minister, of recapturing something of the atmosphere of 100 years ago, by the choir acting as the precentor and singing the first verses of the old Scottish psalms alone, after which the congregation joined in.

A plaque was placed on the west wall of the church by Mrs Dickson in memory of her husband, Dr. D. E. Dickson, who practised in Lochgelly from 1897 till his death in 1940, and who was a member of the Macainsh Church throughout that period. The plaque bears the inscription:—"In loving memory of David Elliot Dickson, J.P., M.D., F.R.C.S.(Edin), born 5th July, 1874, died 6th July, 1940. He attained the highest honours in his profession and was eminent in its counsels, yet the first place in his heart was his love for this community in which for over 42 years he proved himself a trusted adviser and a devoted friend."

A Baptismal Font and Communion Table, both of carved solid oak, were presented in 1933 from a fund raised through Miss Currie, Church Sister, by the children of the Sabbath School. They were unveiled by Mrs May Clark.

The original Font, a small silver vessel, which was hung on the pulpit when needed, was presented by Mrs Clark's grandfather, Thomas Dick, when the church was opened, and the first time it was used was at the baptism of his daughter, Jemima (Mrs David Philp), Mrs Clark's mother. This vessel was appropriately fitted into the bowl of the new font, thus perpetuating a relic of sentimental value.

LEGACIES

Rev. Peter Macainsh — £500 (to Church's Sustentation Fund Contribution)

Kay Bequest (Bi-Annual)

Andrew Malcolm Bequest — £100

Mrs Helen C. Harrower or Williams — £500

Mary Beatson — £100

Notes on the Ministers
1856 - 1957

Throughout the century, the Macainsh Church has had ten ministers. The first two served for fifty years and eight in the second half. They all resigned for other charges and it can be truthfully said that the congregation would have preferred that they should have stayed on.

In the eight is included one who held the position for only six weeks, the Rev. George Steel. An accident in the Manse occasioned his removal to hospital where he died the following day. It was a grievous loss to the congregation who showed much sympathy to his parents. It was a tragic end to a useful and promising life. His death took place on the eve of his marriage.

REV. PETER MACAINSH

The Rev. Peter Macainsh was born in 1824 in the Parish of Monzie, situated between Crieff and the Sma' Glen. He was the first minister.

He came to Lochgelly as a Probationer. A mission had been started in the then village in 1849 by Kirkcaldy Free Presbytery. The district was reported to be in "a state of great spiritual destitution" and it looked a likely place for expansion of the Free Kirk.

Mr Macainsh had been serving as a Probationer at Methil and Leven. When the Free Kirkers here applied for his transfer the Presbytery approved and he arrived in Lochgelly in 1855. His appointment proved a milestone in the history of the town.

Probationers' salaries were then £60 a year, paid half by the Home Mission Committee and the other half by members of the mission. To raise this sum was a bit of a struggle but united and earnest, and fired by the enthusiasm of the young missioner, they not only accomplished it but soon found the nucleus for building a church. Within a few years it became self-supporting and has so continued and in general has contributed more to the church funds than it received.

The Macainsh congregation was, and is, working class and democratic in all its ways. It has exercised a profound influence for good over the community.

Rev. PETER MACAINSH

Mr Macainsh's work was not confined to the village (Lochgelly became a Police Burgh in 1877). All over the surrounding district, comprising the Parishes of Auchterderran, Ballingry and part of Beath, he carried forward the Christian message and by means of open air and cottage meetings led many to happier and purer lives. Such villages as Cowdenbeath, Lumphinnans, Cardenden and Lochore depended on Lochgelly as a centre for spiritual guidance in Free Church tenets. That the work was fruitful is evidenced by the churches that later sprang up there.

He was much thought of in the Presbytery (of Kirkcaldy then). Three years after his ordination he was elected Moderator. His advice and help was often sought by other Churches. He could have had a more prominent charge, but like the parson of Goldsmith's poem—

> *"Remote from towns he ran his Godly race*
> *And ne'er changed, nor sought to change his place."*

He served his congregation faithfully and zealously and continued as minister till he died in 1913. For the last two decades he had a colleague and successor.

For years before he relinquished the active ministry, he engaged student assistants. He paid their salaries. It was a former assistant, the Rev. Duncan Brown, M.A., who was chosen as his colleague and successor.

Mr Macainsh took an interest in the founding of the Free Kirk congregation at Cowdenbeath; and, in conjunction with the late revered Rev. Charles Mason laid the foundation of the congregation of Lochcraig. This church was built when Glencraig Colliery was developed. He had been associated with Mr Mason in a Mission in that area. Services had been held for years on Sabbath evenings in a school north of Lochore, known as Flockhouse. He had a number of members in the landward part of Auchterderran parish, and they and Kinglassie members formed the nucleus of the Free Church at Cardenden which connected with the Free Church at Kinglassie.

His extensive parochial responsibility made him a kenspeckle figure in the village and district. Of average height, he was stoutly built and invariably wore clerical dress and a soft black hat, and a white muffler round his neck. His broad face, emphasised by a beard round the chin, kindly eyes, and genial smile, beamed benevolence.

In his topcoat skirt pocket he carried packets of tea which he handed out to the sick and aged. By sustained visiting, he maintained personal contact with his people.

> *"He was a man to all the country dear"*

Round such a personality stories are inevitable. Reference has been made to his cottage meetings in the early years of his ministry.

On one occasion he sent word to the Baltic Cottage (between Lochgelly and Lumphinnans, now demolished) the residence of the miner member, James Thomson, better known as "Curly", that he would be holding a meeting in their house that night.

The Thomson family was connected with the church from the start. They were also keen volunteers and good riflemen with the Fife Volunteer Battalion started in 1859 on the threat of an invasion. Lochgelly village supplied one of the eight county companies, almost entirely comprised of muscular miners.

"Curly" was a perfect attender at parades and when he retired as sergeant after 20 years' service he had an unbroken record. On returning from the pit that day and getting the message from Mr Macainsh he said to his wife: "Ye'll better send word to the minister that it'll no suit me. Maister Macainsh surely does'na ken this is a drill nicht." So that service was cancelled and "Curly" kept his drill record intact..

When Lochgelly quoad sacra Parish School Board was formed in 1872 on the passing of the first Scottish Education Act, the local Board of seven members comprised the then three clergymen in the town (Macainsh, Free; Dewar, Parish; and James Brown, U.P.); the laird of Glencraig, G. W. Constable; the manager of Lochgelly Iron and Coal Coy. (Andrew Landale); the Union Bank Agent (William Cameron); and Lumphinnans was represented by Henry Mungall, coalmaster.

In that connection a controversy arose at a meeting at which Mr Dewar claimed a privilege in that he was minister of the Parish, to which Mr Macainsh retorted: "You may be minister of the Parish, Mr Dewar, but I am minister of the People."

Two stories were given to me by Mr Alex Hunter ("Auld Eck"), a sturdy Fife miner now in his ninety-third year. I give the stories in his own words: "When Mr Macainsh was visiting one day in Park Street, he knocked by mistake at the wrong door which in the row were much alike. The house was occupied by an old Irish woman, named Ann Downie. He had intended to visit the house next door. When she saw the figure in the doorway she got up and shouted—'Go away, you big fat Macainsh. We don't want you here; we've got a praiste of our own.'

"He explained how he had made the mistake, then put his hand into his big pocket and offered her a packet of tea. She cooled down and was very profuse in her thanks. Next morning she told her neighbour about it, and added—'Sure, Mr Macainsh is a very fine gentleman.' "

Auld Eck's other recollection runs: "Mr Macainsh married me in 1890. When the first of the family came I went to the manse to arrange about baptism. He wanted me to have it done in the Church. I had not the courage to face that and I made the excuse that my wife did not have a pretty enough dress to wear. He said: 'Oh, but we still have Hannah's (his daughter) dress in the drawer and you can get it.' "

Then continued Eck: "I told him my real reason. My wife, like every other wife, when there are sisters to carry the baby, had to get everything of the best. Mr Macainsh also baptised my next baby (Alexander), and Duncan Brown, then the minister, baptised the others, which were twins. He wanted to say he had baptised twins in the Church. He got his way and a paragraph appeared in the 'Lochgelly Times' about it."

Mr Macainsh was married in 1871. His bride was Hannah Brown Johnston. She died in 1919. There was one child of the marriage, Hannah, who married the Rev. Hugh Elder in 1900 at Crieff. The bridegroom was then minister of the Forman Free Church, Leven, and later of Stockbridge, Edinburgh. Of a family of seven, two were boys. One died in infancy. His name was Peter Macainsh Elder. The other son, Hugh Elder, is the headmaster of the Merchants Taylors' School, Middlesex. He had a memorial tablet placed in the church where his father ministered and where his grandfather started as a Probationer.

Mr Macainsh's jubilee as a minister and the jubilee of the opening of the Church were celebrated at a social gathering in a packed church in October, 1906, and special services on Sunday were taken by Professor Stalker and Mr Brown. Mr Macainsh was too infirm to travel.

In a tribute to his work, Mr Brown said of him: "He was greater than anything he said or did. Wherever he went, people could not but feel the better of his presence. He raised the tone of life all around him. He had the power to win the careless, to inspire the hesitating, and rebuke the evil-minded."

Mr Macainsh was traditionalist in doctrine and evangelical; like most Scots of his period he was conservative in the older forms of church worship, but a Liberal in politics. There was no instrumental music in the Church till after he left Lochgelly; psalms were preferred to hymns unless in the Sunday School. He would not have a Christmas tree for the children's soiree and the Macainsh bairns had to be content with a magic lantern. The summer picnic was to places within walking distance while those of the other churches had the excitement of a hurl in a corn cairt. The reason, I was told, was because in the early years there had been a picnic to Aberdour in carts and a boy was seriously injured. Henceforth, Mr Macainsh took no risks.

In middle life, Mr Macainsh received a legacy which removed him from financial worries. From notes in another part of this booklet it will be seen that the congregation benefited materially. On his retiral as senior minister, he built a house at Crieff situated midway between Knock Hill and the River Earn, appropriately named "Knockearn." There he spent the evening of a strenuous life in the beautiful district which was his cauf country, and with which he had sentimental recollections. There he died on 17th February, 1913, at the ripe old age of 89 years.

A memorial was placed on the vestibule wall of the church by the congregation; but the work he did and the example he set is his finest memorial. His memory will be carried down by tradition to generations who knew him not.

THE REV. DUNCAN BROWN, M.A.

Mr Brown was a native of Killin, Perthshire, where he served his apprenticeship as a baker. He trained in Arts and Divinity in Glasgow University and came to Lochgelly as an assistant to Mr Macainsh. They were much attached to each other and there is no doubt that Mr Macainsh had him in mind when he asked for a colleague and successor and was greatly pleased when the congregation fulfilled that desire. For a short time previously Mr Brown had laboured at Clackmannan.

Tall and sparsely built, Mr Brown had an austere appearance which belied his nature, which was warm-hearted and sociable. He had a cultured mind; an intellectual; and he had a keen sense of humour. In general character he followed in Mr Macainsh's footsteps. Much inclined to the study, he was well informed and well versed in the classics and theology.

A reader and speaker of the Gaelic tongue, he was attracted to the numerous Celtic place names in the district.

A feature of his ministry was his interest in adolescents. His Bible Class was tremendously popular. The Hall, built in 1884, proved inadequate and that was the immediate reason for a larger hall being built. He lectured on various subjects. Sankey's Hymns were used at the Bible Class and under the conductorship of the late James Williamson (one of the outstanding officebearers of the Church) they went with the swing of a revival meeting. In the interval to the opening of the larger hall, the Bible Class was held in the Church where orchestral music was introduced.

Mr Brown was a bachelor and his sister, who had been a nurse, looked after him with devoted care.

Rev. DUNCAN BROWN, M.A.

His death was unexpected. It occurred in 1916 and came as a shock to the congregation.

THE REV. W. McLEOD, D.D.

The Rev. W. McLeod had experiences of charges before being unanimously called to the Church.

He attended Edinburgh University and Princeton University, U.S.A., and held the degrees of B.D., Ph.D., F.S.A. (Scot), and D.D. His first charge, in 1904, was Mellness in the Presbytery of Tongue, thence to Stratherrick (Inverness) in 1910; Whiting Bay (1912); Lochgelly (1916); Fort William (1922); Cowcaddens, Glasgow (1924); St. Bruoc, Port Bannatyne (1928-1945).

Mr McLeod was a Gaelic preacher and moved into charges at the request of the Assembly.

He gave a convincing impression of a man of great piety. His devotional prayer meetings were largely attended and he held the affection of the congregation. During his incumbency the average attendance at Church reached its peak.

Before he left Lochgelly he had two calls, one of which he turned down at the earnest request of a deputation sent to him by a large turnout of the congregation. Later on, an urgent request from the General Assembly, to take a Gaelic Church, was made and he felt it was his duty to comply. He left Lochgelly leaving behind the memory of a pious and devoted pastor. His degrees testify to his scholarship.

He retired in 1945 and went to reside in Edinburgh. He was loth to give up his work and in 1948 accepted a call to his first charge, Mellness. Mrs McLeod died there in 1950.

In 1953 he again retired and made his home in Edinburgh. There he died very suddenly on 9th January, 1956, and was buried beside his wife in Mellness. Mr McLeod's only daughter, Marie, is at present a teacher in Glasgow.

THE REV. HARRY LAW, M.A.

Mr Law was a native of the Bishopshire, the birthplace of Michael Bruce; attended Dunfermline High School and graduated Master of Arts at Edinburgh University. He went on to the New College for his Theological Training. Licensed by the Presbytery of Dunfermline and Kinross, he held two assistantships—Union Church, Edinburgh, and St. Paul's, Dundee. In 1914 he

Rev. WILLIAM McLEOD, D.D., B.D.

Rev. HARRY LAW, M.A.   Rev. JONATHAN D. BROWN, M.A.

Rev. JOHN D. McLENNAN, B.D.

Rev. NIGEL R. MacLEAN, B.D.

Rev. GEORGE STEELE, M.A.

Rev. DAVID ROSS, B.D.

was ordained and inducted minister of Panmure Church, Monifieth. On the resignation of Mr McLeod in 1922 he received a call to the Macainsh Church and five-and-a-half years later was translated to Ruchill, Glasgow. His last charge was the United congregations of St. Ninian's and Priory, Whithorn. While there, illness compelled him to retire from the active ministry. He died in Dundee on 4th November, 1952.

Mr Law had a distinctive personality, and a most gracious and winsome character. He served the church faithfully and devotedly and found time and the inclination to devote to social work.

As secretary of the two West Fife Evangelistic Campaigns he put his whole heart into the effort to win the miners whom he understood and loved. He pleaded their cause in the General Assembly.

During the First World War he served with the Y.M.C.A. at home and abroad. In Glasgow he initiated and carried on splendid work in the dark days of the depression. Temperance and civic affairs were included in his interests in Monifieth and Whithorn.

An enthusiast for the vernacular, he attracted large audiences to hear the Gospel in the Mither Tongue and as a lecturer he was much in demand. His passing left a great blank in many hearts. His widow, who was an active help-mate and interested in his work, now resides in Dundee and recently opened a Church Bazaar in the Town Hall, Lochgelly.

THE REV. J. D. BROWN, M.A.

Mr Brown was educated at Hutchison's Grammar School, Glasgow, Glasgow University and Trinity College. His studies at the University were interrupted by the 1914-18 war during part of which he served as a combatant in the Machine Gun Corps.

His first charge was St. Abbs, Berwick on Tweed, to which he was ordained and inducted in 1923. After about five years in the fishing village and holiday resort, he received in 1928 (he was then aged 29) a call to Macainsh Church. At the date of his induction he had been married one week. From Lochgelly he was called to High Hilton, Aberdeen, as first minister of what was then an Extension Charge. It is now a well established congregation with about 1,500 members. His success led to his present charge, Portobello Old Parish. This congregation four years ago was joined with the neighbouring congregation of Portobello Old and Regent Street.

Mr Brown's term in Lochgelly was very successful. In a covering note from him regarding the Centenary, he says: "It lets the thoughts fly back across the hundred years of the church's existence, widening thoughts of pride and thankfulness in its splendid record of service and achievement. Yet while we glory in the past, let us draw guidance and inspiration that will enable us to face worthily the duties and demands of the present."

THE REV. J. D. McLENNAN, M.A.

Mr McLennan was inducted in the Macainsh early in 1936. He was full of the vigour of youth and specially attracted the youth of the congregation. Lochgelly was his first charge and there was general regret when he transferred to Rockcliffe Church, Glasgow.

He was educated at Clydebank High School, Glasgow University and Trinity College. His first appointment was that of lecturer at Westhill Training College, Glasgow. From there he came to Lochgelly.

During the second world war he obtained leave of absence to act as an Army Chaplain and was posted to the Royal Scots Greys. On demobilisation, he accepted a call to Rockcliffe Church, Glasgow which is his present charge.

He is a member of Glasgow Education Committee.

Mr McLennan is married to Ella Doig, second daughter of Mr Andrew Doig. She was a member of the Macainsh Church in which her father is an elder, as was also her grandfather, James Adamson.

THE REV. NIGEL R. MacLEAN, B.D.

Mr MacLean is a son of the manse, his father, the Rev. A. C. MacLean, J.P., F.S.A.(Scot.), a well-known writer upon the history of Northern Scotland, archaeologist, poet and Gaelic preacher, and was minister of the Parish of Contin for over 30 years.

Following attendance at the local school and at Dingwall Academy, Mr MacLean entered upon his studies at Aberdeen University, graduating M.A. 1937 and B.D. in March, 1940. During student years he was interested in athletics and captained both the Harriers and Athletic clubs, and was awarded his blue for performances associated with each club. In 1937 he was elected a member of the Atalanta Club.

Macainsh Church called him to be its minister in April, 1942. In 1944 he entered upon a period of National Service and spent a considerable period with the Church of Scotland Huts and Canteens, serving H.M. Forces. He was associated mainly with the R.A.F. stations in south-west Scotland. Mr MacLean was a keen supporter of Toc H. There was general regret when he left. Five years after coming to Lochgelly he was called to Barony North Church, Glasgow. This charge was centrally situated with a congregation scattered throughout the city, a large proportion of the membership being accommodated in the new housing areas, and during 1950 he was area convener of the Presbytery's open-air mission. After over seven years at the Barony North he accepted a call to St. Paul's Perth, where he was inducted in 1954. In 1949 he married I. C. Vallance, daughter of a Glasgow minister and there are two children.

THE REV. DAVID W. ROSS, B.D.

Mr Ross is a Ross-shire man, born at the fishing village at Balintore. He was educated at Tain Royal Academy and graduated at Aberdeen University: M.A. in 1935, and B.D. in 1938.

He started his ministerial career as an assistant at Montrose Old Church, 1938-41 and was ordained and inducted to the Barony Church, Auchinleck, Ayrshire.

He was called to Lochgelly in 1948 where his ministry was highly appreciated, and in June, 1953, he was inducted to Mains Parish Church, Dundee. The Men's Guild was started on his initiative.

In a message he recalls that Mrs Ross and himself have happy memories of their stay in Lochgelly and it was with real sincerity they wished God's highest blessing on the minister, office-bearers and members of the Macainsh Church. They earnestly pray for many more years of successful work there.

THE REV. GERALD B. MACALLAN

The Rev. Gerald B. Macallan, the present incumbent, is a native of Troon, Ayrshire, and received his secondary education at Marr College there. He proceeded to Glasgow University to study for the degree of B.Sc. in Engineering. This course was interrupted by the war in which he served in the R.A.F. as a flight mechanic and later as an engineer fitter.

After demobilisation he felt a call to the Ministry and in March, 1953, completed the War Service Course in Divinity at Glasgow University. During part of his time at University and until coming to Lochgelly, he served as Assistant Minister in St. Nicholas Church, Prestwick. It is interesting to note that the Rev. G. McLeod Dunn, whose assistant he was, had himself baptised Mr Macallan as a child at the start of his ministry in 1927.

Mr Macallan has taken a special interest in youth. He spent several summers at campaigns and seaside missions under the Rev. D. P. Thomson and the Rev. Tom Allan. It was while working with the latter at Ayr that he first became conscious of a call to the ministry and while at Kintyre with Mr

Thomson he became certain that this was the work God intended for him. Since coming to Lochgelly he has twice taken a team of young people to Prestwick to conduct a seaside mission there and hopes to do so again this summer.

During the Kintyre campaign he met the young lady who is now his wife. An Aberdonian, she was leader of the Primary Sunday School in Torry U.F. Church and taught in the Infant Department of King Street School.

Since coming to Lochgelly, two children have been born to Mr and Mrs Macallan: a boy and a girl, and having two "Fifers" in the family has given them a real tie with the district and has made them feel more than ever that this is their home.

Members who entered the Ministry

Several members of the church became ordained ministers, but only one entered the Free Church. He was the Rev. Alexander Westwater, M.A. Coached by Mr Macainsh, he graduated at Edinburgh. His first appointment was assistant at Mayfield Church, Edinburgh. From there he was appointed and inducted at Hawick and thence to Prestonpans. After retiral, he lived on at Edinburgh and acted as secretary of the Carlyle Society. He died at Edinburgh where his widow survives. His eldest daughter, Agnes, was a missionary in India (Madras). She retired a few years ago.

Another of Mr Macainsh's proteges was the late James Moyes. He joined the first American mission to Tibet. They were attacked by the natives and had to flee for their lives. Several were killed. Mr Moyes escaped and went to Canada where he became a minister in a church there.

Samuel Blair, who was coached by Mr Duncan Brown, became a student at the Bible Training Institute in Glasgow. He went out on Mission work to Australia. After two years he returned to Glasgow to amplify his training and was appointed assistant at Rockcliffe Church, Glasgow. He married a student at the college. His next appointment was missionary assistant at Egresmont, Liverpool.

He was induced to return to Australia and spent three years at the Divinity College in Melbourne. His first full charge was at the mining town of Wantaggi. He found many people from this district resident there. He accepted a call to a larger church in Melbourne and died there nine years ago. All his three sons entered professions.

William Simpson, like Mr Blair, was active in local evangelistic work with Mr Brown. He, too, went to Glasgow Bible Training College and later proceeded to Australia where he was inducted to the same church as Mr Blair started his ministry, Wantaggi. During the last war, he several times sent parcels of food for distribution among the old folks of the Macainsh congregation.

The Rev. David Moyes, who was an elder and did active work in the Macainsh congregation, was a keen opponent of the Union of 1929. He was appointed organising secretary for Scotland for the minority section. Following the union, he was ordained a minister of the U.F. Church continuing and appointed to a church in Orkney. He later transferred to Stanley in Perthshire and thence to Colmonell in Ayrshire. He died two years ago.

Miss Dorothy Malvenan, elder daughter of Mr Alex. Malvenan, has been associated with religious and social work at home and abroad. After training at St Colm's, she was appointed probationer under Dunnikier Church, Kirkcaldy. After eight years in that post, she served the Scottish Factory Girls' Association in the Scottish Midlands; thence to Scottish Command Highland Division, 1945; appointed Welfare Officer and Warden for Stobcross Community Centre under the Rev. Dr. Jardine, Wellington Church.

She later saw service in Egypt as Chaplain Assistant to W.R.A.C. and W.R.A.F. (1948-51); in Germany, 1953-55, and is at present on similar duty at Singapore, Malaya.

The late Rev. John Robertson was a minister in Lauder. He was a native of the town, and a member of Lochgelly Free Kirk, before proceeding to the University. While residing at Lochgelly, he served apprenticeship in a Kirkcaldy law office. For a time he walked the seven miles daily.

Another who has engaged in religious work is John Adamson, at present in charge of the Evangelical Church, Kirriemuir. Previously he served eight years in China with the China Inland Mission.

His sister, Jenny Adamson, was also a Missionary with the Kurku Mission in India. Her service there over a long period included part of the last war.

Their father, David Adamson, was for many years an elder in the Macainsh Church. They had transferred to Lochgelly Baptist Church when they took up Mission work.

The Church To-day

The high standards set by the founders of the church are well maintained. Under its present incumbent and office-bearers, as well as the heads of its various organisations, it plays a leading part in the spiritual and moral life of the community.

For a working class congregation, its givings are high as they have always been, and from a turn-over which this year amounts to £1697, it is able, over and above its obligations, to contribute much to Christian giving.

The Roll of members is 774 (recently purged).

Message from the Minister

My Dear Friends,

The Centenary of a congregation is a wonderful time, at once moving, inspiring, humbling.

It is a time to pause, as it were, in the course of a journey and, looking back, to marvel anew at the way in which God had led us before setting out again towards the dawning of that day when the Kingdoms of this world shall become the Kingdom of our God and of His Christ.

Sometimes, as we journey, we become footsore and weary. Sometimes we become disgruntled because the way seems long, the going slow and difficult. Sometimes we complain that the harmony has dropped from our pilgrim song, making us an ineffective rabble rather than an army on the march.

It is good at such moments to have an opportunity like this.

The way seems long but see how far God has enabled us to come. Much lies before us to be conquered but see how God has caused us to triumph in the past.

You see, that is what the backward look does. It shows us God, leading, guiding, blessing, strengthening.

So let us take heart and, with our Leader at the head, resume the march and press on to greater triumphs still.

With every blessing,

GERALD B. MACALLAN

Rev. GERALD B. MACALLAN

SESSION CLERKS — 1857 - 1957

WILLIAM SMALL - - - - - - 1857-62
JAMES ARNOT - - - - - - 1862-67
JOHN McINTOSH - - - - - - 1869-72
ALEX. NAYSMITH - - - - - 1885-88
(First Member of Session to act as Clerk)
HENRY GEDDIE - - - - - - 1889-92
DAVID PHILP - - - - - - 1892-1919
JAMES WILLIAMSON - - - - 1919-42
JOHN SWAN - - - - - - - 1942-47
ALEX. MALVENAN - - - - 1947-55
ARCHIBALD COOPER - - - - 1955-

The present representative to the Presbytery is Mr Robert Blair. He succeeded Mr Alexander Malvenan who is now feeling the infirmity of age. Mr Malvenan has to his credit many years of devoted and highly appreciated service to his Faith and the Church.

A valued elder who died recently and whose interest in the church will not be forgotten is the late William Ritchie. He was ever ready to sacrifice time and labour in the interests of the church, and in every way sought to live up to the principles of his Faith.

PRECENTORS — 1856 - 1957

JAMES KINNELL - - - - - - 1856-88
DAVID LOW (£12 per annum) - - - 1888-1902
(Stewart Millar occasionally deputised for Mr Low)
New Hymnary introduced - - - - 1899
Organ introduced - - - - - 1901
THOMAS WATSON (£15 per annum) - 1902-03
ALEX. PATRICK (£17 per annun) - - 1903-10
PETER MORRIS (£20 per annum) - - 1910-17
(Mrs Thomson and Mr Williamson acted as Organist and Choirmaster respectively during period of war service of Mr Morris and for a time thereafter).
A. K. PATRICK (£30 per annum) - - 1918-20
Mr. SIMPSON (£35 per annum) - - 1920-25
J. M. HUGHES - - - - - - 1925-26
                                    1926-28
D. BROWN - - - - - - - 1928-34
CHARLES BLACK - - - - - 1934-46
Miss LILY STEWART - - - - 1946-48
WILLIAM H. RITCHIE - - - - 1948-

ORGANISATIONS and LEADERS

Sunday—
10 a.m.	Junior Bible Class	Rev. G. B. Macallan
11.15 a.m.	Primary Sunday School	Miss Ella Lumsden
12.30 p.m.	Senior Sunday School	Mr Robert Crawford
7.30 p.m.	Youth Fellowship	Miss Margaret Doig

Monday—
6 p.m.	Brownies	Miss Nan McKinlay
7.15 p.m.	Girl Guides	Mrs James McIntosh
7.30 p.m.	Men's Guild	Rev. G. B. Macallan
	(Fortnightly)	

Tuesday—
7 p.m.	Woman's Guild	Mrs G. B. Macallan

Wednesday—
6 p.m.	Wolf Cubs	Mr James McIntosh
7.45 p.m.	Boy Scouts	Mr James Simpson

Thursday—
6 p.m.	Junior Choir	Mr Wm. H. Ritchie
7.45 p.m.	Senior Choir	Mr Wm. H. Ritchie
7 p.m.	Men's Guild	

Friday—
7 p.m.	Youth Club	Mr John Keddie

THE WORK PARTY

The Work Party was formed in the nineties: its main purpose was raising funds for the Foreign Mission and it also contributed to the general congregational finance.

Its first president was the late Miss Blackwood. She was followed by the late Miss Helen Steedman, a lady of specially high attainments. The organisation proved a valuable adjunct to the congregation. The president was generally the lady of the Manse.

After the Union of 1929, it ceased to function on being merged in the Woman's Guild. The reigning president is Mrs Macallan, and the vice-president, Mrs Nisbet. When there was no lady of the Manse, other women have also held office. The late Mrs Reekie, and Mrs Annie Aitken were presidents for a number of terms.

Back Row — J. Mathewson, W. Ritchie, J. Christie, W. Scott, D. Pollock, R. Lawson, A. Laing, A. Keddie
Middle Row — G. Logan, D. Yule, R. Lumsden, J. M. Mitchell, R. Gray, H. Pollock, J. Swan, A. McMillan, D. Kerr, A. Davidson,
G. Kerr, D. Gerrard, J. McLean (Jun.), D. Seaton, J. Baxter, R. McMurray
Front Row — R. Baxter, A. King, R. Swan, J. McIntosh (Clerk to Deacons' Court), Rev. G. B. Macallan, A. Cooper (Session Clerk),
J. McLean (Treasurer), D. Smith, R. Blair (Presbytery Representative)
Inset — T. McLean (Died 13th February, 1957) and A. Malvenan.   David Stein absent through illness

Members of the Church Courts
1856 - 1957

ELDERS

7.12.1856
ANDREW BEVERIDGE
THOMAS DICK
GEORGE DOWIE
JAMES NEIL
ALEXANDER WESTWATER
10.2.1861
ROBERT FAIRFOUL
JOHN WHITE

22.11.1868
WALTER DRYBURGH
ALEXANDER MAILLER
DAVID HENDERSON
3.12.1871
HUGH McDIARMID
JOHN HARROWER
JOHN SEATH
DAVID SHARP
5.1.1879
CHARLES RATTRAY
WILLIAM ARNOTT
WILLIAM BARROWMAN
JOHN HUNTER
22.2.1885
JOHN ANDERSON
WILLIAM DRYBURGH
MURDOCH GAIR
HENRY GEDDIE
ALEXANDER NAISMITH
ALEXANDER SKENE
7.12.1887
NEIL SMITH
20.3.1892
PETER WILLIAMSON
DAVID PHILP
DAVID WILSON

21.6.1896
ALEXANDER KERR
JOHN LAIRD
JAMES NAISMITH
JOHN ROLLAND
26.10.1902
JAMES ADAMSON
JOHN BURLEIGH
S. LAWSON
JAMES WILLIAMSON, Jun.
JAMES FORSYTH

17.6.1906
DAVID ADAMSON
DAVID FOOTE
JOHN SNEDDON
SAMUEL STEWART

22.6.1919
GEORGE AITKEN
JAMES BLAIR
WILLIAM L. HOWIE
DAVID KERR
DAVID MOYES
WILLIAM RITCHIE
DAVID SMITH
5.11.1922
JOHN CAIRNS
JAMES DONALDSON
ARCHIBALD KERR
DAVID LOW

**No record at present available
of years between 1922 and 1945**

14.1.1945
JOSEPH ADAMS
JOHN BURLEIGH
JAMES MITCHELL
DUNCAN SEATON
10.10.1948
ARCHIBALD COOPER
R. LUMSDEN
ROBERT McMURRAY
D. McGREGOR
ROBERT M. GRAY
JAMES McINTOSH
DAVID DUFF
THOMAS BONNAR
J. M. MITCHELL
DAVID STEIN
DAVID GERRARD
25.11.1956
GEORGE KERR
GEORGE LOGAN
JOHN McLEAN
ALEXANDER McMILLAN
DAVID YULE

DEACONS

18.1.1857
JOHN WILKINSON
JOHN HODGE
THOMAS McKEE
WALTER DRYBURGH
ROBERT TURNER
ALEXANDER NAISMITH

10.2.1861
WILLIAM SMALL
ALEXANDER MAILLER
JOHN HARROWER
DAVID HENDERSON
JAMES ARNOTT
JOHN DRYBURGH

10.4.1864
WILLIAM ARNOTT
JOHN SEATH
WILLIAM McQUEEN
JAMES LUMSDEN
JOHN WESTWATER

22.11.1868
DAVID SHARP
COLIN McDIARMID
ANDREW DRYBURGH
DAVID DRYBURGH
JOHN CAMPBELL
JAMES WEBSTER
ALEXANDER WEBSTER

3.12.1871
JAMES STEVENSON
WILLIAM BARROWMAN
MURDOCH GAIR
JOHN HENDERSON
JOHN McLEAN
JOHN HUNTER

5.1.1879
A. SKENE
H. GEDDIE
T. TRAILL
J. GREENHILL
WILLIAM DICK
J. HENDERSON
D. WILSON
R. DICK

22.2.1885
ROBERT GARDINER
JOHN GILBERT
JAMES HUNTER
ALEXANDER KINLOCH
DAVID PHILP
WILLIAM SIMPSON
GEORGE THOMSON
JAMES WILSON
PETER WILLIAMSON

24.4.1892
COLIN LAIRD
JOHN LAING
JAMES WILLIAMSON
JAMES NAISMITH
ROBERT HEIGH
ANDREW DICK
WILLIAM FOOTE
JAMES WHITE
DAVID GREENHILL

12.7.1896
SAMUEL LAWSON
JOHN ADAMSON
SAMUEL BLAIR
WILLIAM SMITH
GEORGE WESTWATER
JAMES ADAMSON
JAMES WILLIAMSON
WILLIAM STEWART

16.11.1902
DAVID ADAMSON
ANDREW DICK
DAVID FOOTE
HENRY FORRESTER
DAVID LOW
DAVID SMITH

22.7.1906
GEORGE AITKEN
JAMES BLAIR
DAVID KERR
JAMES LOCKHART
ANDREW MALCOLM
WILLIAM RITCHIE
GEORGE SMITH
ROBERT WESTWATER

19.10.1919
WILLIAM BAIN
JOHN CAIRNS
JOHN CRAWFORD
JOHN CURRIE
JAMES DONALDSON
ARCHIBALD KERR
ALFRED W. PHILP
WILLIAM REEKIE
WILLIAM SIMPSON

24.12.1922
ROBERT BLAIR
JAMES DAWSON
JAMES DEWAR
ANDREW DOIG
JOHN GRAY
WILLIAM LINTON
ROBERT McLEAN
ROBERT SWAN
ALEXANDER WESTWATER
PETER WILLIAMSON

No record for years 1922-42.

9.3.1947
FRED G. WILSON
JOHN MILNE
ARCHIBALD COOPER
CHARLES A. McMILLAN
ROBERT M. GRAY
GEORGE H. KERR
RICHARD LUMSDEN
WILLIAM SCOTT
DAVID DUFF
JAMES McINTOSH

—.9.1950
WILLIAM H. RITCHIE
JAMES CHRISTIE
GEORGE LOGAN
ROBERT CLYDESDALE
JAMES L. McLEAN
D. B. G. POLLOCK
JOHN McLEAN
WILLIAM BARCLAY
PETER PLAYFAIR
THOMAS DURHAM

17.4.1955
JOHN McLEAN
ALEXANDER KEDDIE
ROBERT LAWSON
ALEXANDER LAING
JAMES LUMSDEN
PETER McMURRAY
ALEXANDER McMILLAN
JOHN MATHEWSON

The following Deacons are first mentioned on the dates given—

16.1.1925
A. NISBET
T. HUNTER
R. BAXTER
R. LAIRD
J. COOPER

19.9.1930
H. POLLOCK
W. PATRICK
A. MARSHALL
R. DEY
G. ADAMSON
A. FLEMING
J. CLARK
A. LYALL
W. SPENCE

21.12.1934
A. KING
R. McKAY
W. HOWIESON
J. CURRAN

15.3.1935
J. B. McLEAN
R. McMURRAY
D. YULE
J. SWAN
D. DAWSON
J. DAKERS
T. McLEAN
P. McQUIRE
A. BLAIR
T. THOMSON
R. CRAWFORD
T. ARMSTRONG
A. DAVIDSON

29.6.1939
R. CLARK
J. MITCHELL
J. ADAMS
T. B. EWING
R. PENMAN

"LEST WE FORGET"

The following are the names inscribed on the Church's two War Memorials:—

"In honoured memory of those members of this church who gave their lives in the cause of freedom."

1914 - 1918 War

James Barnes, John Baxter, Robert Bolt, Peter Carrie, Douglas Causer, Andrew Clark, R. Cunningham, George Dewar, Alex. Duncan, James E. Foote, Murdoch Gair, A. Galloway, David Gibb, John Gillespie, James Gillies, Alex. F. Hunter, John Jackson, John Jardine, John Johnstone, Alex. Keddie, David Kinnell, Alex. Laird, William Lindsay, Andrew McEwan, James McKee, John McLay, James T. Forsyth, Robert Gray, William Gray, Andrew McLean, Andrew C. McLean, Robert McLean, William McLean, W. D. Melville, David Mollison, Robert Morton, James Naysmith, Andrew Neilson, Archibald Nicol, John Nicol, Charles Potter, John Robertson, John Rodger, Alex. Scott, David Shand, Robert Shand, David Sharp, Robert Steele, Andrew Summers, George Swan, Charles Todd, John Whyte, William Wilkie, Alex. Wilson, Andrew Wilson, John H. Wilson.

1939 - 1945 War

Andrew Beveridge, James Collins, Peter Green, John Jackson, David McLean, Robert McLean, George Melville, John Paterson, Alex. Scott, George Stewart, Andrew Thomson, William Wilson.

"They died that we might live."

THE MANSE.   The Rev. G. B. and Mrs Macallan and Family

ADDENDUM

"ICHABOD"

In the vestry of Macainsh Church, Lochgelly, hang printed verses in a frame. They bear the title "The Old Wooden Church of Monzie" and connect with an incidental impulse by Mr Macainsh. Monzie was his native parish.

In the time of the Disruption, Mr Macainsh was a student, and like most others, threw his lot in with the Free Kirk.

On the day when the people of the Established Kirk left it to worship in a wooden church on a Communion Sabbath, 27th August, 1843, there appeared on the door of the Auld Kirk of Monzie the Word "Ichabod" (Thy glory is departed).

THE FIRST FREE KIRK—MONZIE

The Free congregation had met and the Action Sermon had been preached in the open air on the grassy slopes in front of Craigentor. The "Tent" or Wooden screen for the Pulpit was pitched near an old elm tree where tradition says Ebenezer Erskine preached in the middle of the previous century. The weather, however, became threatening, and the people moved across the road into the Wooden Church, barely finished. The first "Table" served there was by their own minister, the Rev. John R. Omand of Monzie. The present beautiful little church was built in 1869. On the tower, near the western door of the church, two texts were engraved. One is from Isaiah, "The Lord is our Judge; the Lord is our Lawgiver; the Lord is our King." The other is from the Prayer of Solomon in 1st Kings—"The Lord our God be with us, as He was with our fathers; let Him not leave us nor forsake us."

Suspicion for the word on the auld kirk door fell on one who has since risen to honour and given good service as a minister of the Free Church of Scotland. Mr Macainsh later acknowledged the authorship.

On an occasion later in the Kirkcaldy Presbytery when the Sustentation Fund was sagging a bit, Mr Macainsh read out the following verses, doubtless to stimulate interest in the Fund

I.

It was weel-kent grund in Scotland that we took in the Forty-Three;
It was nae new word amang us that Christ's kirk maun be Free;
It cam frae the mosses and ferns that are flowered wi' martyrs' graves;
It cam frae the Water o' Blednoch wi' the sough o' the Solway waves.
We read it in deep-cut letters where the bluid o' God's saints was shed,
Where Anwoth, an' Ken, an' Cairnsmuir have the keeping of our dead.

The witnesses and the worthies in the days of the peril and strife—
They set their seal to the record that we read in the Word of Life;
That men maun honour the ruler, but first they maun honour the Lord;
That the laws for the House of God on earth are given us in His word;
And not for fear nor favour, nor gowd nor earthly thing,
Main ither voice be hearkened where Christ alone is King;
That His folk behove to serve Him, though they meet on the mountain sod,
And the law of an earthly king is nought when it crosses the Law of God;
That the kirk maun be free to guard the richts that were bought wi' a bluid unpriced,
And that Christian folk in Scotland maun be free to follow Christ.

II.

The Moderates and the Southrons they geckit us laigh an' hie,
An' whiles they said it was havers, an' whiles it was Papistrie,
What kent they or cared for our conflicts, for the breach of a nation's faith,
For the truth an' the life o' the Gospel, an' the men that were faithful to death;
What recked they for richts o' the people? though the lesson was eith to learn,
Gin they speired at the folk o' Marnoch, an' Stewarton, an' Strathearn.
Our ain folk in the Commons they spak oot stieve and strang,
It wasna' the Scottish members had the wyte o' Scotland's rang.
But the Southron Lords and Commons they jeered them on the flure;
They scorned at guid Bredalbane, and' the heir o' auld Panmure.
What needs it to speak o' that battle that was focht ten years an' mair
By our wisest an' best, wi' the tongue an' the pen—by the puir o' the land wi' prayer,
They pled wi' the Lords in London; they pled in the Commons' Ha';
On the steps o' the throne they laid it, their claim in richt an' law.
An' little they wan wi' their pleadin', but muckle o' dule an' care,
Till they cam' tae the Commons o' Scotland, an' they got their answer there.
There was monie an ane that sneered an' leugh, an' said that it widna stand;
But they kent the hearts o' their ain folk, an' we lippened then burgh an' land.
There were foes ahint an' the sea before, an' the way was dark an' dim;
But the Lord in the cloud went forward, an' they boud to follow Him.

III.

Sae the ministers left their manses, wi' their livin's an' earthly store,
An' they set their face to the wilderness, wi' the Pillar of Cloud before;
An' they that had gaen to the heathen, an' countit the warld but loss,
There wasna' ae man o' them wantin', for they kent "the way o' the Cross."
They sawna' the bread for the morrow; they kentna' the path they trod;
But they lippened themsels an' their bairnies to the faithfulness of God.
An' the best o' the land went wi' them, ilk ane that was trusty an' true,
It warms my heart in me to mind on't, though I'm matchless an' auld enoo.
Aye, we were proud o' them, lassie, an' weel we had richt to be;
Aye, we were proud o' the Kirk o' Scotland, that micht suffer, but maun be Free,
An' frae monie a cottage altar, I wot there was praise that day
For the men that had grace to be faithful, an' the Lord that had opened the way;
An' greetin' there was wi' monie an' ane, that was used wi' nae sic thing,
When we thocht on them that had gien their a' for the honour o' sic thing,
When we thocht on them that had gien their a' for the honour o' Christ the King.
Sae we lifted our Psalms and our Bibles frae the seats, an' we gaed our ways;
An' we took to the bent an' the braeside, as they did in the Covenant days.

On the yetts o' the puir auld biggin', as we left it there cauld and toom,
The hand o' some fordersome callant had written the words o' doom.
But oh! it was bonnie that simmer, the simmer o' forty-three!
The lift was sae blue, an' the sun sae bricht, an' the Kirk that we lo'ed was Free.
The lilt o' the muirland mavis cam' saftly stealin' in,
An' saft frae the glen o' the Shaggie cam' the sough o' the "Ceichin' Linn,"
An' the grace o' the gracious spirit cam' doun like a simmer shower;
For the hearts o' the folk were open, an' the Word o' the Lord had power.

IV.

Oor laird he was aye in the thrang o't—a gallant like man to see—
'Twas a weel-kent name in the country then was Campbell o' Monzie.
He tirred a seete in his southmost park, where the birks on the knowes were fair,
An' oor lads they wrocht wi' a richt guid will, an' we laid the buirds wi' prayer.
The posts an' the joists were o' well waled pine frae Norroway ower the sea,
An' the buirds an' the seats an' the lave o't were the larches o' Monzie.
Like the Tent o' the Lord in the desert, wi' its buirds o' the Shittim wood,
Where He promised to meet wi' His people, to bless them and do them good.
There was biggin' o' kirks frae the east tae the wast, frae the south to the Shetland sea;
But the first o' them a' to be open was the spail kirk o' Monzie.

V.

When the rowans grew red in the fa' o' the year, an' the bracken was yellow an' broun,
An' like tokens flung free frae the fairy folk, the leaves cam' flichterin' doun,
Our first Communion Sabbath, in th' autumn o' 'Forty-three,
Was the hanselin' day, an the arles as weel, o' the Free Kirk o' Monzie;
Aneath the strang pine rafters we held our solemn tryste,
An' there, in the Sabbath stillness, His people met wi' Christ.
I seem to see the faces yet that are seen on earth nae mair—
To see the guid auld Elders, and hear the Action Prayer.
Ay, better bread we tasted there, and love was mair nor wine,
An' fand a blessing in the place that has gladdened our days sin' syne,
An' there, in that first snell winter, how we gathered frae muir an' glen,
Wi' the lichtsome trip o' bairnies fit, an' the tread o' stalwart men;
An' we saw Benvoirlich, cliff an' scaur, a' glancin' fair wi' snaw,
White as the robes in Paradise that they wear that's awa'.
There's nae freends like the auld freends ye hae tried in the shower an' the shine;
There's nae words like the auld words that I mind in the days lang syne.
Aye, lassie, it's bonnie an' gentle your new kirk on the brae,
Wi' its tower an' its porch and the lave o't—may it staund for monie a day!
But an antron thocht comes ower ane whiles, an' ye maunna think hard o' me
That I'm mindin' yet on the auld kirk an' the simmer o' 'Forty-Three.

D.D.B.

Monzie, September, 1883.

Book
of
Lochgelly Bowling Club

By
Alex. Westwater, J.P., F.S.A.Scot.
1947

Contents

Foreword

IN OFFERING this Brochure as a Souvenir of the Jubilee of Lochgelly Bowling Club the Committee feel that it will bring back happy memories to those of our oldest members still able to actively participate in the game; to those not so fortunate, because of physical disability, it will recall the doughtier deeds of many now gone from amongst us; to the present generation of young bowlers it is offered as an inspiration to go forward and emulate the feats of those worthy champions who have so ably upheld the honour of the Club in the years now past.

No abler compiler of this Souvenir could have been found than Alexander Westwater, one of our oldest members. He has spared no effort in his research, and grudged no minute of his time in making this production worthy of the occasion.

To Mr Westwater we wish to record our grateful thanks.

J. G. DOUGARY,
President.

Preface

To use a hackneyed phrase, the writing of this booklet has been "a labour of love". It has recalled, as I hope it will to others of the older members, scenes and incidents, and the men who figured in the pageant of those fifty years. That pageant, which I have had specifically favourable opportunities of witnessing and participating, conjures up memories of pleasant days and happy personal associations.

The book has been extended beyond its original conception, but there is nothing extraneous to its purpose.

To the younger members, may I say that they too are making history; and that when the club's centenary comes round, some scribe may be able to record that the fame and traditions of the club to its Jubilee have been fully maintained.

Acknowledgement is made of the readiness of Alfred Rodger, the secretary, and John Wilson, former secretary, in providing me with minutes and other data at call.

A.W.

Notes on Lochgelly Town

Unlike most mining communities, Lochgelly is not of mushroom growth. Back from the water edge it is the oldest township between Dunfermline and Kirkcaldy, with a communal existence back to the fifteenth century. Reference to the " Tafts of Lochgellie" around 1450 show that a hamlet must then have been in existence, or probably earlier. After the break up of the large Barony or Shire of Lochore, which stretched from Benarty to Auchtertool, and, succeeding the ownership of the Boswells of Balmuto, the lands of Lochgelly were reduced to comparatively small estates, "Easter and Wester Lochgellie." These eventually came into the ownership, in the early eighteenth century, of the Kinninmonts of that ilk (near Kinglassie) and ended in an heiress who married into the Border family of Elliot of Minto. Her husband was Sir Gilbert Elliot, and they were the parents of the first Earl of Minto. The estate, which was later added to by the purchase of lands in Auchterderran Parish, still remains in the possession of the Minto family. The bowling green is on their land. Minto is indeed the superior of almost the whole of the town and most of the parish. Sir Gilbert and his bride took up residence at the Lochgelly House which became uninhabitable over a century ago, to be succeeded by the present mansion, now too, only partially habitable owing to mining subsidence. It has a delightful situation overlooking Loch Gellie (from which the town got its name), with a fine southern prospect to the Cullaloe hills and glimpses of the Firth of Forth.

From the agricultural hamlet of its origin, Lochgelly grew to a village where most of the inhabitants were engaged in weaving and husbandry. In the later part of the eighteenth century coal was discovered and worked in the primitive way of the period by the Superior, who continued as the coalmaster till the next century was well advanced. Up till then only a few dozen miners were employed, including women. They resided, not in Lochgelly, but in the then distant row called Launcherhead. For a few decades later, ironstone was the principal production of the Lochgelly mines, providing the raw material for Lochgelly Iron Works, closed down about sixty years ago. Ironstone production gave way to bituminous coal, and this led to a considerable development. The village increased, and in 1877 was raised to the status of a Police Burgh. The population was then fully 4,000. Through the intensive mining developments round the turn of the century, Lochgelly further increased in size, and at the outbreak of the first world war its population was just short of 11,000. Since then it has fallen again to under 9,000.

Recently it was decided to build a new town to the south of the present one, with its western boundary coterminous with Cowdenbeath Burgh.

Bowling – An Ancient Game

While curling and golf can be accepted as the traditional Scottish games, bowling is probably more ancient than either, though this does not apply to Scotland. Claim is made that bowling was introduced to England at the period of the Norman Conquest, and it is referred to in English documents down the centuries. Just as football was prohibited by the Scottish Parliament because it interfered with the practice of archery, so in England bowling was prohibited for the same reason. Kings have indulged in the pastime (Charles I, who was born at Dunfermline, is said to have been an enthusiast), and there is, of course, the well-known story of Drake waiting to finish his game of bowls before proceeding to finish off the Spanish Armada. In Scotland we cannot find trace of it till the eighteenth century. Modern bowling in Scotland seems to have been mainly associated with the south-west of the country. Before the middle of the century it was established in Fife, first at Dunfermline and shortly after at Kirkcaldy. It developed gradually.

In our own county it got an impetus from the formation of the Fife Bowling Association, and in the country generally by the institution of the Scottish Bowling Association twelve years later. To-day there are 50 clubs in Fife and 650 members of the Scottish.

Early Days of Bowling in Lochgelly

THE GAME OF BOWLS is older in Lochgelly than the present club or green. The first Bowling Club was founded in 1873, and the first President was Dr. Mungall, who resided in Viewfield House, Lumphinnans, and was the colliery doctor for the district. He was a kinsman of Henry Mungall, chairman of the Cowdenbeath Coal Company, which merged with the Fife Coal Company about half a century ago. The green was in private ground belonging to the Minto Hotel. It had three rinks, and play was only possible from east to west.

The Club at that time was somewhat exclusive – caste was more in evidence in that period in Lochgelly than it is to-day. Its membership mainly comprised professional and business men, with a sprinkling of whom were then called "the aristocratic colliers". Matches in the early days were played with Kirkcaldy and Dunfermline Clubs, the only ones then in existence in the adjacent area. This first Lochgelly Bowling Club was the nucleus of the present club, of which most of the old club members were founders. No written records of this Club are extant, but from a search of the minutes of the Fife Bowling Association we find that it was one of the eight clubs that met at Kirkcaldy and founded the County Association. That was on 4th August, 1879, when the first county tournament was arranged on constituted lines. The eight clubs were Newport, Kirkcaldy, Cupar, Lochgelly, Dunfermline South, Markinch and Leven. The Lochgelly representatives at the meeting were William Cameron (Agent of the Union Bank) and James Cook (Baker), the latter of whom had recently been elected to the first Lochgelly Police Commission on the formation of the Burgh and who was later a Magistrate.

At a meeting held at Markinch the Association considered the purchase of a County Cup for annual competition: £25 was voted to purchase the cup. Entry money was fixed at 10s. per rink, and prize money at £3 10s. for the winners and £1 10s. for the runners-up. Play was to start at 8.30, and the rules to be observed were those of "Mitchell's Bowling Annual." (Note.–The Association adhered to these rules for many years, regularly turning down a proposal to adopt the rules of the Scottish Association.) The one exception made to Mitchell's rules was that opponents could object to play if the jack was thrown more than 20 yards. The first tournament was played on Leven green. At the Markinch meeting Lochgelly was represented by Andrew Galloway, a well known Lochgelly man who was an official of the Lochgelly Iron and Coal Company, and the first active R.W.M. of Minto Masonic Lodge, founded in 1858.

There seems to have been a time lag in Lochgelly's interest or connection with the Association. No representative attended the annual meeting from 1887 till 1902, when Antony Walker (later to be President of the Association) represented the club. In 1890 Lochgelly Club was written to regarding non-payment of the annual subscription, and there is no record of their having taken part in the County Competitions till 1895. In this year, after another lag, the new Lochgelly applied for readmission. This was accepted "without extra fee," and so Lochgelly appeared once more in the draw for the cup, and has continued without break since then. Both rinks must have lost in the first round that year, for neither were in the second round draw. There is no record of any County ties having been played on the first Lochgelly Green. It would doubtless be reckoned unsuitable for ties, and from our personal recollection of it at that period this is not to be wondered at.

It was only now (1895) that the Fife Association decided to adopt the rules of the Scottish Bowling Association as against "Mitchell's Annual," under which they had played up till then. The Fife Single-hand Competition was started in 1902.

The formation of the present club and green was occasioned by the growing population of the town, which greatly accelerated in the nineties and round the turn of the century. As already indicated, the new Club evolved from the old one. It is unfortunate that the early records of even the present Club, as well as the older one, have been lost, and for the six years from the scheme being initiated in 1894 till 1901 no club records are available.

Such notes as we are able to present of these years have been gathered from other sources, in part from personal memory, in part from files of the local newspaper the *Lochgelly and District Times,* and in a lesser degree from the minutes of the Fife Bowling Association. From 1901, however, the Club minutes have been kept. They tell the prosaic story of administration, dealing with matters which though they look small and domestic are nevertheless important to the carrying on of an institution.

The Club has been well served by its officials, seeking to provide the best sport and the best facilities measured by the yardstick of their resources. Competitions figure largely in the story of the years; on their own green, where they tended to raise the standard of play of this fine pastime; and in the bigger world outside, where Lochgelly bowlers have gained a measure of distinction much above the average.

It is in 1893 we get the first inkling of a move to put bowling on a wider basis in the town. In that year letters appeared in the local paper suggesting such a development. The correspondence led to action, and the old Club formed a committee to consider the matter. Progress, however, seems to have been slow, as indicated by further letters to the newspaper. In 1895 a correspondent writes, "Surely there is a slackness among the promoters as, in my opinion, a meeting of all bowlers in the district ought to have been held before now to ensure their support and co-operation." In the following issue of the paper two letters appeared – one from a promoter, which stated that collectors were doing their utmost, but suggesting that a more energetic committee should be appointed. The other letter said that there was no flagging, but "as we have a lot of members who are keen curlers, we think it advisable to let them get through with their curling first."

This was the year (1895) of the intense and prolonged frost, when the roarin' game was played every day on the Loch from the beginning of the year till March. "I may add," continues the writer, "the hope that the general public of Lochgelly (male and female), though not bowlers, will give this laudable object their support, seeing it is to be a public benefit. As I understand the scheme for the new green, it is intended to be what we may term a semi-public park, where each member will have a key and can spend an enjoyable summer evening, if not playing being a spectator."

Early in March, 1895, the provisional committee of the new Club held a meeting, when the Secretary (Tom B. Allan, an accountant in the Union Bank) tendered his resignation and William Walker Bethune (grocer) was appointed to that office.

The first annual meeting was held on April 24th, 1895, when the following office-bearers were appointed – President, Hugh Drysdale; Vice-President, Alexander Irvine; Secretary, W. W. Bethune; Treasurer, David Philp; Committee – William Drysdale, Peter MacDuff, Robert Galloway, William Penman (Curly), William Russell, Robert Suttie (tailor), and George A. Taylor (painter). It was reported that the arrangements for the new bowling green in North Street were being energetically pushed forward. The ground had been staked off and specifications would be ready shortly.

During the 1895 season matches were played by the old green members against Crossgates, Kelty, Orwell (Milnathort), Burntisland, West End (Kirkcaldy), and Dunfermline. The skips engaged in these matches were William Russell, Robert Suttie, W. Bethune (baker), W. W. Bethune, Robert Galloway and George Swan (the last mentioned a noted marksman who shot at Wimbledon and Bisley).

The contract for making the green was given to William Russell who was assisted by David Swan and Walter Rolland and the turf was brought from Tollie Hill, west of Lumphinnans Farm, later the site of Cowdenbeath Golf Course. Andrew Wilson, builder, Cowdenbeath, secured the contract for building the clubhouse and Green walls. A start was made on this work in June, 1895. To help the fund, concerts were organised and a bazaar on a big scale was held.

The first of the concerts (in September), in the Drill Hall, was very successful. Among the entertainers were Dr. Cumming, Lochgelly; Peter Donald, Dunfermline, a well known exponent of Negro minstrelsy; Hugh Kelso, Cowdenbeath, a leading bass singer; and Cecilia Burgess, a delightful singer, who died two years later. The Bazaar was held in the Drill Hall on 19th October. It was opened by Provost James Melville (Lochgelly's second Provost). The drawings amounted to £173 6s., of which £78 was from a prize drawing. The first prize was a bridescake valued at £12 10s. The stall-holders were Mrs. Cumming and Miss Drysdale, Mrs. Philp and Miss Gillespie, Mrs. Binning and Miss Shaw, Mrs. Penman and Mrs.Dewar. Office-bearers for the next year (1896) were mostly the same, except that John W. Osborne (jeweller) was made secretary. Later in the season he was replaced by George Erskine, jun.

The new green was formally opened on June 9th, 1897, in the presence of a large company of members and visitors. Dr. Dendle called on the president, Hugh Drysdale, to perform the opening ceremony. A five-rink match took place between the President and the Vice-President (Peter MacDuff), and the latter won 57-51. The skips at the opening game were:– President's side – W. W. Bethune, Robert Philp, W. Wilson, W. Bethune, Robert Suttie. Vice-President's side – Andrew Hunter, Andrew Galloway, Alexander Thompson, William Russell, and P. MacDuff. Cake and wine were supplied in the club-house. The President intimated that he would present a Jubilee Medal (it was the year of Queen Victoria's Diamond Jubilee) to be played for in pairs.

One of the club matches engaged in in 1897 was against Dunlop, Edinburgh, a fixture which continued for many years. The first greenkeeper was James Baker Clark, who had a salary of £10 a year. William Russell was green ranger. In 1899 another trophy was presented for competition – a silver flower vase by James Cunningham (butcher) on his leaving for Australia. It had to be won three times in succession, before becoming the property of the winner.

In July, 1899, Lochgelly won their first trophy – the Consolation Cup in the Fife County Competition. The rink was skipped by James Forrester. They won their first round 18-2, the second 16-7, and the final 15-14.

Lochgelly did not win the Fife Rink Championship until 1905, when the rink skipped by Dave Campbell, with Tom McDonald, William Johnstone, and John Crawford blazed the trail for further successes. When the result came to the town a crowd set off down the Avenue to meet the waggonette with the players. With the cup held aloft they entered the town from the Kirkcaldy road under circumstances like a Roman triumph. Great enthusiasm greeted them when they unyoked at the Minto Hotel and the cup was filled and passed round. A year or so earlier Lochgelly narrowly missed winning the cup when they reached the final, and the skip had the winning of it. Overcome, doubt-less, by the excitement of the occasion, he failed to draw in an open end. This rink comprised four noted earlier players–William Russell (who skipped), William Penman (Curly), William Johnstone, and Dave Campbell. It was to be the happy lot of the son of William Russell to skip the winners on two later occasions.

Opening of New Green, May, 1897

Top Row—J. Greenhill, D.Stevenson, D. Burt, Dr. Dendle, Rev. T. Dewar, J. Mitchell, J. Williamson, J. Laird, J. Hamilton. Second Row (standing)—J. Wilson, R. Reekie, R. Philp, R. Wood, J. McGruther, F. Stiven, G. Gillespie, J. Laing, A. Thompson, A. Splitt, W. Bethune, D. Campbell, D. Penman, Rev. J. Hunter, Dr. Dewar, W. Duncan, W. Gammie, W. Reid. Third Row (sitting)—C. Burgess, J. Forrester, R. Suttie, J. Clark, W. Drysdale, W. W. Bethune, A. Irvine, J. Paton, J. Houston, G. Mark, D. Penman, W. Blyth. Front Row—W. Russell, G. Taylor, H. Drysdale, P. MacDuff, J. Adam, J. Stewart, J. Connell.

A Sporting Community

Athletic sport has always made an appeal to Lochgelly youths. Cricket at one time had a strong hold. The village had several clubs – senior, junior, and school. The former had fixtures with Dunfermline, Kirkcaldy, Cupar, and Burntisland. In the Fife Junior League in the nineties Lochgelly cricketers won the championship three years out of four. Football started in the town in the eighties, and in two decades it almost completely ousted cricket. The decline of the latter was rapid, and has long since ceased to interest our youth. Several efforts were made to resuscitate it, without success.

Field sports were popular – running, jumping, vaulting – and many Lochgelly athletes figured in county games and national gatherings. In this, too , there has been a decline almost to extinction.

The oldest organised game in Lochgelly is curling, with a club instituted in 1831 and still going strong – only that the traditional and robust play on the Loch has given place to the more comfortable atmosphere and easier, if more skilful, game on the indoor rink.

Bowling started in 1873, and a golf club was formed in 1896. For a short time, between sixty and seventy years ago, Lochgelly had a tennis club which had a somewhat rough court in the south-west corner of Cooperhall Park, and about the same time an archery club practised there. There, too, was the pitch of the school cricket club sixty years ago. Cooperhall Park has indeed played a big part in local sport, especially cricket and football; it became a golf course, and for many years it was the site of the annual games.

The town for nearly a century, with several lapses, has had a Brass Band. Fully forty years ago the band won the Junior Championship of Scotland, and went on to win an even bigger distinction in carrying off the Junior Championship of Great Britain. Piping became a force in the town previous to the First World War; Lochgelly Pipe Band has had notable successes both in Fife and in national events, one of which was a Championship at the Cowal Gathering.

INTERNATIONALISTS.

Lochgelly has been prolific in internationalists and national champions; indeed it might reasonably be claimed that, if not quite unique, it has produced for its size an exceptional number in that respect. They range over a wide field of sport and pastime and add up to the number of 39, as follows:-

Football–Senior–
   George Wilson, Archie Devine, John Duncan, Charlie Geatons, Robert Davidson and William Liddell.

Junior–
   Donald Cameron, William Nicol, Jackie Whyte, William Archibald, Tom Dryburgh.

Juvenile–
   John Wallace.

Schoolboy–
   Alexander Wood, Arthur Barnes, David Calder, Alfred Melville (who is a member of Lochgelly Bowling Club), James Bremner.

Amateur–
   Robert (Piper) McKay.

Rugby–
   Harry Lind.

Hockey–
   Margaret Dickson (Mrs. Webster), Dr. David Dickson, Dr. James Dickson.

Angling–
   Dr. D. E. Dickson, John Dawson, W. Duncan

Boxing–
   Tommy Dunn, Patrick Healy, Eddie Starrs.

Bowling–
   David Campbell, Tom McDonald, John Hynd, John Clark, John Simpson, William Splitt, John Sinclair.

Chess–
   James Aitken.

Rifle Shooting–
   George Swan.

Quoiting Champions–
   Alexander Gillespie, William Watters.

Annals of the Club

The following brief notes are extracted from the Minute Books, the earliest record beginning in 1901. The notes are not dated, but are in chronological order.

The membership subscription in 1901 was 12s. Occasionally members were admitted on payment of 3s. per month. At that time a debt existed amounting to £100, balance of the making of the green and walls and the erection of the clubhouse. The debt was reduced by £15, notwithstanding the purchase of a lawn mower, mats, etc. John Mitchell, sen., was appointed greenkeeper at £15 per year.

Trophies then competed for were the Cook Cup, the Cunningham Vase, and a Medal. It was customary for the President to give a pair of bowls to the Champion. Two other pairs were presented that year by Peter Wildridge and David Webster (the latter a Lochgelly native, then schoolmaster at Glen Lyon). A fourth pair of bowls was given shortly afterwards by David Burt, late Chief Constable of Airdrie and later a grocer at Auchterderran, and Antony Walker.

Difficulty was experienced in getting members to pay their fees.

A proposal was put forward in 1904 to apply for a club licence under the new Licensing Act. It was dropped on a recommendation from the Scottish Bowling Association advising no action.

On account of the delay in finishing competitions, all who had not played their ties were disqualified. A meeting of protest against this rule was held, but the committee's action was upheld.

In the following a year a petition, on the suggestion of A. Walker, was sent to the S.B.A. asking them to make representation to the Secretary for Scotland to have the provisions of the new Licensing Act amended so that bowling and similar clubs would be exempt from the Acts.

The committee proposed to hold a prize drawing to clear off the Club's debt, but owing to a recent decision of the Lord Advocate declaring prize drawings illegal the matter was delayed.

David Campbell and his rink (T. McDonald, William Johnstone and J. Crawford) were congratulated on having for the first time in the history of the

Club won the Fife Bowling Association Cup, and also the splendid results the rink had attained in the Scottish Competition. Mr. Campbell presented a framed photograph of the rink to the Club.

William Russell and William Penman were selected to represent the Club at the Jubilee of Kirkcaldy Bowling Club (1908).

Concern was expressed by members on the report that matches were being played for money stakes. The committee expressed strong disapproval of this practice, and power was given by the members to enforce Rule 12.

Four seats for the green were presented by the Lochgelly Public House Society.

The question of registering the Club under the Licensing Laws again came up. It was put forward by Tom McDonald, but did not get the support of the members.

Members who had not paid their subscription by July were debarred from competitions.

At a special meeting A. Westwater moved an extension of the clubhouse (1911). P. MacDuff moved delay. The proposal was carried and a deputation was appointed to meet Peter Henderson with a view to getting plans. At a later meeting in the *Times* office plans were submitted and approved, and it was decided to fit the premises with gas, if not too expensive. The contracts for the extension were fixed as follows:–Brickwork, £17 15s.; Joiner, £31 5s.; Slater and Cement, £19 1s. 8d.; Plumber, £10 10s.; Gas Fittings and Stove £1 15s. It was agreed to raise money by the issue of £1 shares with interest at 4 per cent., said shares to be repaid by ballot when funds were available.

The Club was represented at the opening of Bowhill Institute and Bowling Green.

A rule was made that all publicans who were members of the Club should get turn about in supplying refreshments for club matches and that a "Tumber" Fund be started wherein any odd money over the accounts for matches should benefit the Club.

A member was called before the committee to answer a charge of abusive language towards the secretary. He explained it was a result of losing his temper, and he was sorry. He refused, however, to withdraw a further remark imputed to him regarding the Secretary, and the committee decided they would not proceed further with the matter.

The debt over the Club was considered. It was decided to approach the Lochgelly Iron and Coal Company for a donation and they later sent £25 (1913).

It was decided not to admit any more members after the number reached 110.

The Secretary was instructed to put up notices prohibiting spitting on the green and in the ditches.

The greenkeeper's salary was fixed at 23s. per week.

Support was given to an appeal by the S.B.A. to secure a modification of the Property Income Tax on bowling clubs, and the local M.P. (William Adamson) was asked to support the appeal.

The green ranger was suspended following on alleged abuse he had given the green keeper.

During the war years the Red Cross Fund figures largely in the club's interests. Dr. Stephen was President at that time, and doubtless it was due to his stimulating enthusiasm that Lochgelly raised more money for that fund than any other club in the county. That revered Lochgelly lady, the late Helen Steedman, co-operated with a Ladies' Committee.

The Club, on the suggestion of Dr. Stephen, decided on a War Memorial for members who had fallen in the late war. The marble slab which stands near the entrance to the green was the outcome. It bears the following names:–Bdr. W. Campbell, Bugler D. Gibb, Ptes. James Gillies, John Thompson, John Rodger and James Logan. It was unveiled the following year by Lieut.-Colonel MacDuff, a member of the Club who had served throughout the war. Lochgelly Brass Band attended and played appropriate tunes.

At the same time the Club undertook to take steps to support the Town War Memorial Fund.

The membership was closed for the year.

An offer to visit the green by the Caledonian Bowlers was cordially accepted, and the game took place in August. Minutes are silent as to the result.

A personal controversy between two members of the Club led to some feeling and the suspension of a prominent member. On a requisition a special meeting of members was called and the suspension was raised unconditionally.

Lochgelly refused to join a proposed Fife Bowling League though a considerable number of members favoured it.

An application by the Police, of whom large detachments were stationed in Lochgelly this year (1921–the miners' strike) to be admitted as occasional members was granted. They donated £10 for the privilege.

The Rules of the Club were revised (1922).

The Cook Cup, which was won outright under the condition of being thrice won by the same person, was handed back to the Club by John Hynd. The Club decided to present Mr. Hynd with a gold badge in acknowledgement.

Antony Walker gave a clear receipt for the shares he held in the Club.

All the share capital which had been given by members to cover the Club's debts was paid off (1924).

An addition to the clubhouse was decided on, and a further share capital raised by units of £1. This was the last addition and added the hall on the north side.

Bridge became a favourite clubhouse game, and in January 1925, a weekly tournament was started. The Club, however, declined to join a Bridge League in the town.

A list of Past-Presidents was compiled. Help in this was given by an old member, W. W. Bethune, U.S.A.

Dr. Stephen was congratulated on his election as President of the Fife Bowling Association.

A gold watch, at a cost of £14 10s., was presented to James Henderson, who had acted as architect in the buildings extension.

William Clark was appointed to represent the Club in the match with the South African touring team at Kirkcaldy.

The Club decided to become members of the newly-formed Lochgelly Ratepayers' Association.

Rules for the conducting of the clubhouse were approved. It was particularly stipulated that no drink was to be supplied to visitors or sold outwith statutory hours.

A proposal to close the green each evening at ten o'clock was turned down.

An automatic machine agency asked permission to erect a chocolate machine on the premises. The request was unanimously refused.

A billiard table was presented by Mr. William Duncan, Vice-President.

A serious accident befell one of the leading members, Tom MacDonald. A letter of sympathy was sent him in hospital.

Lochgelly Town Council asked to renew the annual game with the Club (suspended before the war), and this was cordially agreed to.

On the initiative of the then President (John Wilson, 1929), the presentation of prizes took the form of a social and dance in the Co-operative Hall. (This innovation was continued for several years.)

The Club was congratulated by the S.B.A. on raising £28 for the Edinburgh Royal Infirmary Special Extension Fund.

Consideration of extension of green led to an application to the Town Council for an option on the feu on the north side, also to the proprietor of feu adjoining.

Fife Police were granted the use of the green for their County Championship finals.

The price of port wine sold in the bar (1934) was fixed at 6d. per glass and 4s. per bottle.

Bailie Wilson was nominated for a place in the team against the South African touring side against Fife. Two guineas were granted to the match fund. He was asked to put forward Lochgelly Green for the match.

A private lottery was started on behalf of the members, after consultation with Charles Hornal, solicitor. Strict regulations were laid down.

With a view to extending the club premises, an approach was made to the several feuars of property on the east side of the bowling club feu. The intention was to purchase one or other of the properties. (Nothing came out of any of the extension proposals.)

Furnishings were purchased for the smoke-room adjoining the bar, including 20 tub chairs at 16s. each, and four glass-topped tables at 29s. 6d. each. Linoleum was given by the President (Alexander Forrester) free of charge.

The condition of the boundary wall at the entrance passage led to an estimate of cost from Alexander Lumsden and a proposal for joint action with the other proprietor (1937). (The estimated cost was £31.)

Permission was given for the East of Scotland Police Championship to be played on the green.

Acknowledgement is made of a small clock for the bar, presented by the Secretary (D. R. Lyall).

Lochgelly Town Council paid £26 11s. 6d. in respect of their share of the mutual boundary wall on the west side of the green, where dwelling-houses had been built by the Town Council.

A change was made in the method of entries for the club championship. Previously all members' names were in the draw, now only those who put down their names would be held as entering.

A proposed increase in the membership fee to 17s. 6d. on entrance was negatived by 44 votes to 28.

John Sinclair was nominated to play in the Empire Exhibition Tournament (Glasgow).

In view of the lighting restrictions (1939) and other difficulties it was decided that the club premises would be closed during the winter months.

The request of the S.B.A. that the Club should join in the Bowling War Relief Fund was approved. A committee was appointed to promote funds to that end.

Recommendation was made to the S.B.A. to dispense with international matches during hostilities.

The courtesy of the green was extended to James McKenzie in view of his long connection with the Club.

The Special Constables were granted the use of one or two rinks on selected nights.

A new flag was authorised to be purchased, coloured blue, and measuring 6 feet by 4 feet; cost 32s. 6d., and a Scottish Standard at 13s. Alexander Forrester presented a new flagstaff.

Entertainment for troops who might be billeted in the town was considered. A suggestion was made that the clubhouse be made available for recreational purposes, but the matter was left over pending the arrival of troops.

The club premises came under the War Fire Prevention Order and a committee was appointed to deal with the matter of fire watchers.

Owing to the growing scarcity of liquor, it was suggested that the bar stock be increased, but this was not approved.

At the annual meeting in 1941 the membership fee was increased by 5s. to 20s. The greenkeeper's wage was fixed at £3 5s.

Consideration of the war conditions led to the cutting down of fixtures. Only clubs in the immediate neighbourhood would be played, and in view of the difficulty of catering, teas were dispensed with.

Beer supplied to the bar was reported to be in bad condition. It was sampled by the committee, and found to be undrinkable. A test of putting a bottle under cold water was decided on.

It was decided that henceforth dogs would be debarred from the enclosure. All entry money for points competition was handed to the War Weapons Savings Campaign Fund.

In 1940 Provost John Wilson was paid the signal honour of being appointed President of the S.B.A., and he was cordially congratulated. As a compliment to him the S.B.A. Council visited Lochgelly on Saturday, 22nd June, and played a five-rink match with the Club. The visiting players included a number of internationalists. The Lochgelly skips were James Paul, William Clark, A. Westwater, T. Timmons, and J. Sinclair. The game resulted: S.B.A., 96 shots, Lochgelly 95. An official reception was held in the Masonic Hall, and the teams lunched together. Scottish buttons were presented to all the Lochgelly players. Later Provost Wilson was the recipient of a handsome pair of bowls with silver buttons and inscriptions through Alexander Westwater, who spoke of Provost Wilson's progress in the bowling world, leading to the highest honours.

Members were ordered to wear bowling shoes when marking ties, and to refrain from spitting and throwing cigarette ends on the green.

During the season the sum of £33 8s. 7d. was collected for the local Red Cross Fund.

A rule was passed that all refreshments given gratuitously were to be paid in cash by the Treasurer to the barman.

The local constabulary were granted the use of the green for a tournament intended to help the "Wings for Victory Week" Fund.

Members using bowls belonging to the Club were warned not to lock them in boxes.

At the close of season 1943 the Club sent £20 to the Duke of Gloucester's Red Cross Fund, and £33 to the local Red Cross Fund; £3 3s. was sent to the local Stalingrad Hospital Fund.

The price of whisky and gin sold in the bar was fixed at 3s. per glass, and rum at 3s. 4d.

In recognition of his honorary work of auditing the Club's accounts Patrick Shaw, C.A., was handed two certificates for each of his children.

The President, John Sinclair, intimated that he intended to present a Cup for competition.

A letter from Cowdenbeath Miners' Welfare Bowling Club was read with reference to forming a Bowling League. The scheme was not approved.

Lochgelly Brass Band applied for the use of the pavilion to provide teas for a visiting band, but as the premises were not open on Sundays it was decided to refuse the request.

The matter of the Club's Jubilee was raised by A. Westwater. It was founded in 1895, but as the green was not opened till 1897 it was decided to postpone any action.

The committee, on the suggestion of the President, agreed to thank Mr. Milligan of the Lochgelly Iron and Coal Company, for having the board containing the rolls of the Club Champions and Presidents reconstructed and repainted, and also Mr. William Ritchie for carrying through the painting work.

At the 1946 Annual Meeting it was decided to mark the Jubilee of the opening of the green in 1897, and a small committee was appointed to draw out a preliminary programme.

The question of purchasing a motor mower to replace the present electric mower was considered and dropped as the price was considered prohibitive.

A report was given by John Dougary on the recommendations of the special committee on the Jubilee celebrations as follows:– June 23rd – Invite representatives from clubs near Lochgelly; June 24th – Invite representatives from clubs in Fife further afield; June 25th – Members, afternoon and evening; June 26th – Fife Association night; June 27th – Social for members and lady friends; June 28th – Visit of S.B.A., followed by social and presentation of prizes won during the week.

John Sinclair was congratulated on being chosen to play in the British Bowling team to tour the United States.

THE FIRST LOCHGELLY WINNERS
OF THE FIFE CUP–1905

Tom MacDonald (Second player);	John Crawford (Lead.)
David Campbell (Skip);	Wm. Johnstone (Third player).

Opening of Extended Club House, May, 1912

Back Row–J. Devlin, W. Campbell, R. Small, W. Barclay, W. Duncan,——– H. Kelso, And. Clark, A. Hodge,——– R. Goodwin, J. Gillies, J. Wilson (Chapel St.) P. Spence. *Middle Row*–D. Wishart, H. Naysmith, J. Hynd (baker), T. MacDonald, J. Logan, W. Reekie, W. Frew, D. B. Gibb, J. Williamson (President), A. Westwater (Vice-President), Antony Walker (Past President), R. Woods, J. Rattray, H. McNeil, W. L. Hourie, J. Adam, J. Spence, A. Thomson. *Sitting*–Jas. Wilson, A. Clark ("Manchester"), W. Clark, J. Beveridge, R. Greig, J. McEwan, J. Jackson, J. Dick, J. Crawford, Jas. C. Thomson, W. Band.

Roll of Presidents

1897	–	HUGH DRYSDALE
1898-99	–	PETER MacDUFF
1900	–	ANDREW MALCOLM
1901-02	–	ANTONY WALKER
1903-04-05	–	ANDREW MALCOLM
1906	–	JOHN PAUL
1907-08-09	–	DAVID CAMPBELL
1910	–	ANDREW MALCOLM
1911	–	ANTONY WALKER
1912	–	JAMES WILLIAMSON
1913	–	ALEXANDER WESTWATER
1914-15	–	WILLIAM CAMPBELL
1916-17-18-19-20	–	Dr. ALEXANDER STEPHEN
1921	–	WILLIAM CLARK
1922	–	ANDREW ANDERSON
1923-24	–	JOHN HYND
1925-26	–	JOHN CLARK
1927	–	DUNCAN B. GIBB
1928-29	–	JOHN WILSON
1930-31	–	WILLIAM DUNCAN
1932-33	–	PETER HENDERSON
1934-35	–	ALEXANDER WESTWATER
1936-37	–	ALEXANDER FORRESTER
1938-39	–	Dr. WILLIAM FOOTE
1940	–	JAMES PAUL
1941-42	–	TOM TIMMONS
1943-44	–	JOHN SINCLAIR
1945-46	–	DAVID R. LYALL
1947	–	JOHN G. DOUGARY

The Presidents – Biographical Notes

Dating from the opening of the green in 1897 the Club has had 25 individuals as Presidents. The list is representative of the various occupations and interests of individuals who played a considerable part in the general life of the community. Of the 25, only 6 were natives of Lochgelly. This reflects the increase that marked the development of the town in the forepart of the century. All who held the office of President previous to 1913 have passed away and six have died since that year, so that just under half are still to the fore.

The position of President is important to a club in that its success is reflected in the way he exercises his authority and guides the counsels of the management towards stability and success. In this respect Lochgelly Club has been well served. It may therefore be opportune now to put on permanent record short biographical sketches. Everyone on the list was, or is, known intimately to the writer, so that the notes are from first-hand knowledge.

HUGH DRYSDALE.   1897

He came to Lochgelly from Perth about 1890 on purchasing a large bakery business adjoining the Minto Hotel long carried on by Bailie James Cook. Interested in the game of bowls, he became a member of the club, which then played on the Minto Green. In the formation of the new Club and Green he gave a lead and took a considerable part. On retiring to Kinghorn he was associated with the bowling club there. The Kinghorn green was laid with the same turf as Lochgelly – taken from Tollie Hill, later site of Cowdenbeath Golf Club –and laid by the same contractor (Wm. Russell).

PETER MacDUFF, J.P.   1898-99.

A native of Strathbran, he was appointed headmaster of Lochgelly East (Senior) School in 1889, and was a well known and popular personality in the town till his retiral two years after the end of the First World War, in which he had taken a conspicuous part. On his retiral he went to reside at Lundin Links, where he later died. A Volunteer when he came here, he joined "L" Coy. (Fife Battalion) with the rank of 2nd Lieut., and from this rank he advanced progressively to command the Company as Captain, later to be Second in Command of the 7th (Fife) Battalion The Black Watch. He had a fine military bearing and looked (and was) every inch a soldier. In 1915 at the age of 56, he went to France with the Battalion. Later he was posted to a Salvage Corps and then, with the rank of Lieut.-Colonel, to the Command of the 7th (Reserve) Black Watch at Ripon. An excellent marksman, he took part in Company, County, and National competitions and once or twice shot at Bisley. A keen curler, he acted as Secretary for Ballingry Club and Minto Bonspiel.

ANDREW MALCOLM.   1903–04–05; 1910

A solicitor and native of Dunfermline, he started the first legal business in Lochgelly near the close of the century. The town benefited from the interest he took in the various institutions – Sport, the Kirk, Freemasonry. He left a legacy to the Free Kirk, and in the Masonic connection was a founder member and Treasurer of Minto Knights of the Temple. For a number of years he served as a junior officer in the Lochgelly Volunteers. He held the agency of the Commercial Bank. A happy, genial type of individual, his death in 1926 was much regretted.

ANTONY WALKER.   1901–02; 1911.

Came from Dunfermline on purchasing the Minto Hotel from David Cook. The hotel had then the reputation of being one of the best hostelries in Fife, and continued as so under the new proprietor. A keen bowler and curler, he was also President of Lochgelly Curling Club. Entering the Town Council, he attained to the position of Provost and took an active part in county affairs. Foresight was one of his characteristics. It was on his suggestion that the Glen Devon water scheme was set afoot. He failed to get Kirkcaldy District Committee to act, and while they deliberated over it Dunfermline stepped in and secured it. A courteous man and a ready speaker, he was prominent in the social and public life of the community.

JOHN PAUL, J.P.   1906.

Was Provost of Lochgelly during the years of the First World War. Initiated for the Burgh the first municipal housing scheme in Scotland. A native of Lanarkshire, he came to Lochgelly to be general mining manager of the Lochgelly Iron and Coal Company. In addition to the Town Council, he served on Lochgelly School Board and was a prominent member of Fife County Council and Convener of the Road Board. Nearly all local activities had his support, with special emphasis on the United Football Club. In addition to bowling, he was a keen curler and was President of the Ballingry Club for a number of years. Retiring some years before the last war, he went to reside in

Dunfermline, where he died a few years ago.

DAVID CAMPBELL.   1907–08–09.

David Campbell was one of the Presidents who was also an expert bowler. He ranks as the fifth Champion of the Club, but perhaps more notable is the fact that he skipped the first Lochgelly rink to win the Fife Cup, while on two occasions his rink gained the district championship to take part in the Scottish finals. He was, too, a generous donor and supporter of the Club. A keen sportsman, he owned a licensed house in Lumphinnans. For a term he served on Lochgelly School Board.

JAMES WILLIAMSON.   1912.

A very likeable person both on and off the green, and a good player, James Williamson was also Treasurer of the Club for some years and was precise in all his works. A draper with a shop in Bank Street, he spent his leisure time between bowling, golfing, and the Kirk. When the present Lochgelly Golf Club was started he was appointed Treasurer, and continued without a break until parted by his death four years ago. To the Kirk, of which he was an elder and session clerk, he gave of his best. He was musical, and one of the founders of Lochgelly Choral Union when it was reconstituted in 1894, and long treasurer of the Society. It is not given to many to seek so earnestly to put into practice the ethical standard of the Christian life.

ALEX WESTWATER, J.P.   1913; 1934–35.

Is the oldest still in membership of the Club, joining when the present Club was formed in 1895 but did not play much for a year or two till 1899. As the notes in this section are biographical rather than autobiographical, we pass on.

WILLIAM CAMPBELL.   1914–15.

Like his Uncle Dave, already referred to, William Campbell was a good bowler and a good all-round sportsman and athlete. A product of Cowdenbeath, he owned the Railway Tavern in Lochgelly. Unfortunately Willie was killed by a bomb in the First World War while on his way home to qualify for a commission. A left-handed player, he ranked among the best club players of his day, and was a popular figure on the green.

DR. ALEX. STEPHEN.   1916–17–18–19–20.

Most of his five years' continuous Presidency covered the First World War, in which he did duty for a period as a M.O. in France. A feature of his terms was the fine work done by the Club for the Red Cross. His enthusiasm stimulated the schemes, with the result that Lochgelly Club raised more than any of the Fife clubs for that great beneficent purpose. His interest in the Club was keen. It was mainly due to him that the third extension of the clubhouse was set afoot, and the war memorial at the entrance with the names of the members who fell in the First World War was pretty much a personal gift.

The town has felt the benefit of Dr. Stephen's initiative and enterprise in many directions – music (vocal and instrumental), ambulance training, sick nursing, and in the various grades of the Masonic Order. During the late war his activities in Civil Defence are recalled, the well-equipped First-Aid Post, the training of its staff, and, in addition, the duties of Medical Officer of the Battalion Home Guard. Keen on natural history and archaeology.

WILLIAM CLARK.   1921.

William Clark holds the double honour of being both President and Club Champion. He belonged to a family closely connected with Lochgelly life and sport in general – a brother of "Manchester". A keen curler, he was for many years Secretary of the Lochgelly Club. He left Lochgelly to take over a business in Kinross, and died a number of years ago.

ANDREW ANDERSON.   1922.

Andrew came from Shotts with a bowling reputation – he was club champion there. Next to his work as manager of the Mary Pit, bowling filled his leisure. He too held the double honour of President and Club Champion. Andrew was a tasteful and skilful player. Personally he was very likeable. A man without sophistry, kindly and obliging, a singer of auld Scots Sangs, which he sang with emotional sentiment. He died fully a year ago.

JOHN HYND.   1923–24.

One of the most versatile players in the history of the Club. He gained the double honour as skip of winning the Fife Rink Championship and of winning the County Single-handed Championship on two occasions. His rink also won through the Scottish District ties to qualify for the finals at Queen's Park. He reached the semi-final of the blue riband of bowling. In club and outside competitions he was conspicuous. He was champion of his own club five times, and won the Gilmour and Minto Trophy competitions as skip. In 1926 he was chosen to play for Scotland in the internationals of that year. His record is unsurpassed in the Club. In his earlier years, John was a noted pedestrian when walking matches were popular thirty to forty years ago. A native of

Cowdenbeath, he died at a comparatively early age.

JOHN CLARK.   1925–26.

A prominent member of the Club. Had a baker's business in the town, and now resides at Slough, near Windsor. He took a special interest in the Scottish Bakers' Bowling Association, of which he was president and winner of trophies. His reputation as a player gained him an international place in the matches of 1926.

DUNCAN B. GIBB.   1927.

A well-known Lochgelly man. Before starting bowling he was best known in instrumental musical circles. In his youth he played in both Lochgelly and Kirkcaldy Trades Brass Bands, and was a member of the latter in its championship years. He started a band in Lochgelly known as "Lochgelly Temperance." Was in business as a music seller. Though an octogenarian, he is still very keen on his favourite pastimes – bowling and curling. In both he has long been a skip, and is presently president of Ballingry Curling Club; has acted as secretary of the Minto Bowling Trophy since its inception 35 years past, and has won the trophy several times. Duncan, like his friend Jimmie Williamson, is a sort of Peter Pan. Both seem to have the secret of perpetual youth.

JOHN WILSON.   1928–29.

Known far beyond Lochgelly in the administration of the game of bowls, he has been president of the Fife Bowling Association and later had the special honour of being elected president of the Scottish Bowling Association (1940). His ain folks paid tribute to his general service to the Club and to the game by the presentation of an inscribed pair of bowls. A native of Ayrshire, with that county's characteristics, he came to Lochgelly at the beginning of the century as a contractor pit sinker. He early joined the bowling and curling clubs, and is an expert on the ice as well as on the green. In 1927 he was elected to Lochgelly Town Council. Later he became Provost and held that office for nine years to his retiral in 1945. As a member of Fife County Council for sixteen years he held for a period the responsible position of vice-chairman of the County Finance Committee. Is a member of the Caledonian bowlers and toured with them previous to the war. Throughout the war years he gave unstinted service to Civil Defence. He has given notable service in many directions, and his name is one to conjure with in Lochgelly.

John Wilson, Past-President of the Club, of the Fife Bowling
Association and of the Scottish Bowling Association.
Provost of Lochgelly, 1936-1945.

WILLIAM DUNCAN.   1930–31.

When Willie Duncan's health gave way the green lost a kenspeckle figure, a much esteemed personality. He was reckoned among the best of the Club's leading single-hand players, and he took a great interest both in the administrative and the more active playing side of bowling. He was Champion in 1899. For six years he acted as Secretary of the Club (1905-11), and was almost continuously a member of the Committee. He had two other pastimes – angling and flowers. As an angler he had much skill and fished in the Loch Leven National Championship; and in the cultivating of flowers he had much delight. By occupation he was cashier to Lochgelly Co-operative Society, a responsible position he held with credit for half a century. He did not long survive his retiral, and the Club lost one of its most respected members. He was a native of Lochgelly.

PETER HENDERSON.   1932–33.

Now retired and resident in Kirkcaldy, where he is a member of the Kirkcaldy Club. His connection with the Lochgelly Club dates back to the beginning of the century when he joined Lochgelly Coal Company as a mining surveyor. His professional duties limited his opportunity for play, though he was keen on the game and is a good and modest player. The Club benefited in many ways through his interest and influence. A popular fixture which he promoted was that of the pit matches – workers in the various Lochgelly pits playing against each other followed by a get-together social. Before his retiral he held the responsible position of general mining manager of Lochgelly Iron and Coal Company Ltd.

ALEX FORRESTER, J.P.   1936–37

Thirty-five years ago Alexander Forrester came to this district from the West Country to assist his father who had taken the farm of West Cartmore. Later, with his brother Robert, he branched out in motor transport, passenger and commercial, and by work and enterprise they built up a business with a national connection. He joined the Bowling Club but in these early days of limited leisure he got few opportunities for play. Later, however, he was able to take up the game, and also curling, of which he is a keen and skilful exponent. In public life he gave great service to the burgh as a Town Councillor and Magistrate, and among several directorships he holds that of Lochgelly Gas Company Ltd. While President of the Bowling Club his business experience and acumen were, as in other directions, of great value. The Club has felt the benefit of his interest, too, in a material way.

DR. WILLIAM FOOTE.   1938–39

A native of Lochgelly – he is the only son of ex-Provost Foote – and seeks such pastime as a doctor is permitted in bowling in the summer and in chess and bridge in the shorter days. At chess he is earning something of a reputation in the Scottish Team Championship as the leading player in the Cowdenbeath team. His professional duties limit his opportunities for bowling. He generally plays, however, in the competitions. During the last war, he served for five years as a Medical Officer in the Forces.

JAMES PAUL.   1940

The only instance of a son succeeding his father as President. He completed only one year, due to his changing from the managership of Dundonald Colliery to a similar post in the West. Jim was a cheery, friendly man, a keen sportsman fond of all games, football, tennis, golf – he played them all well. It was with much regret that his bowling and other friends in Lochgelly heard of his sudden death.

TOM TIMMONS.   1941–42.

He came from Dundee to Lochgelly to take up the managership of the local Cinema, a popular place of entertainment which he still continues to run. He served long on Lochgelly Town Council, and in 1933 was appointed Provost. He was also a member of Fife County Council and Education Committee, of which he is at present a co-opted member. Fond of all sports, he now concentrates on bowling and curling. The old age pensioners have had in him an active supporter, as also has the Sick Nursing Association, of which he is president.

JOHN SINCLAIR.   1943–44

In John Sinclair the Club has an outstanding player and member. He has gained many bowling honours. In his own club he has been champion as well as president. His skill with the woods has been recognised much further afield, leading to his selection on occasions to play for Scotland in international games. Perhaps the highlight in that connection was his inclusion in the British team which recently toured the United States and in which he proved one of its greatest assets both in a playing and social sense. Notwithstanding a severe illness, he pluckily accepted the invitation. John is a first rate vocalist and has given invaluable service to his native town in that connection. He is president of the Lochgelly Musical Association, of which he might be termed the mainstay. In bowling administration he acts as representative for West Fife on the Scottish Bowling Association Council. His fellow-members in Lochgelly Club are very proud of the position he has attained in the bowling world.

DAVID R. LYALL. 1945–46

David Lyall demits office as President on the eve of the Jubilee celebrations which he initiated. A native of Kelty, he has spent his life in the area on Local Government work. He succeeded the late Robert Small as Parish Clerk and Registrar, and is now an area official of the County Council in their offices and as Clerk to the District Council. The Bowling Club has found him willing to act *pro tem* both as Secretary and Treasurer. During the war years he was closely and actively identified with the County Civil Defence schemes, in which, as indeed in other directions, he showed ability for administration. One of his duties was to organise the Warden Service over the Lochgelly area, and he did much spadework in the organisation of first the Local Defence Corps and later the Home Guard with rank of Major. His service to Lochgelly has been wide; indeed, there are few institutions in the town in which his active assistance has not been felt to advantage. Since starting to play bowls and curling he has shown considerable aptitude in both games.

JOHN DOUGARY, J.P. 1947.

He may be called the Jubilee President in that the responsibility in this special year in the Club's history will fall on his broad shoulders. John is competent to handle tactfully and efficiently anything that falls to his lot. A schoolteacher by profession, he is headmaster of Glencraig School. He first came into prominence by the interest he took in schools football. He was the spearhead of the movement in this district. From the County Association he graduated to the Presidency of the Scottish Schools Football Association, and later had the signal distinction of filling a similar office on the British International Board. He plays all sorts of games – football, cricket, golf, bowling, curling. He has a special knowledge both of rules and technique in sport; a good organiser, administrator and participator – altogether a very versatile chap. With an honourable career in the First World War as a commissioned officer, it was natural that he should take to the Home Guard – and he did. His enthusiasm drew the attention of the V.I.P., and at their instance he was relieved of his scholastic duties to take on the job of Adjutant of the Fife Battalion. His organising experience and the geniality of his temperament will be a special asset for Jubilee Week.

Club Champions

1897 and 1898 – – –	WILLIAM RUSSELL
1899 – – – –	WILLIAM DUNCAN
1900 – – – –	ROBERT WOOD
1901 and 1902 – – –	WILLIAM RUSSELL, Jun.
1903 – – – –	DAVID CAMPBELL
1904 – – – –	HARRY SUTTIE
1905 – – – –	JOHN BAND
1906 – – – –	WILLIAM JOHNSTONE
1907 – – – –	ROBERT SUTTIE
1908 – – – –	DAVID BOGIE
1909 – – – –	JOHN HYND
1910 – – – –	JOHN BEVERIDGE
1911 – – – –	WILLIAM CAMPBELL
1912 – – – –	WILLIAM CLARK
1913 – – – –	JOHN BEVERIDGE
1914 – – – –	ARCHIBALD HODGE
1915 – – – –	DAVID ALLAN
1916 – – – –	ANDREW ANDERSON
1917 – – – –	WILLIAM RUSSELL, Jun.
1918 – – – –	JOHN HYND
1919 – – – –	ANDREW ANDERSON
1920 – – – –	JOHN HYND
1921 and 1922 – – –	JOHN CRAWFORD
1923 – – – –	WILLIAM RUSSELL, Jun.
1924 – – – –	JOHN HYND
1925 – – – –	ARCHIBALD HODGE
1926 – – – –	THOMAS McKINLAY
1927 – – – –	JAMES McKENZIE
1928 and 1929 – – –	ARCHIBALD HODGE
1930 – – – –	JOHN I. SIMPSON
1931 – – – –	ARCHIBALD HODGE
1932 – – – –	ANDREW CLARK
1933 – – – –	JOHN HYND
1934 – – – –	THOMAS McKINLAY
1935 – – – –	JOHN I. SIMPSON
1936 – – – –	ANDREW CLARK
1937 – – – –	ROBERT GRAY
1938 – – – –	JOHN SINCLAIR
1939 – – – –	JAMES GAIR
1940 and 1941 – – –	JAMES LAING
1942 – – – –	ROBERT WHITEHEAD
1943 – – – –	JOHN CLARK
1944 – – – –	GEORGE STEELE
1945 – – – –	JOHN CLARK
1946 – – – –	JAMES HEMSWORTH

John Sinclair, Past-President and ex-champion of the Club
and International player. A member of the British Team
which toured the U.S.A., 1947.

County Champions

The club has figured prominently in the Fife and Scottish Competitions–

FIFE RINK COMPETITION

1905	–	–	–	DAVID CAMPBELL (Skip).
1908	–	–	–	TOM MacDONALD (Skip).
1909	–	–	–	TOM MacDONALD (Skip).
1911	–	–	–	WM. RUSSELL (Skip).
1919	–	–	–	WM. RUSSELL (Skip).
1932	–	–	–	JOHN HYND (Skip).

GILMOUR TROPHY   –   1909 and 1921

FIFE SINGLE HANDED COMPETITION

(Started 1902; discontinued from 1903 to 1909)

| 1920 | – | – | – | JOHN HYND. |
| 1923 | – | – | – | JOHN HYND. |

The club has not yet had a Scottish honour, though in both Rink and Single Hand, it has been represented a number of times in the finals at Queen's Park.

Personalities in the Earlier Club

Lochgelly in earlier days was rich in Worthies – men with clean-cut characteristics. Many of that type were to be found in the ranks of the early bowlers as well as in the Curling Club and Freemasons. There seems to have been some affinity in that trinity. Among the bowlers of the last century, too, was a connecting link with the old order, the Lochgelly of early and mid Victorian days; men reared in the tradition of Scottish life of the period with emphasis on oatmeal and the kail-pat, the Shorter Catechism and the Kirk. They were dogmatic and strong-minded, not given to compromise in their opinions and beliefs. Such was the type which laid the foundation of our modern communal life in general, seeking to advance not by extreme change but by the more permanent methods of progressive reform.

While our Jubilee is an important milestone along what we hope will be a long and pleasant road, and an occasion for rejoicing, it is also an occasion for reflection on the road we have already travelled. Looking back we see many animated pictures of scenes on the green and think of those who played their part in the picture. Many of them have fallen by the way, gone the road from which no traveller returns.

The present seems opportune for such brief notes as space will allow to put their names on record. This list is by no means complete, for memory is a fickle jade. Here we recall a few of the pioneers.

DAVID COOK succeeded Mrs. Morris in the Minto Hotel and thereby became the proprietor of the Bowling Green. Previously he had a draper's business in Main Street. He wore gold-rimmed spectacles, usually peering over the top of them, and he generally had a cigar in his mouth. The hotel was a favourite with commercial travellers before the Forth Bridge and motor car made possible the daily return to homes in the cities. The hotel had an atmosphere of rigid discipline. Local worthies made it their howff – no bars then – generally occupying the kitchen. In these spacious days a bottle of whisky was placed on the table and each helped himself.

DR. NELSON belonged to Lochgelly. His father did much to make the village roads possible for vehicular traffic round about 100 years ago. President of the curling club, it was his practice to appear at the annual dinner as "My Lord" dressed up as Satan, with horns complete. Always seeming short of breath, his puffing was often mimicked.

WILLIAM CAMERON, agent of the Union Bank, was an Ayrshire man with a distinctive character. He had two hobbies – making fiddles and walking sticks. Entering the bank at almost any hour of the day, one would find him whittling at wood. One of the original members of Lochgelly School Board when it was formed in 1873, an elder in the Auld Kirk, and a man of strong character.

DR. MUNGALL was the doctor for Lumphinnans and Cowdenbeath collieries, then owned by his kinsman, Henry Mungall. At that time Lumphinnans employed many miners resident in Lochgelly, and he was a familiar figure here. A robust personality.

ALEXANDER THOMPSON, at one time grieve for Lochgelly Iron and Coal Company at Westerton Farm, and buyer of pit ponies and their feeding stuffs. Bowler and curler, but keener on the latter game. He celebrated his jubilee as a curler about forty years ago and was presented with a comfortable armchair.

ANDREW GALLOWAY was a sort of Master of Works to the Lochgelly Coal Company. The first R.W.M. of Minto Lodge, though that office was nominally held by Lord Loughborough. Represented Lochgelly Bowling Club at early meetings of the Fife Association. A finicky person and typical of Scots dourness.

WILLIAM BETHUNE, native of Largo, was an early member of the Club. He took over a licensed grocery business in Bank Street from William Henderson in the early seventies. Was elected a member of Lochgelly Police Commission on the formation of the Burgh in 1877. An active Freemason and R.W.M. of Minto Lodge. Introduced a popular brew of whisky which he called "The Auld Hoose". An office-bearer in the Parish Church.

DR. STEELE, a native of Dunfermline. Lochgelly and Raith Colliery doctor. First to occupy the Oaks when the Coal Company built that property in the late seventies. A plain spoken typical Scots doctor with a pawky vein. He attended the Parish Church and generally arranged for his coachman to call him out before the start of the sermon. Married a daughter of James Bethune, grocer and postmaster, and on retiral went to stay in London.

ANDREW HUNTER, brother of Provost John Hunter, was one of the early bowlers. He belonged to the town, and took a great interest in its public affairs. A relative of Professor Page, the eminent geologist, he made a particular study of that science. For many years he served on the Town Council, later as a Magistrate. Took a great interest in Lochgelly Brass Band, of which he was long president. His words were brief and to the point and generally characterised by sound common-sense.

Others of the early bowlers were Thomas Brand, William Binning (plumber), William Bethune (baker), James Connel, Robert Suttie (tailor), Robert Philp (saddler), James White, Sen. and Jr.

OTHER OF THE OLDER MEMBERS

Having dealt with some of the personalities of the earlier bowling days, we turn to record the names of individuals identified with the Club from the opening of the present green in 1897, excluding such as are already mentioned elsewhere in this book.

WILLIAM RUSSELL, the first leading skip, laid out the green. By occupation he was a contractor in the pit. Will took his bowling seriously and woe betide any of his rink, who failed to attend to his martinet instructions. A great ambition was to win the Fife Cup, but it eluded him. On one occasion he had the winning of it with his last bowl. He never forgot nor forgave himself for failing to seize the occasion.

WILLIAM PENMAN, better known as "Curly", was a grand third player, specially adept in trailing the jack. He is probably best remembered for his dry pawky humour, traditionally Scottish. He was one of the founders of the Gothenburg, and for some time chairman of the Lochgelly Gas Company.

DAVID PENMAN, a younger brother of "Curly", and another of Russell's bowling and curling cronies. Good player and keen on the game, he figured much in competitions and tried his hand at tournament play, for which however his temperament was not suited. After he delivered his bowl he followed it in a wide semi-circle which took him over the banking. He was irascible with slow players, but it generally ended in a loud, hearty laugh. Dave's sons took to the game. Alexander, perhaps the most outstanding, had a promising bowling career cut short by an affliction to his eyes, the result of an accident in the pit. Another of the bowling family, George, is an M.B.E.

WILLIAM JOHNSTONE. Will was a tower of strength in match play in the early years of the century. He was one of the rink which first won the Fife Cup. Succeeded "Curly" as our best third player. He was Club Champion in 1906.

WILLIAM BARCLAY was the oldest in membershp of the Club when he died two years ago. A pit lad, he studied hard and came to be the manager of Minto Colliery. He enjoyed the game for the game's sake, and troubled little about competitions. A well-informed man, he liked discussion, especially on politics.

A keen Liberal in the Gladstonian tradition. He played in the first club competition.

Tom MacDonald in his day had few rivals at skip. He brought several honours to the Club. His reputation as a bowler won him an international cap. Tom took a great interest in new players, and spent much time coaching them in the points of the game. Long leading skip in the curling club, he was also a good shot. Died within the last year at the age of eighty.

John Crawford, champion in 1921 and 1922, who died last year, was one of the most familiar figures on the green. He figured much in competitions – Club, County, and Scottish. A cool player, few were better at playing a testing shot. He dearly loved to argue. His tall sparse figure with military moustache and a wee "cutty" stuck in the corner of his mouth, moving across the green with slow, steady gait will not readily be forgotten.

Andrew Clark, now an octogenarian, has long forsaken bowls for the indoor pastime of dominoes. Best known as "Manchester", his burly figure is regularly to be seen in the clubhouse, where he generally has a "horse in the stable".

Tom Clark, a younger brother of "Manchester", died suddenly a long time back. He had an entertaining personality. "The banking" greatly missed his wisecracks and the happy atmosphere which his genial presence induced.

James C. Thompson was a prominent bowler, curler, and marksman. Jim specialised in "bounce" matches, and along with his friend John Dick (Dickey), a fine sportsman, there was never any lack of liveliness on the green.

James McKenzie died some years ago over 85 years of age. He won the Club Championshp in his 70th year. Versatile in sport, Jim was one of the pioneers of football in the town; a good wicket-keeper for Lochgelly Cricket Club in its hey-day; and claimed to have won in his youth the Hurling Championship of Scotland.

John Wilson (Chapel Street) was Secretary for close on twenty years, the longest term held by any of the club's Secretaries. He took a great interest in his duties, and particularly in tabulating the results of games and competitions. We are indebted to him for much information in that connection.

Andrew Dick, another of the old school, was keenly involved in public affairs, member of the Town Council and a Magistrate, the County Council and Education Authority. He was chairman of a Scottish brewery company and a director of Lochgelly Gas Company.

ARCHIE HODGE, one of the Club's best players in his day, was the winner of many games, took part in County and Scottish competitions, qualified for the Scottish single-hand finals, and was a Club Champion. When he removed to Methil it was a loss to Lochgelly's playing strength.

WILLIAM RUSSELL JUN.–In a bowling sense the mantle of the father fell upon the son. Will was twice Club Champion, and a good skip. In that position he won the Fife Cup in 1911 and again in 1919. He died comparatively young – another loss to the Club's playing strength.

GEORGE ERSKINE was one of the founder members of the Club and prominently identified with it in its early years. He filled the office of Secretary and Treasurer. Cashier to Lochgelly Iron and Coal Company, Ltd., he continues under the N.C.B. Over a long period he was organist and choirmaster in the Parish Church, and also acted as session clerk.

JOHN HYND was perhaps the most versatile of our players, with many shots in his locker. He excelled both at single-hand and skip play. No better evidence of his skill at bowls is needed than his record – Club Champion five times, single-handed Champion of Fife twice, rink championship of Fife (skip) three times; and on two occasions he skipped the rink which won the District Championship to qualify for the Scottish finals. He was an Internationalist and President of his own club. His record in bowling circles was indeed outstanding. A native of Cowdenbeath, he was a noted pedestrian when walking contests were popular more than forty years ago.

JAMES KINLAY looked on bowling as a pastime. His geniality won him many friends. Prominent in Masonic circles, he was well known all over the Province. The comparatively early death of this fine gentleman was a personal loss to all who had the privilege of his friendship.

WILLIAM STEWART was for a short time Vice-President of the Club. He resigned on leaving the district, but rejoined later. In his later years he found congenial companions in the clubhouse. A well read man, he was very keen on politics and was president of the local Liberals.

JAMES DONALDSON, another of the older members, died suddenly on the green while watching play. A highly respected citizen, he had retired from the game but continued his interest in the Club. A Past Master of the Minto Lodge, and a keen Freemason.

GEORGE STEELE played third in the rink that last won the Fife Cup, and he figured in other competitions. A good player and an unassuming man, George Steele had many friends, for he was the type that induced confidence and affection. Specially well known in Masonic circles, he was long secretary of Minto Lodge.

WM. WALKER BETHUNE took an active part in the formation of the present club. He was manager of his father's licensed grocery business, Bank Street. Keen on games, he played cricket and curling as well as bowling. A past R.W.M. and secretary of Lodge Minto, he emigrated to America where he died some years ago.

TOM SPLITT has long been a leading player. He skipped and played in many representative rinks. In the championship he has invariably done well but the actual winning of it has always eluded him. A good all-round sportsman, he was a keen cricketer in his younger days. His eldest son has appeared frequently in the Scottish Single Hand Finals, and in Internationals.

Other well known members of the earlier years include (apart from those mentioned elsewhere) Dan McArthur (butcher), John Mitchell (Co-operative Manager), John McGrouther (teacher), Dave Swan, Walter Rolland, David Hood, David Wishart, John Paton, A. Splitt, J. McQuillen, Andrew Nicol, James Hugh, Thomas McKinlay (Senior), Peter Wildridge, Andrew Nisbet (General Manager, Coal Company), John Guthrie (gas manager), Alexander Duncan, Robert Wilson, David Webster (teacher), Dave Penman (chemist), D.A.B. Leadbetter, William Lonie, Robert Suttie (also quoiter and director for W. Watters in his championship games), Henry Suttie, George Aitken (treasurer), Dr. Dickson, Robert Small (town clerk), Peter and James Spence, D. Bogie, John Beveridge, Hugh Kelso, J. M. Morrison, James Armstrong, David Cook, Angus Falconer, Willie and James Suttie, D. Moffat, John Laird, Wm. Frew, Wm. Bauld, Alexander Nisbet, Andrew Seath, Andrew D. Mackie, W. B. Crombie, Alexander Lumsden, John Hynd (baker), Murdoch Gair, T. Frame, James Gibb, Harry Naysmith, Harry McNeil, R. Wallace, Dave Allan, J. Japp, Andrew and George Thompson, Alexander Robertson, Ex-Provost Foote, Robert Park, John Adam (plasterer), Geo., Dave, Archibald and Tom Penman, Dave Richardson, John Rattray, J. Jackson, P. Sinclair, John McEwan, Geo. W. Dick, Alex. Young, Wm. Watters, J. McLean, L. Milne, N. Walker, Andrew Scott, T. Watson, W. Watson, A. and J. Duncan, Mungo Brown, James Shand, Alex. McPherson, James Williamson, J. Hemsworth.

Visit of Scottish Bowling Association to Lochgelly, June, 1940

Back Row—C. Hornal, J. R. Merrilees (S.B.A.), P. Sinclair, W. Barclay, W. Murray (S.B.A.), W. Duncan (S.B.A.), Robt. Laing (S.B.A.), J. Westwater, R. Forrester, J. Sinclair, W. Clark, J. Dougary. *Second Row*—G. Steele, W. Graham, W. Hendry, T. Watters (S.B.A.), J. Laing, R. Wylie (S.B.A.), A. Scott, A. Westwater, W. Mair (S.B.A.), A. Forrester, P. Henderson, R. Park, D. R. Lyall, A. T. Paul (S.B.A.), A. M. Wallace (S.B.A.). *Seated*—M. Hook (S.B.A.), H. Webster (S.B.A.), D. Kilgour (S.B.A.), D. Fairfoul (S.B.A.), T. S. Logie (S.B.A.), J. Paul, J. Wilson, W. Tait (S.B.A.), T. Timmons, S. McGill (S.B.A.), G. McGregor (S.B.A.), R. McGhee (S.B.A.).

Minto Masonic Trophy Association

Closely linked to Lochgelly Bowling Club is the Minto Masonic Trophy Association. It not only had its inception in Lochgelly, but under its rules the semi-finals and finals must be played on Lochgelly Green and the President and Secretary must both belong to Lochgelly Club.

On May 12, 1911, a meeting was held in the Clubhouse at which Alexander Westwater presided, when the advisability of a Masonic competition was discussed. A week later another meeting, at which Tom McDonald presided, agreed to write to the following clubs with a view to forming an Association: Auchterderran, Lumphinnans, Cowdenbeath, Kelty, Crossgates, Hill of Beath, Kingseat, Wellwood, Dunfermline South, Dunfermline North, Townhill, Inverkeithing and Charleston. After reports from the various districts, the project was proceeded with. The following clubs took part in the first competition: Crossgates, Dunfermline North, Cowdenbeath, Lochgelly, Kelty, Dunfermline South, Kingseat. The final was played between Dunfermline (John Devlin) rink and Kelty (A. Buist) rink, and the former had the honour of being the first name to be engraved on the trophy, winning 31-18. Bailie Walker presented the trophy and gold badges to the players of both rinks.

The trophy cost £18 4s. It was subscribed for by members of Minto Lodge. The amount raised fell short, and the balance was made up by John Wilson.

The highest entry during the 36 years of the competition was in 1919, when 52 rinks took part.

It is worth noting that the office of Secretary and Treasurer has been held by D. B. Gibb throughout those 36 years. He won the trophy on three occasions. The Presidents have been Alex. Westwater, William Campbell, John Wilson (a second and long term), A. Westwater (1947).

The rinks which won the trophy presented a photograph to the Club.

Winners and Skips of the Minto Masonic Trophy since its inception are:–

1911	–	Dunfermline	(J. Devlin)
1912	–	Lochgelly	(D. B. Gibb)
1913	–	Cowdenbeath	(A. R. Dick)
1914	–	Dunfermline North	(W. Adamson)
1915	–	Leslie	(J. Carmichael)
1916	–	Townhill	(J. Campbell)
1917	–	Crossgates	(Archibald Allan)
1918	–	Dunfermline North	(J. Ritchie)
1919	–	Lochgelly	(T. McDonald)
1920	–	Townhill	(D. Izatt)
1921	–	Townhill	(J. Campbell)
1922	–	Kinross	(W. Harkness)
1923	–	Townhill	(Chas. Findlay)
1924	–	Dunfermline North	(J. Barclay)
1925	–	Crossgates	(A. Allan)
1926	–	Hill of Beath	(Peter Mitchell)
1927	–	Crossgates	(A. Allan)
1928	–	Lochgelly	(John Hynd)
1929	–	Lochgelly	(D. B. Gibb)
1930	–	Lochgelly	(J. Hynd)
1931	–	Townhill	(D. Adamson)
1932	–	Lochgelly	(George Penman)
1933	–	Cowdenbeath	(R. Sinclair)
1934	–	Thornton	(W. McTaggart)
1935	–	Hill of Beath	(P. Mitchell)
1936	–	Kinross	(F. Fitzsimmons)
1937	–	Cowdenbeath	(Peter Drylie)
1938	–	Lochgelly	(D. B. Gibb)
1939	–	Lochgelly	(J. Stewart)
1940	–	Lochgelly	(J. Crawford)
1941	–	Lumphinnans	(D. Cairns)
1942	–	Lochgelly	(R. Whitehead)
1943	–	Cowdenbeath	(Robert Muir)
1944	–	Lochgelly	(R. Whitehead)
1945	–	Bowhill	(J. C. Robertson)
1946	–	Cowdenbeath Welfare	(R. Lindsay)

Club Internationalists

The following members of Lochgelly Club represented Scotland in International matches:–

David Campbell	–	1908
Tom MacDonald	–	1914
John Hynd	–	1926
John Clark	–	1929
John I. Simpson	–	1931, 1932, 1933, 1934, 1937 (now a member of Craigmillar Park, Edinburgh).
William Splitt	–	1935, 1936, 1937, 1938 (now a member of Canmore, Forfar).
John Sinclair	–	1939 (the latter was a member of the British team which toured the United States of America this year).

Secretaries of the Club   1897 - 1947

GEORGE ERSKINE	–	–	–	1898-1904
WILLIAM DUNCAN	–	–	–	1904-1911
DUNCAN B. GIBB	–	–	–	1911-1919
JOHN WILSON	–	–	–	1919-1937
DAVID R. LYALL	–	–	–	1937-1940
WILLIAM HENDRY	–	–	–	1940-1941
TOM FRAME (pro tem)	–	–	–	1941
JOHN WILSON	–	–	–	1941-1943
TOM CAMPBELL	–	–	–	1943-1944
D. R. LYALL (pro tem)	–	–	–	1944
ALFRED RODGER	–	–	–	1944

Treasurers

DAVID PHILIP	–	–	–	1897-1898
GEORGE ERSKINE	–	–	–	1898-1910
JAMES WILLIAMSON	–	–	–	1910-1912
GEORGE AITKEN	–	–	–	1912-1922
GEORGE BELL	–	–	–	1922-1937
ROBERT WHITEHEAD	–	–	–	1937-1940
JAMES THOMSON	–	–	–	1940
JOHN CURRIE	–	–	–	1941
WILLIAM CLARK	–	–	–	1941

John Dougary, President, 1947.

David R. Lyall, Immediate
Past-President.

The Club To-day

This year of Jubilee finds the club in a very favourable position in every way. Their assets, buildings, green, tools and appliances are completely written off. In addition, there is a substantial credit balance and investments in the War Loan.

At one time the membership was limited to 120. The ceiling was gradually raised and it has now reached its limit of 140 with 20 applications for vacancies. Eight members and two former prominent members died during the year–a comparatively large death roll, and this made the number of vacancies higher than usual. Of those who passed away, five were ex-champions – James Gair, John Crawford, Tom MacDonald, Andrew Clark and Andrew Anderson. The others were David Bonthrone, Allan Lind, George Smith, Robert Wyse and Andrew Adamson.

Office-bearers, 1947

President, J. G. Dougary

Vice-President, Tom Timmons.   Past President, D. R. Lyall.

Treasurer, W. Clark (David St.)   Secretary, Alfred Rodger.

Associations Representative, Alex. Westwater.

Committee–J. Sinclair, G. Bell, Ex-Provost Wilson, Arch. Young, J. Weir, J. Haig, D. B. Gibb.

Green Committee–D. B. Gibb (Ranger), Tom Timmons, J. Kinnell.

Skips–Scottish, J. Smellie.   Fife, John Clark, R. Whitehead.

Club–J. Weir, J. Dougary, J. Laing, R. Lawson, A. G. Gibb, J. Cant, D. R. Lyall, G. Bell, J. Shand, W. Clark (David St.) A. Hunter, W. Clark (Lochore), A. Honeyman, J. Sinclair, J. Kinnell.

Scottish Representative, J. Hemsworth.

Fife Singlehand, D. McLean.

Roll of Members–1947

David Allan

John Barclay
George Bell
Arthur Brand
Robert Bauld
George Black
James R. Boyd
Daniel Beveridge

Thomas Cree
W. Clark (Lochore)
W. Clark (Whyte St.)
W. Clark (David St.)
Robert Cairns
Alex. Crawford
David Cook
John Clark
Tom Campbell
W. B. Crombie
James Cant
James Carstairs
Wm. Chalmers
Andrew Clark

John G. Dougary
Alex. Duncan
John Danskine
David Dewar
Robert Donaldson
Thomas Davidson
George W. Dick
John Ditchburn
Robert Donaldson

Andrew Evans
Robert Evans
John Ellis

Thomas Frame
Martin Finnie
Andrew Foote
Alex. Forrester
Robert Forrester
E. Fleming
Alex. Ferguson
Dr. W. Foote
G. Findlay

H. Ghilone
D. B. Gibb
Alex. Gibb
Harry Goodall

James Heggie
Jack Haig
Andrew Honeyman
Jack Harrison
Thomas Harding
James Hemsworth
Peter Henderson
James Henderson
James Haynes
James Hamilton
Alex. Hunter

Robert Jackson
George Johnston
Alex. Jack

James Kerr
James Kinnell
David Kirk
John Kinlay
James Kyle

D. R. Lyall
James Laing
Alex. Lumsden
Robert Lawson

George Marshall
Lewis Milne
L. R. Milligan
John Maxwell
Alfred Melville
Alex. Maxwell
Wm. Melville
H. Milne
W. H. Martin

David McLean
James McCormack
Tom McKinlay
Tom McDonald
M. McVean
John McEwan
Alex. McPherson
John McLean
Wm. McPherson
Wm. McKay

Andrew Nisbet

P. O'Donnell

George Penman

James Paterson
Robert Paterson
Arch. Penman
Thomas Penman
Wm. Paul
David Palmer

Alfred Rodger
David Richardson
Thomas Ramage
Wm. B. Reid
John Russell

Thomas Scott
Dr. Sinclair
James Suttie
John Simpson
George Steele

John Sinclair
Andrew C. Stewart
John Stewart
Walter Stewart
Dr. A. Stephen
Hugh Stewart
Tom Splitt
James Stiven
James Smellie
James Shand
Robert Shand

Tom Timmons
Andrew Thomson
Hugh Taylor
John Thomson

Alex. Westwater
Jack Westwater
Robert Wyse
James Williamson
Jack Weir
J. Wilson (ex-Provost)
J. Wilson (Chapel St.)
Robert Whitehead
William Watson
Robert Wallace
James C. Watson
James Wilson
J. Wilkie

Arch. Young
Andrew Young
Bruce Young

Office-bearers, 1947.

Back Row—George Steele, John McEwan, Jack Haig, Archibald Young, George Bell, Jack Weir, James Kennedy (greenkeeper), Patrick O'Donnell. *Second Row*—Alfred Rodger, John Wilson, Tom Timmons, John Dougary, David R. Lyall, John Sinclair, William Clark. *In Front*—Duncan B. Gibb, James Kinnell. (Inset) Alex. Westwater.

Lochgelly Burgh in 1897–A Keek Back

SOME GENERAL NOTES.

"Nothing in the past is dead to the man who would learn
how the present came to be what it is"

Comparisons are said to be odious, nevertheless they are interesting and at times necessary. Only by comparison can we know things. By recalling the state and affairs of the town in 1897, therefore, we can better appreciate the changes during the past fifty years.

The year 1897 was the centre of a decade which saw Lochgelly grow from a large village to a moderately sized town. These ten years introduced a coal mining development that has kept us going up to the present time. No new collieries have been started since. In our immediate neighbourhood in the 1890s came the resinking of the Nellie Pit and the "Wee Mary", the opening out of Glencraig, North Lumphinnans ("The Peeweep"), and the Aitken; while the blue prints were being prepared for the Minto (Brighills); Dundonald extension, and the Fife Coal Company's enterprise of the Mary, Lochore.

Such a development added, of course, to the population, and the consequent demand for more service and more houses. For a time the new population was of a migratory type. To meet its needs large lodging-houses were built and new shops were opened. The public-houses were overcrowded and it was at this time the "bar" system displaced the inn kitchen or the wee room, and so perpendicular drinking superseded the companionship of the howff – a retrograde step in our social life. Overcrowded bars led to quarrelsome tempers, and disturbances, especially on a Saturday night, were frequent. Never a Monday morning passed without a Burgh Court being held; indeed there was a period when the reporter could reckon on getting court copy almost every day of the week. The charges were, however, not serious – offences rather than crimes – and there is no record in this particular year of any charge that did not come within the Burgh Police Act.

Besides the floating labouring population, others came to reside in the town and settled down to become some of the town's best citizens.

In the decade centred in 1897 Lochgelly doubled its population. The town was overcrowded and, as indicated, four model lodging-houses gave accommodation to several hundreds. New feus for dwelling-houses were, however, being taken. An idea of the development that was started, or about to take place, can best be understood by a brief description of the town then. On the east side of Bank Street and Station Road to the north no buildings but one at the corner of Chapel Street were in existence. With that exception green fields stretched from the Co-operative Store to the old houses near the railway station. On the opposite side of Station Road (the west) the first house from the school northward was Lomond View, and from the Manse there was another blank to Launcherhead. Landale Street, Chapel Street, and David Street were being opened up, and Melgund Place came later. Melville Street and Hunter Street ("The Happyland") were still in the offing, as was the long row of single-storey houses on the south side of Auchterderran Road. So too with Main Street, where hitherto no houses existed on the south side from the Free Kirk westwards. School Lane and Ballingry Lane, however, were by then in being, but nothing beyond Cartmore Road to "Number Four." Changes were less in evidence on the south side of the town. Well Road and Mid Street bounded the west side. The Birnie Braes, a rough open space, had lost its usefulness for supplying water from its three pump wells, as a quarry for sand and as a site for the circuses, and had become a dump for the town refuse.

The schools, the East and West (both of which were later greatly extended) provided educational facilities. Another decade or more was to pass before the South School and St. Patrick's were built. The latter at that time was sited at Lumphinnans "Tunnel." Peter MacDuff was head of the East (Senior) School, and Helen Steedman head of the West (Infant) School.

The Presbyterian Churches were as to-day – the Established, U.P., and Free, all now with different names. The Baptist Church was built much later. The ministers were – Parish, Rev. Thomas Dewar;- U.P., Rev. James Brown; Free, Rev. Peter Macainsh (senior, retired) and Rev. Duncan Brown; R.C., Rev. P. McMahon. Only one extra licence has been granted in the Burgh during those fifty years. We have therefore the fact that only in the case of the kirks and the licences has there been practically no change, and that in both cases they are apparently sufficient for the spiritual and spirituous needs of the populace.

The most popular sport in 1897, as now, was football. Lochgelly United was taking its place in the higher Scottish circles. The team comprised nearly all home products – stalwarts such as Tom, Sandy and Peter Vail, Tom Greenhorn, John and Charlie White, Jim Eadie, Andrew and John McNeil,

Dave McLean, John Campbell, A. Linton, C. Heffron, John Guy, Dod Kinnell, Dave Smith, A. Nicol, J. Devine, P. Gilmour, C. Morrison, Jimmy Hamilton, and Jock Wilson. There were a Junior and two Juvenile clubs which proved good nurseries for the Seniors.

Cricket still retained a hold. In 1897 Lochgelly won the Fife Junior Championship. Some fine players turned out for the club among whom may be mentioned John H. Melville, George A. Russell, William Smellie, John Simpson, Archie Burt, W. Arnott, Tom Vail, Dave Scott, James and John White, Bob Woods, James McKenzie, W. Bowman and John Bain. John Anderson, a leading batsman, had just left for South Africa.

It was a good year for the curlers. Lochgelly could then enter five rinks for the Bonspiel with such skips as Alexander Thompson, R. Suttie, John Adam (Mason) and Andrew Hunter.

Willie Watters this year lost his title as champion quoiter of Scotland to Robert Kirkwood, Banknock, who defeated him 61-59. The stake was £100. (Watters later regained the title.)

Golf was in its teething stage. The new club played on a large field on Spittal Farm. They had matches with Cowdenbeath and Kelty, lost to the former by 41 holes and beat the latter.

Cycling was popular. The pastime was organised in a club termed Lochgelly Thistle. A noted local cyclist that year was Andrew McConnell, who had a number of successes as a professional.

Lochgelly Brass Band crops up often during the past fifty years. The year 1897 saw the start of their long run of successes in contests. In June they carried off first in a Scottish contest at Broxburn. Later in the year they again gained first at Portobello.

The noted "L" Company Volunteers was, as usual, prominent in rifle shooting. At the Fife meeting at Kincraig, Lochgelly shots won a large proportion of the prize money. They included Sergt. Andrew Nicol, Pte. J.C. Thompson, Cpl. D. Swan, Ptes. Mungo Brown, Tom MacDonald, Lieut. Peter MacDuff, Pte. Peter Miller, Cpl. James Nicol, Pte. A. Wilson, Pte. T. Johnstone, Pte. T. McKinlay, Pte. J. Thompson. It may be worth mentioning that they were inspected in the battalion that year at Ladybank by Colonel Wavell, Commanding the 42nd Regimental District.

Devotees of the game of draughts were fairly numerous, including the now veteran Willie Greig. The champion, Freedman, gave an exhibition in the town this year. Against Dunfermline in the Fife Cup Lochgelly had 7 wins against 4 and 14 drawn games.

In public affairs the school board election held first place. Excitement ran high, and meetings were packed and lively, and personalities bandied about. The successful candidates were:– Alexander Reid (spirit merchant), Alexander Graham (chemist), Robert Philp (saddler), John Laing (hairdresser), John Cunningham (oversman), John Hunter (miner) and William Shaw (miner). The other candidates were Mrs Moodie (the first woman to stand for a local body in Lochgelly) and Harry M. Stiven.

Ex-Provost Andrew Landale (a name to conjure with in the building up of Lochgelly) met with a serious train accident. He was then eighty years of age.

The Co-operative Society had a membership of 1,005, a share capital of £13,000, and a turnover of £50,000 a year.

The Choral Union gave a performance of "The Maid of Lorn." Among the soloists was the late Hugh Kelso, Minto Hotel.

Keir Hardie gave a lecture in the Drill Hall on "My Native Land". "We stand," he said, "an unconquered people, but the land must be restored to the ownership of the people. Scotland, the pioneer of freedom, shall yet take its place in solving our social problems." Alexander Kerr was chairman.

A proposal was made to transfer the meetings of Auchterderran Parochial Board to Auchterderran alternately with Lochgelly. The sponsor, Dr. David Rorie, withdrew his proposal.

The Police Commissioners discussed taking over the upkeep of the roads and streets from the County Council. It was stated that it would cost £1 a week for a roadman, besides buying a roller and scraper, and the idea was rejected.

Lochgelly Merchants' Association was formed this year, Bailie Laing being president and W. W. Bethune secretary.

The visit of Lord Rosslyn, the new Provincial Grand Master, to the Minto Lodge was a big occasion. He eulogised George Syme, who had been R.W.M. for eleven years. Later in the year a special train carried the Fife Masons to Rosslyn, where his Lordship was installed in his ancestral chapel. Many members of Minto Lodge and their lady friends joined the excursion.

The Miners' Gala Day was held at Dundee. James Innes was president, and the principal speaker was Augustine Birrell, M.P. for West Fife. The chairman alluded to the Cowdenbeath Coal Company insisting on working eleven days a fortnight, but though the company might succeed they had defeated their own ends for the men would not agree to such a rule. John Weir, secretary, condemned the Government for throwing out the Eight Hours Bill. But they must make sacrifices to attain beneficent reforms. He claimed that the radical wing of the Liberals had been the means of promoting every reform.

The water supply in June was so short as to necessitate it being cut off entirely for twelve hours a day–7 p.m. to 7 a.m.

There was much temperance activity by several associations. The "Rescue" I.O.G.T. reported increasing membership.

St. Finnans Episcopal Church (Lumphinnans Road) was dedicated by the Lord Bishop of St. Andrews and Dunkeld.

Owing to a health breakdown by the Clerk to the Police Commissioners (John Small) the Commission appointed his son, Robert Small, as assistant.

A new postmaster, Robert Hutton, was appointed to succeed Alexander Irvine, who had followed James ("Postie") Bethune.

The Golf Club, which had played at the Spittal, opened at the end of the year a new course at Cooperhall Park. This park was twice a golf course.

Changes among trades have been numerous. Of some forty odd businesses fifty years ago, only four remain in the same family; two of them Public Houses, the remaining two businesses are in Bank Street.

Few facilities for travel made for a more homogeneous community life. The motor car hadn't yet appeared in our town and the tramcar and motor bus were still a decade away. Charlie's Bus, however, a covered horse-drawn waggonette, took passengers to Dunfermline, and as for other means it meant the train, the bicycle, or Shank's Naigie.

The year 1897 saw a greatly increased output of coal in Fife. Wages were $12^1/_2$% above the 1888 rate and so had increased to 4/6 a day. At the end of the year, the men were demanding another $12^1/_2$% increase.

Wednesday half-holiday drives to Aberdour at 1/- return in a two horse brake never lacked patrons. The promoter was Sandy Campbell, Cowdenbeath.

Many tailors and dressmakers were employed. A ready made suit was rarely bought. It was shoddy stuff, and it was sound economy to have the suit "made to measure". The same applied to women's frocks. Most under-garments were hand knit. Women's hats were "trimmed" by the milliners – large contraptions of flowers and feathers. Hand made or "trysted" boots were more in demand than ready-mades, but this did not now apply in the same degree to pit boots. Strong boots, rather than shoes, were worn by both sexes; stout footwear was needed for Lochgelly roads in these days when we had not yet reached the day of the granolithic pavement.

Nearly every house had a garden, large or small, and it was unusual to see a garden uncultivated. The annual flower show (an old institution), was a big occasion. Competition was keen, though prizes were merely nominal. The show this year was in the East School and was opened by ex-Provost Landale who had been its active patron from the start. It was open to a wide area. There were 115 classes in the flower section, 5 for fruit and 50 for vegetables. Twenty classes were provided in the Women's Industrial Section as well as competitions for baking and fretwork, and for children.

A tie with Kirkcaldy at School Park was "wired off", as it was thought that quoiting matches would detract from the "gate".

The year was notable in local quoiting history in that it was the first time Lochgelly Club took part in the Scottish team competitions. They were beaten at Larkhall. The Lochgelly players were John Bain and Thomas Welsh, William Watters and Andrew Wilson; Robert (Carry) Suttie and Dave Hutton, James McLean and Alexander Foley.

The total Burgh rate in 1891 was 2s. 11d., of which 1s. was for schools.

John Hunter was appointed Provost, and George Erskine and Alexander Reid, Bailies.

R.G.E. Wemyss, Unionist candidate for Parliament, told a meeting in the Drill Hall that the man they should vote for was the one who made the fewest promises.

The ownership of the Mine Well Green (where the Miners' Institute now stands) presented a problem to the Police Commissioners, who wanted to be refunded for the cost of repairing the wall. Lord Minto denied liability. Some feuars claimed a right to use it for bleaching clothes, but refused to foot the bill, so the Council had perforce to pay the bill from the rates. At an earlier date they drew 5s. a year for the grazing from David Paton, whose public-house adjoined. At one time the Mine Well was the principal source of water supply for the north side of the village.

Lochgelly Police Commission (later the Town Council) in 1897 comprised James Melville (Provost), John Laing and John Hunter (Bailies), David Williamson, George Erskine, John Raeburn, James Houston, James Henderson, and Alexander Reid. At the November election Michael Lee took the place of David Williamson, who had retired.

In social as well as economic life the town in 1897 had a different pattern than to-day. Young folks made their own entertainment to a greater extent; less was done for them, and consequently they were more self-reliant. In summer their games were varied. Sport requisites, even football, were beyond their purchasing power, but they improvised. The nights of winter were often dreary; no regular nightly entertainments such as pictures, dances, and spectacles. Yet there were many breaks in the monotony, and because they were scarce were anticipated and enjoyed with the greater relish. Dances were held on Saturday nights in Henderson's (formerly Littlejohn's) hall. In summer nights in the open air the lads and lassies made the welkin ring with hoochs and shouts, dancing to the music of the Brass Band. The Miners' Gala was attended by nearly everybody with much merrymaking on their return.

The high spot of the winter was the series of balls. First came the Volunteers', then the Freemasons', followed by the Gardeners' and the Foresters, all conducted in the majestic Victorian fashion with courtesy and politeness. How the lassies looked forward to them, planning their dresses months ahead. Good concert and theatre companies made regular visits, and occasionally the old-fashioned circus on the Birnie Braes – W. F. Frame, MacDonald's Merry Makers, the versatile Brescian Family, while Rushbury provided the drama. Durward Lely, then at the height of his fame, gave a concert this year in the Drill Hall, to which people drove from as far away as Kinross. Sunday School picnics in summer and the soiree in winter were events for the youngsters. At the latter the principal attraction was usually the magic lantern. The Kirk soirees were well attended.

Animated pictures had not yet reached Lochgelly, but a year or so later one Calder, an Aberdonian, brought the first movies to the Drill Hall. They were literally the "flicks" in these days. The Choral Union had a large membership, with star soloists at their productions, and choir practices provided a further outlet for the musically minded.

Youths with the proverbial Scots thirst for knowledge attended "Mutual Improvement Societies" run in connection with the Kirk, and good lectures were provided in the old Co-op. Hall by the Educational Committee. It was just about this year that the first billiard table was installed in the town. It was a three-quarter size. There was also a Co-op library, the nucleus of which was a village library started decades earlier by Andrew Landale.

Friendly Societies, that magnificent feature of the nineteenth century non-political achievement by the wage-earners, were flourishing.

Wages were low compared with present figures. The value of the miner had not yet been given proper recognition by the country. Nevertheless the wages were real wages, not fictitious, as in a great measure pertains to-day. Money had perforce to be wisely spent; the Scot still retained the traditional economic sense of true values. There was not, of course, the temptation to spend money on modern amusements, on dog racing, travelling, or spectacle; such facilities did not then exist.

Cigarettes were no problem then; very few were used. The smoke was through the clay pipe, with bogie roll at $2^1/_2$d. or 3d. an ounce with the pipe thrown in (the cleanest smoke).

Space prevents us extending the keek back, but doubtless a sufficient outline has been written to enable the younger generation to focus their minds on the fact that the privileges they are enjoying to-day were made possible by the hard work, by the thrift, and by the more natural life of their forebears. Many changes have been made for betterment in public health by hygiene and science. Through these agencies, for which their forebears struggled and laid the foundation, a great advance has been made. The march of progress cannot be stopped. No one would want it to be.

Nevertheless let it be fully appreciated that Lochgelly fifty years ago, even without the desirable amenities of to-day, was a grand place to live in, a neighbourly, happy and healthy community. And over all it was the sense of freedom; the day of absolution of a bureaucracy was yet of the future.

The Club's Feu Charter

We had difficulty in tracing the Feu Charter but eventually it was found in the strong room of the Union Bank. It is dated 9th September, 1895. The extent of the feu is 150 ft. x 155 ft. The Charter is signed on behalf of the club by Hugh Drysdale, baker, Langley Villa, president, David Philp, clerk, Berry Street, treasurer, Wm. Walker Bethune, grocer, Bank Street, secretary. Witnesses were Alex. Westwater, printer, Bank Street, Robert Blyth, grocer, Main Street, David Mitchell jr., baker, Hall Street, John Band, baker, Berry Street, Robert Wilson, miner, Berry Street, James Clark, miner, Berry Street.

The ground on the south and east sides had already been feued, the former by Geo. A. Taylor, and the latter by David Johnstone, and others. As usual in all Lochgelly Feu Charters of that period and since, the superior reserves "all ironstone, clay, marl, shale, limestone and all metals and minerals of every description with power to work these; only that they will not be entitled to sink pits in the ground." They reserve power, however, to lower the surface of the ground and in the event of any damage being caused to the ground or buildings on the feu, no claim for damage or recompense shall lie against the landowner.

The feu duty is £5 per annum.

FOR THE BEST VARIETY OF
SPIRITS, WINES and ALES

MATHIESON'S RAILWAY TAVERN, LOCHGELLY

COMMODIOUS BAR
and SITTING ROOMS

'Phone—199.

TOURING BY BUS

On account of the many restrictions, we cannot at present provide all the touring services which we would like to, but we are all set for the happier times which lie ahead and then we will again have what has always been our well justified claim—the best touring facilities in the country.

W. Alexander & Sons, Ltd.

LOCHGELLY DEPOT—AUCHTERDERRAN RD.

Phone 19.

STATIONER

AND

NEWSAGENT

JOHN McEWAN

TOBACCONIST

AND

CONFECTIONER

MOTION STREET, LOCHGELLY

Local Weekly Newspapers

56th Year of Publication

" Lochgelly and District Times "

Bank Street, Lochgelly

" Cowdenbeath Advertiser and Kelty News "

285 High Street, Cowdenbeath

LARGE CIRCULATIONS IN THEIR RESPECTIVE AREAS

EXCELLENT ADVERTISING MEDIUM

Telephone—Lochgelly—Office, 42 ; House, 141
Cowdenbeath—Office, 2139 ; House, 3106

Publishers—
JOHN WESTWATER & SON, LTD.

1858 – 1958

FREEMASONRY

in

LOCHGELLY

By ALEXANDER WESTWATER, P.M.

Centenary of
Lodge Minto, Lochgelly, No. 385

Printed by John Westwater & Son, Printers & Publishers, Lochgelly
Published by the Committee of Lodge Minto, Lochgelly, No. 385

CONTENTS

Photographs (interspersed with text).

Roll of Members.

PERSONAL

It is a privilege vouchsafed to me by the Great Architect of the Universe, to put on permanent record in my 84th year, a digest of the history of my Mother Lodge.

I was born seventeen years after the Lodge was founded and initiated in January, 1897, and I knew intimately all the Masters of the Lodge excepting the first honorary Bro. Lord Loughborough.

They were men typical of the Victorian era – hard-headed, with their feet firmly on the ground; eager for advancement, but with the restraining influence of promoting their aims by reform conforming with their resources. These men were an example in fidelity and an inspiration to those who came after.

Many of the pioneers of Freemasonry were also leaders in the town's development, making haste slowly, and thereby building on a solid foundation.

The text of this book will confirm these opinions and may serve to keep their example fresh in honoured memory.

I wish to acknowledge the co-operation received from the secretary, Bro. Andrew Dewar. He put at my disposal all the necessary records and documents and furnished me with any information required. He also provided the roll of members over the 100 years. I also wish to acknowledge the assistance received from the Grand Secretary (Bro. Buchan) and the P.G.S (Bro. Sloss).

BRO. JOSEPH ADAMS – THIS YEAR'S R.W.M.

Bro. Adams occupies the chair in an historic year which involves extra responsibility and time. In this he has not been found wanting and along with the secretary has directed much thought to the Centenary Celebrations. Bro. Adams is a native of Coatbridge. Since joining the Lodge his progress has been rapid and justified. He is an official in an important position on the N.C.B. staff.

OFFICE-BEARERS CENTENARY YEAR 1958

Back Row – Richard Kent, William Speed, Robert Mackay, Robert Dick, Robert Aitken, Robert Wilson, John Kerr, Ebenezer Robertson.
Middle – Frank Kennedy, Thomas Peel, William Wilson, Andrew R. Dewar, Charles Shand, Peter Kinlay, Hugh Harrower, Thomas Russell.
Front – Walter Davie, William Robertson, Alfred Melville, Joseph Adams, Alexander McKay, James Kinnell, Hugh Honeyman.

Lodge Minto Lochgelly, No. 385
Consecrated 1858

THE BACKGROUND

THE VILLAGE AND TOWN OF LOCHGELLY.

When Minto Lodge was started, Lochgelly was a large village – the largest within a radius of eight miles. It was raised to the status of a Police Burgh in 1877. It had developed rapidly from the beginning of the century with one main industry – coal mining. The discovery of iron stone in the coal measures led to the erection of large iron works, with four blast furnaces. These were closed down in 1876 for a double reason – the iron stone was in the course of exhaustion and the importation of iron ore from Spain made the industry uneconomical.

The name of the town derives from Loch Gellie, a water 2½ miles in circumference, half a mile to the south. Authorities are agreed that the place name is Gaelic and must be ancient, dating to the time when Fife was Celtic territory. Incidentally, nearly all the old place names in Fife have a Gaelic origin.

The loch was the cause of a dispute over fishing rights between contentious lairds at the end of the sixteenth century. The family of Wemyss of Wemyss owned (and still own) the lands of Lochhead on the south side and the Boswells of Balmuto owned the north side. The dispute almost brought about an armed conflict. Each party mustered their retainers with the purpose, as so often happened in those days over land disputes, of settling the matter by arbitrament of the sword. Other counsels prevailed and it was decided to refer the dispute to King James VI. That monarch, in his credited wisdom, settled the affair without the necessity of bloodshed. In the present year the Loch has been adopted as a centre of Fife water skiers and is at present the only inland ski-ing centre in the county.

The town had its beginning as a hamlet, comprising "tafts" which are mentioned in documents of the fifteenth century. It gradually became a village of importance with cattle markets and fairs and the inhabitants engaged in weaving and husbandry. It had also a large brewery. The discovery of the coal measures, about 200 years ago changed its character to an industrial community.

The coalfields were worked at first by the Superior, Sir Gilbert Elliot of Minto who had acquired Lochgelly Estate by marriage with the heiress, Agnes Murray Kinninmont of that ilk (near Kinglassie). Tradition has it that Sir Gilbert noticed when snow fell on a part of the estate that it soon melted. He conjectured this was due to burning mineral underneath. The surmise proved correct and led to the start of the primitive "water level" surface mines. He carried on the works himself and employed a "grieve" or manager and with twenty colliers. Later he leased the minerals to a series of investors. It was a period when much money was spent in coal speculation.

In 1847 seams of iron ore were discovered and when the iron works were erected the furnaces produced 50 tons daily.

The railway, between Thornton and Dunfermline, was opened in 1849 and a year later the partners of the collieries formed a company under the name of Lochgelly Iron Company. With the exhaustion of the iron stone seams the production of bituminous coal became the main production. A limited liability company was registered in 1872 and the name changed to Lochgelly Iron and Coal Company. It was then the principal centre of coalmining of Fife. A large proportion of Lochgelly coal was shipped from Burntisland to Baltic ports.

Throughout the century the population increased greatly, five-fold in 50 years. The Company built houses for their employees, mostly in the Muir district to the north-east of the village. The situation by then called for amenities of an urban type. The village was still under the administration of Auchterderran Parochial Board, but it was not till 1877 that Lochgelly became an ad hoc municipal authority by Act of Parliament which created it a Police Burgh. The new authority was fortunate in electing as its leader and head a very enlightened chief magistrate in the person of Andrew Landale, managing director of the Iron and Coal Company. He continued as Provost for 16 years. His influence for good had already been felt. His position gave him considerable power and he used it wisely. Included in his good work was the erection of a school for miners' children in 1859. It was known as the Iron Company's School, and as governor he gave it great attention. It was described, by a national educationist, as one of the best seminaries in Fife. Mainly on his initiative Lochgelly was disjoined from Auchterderran parish and formed into a quoad sacra parish. Previously a Chapel of Ease was erected in 1855 and became a full charge as Lochgelly Parish Church. He encouraged horticulture by the cultivation of gardens and by starting an annual flower show. He also started a village library, the Mutual Improvement Society, and laid the foundation of other valuable traditions.

HOW THE LODGE WAS FORMED.

It was in such an atmosphere that Minto Lodge was started. Initial steps were taken in the spring of 1858 when a meeting of resident members of the craft was held in the village hall.

At the preliminary meeting, Andrew Galloway, a master mason of Kirkcaldie, No. 72, was called to the chair and the following Freemasons residing in the village were present – William Steedman, George Gilmour, William Suttie, William Young, Thomas McKee, William Smith, all Master Masons and Thomas Brand, John Inglis and Alex. Suttie, apprentice masons.

The chairman explained the purpose of the meeting; to consider making application to the Grand Lodge of Scotland for a Charter to constitute a Lodge in Lochgelly. The reason he gave for this step was "that living at such a distance from any Lodge of Free and Accepted Masons meant they had few opportunities of practising the ancient and honourable craft".

The nearest Lodges were at Dunfermline and Kirkcaldy eight miles distant.

The chairman added that if the brethren present were prepared to assist and aid each other by their advice and contributions there was nothing to prevent them getting a duly constituted Lodge. The decision to apply for a Charter was unanimous.

A further meeting was held on 8th June, 1858, when it was resolved to make application. Bro. James Gilmour moved that they draw up a subscription of one shilling each per month to assist to defray expenses. An agreement was drawn up and signed by all present, binding each to uphold and support the Lodge.

The petition was duly forwarded to Grand Secretary and from Grand Lodge minutes we extract the relevant quotation: "The Grand Secretary presented petition for creation of a Lodge at Lochgelly to be called 'Lodge Minto', and reported that the proper number of names was appended to it with the usual certificates from the Provincial Grand Master of Fifeshire and the Masters and wardens of the two nearest Lodges. The fees had been deposited with him. It was found that the requirements of Grand Lodge had been complied with and recommended that body to grant the Charter as craved."

The application went forward to Grand Lodge. At a meeting on 6th July, 1858, the following first office-bearers were unanimously appointed – The Rt. Hon. Lord Loughborough (Later Earl of Rosslyn) to be R.W.M; Andrew Galloway, D.M.; William Steedman, S.W.; George Gilmour, J.W.; Thomas McKee, Treasurer; William Young, Secretary; William Smith, S.D.; Thomas

Scott, J.D. A deputation comprising A. Galloway, G. Gilmour and Thomas McKee, was appointed to purchase the necessary jewels, paraphernalia, etc. It was further decided to raise money by bill or otherwise to settle accounts. A lease of the hall as a Lodge-room was accepted at a rental of £8 per annum.

It was decided to name the Lodge "Minto" after the Superior of the lands of Lochgelly, the Border family of Elliot, who acquired the Lochgelly Estates about 200 years ago along with that of Melgund, in Angus, by marriage.

The consecration of the new Lodge was fixed for 5th November, 1858. On that date, at one o'clock, the ceremony of consecration was carried through by the Right Worshipful Provincial Grand Master, John Whyte Melville, of Mount Melville and Bennochy. Deputations were present from Lodges No. 1 St Mary's Chapel, Edinburgh; No. 2 Canongate Kilwinning, Edinburgh; No.19 St. John's, Cupar; No.25 St. Andrews; No.26 St John's, Dunfermline; No.72 Kirkcaldie, Kirkcaldy; No.91 Elgin, Leven; No.250 Union, Dunfermline; No.327 St. Serf, Kinross; No.291 Celtic, Edinburgh. The attendance numbered 120. After the ceremony the brethren marched with the P.G.M. to the Railway Station, where he addressed them. Kelty Instrumental Band headed the procession. Dinner was served in the Lodge-room at four o'clock when Bro. Galloway, D.M., presided. Under his direction the Lodge was opened for the first time. Later he called the Lodge from labour to refreshment, and "a happy afternoon was spent."

And so Lodge Minto set out on its long journey of a hundred years during which it has played a notable part in the history of the town. Local and national movements met with generous support. There was a close liaison with St. John's 540, Crossgates. The reason for the connection was that both the latter and Minto Lodge had members from the then village of Cowdenbeath previous to the setting up of Lodge Thane of Fife. Cowdenbeath, in the centre of the two lodges, was sometimes used for a joint meeting. Generally the brethren marched to the rendezvous in regalia, headed by a Brass Band with the Tyler on horseback and accompanied by a multitude of young folks.

The Lodge, as will be seen for the minute extracts, was represented at many Foundation Stone laying ceremonies, the first of which was in 1863 in Church Street to which the congregation moved from their original Burgher Church in Mid Street. It was then a U.P. Kirk and is now Churchmount Church of Scotland.

DIGEST OF LODGE TRANSACTIONS

We have extracted from the minutes (which have been well kept), and other sources, the more or less outstanding business transactions in the Lodge throughout the century.

The first Initiation took place on 7th December. The candidates were John Couper, grocer; John Connell (Lochgelly Iron Company); and Thomas Hugh, vintner.

St. John's Day was celebrated on 27th December, and was preceded by a torchlight procession. Twelve torches were supplied by Lodge Union, Dunfermline. Lochgelly Flute Band led them through the village streets, for which service they were paid 12/-. All the brethren paraded in full Masonic costume, wearing a white tie and white gloves.

Torchlight processions, uncommon at the time in Lochgelly, and held on St. John's evening, attracted a concourse of spectators. They were made the theme of a sarcastic sermon by the minister of the U.P. Church, the Rev. David Reid. Titled "A Rare Noise," he said: "We were not a little surprised at seeing, parading our streets, a large and somewhat tumultuous procession bearing large pieces of blazing ropes and other combustibles which threw a light around them all. They were accompanied by a band of music (the local Flute band). The tune they were playing let us into the secret that this was the Minto Lodge of Free Masons parading in honour of St. John. They were arrayed in sashes and other insignia of their offices and accompanied by all the little urchins jumping and capering, apparently enjoying the grand display far better than any puppet show they had ever seen. This was all very good for the masons who did their best to make the show attractive. But although we happen to be ignorant of the secret mysteries of this popular society, we think such exhibitions are not calculated to contribute to the respectability of the Lodge, but critically, one must imagine in the eyes of the non-masonic public. We are persuaded, however, that had any other body taken into their head to play such a prank, the authorities would have to interfere and make them parade, if parade they did, minus their flambeaux."

In the course of the years Lodge Minto has maintained a high standard earning the respect of the Provincial Grand Lodge and Grand Lodge. Several of its R.W.M.'s have risen to high position in both these authorities. When presenting Oak panels to the Lodge with the names of all R.W.M's the present writer stressed the value of commemorating the men worthy of reverence and respect and he quoted from the Holy Writ which lies open at every meeting and without which no Lodge can function; "Disregard not the landmarks thy Father has set."

The centenary of the birth of Robert Burns was the occasion for a special meeting on 25th January, 1859. Bro. William Suttie proposed the toast. Later a public party met in the hall for the same purpose.

22nd February, 1859. – It was agreed to pay 6d. a month to maintain the Lodge and to hold a course of Instructional Meetings.

6th May, 1859 – The Lodge agreed to take part in the laying of the Foundation Stone of Kirkcaldy's new Corn Exchange.

17th May, 1859 – The practice of holding the meetings on the second Tuesday of each month was decided on. This date has continued throughout the 100 years.

14th June, 1859 – Before Cowdenbeath had a Lodge several residents there joined Minto Lodge. A summer St. John's procession led to a difference of opinion as to whether they should parade from Lochgelly to Cowdenbeath and meet the Cowdenbeath brethren in Bowman's Inn there or meet at Cowdenbeath and march back to Lochgelly. The former was agreed to. (This was the first of many parades in which Cowdenbeath was the rallying point of summer processions.) The parade was "conducted in a very orderly manner." The 40 brethren who took part partook of supper in the Lochgelly Lodge-room.

The first mention of celebrating St. Andrew's Day was of sending a deputation to St. John's, Dunfermline, for that purpose.

25th October, 1859 – A proposal by Grand Lodge that the County lodges should pay £1 annually for the new Benevolent Fund was not favoured.

27th December, 1859 – The brethren paraded the village prior to celebrating St. John's.

10th January, 1860 – Consideration was given for taking a lease of a hall proposed to be erected by Mr Jackson (probably at the old Brewery). Complaint was made for letting their present hall for "certain amusements." Mr Jackson offered to make his new hall agreeable to their plans at a rent of £10 provided he made a smaller room also suitable for Masonic purposes. This room was above the arched gateway. (This was known as the Pend.) At a later meeting, Mr Andrew Landale (Lochgelly Iron Company) told the Lodge that their present hall had been repaired to their satisfaction at considerable expense and that he could not allow them to give it up without compensation. Compensation of £8 was offered but Mr Landale said he would first need to see what it would cost to turn the hall into a dwelling-house. On consulting a lawyer, it transpired that the lease of the old hall was illegal and that they could leave it at Whitsunday. Bros. William Mungall, Thomas Brand and Low were appointed to meet Mr Landale.

At a subsequent meeting a letter from the Grainger Trustees stated that the hall could not be taken off the Lodge's hands. It was then decided to retain the hall and ask Mr Jackson to release them from the other one.

11th December, 1860 – Bro. Andrew Galloway was now R.W.M., and Lord Loughborough became I.P.M. The latter could not come to install his successor and that duty was performed by Bro. Wemyss of Wemyss, R.W.M. of Lodge Kirkcaldie.

6th April, 1861. – It was decided to discontinue the monthly payments of 1/- per month per member. It was agreed to write brethren to pay up arrears, otherwise they would cease to be members.

27th December, 1861. – St. John's. Torchlight procession, headed by Bain's Flute Band.

TEST OF MEMBERSHIP.

11th January, 1862. – Test of membership fee (1/-) adopted, to apply to all members residing within a radius of 10 miles of Lochgelly. Those failing to pay would forfeit the right of speaking and voting in the Lodge. No action was taken in a proposed assessment of £1 per lodge to liquidate the debt on Grand Lodge.

8th April, 1862. – No aid to be given to any destitute brother from the Benevolent Fund but by the Treasurer or Secretary and only after authorised by the R.W.M.

22nd July, 1862 – Thomas Brand. who had acted as Secretary since the opening of the Lodge, was granted £2. The Tyler (John Inglis) was awarded 15/- in addition to his fee of 1/- per initiate.

The annual St. John's "walk" was discontinued this year.

THE NEW U.P. KIRK

5th May, 1863 – The ceremony of laying the Foundation Stone of the new Lochgelly U.P. Church was carried through by the P.G. Master. (It was transferred from the original building in Mid Street.). The paraphernalia of Grand Lodge was used. The two Dunfermline lodges appeared headed by Forth Iron Works Masonic Band, while Kelty Band led the main procession. The ceremony was by Bro. Sir P. Arthur Halkett. Later in the day, the latter was made an hon. member of Minto Lodge.

14th April, 1863. – A Past Master's jewel was presented to Bro. Andrew Galloway for his services. With part of the sum raised (£3), a silver brooch was given to Mrs Galloway.

MEETING AT COWDENBEATH

9th October, 1863. – For the first time, Minto Lodge was opened in

Cowdenbeath (Brunton's Inn) and three candidates initiated.

26th July, 1864.– Three Degrees were conferred in one night on two candidates (Andrew Burt and John Orme) on account of them proceeding to America. At the next meeting, Robert Stewart was given the same privilege on leaving for Australia.

10th December, 1867 – It was decided to light the hall by gas and charge £1 extra rent.

April, 1870 – The schoolmaster of Ballingry, Bro. Kippie, delivered a lecture on "Home." At a later meeting, Bro. James Cook, S.W., read a lecture on Freemasonry.

10th May, 1870 – The filthy state of the Lodge-room. It was agreed to get another Tyler.

INSTALLATION OF H.R.H. THE PRINCE OF WALES

11th October, 1870. – The Lodge was represented by Bro. Henderson at the installation of H.R.H. The Prince of Wales as Patron of the Masonic body in Scotland, and a deputation also took part in the Foundation Stone laying of the new Edinburgh Royal Infirmary.

27th December, 1871. – The Auditors refused to sign the annual financial statement because they had found an irregularity. An inventory was ordered of all Lodge property.

23rd April, 1872 – By a large majority, the Lodge agreed to the proposal of the Grand Master Mason to pay the test of membership dues.

10th September, 1872. – A deputation attended the consecration of St. Clair of Dysart.

BALLOT VOTING ADOPTED

9th October, 1872 – The Lodge resolved to adopt voting by ballot instead of open voting. (That was before the Ballot Act was adopted by legislation for Parliamentary and Municipal Elections.)

12th October, 1872. – The fee for registration and Diplomas issued from Grand Lodge was raised from 8/- to 10/6.

MEETING PLACE CHANGED

12th May,1874. – The Lodge left their hall in Hall Street (reason not recorded) and removed to Bro. James Smith's large room upstairs till we get a more suitable place. (Smith's public-house was later enlarged to what is now the Bay Horse.)

24th June, 1874 – The brethren walked to the west end of Cowdenbeath and met the Crossgates Lodge. In procession they returned to Bro. Crawford's Crown Hotel, where the large room was decorated with evergreens. They had choice of a plain supper at 2/6; supper with dessert, 3/-; and supper with one round of drink, 3/6. They chose the 2/6 supper.

FOUNDATION STONES – EDINBURGH, DUNFERMLINE AND GLASGOW.

26th November, 1874 – Lochgelly Instrumental Band led the Lodge in procession to lay the Foundation Stone of Ballingry Public School by the R.W. M., Bro. Galloway. Back in Lochgelly, they sat down to supper in Bro. Smith's and the Rev. Mr Pennell, minister of Ballingry, presided.

7th December, 1875 – The salary of the Treasurer was fixed at £2 and be responsible for keeping all jewels and sashes. The Secretary was paid £1 10/-.

19th May, 1876. – Eight brethren represented the Lodge at the laying of the Foundation Stone of the Royal Blind Asylum and School at Westcraig.

12th October, 1876. – To the laying of the Foundation Stone of Dunfermline Corporation Buildings they took their flag as well as the working tools. Several brethren also took part in a similar ceremony, that of the new Post Office in Glasgow. The stone was laid by H.R.H. The Prince Of Wales, Grand Master of England.

19th December, 1876. – Complaint was made that of sashes given out for processions some had not been returned and others were very soiled.

LODGE PROPOSED FOR COWDENBEATH

8th May, 1877. – Bro. John McArthur brought before the meeting about the proposed formation of a Lodge in Cowdenbeath. It was unanimously agreed to support the scheme. A Charter was granted to Lodge Thane of Fife in 1891.

DISASTROUS FIRE

13th February, 1877. – The Co-operative Building at the top of Bank Street, in the hall of which the Lodge had lately been meeting, was destroyed by fire, and the Lodge reverted to meeting in Bro. Smith's. It was reported that the Lodge chest, containing the working tools etc., valued at £40 had been lost in the blaze. A fund was opened, and the first donation came from their G.L. Proxy Master, Bro. David Menteith (£5). To replace the Lodge furniture, Bro. William Bethune proposed a grand drawing for money prizes, and it was agreed to draw the numbers in Henderson's Hall on 16th April. Bro. Thomas Laing, Joiner, Cowdenbeath, was entrusted to supply a new chest, etc.

25th June, 1877. – The brethren marched to Crossgates, joining the brethren there in procession and partaking of refreshments at Mr Connelly's Inn.

11th September, 1877. – Though not mentioned in the minutes, the Co-operative Hall seems to have been ready for re-occupation by this date. The rent was fixed at £3 per year. £1 and all the Lodge crystal was given to Bro. James Smith for the use of his inn for meetings for eight months.

12th February, 1878. – It was decided to purchase a safe to hold various documents.

9th April, 1878. – To an objection regarding the sending of P.G.L. dues by the Treasurer before being before the Committee, the R.W.M. said the Treasurer was bound by his obligation to forward G.L. and P.G.L. dues and was in order in doing so.

RIFLE SHOOTING

The R.W.M. read a letter from P.G.L. regarding an inter-Masonic shooting match among the Lodges in Scotland. A committee was formed to get up a team to represent Minto Lodge. Lochgelly Company of the Fife Volunteer Battalion was noted for its rifle shooting. It was acknowledged to be the premier shooting company in the country. The Lodge was largely represented in the Lochgelly Company ("L" Coy.).

A complaint was put before the brethren by the R.W.M. that he had heard that brethren of higher degrees had been in the habit of informing brethren of inferior degrees before they were entitled to such information. If such continued extreme measures would have to be taken.

THE FIRST INVESTMENT

13th May, 1879. – Bro. Walker proposed that the funds be invested to secure a larger interest return. It was later decided to invest the sum of £60 in the Scottish-American Mortgage Company for three years at 5 per cent. This amount was drawn out of the Union Bank from a Deposit Receipt.

January, 1880. – Bro. Thomas Brand, a founder of the Lodge, in which he had taken a great interest, died. The brethren of Minto and St. John, Crossgates, attended the funeral in Auchterderran Churchyard.

9th March, 1880. – As in former years, the brethren of Crossgates were granted the loan of decorations for their Assembly.

24th June, 1880.– Bro. Henry Cook, a Lochgelly member (Secretary of the Fife Miners' Union), was presented with a gold jewel by St. John, 540, Crossgates, of which he was I.P.M., and a silver tea-pot and gold brooch to

Mrs Cook. The function took place at a joint meeting with Minto Lodge in Crawford's Hotel, Crossgates.

14th September, 1880. – Bro. Andrew Speedie, Cowdenbeath, through the fire at the lodge rooms, lost two diplomas and asked that they be replaced. He was told to take action himself to get them replaced.

9th November, 1880.– Bro Henry Cook died the same year, and Lodge St. John asked Lodge Minto to join in getting up a memorial. The matter was left over. Bro. Cook was a native of Lochgelly. He was the first secretary of the Fife Miners' Union and was a P.M. of Lodge St. John, Crossgates.

January, 1881. – One of the earliest Masonic funerals was that of Bro. James Angus, S.W., to the new cemetery.

FLAG FOR PROCESSIONS

14th June, 1881. – It was decided to purchase a Flag for the Lodge to be used in their processions, to be supplied by Bro. David Cook, draper.

24th June, 1881. – A joint procession with St. John's, Crossgates, took place through the streets of Cowdenbeath and Lochgelly, headed by Lochgelly Brass Band. Later a "sumptuous" repast was served in the Lodge-room.

9th August, 1881. – A letter was received from the Fife Miners' Secretary asking subscriptions towards a memorial stone to the late Henry Cook, P.M. of Lodge 540. It was agreed to co-operate with the latter lodge.

15th September, 1881. – Agreed that on meeting nights when there was no particular business there should be instructions in Masonry of a nature that would be edifying to the brethren.

THE DUBLIN ASSASSINATION

9th May, 1882. – A resolution was passed expressing horror and detestation at the recent assassination of Lord Frederick Cavendish and Mr Burke, Her Majesty's Secretary and Under-Secretary for Ireland, at Dublin.

13th March, 1883. – A proposal to introduce the working of the Mark Degree was left over. At a later meeting it was decided to write Grand Secretary for particulars.

27th December, 1884. – Dissatisfaction was expressed at the bad attendance at Grand Lodge of the Proxy Master, and Grand Secretary was asked to procure another Proxy Master for the Lodge. At a later meeting, Bro. William Walker (later R.W.M.) was appointed. The sum of £5 was voted for the new fund of Masonic Benevolence, and a loan to the Scottish-American Mortgage Company was renewed.

LODGE ADVERTISES FOR PROXY MASTER FOR GRAND LODGE

25th December, 1886. – The R.W.M. and Wardens did not see their way to continue as representatives to Grand Lodge, and it was decided to advertise in "The Scotsman" for a Proxy Master.

14th June, 1887 – An invitation was received from the Kirkcaldy lodges to attend a demonstration in the grounds of Raith.

DIFFERENCES OVER A LODGE FOR COWDENBEATH

10th September, 1889.– By this time brethren in Cowdenbeath belonging to Crossgates St. John wanted to have this Lodge transferred to Cowdenbeath. Apparently there was some difficulty over this with Lodge Minto, for a minute of this date stated that a deputation was received from St. John, 540. They asked explanations from Lodge Minto "regarding their attitude towards the Cowdenbeath action during their present dispute"; but on being analysed their surmises were found not to be correct.

11th December, 1880. – The brethren subscribed £6 6/- and the Lodge Fund contributed £2 towards the Grand Lodge Bazaar to be held in Edinburgh; also "a large quantity of work including napery, cases of stuffed birds, field glasses etc,." passed by Mrs James Cook to the Bazaar.

BURNS' STATUE

9th June, 1891– An invitation was received to attend the inauguration of the Burns Statue at Ayr and to the laying of the Foundation Stone of a hospital in Dundee.

11th August, 1891. – The Lodge members had a drive, along with wives and sweethearts, to Perth.

9th February, 1892. – The first reference to the founding of Thane of Fife Lodge, Cowdenbeath, was an invitation to attend their Assembly. (This Lodge was consecrated on 20th August, 1892.)

FIRST CHURCH SERVICE

24th May, 1892.– The start of Church Services took place this year to Auchterderran Kirk. The Rev. A. M. Houston had been appointed Chaplain.

23rd August, 1892. – The brethren and their ladies had a drive to Falkland in brakes. They started at 7 a.m.

ENTRANCE FEE RAISED

8th November, 1892.– The entrance fee was raised to £2 2/-.

28th March, 1893. – The Mark Degree was worked for the first time. Its introduction was opposed by a small majority. Steps were taken to procure regalia and jewels.

9th May, 1893. – It was agreed to march in procession with Lodges St. John 540 and Thane of Fife 780 on the Summer Festival of St. John.

17th July, 1894. – Another Church Service was arranged for Auchterderran Kirk, the brethren to get refreshments from the funds of the Lodge.

4th August, 1894. – One kneeling stool and three pedestals were purchased at a total cost of £5 5/-.

11th December, 1894. – Decided that the R.W.M. and Wardens be representatives to Grand Lodge, the Lodge to pay the fees and that 6/- be allowed each for expenses. This was later changed to railway fare and 1/- extra.

14th May, 1895. – In response to an enquiry from P.G.L. it was intimated that the Lodge had no Benevolent Fund.

PRESENTATION TO BRO. SYME

9th July, 1895 – The affiliation fee was reduced from 7/6 to 5/-. Bro. Dr Dendle, on behalf of the Lodge, presented a purse and sovereigns, along with a silver mounted staff to Bro. George Syme, and a tea service to Mrs Syme in acknowledgment of his great service as R.W.M. Bro. Syme had been R.W.M. for 12 years. He was re-elected in 1902-03 and altogether occupied the chair for 15 years.

G.L. RULING ON DEGREES

11th February, 1896. – Grand Lodge notified alteration in law whereby degrees could, under the plea of emergency and in the discretion of the Master, be conferred in a shorter interval than 14 days between each degree. That privilege had now been withdrawn and two weeks must henceforth elapse.

It was unanimously agreed that, because of the unemployment in the district, brethren of the Lodge should be admitted free to the annual Assembly. Three brethren were appointed to attend the Olive Lodge of Free Gardeners Assembly.

12th May, 1896. – Several brethren agreed to attend the ceremony of laying the Foundation Stone of the new North Bridge, Edinburgh.

29th May, 1896. – A request from the Free Gardeners asking the Lodge to join in a demonstration of the various Orders in the town was turned down.

VETERAN MARKSMAN

10th October, 1896. – The Lodge attended the funeral of Bro. George Swan. They joined the Volunteers at the Drill Hall. The latter's band headed the procession. (George was a prize-winner at Wimbledon and Bisley rifle meetings.)

9th March, 1897. – A subscription list was opened in aid of victims of the Indian famine.

BENEVOLENT FUND

20th April, 1897. – Bro. the Earl of Rosslyn headed a visitation of P.G.L. He told the Lodge they were in breach of the Constitution in not devoting at least one-half of the fee to a Benevolent Fund.

It was agreed to communicate with Bro. Andrew Galloway, P.M., as to an oil painting presented to the Lodge by the late Bro. Lord Loughborough, the first R.W.M.

27th December, 1897. – Bro. Syme, R.W.M., at St John's Festival, gave a lecture of how Masons should conduct themselves at festivals and all through life.

17th May, 1898. – A Mark Degree (the first recorded in the minutes) was conferred on 11 brethren.

MOVE FOR LODGE AT KELTY

14th June, 1898. – It was agreed to co-operate with brethren in Kelty district to secure the formation of a Lodge there.

11th October, 1898. – The debenture bond for £60 with the Scottish-American Mortgage Company was renewed, and the deposit in the Union Bank was transferred to the Savings Bank.

13th November, 1898. – The Lodge contributed £5 to the proposed General Gordon College at Khartoum.

17th January, 1899.– A deficit of £7 was reported on the last Assembly. The Co-operative Society was requested to put shutters on the windows of the Lodge-room. A deputation attended the consecration of Lodge Oak, 877, Kelty.

26th June, 1990. – Bro. the Rev. A.M. Houston, for the Lodge, presented Bro. George Syme, R.W.M., with a gold watch and a gold brooch for Mrs Syme.

QUEEN VICTORIA'S DEATH

30th January, 1901. – A letter of sympathy and fealty was sent to King Edward on the death of his mother, Queen Victoria. Later the Lodge attended a funeral service in the Parish Church, when 79 walked in procession.

26th December, 1902. – The Lodge accounts showed a credit balance of £226. The sum of 24/- was collected at St John's Festival for benevolence.

13th January, 1903. – A Grand Lodge communication stated that a body calling itself "Lodge Christian Zum Palmbaun" at Copenhagen had been declared illegal by Grand Lodge. For any brother to visit it would incur the penalty of a grave Masonic offence.

14th February, 1903.– The brethren attended a Masonic service on the death of Bro. John Hunter, a Past Master and former Provost of Lochgelly. They walked from Glencraig to Lochgelly and thereafter went in brakes to Auchterderran Churchyard.

9th June, 1903. – Grand Lodge intimated that two brethren from an Ayrshire Lodge personified and represented regular members at a Grand Lodge meeting and voted in divisions. They had been suspended from all Masonic privileges, along with the R.W.M. of the Lodge.

PROPOSAL FOR A MASONIC HALL

23rd June, 1903. – At a meeting, specially called, the advisability of erecting a building for Masonic purposes was considered on the motion of Bro. Anthony Walker, seconded by Bro. The Rev. Thomas Dewar. A committee was appointed to go into the question. It consisted of Bros. George Syme, A. Walker, Thomas Dewar, J. Jackson, R. Wilson, sen., David Pryde, William Greenwood, David Wilson, Alex Westwater and W.M. Bethune. Bro. A. Westwater was appointed Assistant Secretary for the Hall Scheme. The Lodge was at that time meeting in the Co-operative Hall at Knockhill Close. Their assets were £120 in the Union Bank.

13th October, 1903. – A proposal from Grand Lodge was received that the names and addresses of all candidates for admission should be stated in open lodge at a previous meeting or submitted in the notice calling the meeting. The Lodge agreed to support only the first part of the proposal.

SITE CHOSEN

13th October, 1903. – Report by the Committee on Hall sites recommended the Union Bank feu in North Street and David Street, moved by W.W. Bethune, seconded by William Stuart, while William Johnston and Andrew

Hunter moved an amendment. The former site was recommended, and the Secretary was instructed to obtain plans and specifications and probable cost. Other sites considered were at the rear of the Parish Church, adapting the old Music Hall in Mid Street, and the purchase of the former R.C. Chapel in Grainger Street.

10th May, 1904. – The minimum fee for initiation was raised by Grand Lodge to £3 3/-.

COST OF MASONIC BUILDING

5th July, 1904. – It was reported that the probable cost of the building to be erected was £1200. Plans were accepted and Bro. John Murray, Kirkcaldy, was appointed as architect. At a later meeting it was agreed to hold a Bazaar in aid of the Building Fund. Ladies were appointed as receivers of work. The Secretary reported that he had written Grand Lodge for patronage for the bazaar. The date for it was fixed for the first week of October, 1905.

24th January, 1905. – Bro. William Stuart, D.M., was given a Masonic funeral.

14th March, 1905. – By the narrow majority of 14 to 13 it was decided to build on the North Street site. On 11th July, the Committee opened the offers and reported that the cost would be about £1000.

12th September, 1905. – An invitation from Lochgelly Town Council was accepted to attend the opening of the Public Park on 2nd October.

FINANCE

26th September, 1905. – The Building Committee was granted permission to borrow £500 which had been offered by Court Robin Hood, A.O.F., Lochgelly at 3¹/₂ per cent. per annum and to enter into leases for any part of the new building, not exceeding 10 years. Code of regulations, cleaning, etc., were authorised to be drawn up. The Trustees of the Foresters' Society were granted the necessary Bond and Disposition as security for the loan.

PUBLIC PARK OPENED

2nd October, 1905. – The brethren marched to the Senior School, where they joined a procession along with other Lochgelly societies, and proceeded to the new Public Park, which was opened by Provost Henderson. The Park was granted to the burgh by the Earl of Minto and the late Provost Landale bequeathed £1000 for its layout.

10th October, 1905. – The Lodge agreed to a levy of 4/9 put on all Lodges in the Province to provide a present to the retiring Provincial Grand Secretary, T.W. Davidson.

14th November, 1905.– The Treasurer reported that the total drawings to date for the Bazaar held in aid of the Building Fund amounted to £479, and expenditure £115, leaving a balance of £364.

NEW HALL OPENED

29th December, 1905. – The first function to be held in the new Masonic Hall was St. John's Festival. Permission was given by P.G.L. to remove to the new Lodge-room, and thereafter the meetings were held there in place of the old Co-operative Hall. The Secretary, Bro. Henry Stuart, resigned and Bro. Alex Westwater was appointed.

13th March. 1906. – It was agreed to hold an open excursion to Aberfeldy, on the motion of Bro. Johnston, seconded by Bro. John Rattray. (This was the first of a series of popular excursions by rail. Profits were devoted to the Hall Fund which benefited considerably.)

A "CLUB" LICENCE

Bro. R. Christie gave notice of motion, seconded by Bro. John Barclay, that the Lodge-room be registered as a Club for alcoholic refreshment. A direct amendment was moved by Bro. John Wilson, seconded by Bro. Mungo Syme.

2nd April, 1906. – The brethren attended the funeral of Bro. William Clark, an ex-office-bearer and one of the oldest members of the Lodge.

10th April, 1906. – When the motion to register as a Club came up, it was unanimously accepted. It was pointed out that it would be a great convenience when the Lodge had visiting brethren.

The annual Test Fee was increased from 1/- to 2/-.

LODGE ROOM CONSECRATED

19th May, 1906.– The new Lodge-room was consecrated by P.G. Lodge. Bro. Henry Hilton Brown, in the absence of Bro. Colonel Cathcart, P.G.M., presided. A large number of Minto brethren and visitors from other Lodges were present Following the prescribed prayer, the former delivered an oration on "The Nature and Objects of Freemasonry," followed by singing, grand honours, chanting and prayers.

10th July, 1906. – The family of the late William Clark presented his photograph.

OFFICE-BEARER'S ELECTION CHALLENGED

25th December, 1906. – The Secretary read correspondence from P.G. Lodge, and copy of a letter from Bro. R. Christie regarding the recent election of office-bearers. The complaint referred to a brother who had taken part in the election and had been elected to office without his test fee being payed. In the election of a S.W. the voting had been equal, and the R.W.M. gave his casting vote. The instruction from P.G.L. was that the offices of S.W., J.W., and J.D., should be declared vacant, and the offices were filled without a division. The death of Bro. David Wilson, former treasurer, was intimated.

Bro. George Arrol was offered the post of hallkeeper but he declined, and Bro. William Stuart was appointed at a salary of £2 per annum and 5/- for all-night lettings.

FINANCE

26th January, 1907. – It was intimated that the Lodge had now a clear credit balance of £700, and of this, £500 had been raised during the past three years. Bro. William Greenwood had been R.W.M. during that time and was the mover of the motion to build the hall.

12th March, 1907. – The annual excursion was fixed for Pitlochry. It was agreed to reserve saloon carriages for the office-bearers. Bro. W.W. Bethune complained that some unauthorised meetings were held on Saturday nights. The R.W.M. (Bro. James Hunter) said they were informal meetings for instruction.

14th May, 1907. – A motion was made by Bro. Greenwood that registration as a Club be discontinued, but later withdrew it.

COMPLAINT FROM COWDENBEATH

The Secretary of Thane of Fife, Cowdenbeath, wrote complaining that they had not been invited to two recent Masonic funerals.

The Summer St. John was marked by a service in the Parish Church, conducted by Bro. the Rev Thomas Dewar. One hundred walked in the procession.

11th June, 1907.– The net profit on the excursion to Pitlochry was £19.

HARMONIUM PURCHASED

It was agreed to purchase a harmonium for Lodge use.

"BLACK -BALLING"

Protest was made that the two who had presented themselves as candidates at the meeting had been rejected by the ballot. Bro. W.W. Bethune condemned

JUBILEE YEAR OFFICE-BEARERS

Back Row – John McEwan, William Stuart, John Wilson, William Paterson, Committee: George Main, Auditor; James Howden, Organist; William McNeill, Jeweller; John Wilson, Committee

Middle Row – George Arrol, Tyler; David Moffat, D.C.; Robert Bain, Steward; John Rattray, S.D., Alexander Westwater, Secy.; Walter Rolland, J.D.; Alexander Young, I.G.; Thomas Vail, Asst. Steward; Robert Wilson, P. Treasurer

Front Row – John Jackson, Treasurer; Andrew Seath, J.W.; James Kinlay, S.M.; John Barclay, D.M.; James Hunter, R.W.M.; William Greenwood, I.P.M.; W.W. Bethune, P.M.; Robert Christie, S.W.; Rev. Thomas Dewar, Chaplain. All but two have "Crossed the Bar."

the action of the minority. The R.W.M. concurred. Such systematic black-balling would stop all progress. The Secretary was asked to write Grand Secretary regarding the matter. At a later meeting the latter said he could not interfere between the brethren and the ballot.

In November a similar incident occurred. On a motion, the ballot was taken over again as possibly a mistake was liable to have occurred. This time the ballot was clear. There was, for a time, much anxiety over this matter.

10th December, 1907. – The Committee recommended salaries as follows-Secretary, 30/-; Treasurer, 20/-; Tyler 20/; Assistant Steward, 15/-; Hallkeeper, £3 and 5/- for all-night lettings; Hall Cleaner, £5.

It was decided to fix a Life Membership fee of £1 5/-.

A CHARGE WITHDRAWN

20th December, 1907.– A brother appeared in response to a summons in respect of certain charges he had made regarding the Committee at the excursion to Pitlochry. He denied making the statements but later offered to withdraw and apologise, and this was accepted.

14th January, 1908. – The Lodge proposed to the Town Council to hold a Masonic ceremony in laying a Memorial Stone at the new Town House.

AN ANONYMOUS LETTER

11th February, 1908.– At a Provincial Lodge visitation, the P.G.M. referred to an anonymous letter he had received regarding Minto Lodge. He had handed the letter to the R.W.M., but his personal inclination would have been to put the letter in the fire.

Bro. John Jackson was appointed Treasurer on the resignation of Bro. Robert Wilson, which the Lodge had received with regret.

The annual excursion was fixed for Callander in June. (It showed a net profit of £13.)

It was agreed to purchase four new sheets and get a carpet laundered. This took the place of a crude method. A Hall Committee was formed.

5th May, 1908.– The Lodge agreed with P.G.L. proposal that each Lodge should pay 1/- for each entrant. A gold watch was presented to Bro. R. Wilson, who had held office for 24 years.

12th May, 1908. – It was decided to take no action on a suggestion by Thane of Fife, Cowdenbeath, with regard to a meeting to consider a uniform system for the admission of candidates.

A candidate's application was ruled out of order as his proposer's test fee had not been paid. Another candidate was rejected on the ballot.

THE GOLDEN JUBILEE OF THE LODGE

Sunday, 2nd August, 1908. – A large church service marked the fiftieth anniversary of the founding of the Lodge. The brethren, to the number of 300, assembled at the Lodge which was opened by Bro. James Hunter, R.W.M., and in procession, with full regalia and headed by Lochgelly Brass Band, marched to the Parish Church. It was watched by a large concourse of spectators. The Rev. Thomas Dewar, Lodge Chaplain, presided and the sermon was preached by Bro. the Rev. T. Angus Morrison, Very Worshipful Grand Chaplain of Scotland. He spoke from the text in Proverbs XV and 3: "The Eyes of the Lord are in every place." In an eloquent peroration he appealed to the brethren to live up to the principles they were taught. The volume of the sacred law was always open in the Lodge; they were taught what it contained and he exhorted them to keep ever in front the teaching thus imparted. He also made reference to the Jubilee of Lodge Minto and the vast amount of good they had been able to accomplish during those 50 years. The Praise was led by Bro. Thomas Crichton and Bro. Alexander Nisbet presided at the organ. The former sung the sacred solo "Nazareth."

The brethren re-formed after the service and at the Lodge room Bro. Hunter thanked the Grand Chaplain for his powerful sermon and the instruction it contained. He added that he intended at the next meeting to move that he be enrolled as an honorary member of Lodge Minto, an announcement that the brethren received with loud applause. The thanks of Minto Lodge were extended to numerous visiting brethren who had helped to make the function such a success. The substantial collection at the Church was placed to the Benevolent Fund.

The visitors sat down to a substantial high tea, purveyed by Councillor Robert Bain, Steward, and the assistant steward, Bro. Tom Vail.

LODGES REPRESENTED

The Lodges represented were No. 5 Canongate, Leith; No.6 St. John, Dunfermline; No.48 Edinburgh, St. Andrews; No.72 Kirkcaldie; No. 145 St. Stephens, Edinburgh; No.166 St John's, Airdrie; No.19 St. Andrews, Cumbernauld; No. 327 St. Serf's, Kinross; No. 400 Dunearn, Burntisland; No. 468 Oswald, Dunnikier; No. 540 St. John's, Crossgates; No. 557 Kilwinning, Blantyre; No. 776 Randolph, Buckhaven; No. 277 Wemyss, West Wemyss; No. 781 Thane Of Fife, Cowdenbeath; No. 827 Hope Budge Castle, Armadale; No. 867 St. Clair of Balbeggie, Thornton; No. 877 Oak, Kelty; and

No. 940 MacDuff, East Wemyss.

11th August, 1908. – A proposal to alter the day of the regular meeting from Tuesday to Wednesday was defeated by a majority. (The plea had been made that a number of members were also members of the Co-operative Society committee, which also met on Tuesdays.)

The cost of the Jubilee celebrations was £36 8/-.

The Lodge agreed to a request by the town to "make" their portion of the road opposite their feu in David Street.

A Jubilee Social was held on 2nd October, but the proposed Torchlight Procession was postponed.

A rule was made that either the proposer or seconder of a candidate should be present in the Lodge when a ballot was taken.

22nd September, 1908. – Lodge Rothes invited the office-bearers to Leslie to "give them a lesson on the working of the Third Degree."

REGRETS

22nd October, 1908.– At a social, celebrating the Jubilee, the R.W.M., Bro. James Hunter, said it was a pity that none of the original members in 1858 were now alive, but it was quite possible that when Lodge Minto celebrated its Centenary some present that night might be alive to take part in the Centenary celebration.

10th November, 1908.– Of 12 candidates for admission, six were rejected in the ballot.

It was decided to pay train fares to the representatives to Provincial Grand Lodge and to give an allowance of 7/6 instead of 6/- to those attending Grand Lodge.

LODGE VACATION

The Committee recommended that the Lodge should be in vacation during the months of June, July and August, and meet twice a month for the rest of the year.

It was decided to purchase a new electro-plated sword for the Tyler, and to get black and white counters for the ballot.

ROYAL ARCH CHAPTER FORMED

12th January 1909. – An application was received from the new Royal Arch Chapter, No. 342, for the use of the hall for meetings, and this was granted free of charge for one year. The Chapter also asked a loan of £60 which was sanctioned to bear interest at the rate of 3$\frac{1}{2}$ per cent.

26th January, 1909. – The initiation of one candidate, who had passed the ballot, was delayed till certain enquires were made.

LODGE COMPLIMENTED

9th February, 1909. – At a P.G.L. visitation, Lodge Minto was complimented by the P.G.M. on the large amount the Lodge gave to Charity.

8th March, 1909. – A more effective scheme of lighting of the hall was authorised, as well as the purchase of 13 aprons for office-bearers. The Assembly in the Opera House showed a net profit of £5 14/2. At a later meeting, 20 jewel collars were ordered.

It was agreed to hold the annual excursion to Aberfeldy on Tuesday, 8th June.

BOWHILL ASKS A CHARTER

27th April, 1909. – It was intimated that Bowhill brethren had applied for a Charter for a Lodge, and they were wished much success. Bro. Robert Christie, S.M., was presented with a gift on leaving Lochgelly to reside in Perth.

LOAN REPAID

13th December, 1909. – The Committee considered a letter from Court Robin Hood, A.O.F., asking repayment of the loan of £500 granted when the hall was built. The Lodge replied that they would hand over the money at once.

An offer to erect a brick boundary wall at 4/4 per square yard, from Thomas Beveridge, was accepted, as also was the offer of Bro. Inch to erect an iron gate for £2.

LODGE ROOMS ACCOMMODATE THE FRIENDLY SOCIETIES

6th April, 1910. – Consequent on a fire at the new Co-operative building in Bank Street, five Friendly Societies asked the temporary use of the Masonic Hall. This was given at the following rents per year – Lochgelly Funeral Society, 30/-; B.O.A.F. Gardeners £5 10/-; A.O. Foresters, £5 10/-; Lodge of Oddfellows, £5 10/-; Rechabite Tent, £5 10/-; also Lochgelly Branch of the Miners' Union, £12.

It was agreed to take part in the Memorial Joint Service in the Parish Church on the funeral of King Edward.

DECORATING THE LODGE ROOM

The painting and decorating of the hall was left in the hands of the small committee who were asked to visit various lodges with a view to selecting a model whereon a specification could be drawn out. It was also decided to erect a platform round the hall, 3ft. broad and 7ins. high and to have a raised dais 18 ins. high in the east. Powers to carry this through were given to Bros. J. Kinlay, J. Hunter, A. Westwater, John Wanliss and John Wilson.

Mrs David Johnstone, David Street, claimed £19 7/6 in respect of making portion of road there. The claim was not admitted.

GRAND CHAPLAIN'S GIFT

Bro. The Rev. Angus Morrison, Past Grand Chaplain of Scotland, who had preached at a service in the Parish Church, presented a black and white etching of the late King Edward's coronation, framed in oak.

LORD LOUGHBOROUGH PORTRAIT

12th September, 1910.– The hall and ante-rooms were closed for all lets, but present agreements were to be completed.

It was agreed to write Lodge St. Clair, Dysart, to get a copy of a portrait of Bro. Lord Loughborough, who was the first R.W.M. of Lodge Minto. It was explained that Lord Loughborough 50 years ago presented his portrait to the Lodge, but it had long disappeared and could not be traced.

10th October, 1910. – Bro. John Wanliss presented a handsome gong, compass and square to the Lodge.

11th November, 1910.– The Lodge rooms were redecorated and refurnished. To inaugurate the extensive scheme of redecoration and refurnishing of the Lodge a social meeting and dance was held. There was a large turnout of brethren.

The R.W.M. (Bro. Kinlay) said it was their aim to make Minto Lodge the finest in the Province of Fife and Kinross. In this he believed they had succeeded. The scheme had cost a considerable amount of money but the finance of the Lodge quite justified the outlay.

THE NEW GRAND LODGE BUILDING

22nd November, 1910. – The secretary read a circular from Grand Lodge in connection with the building of new headquarters in George Street. It suggested that daughter lodges should contribute as they were able towards the cost which was estimated at £30,000.

12th December, 1910. – A committee, consisting of the R.W.M., secretary and treasurer was appointed to negotiate regarding share of cost of street making in David Street opposite the Lodge feu.

Bro. George Arrol offered to plant a tree, brought from Aberfeldy on the occasion of the first annual excursion in 1905 by the father of the R.W.M., in the garden at the rear of the hall and the offer was gratefully accepted.

CORONATION OF KING GEORGE V

8th May, 1911. – The Lodge decided, on the recommendation of the Committee, to take part in the Coronation procession of King George V on 22nd June, to the Public Park.

MASONIC BOWLING TROPHY

12th September, 1911. – The Secretary (Bro. Alex Westwater) said arrangements had been made for the start of the Masonic Bowling Trophy which had been subscribed for by members of Lodge Minto. The competition would be opened to Masons in the district. A rule had been passed by the Association that in the event of the competition becoming defunct the trophy would revert to the custody of Lodge Minto. The initiation of the trophy competition was taken by Bro. John Wilson, R.W.M.

11th December, 1911. – Bro. William Stewart was offered the appointment of hallkeeper and cleaner at a salary of £4 and £5 respectively.

12th December, 1911. – Agreed to open the lodge rooms at week-ends for all members of the Lodge in good standing and furnish papers, books and games.

TWO LODGES JOIN FOR CHURCH SERVICE

25th May, 1912 – Representatives of Lodge Minto and St. Fothad's Auchterderran, agreed to hold a joint church service each year alternatively at Lochgelly and Auchterderran. The first took place in Lochgelly on July 28th, 1912, at the Parish Church. The service was conducted by Bro. the Rev. A. M. Houston, chaplain of Lodge St. Fothad's.

10th September, 1912. – The Minto Masonic Bowling Trophy was won in its first year by the Minto Rink skipped by Bro. D.B. Gibb, who presented a photograph of the rink to the Lodge. The other players were James Gillies, James Kinlay and John Wilson.

CHAPLAIN RESIGNS

15th November, 1912. – Bro. the Rev. Thomas Dewar, Lodge Chaplain, was presented with a handsome Chaplain's jewel and purse of sovereigns on demitting office on account of his leaving Lochgelly. Bro. Kinlay, R.W.M., spoke of the active interest he had taken in the Lodge during his 11 years of office.

12th December, 1912. – The Royal Arch Chapter, No. 342, was granted use of the hall for special degrees at a rent of 5/- per meeting.

A Committee was appointed to purchase a piano, price not to exceed £25, and it was agreed to make an addition to the Lodge building and consult an architect on the matter. For the use of the piano the Royal Arch Chapter would pay 10/- per year.

TYPE OF CANDIDATES WANTED

11th February, 1913. – The R.W.M. (Bro. Wilson) drew attention of the brethren with regard to putting candidates forward that they should be careful to see that none were proposed unless likely to prove a credit to the Lodge and the craft.

He referred to a visit paid by a number of members of the Lodge to the 15th anniversary of Lodge Elgin, Leven, where they heard a most interesting masonic address by Grand Master Mason, the Marquis of Tullibardine.

11th March, 1913. – The R.W.M. moved, and the secretary seconded, the adoption of the following bye-law: "That candidates who may pass the ballot but fail to come forward for nomination within six months after that date, make another application for admission."

4th April, 1913. – In addition to the customary P.M.'s jewel, Bro. Kinlay, on demitting office as R.W.M., was presented with a massive marble clock and side ornaments to match, a gold-mounted walking stick, and a gold bracelet for Mrs Kinlay.

EASTERN STAR ACCOMMODATED

29th April, 1913. – An application by Bro. John Rattray asking the use of the hall for a proposed meeting to form a Chapter of the Eastern Star was unanimously granted.

17th May, 1913. – A communication was read from P.G.L. asking if the Lodge was in favour of a proposal recently brought before G.L. that the minimum entrance fee of three guineas be increased. The Lodge intimated they were not in favour of the proposal.

6th August, 1913. – The visit of Provincial Grand Lodge is of special interest in that it was the first official visit by the newly elected W.P.G.M., Bro. Lord Bruce (later Lord Elgin) to a Lodge in the Province. Minto Lodge took the visit as a compliment. As it turned out it was the beginning of an important career in the masonic hierarchy.

8th September, 1913. – Donations were granted to the Sick Nursing Association and the Ambulance Wagon Association from the credit balance of the excursion to Ayr. Expense in connection with the recent joint Church service with St. Fothad's and Minto Lodge amounted to £27 16/11 payable half by each Lodge.

CULTURE ENCOURAGED

16th September, 1913. – It was agreed to form a literary and recreation society within the Lodge and arrange for a winter session. The secretary was asked to make the arrangements.

14th October, 1913. – The presentation was made from a number of visiting brethren of a substantial and artistic box for clothing and jewels.

21st October, 1913. – Approval was given to the purchase of 60 additional chairs for the halls and ante-rooms and to introduce electricity for lighting and ventilation. A special collection was authorised for the Distress Fund in connection with a mining disaster in Wales.

21st October, 1913. – An invitation was accepted from Lodge Union No. 250, Dunfermline, to a dinner and dance in celebration of the centenary of that Lodge.

8th December, 1913. – It was agreed to purchase a bookcase to be utilised for the Lodge library.

26th December, 1913. – Bro. George Arrol, Tyler presented an inkstand made from old oak taken from Glasgow Cathedral.

10th March, 1914. – The secretary intimated a gift of books for the library – an edition of Scott's Waverley Novels in 25 volumes. They were the gift of Bro. John Wilson, R.W.M. At a later meeting a further gift of fifteen miscellaneous books was contributed by Bro. James Beveridge, and "Gould's History of Freemasonry," in six volumes, by Bro. A. Westwater.

11th May, 1914. – It was decided to proceed with a scheme for electric light and ventilation in the lodge room.

7th September, 1914. – A letter was read from Bro. A. Westwater tendering his resignation in having been called up as a territorial. Bro. H. Fordyce was appointed assistant secretary to carry on the secretarial work in the meantime. The small hall was opened as a reading and recreation room.

LODGE BIBLE PRESENTED

22nd September, 1914.– The brother of the late Bible-bearer, Bro. David Johnstone, presented the Lodge with a handsome Bible. The Lodge decided to have a roll of honour containing the names of members "serving their King and country" hung up in a prominent part of the lodge room.

ACCIDENT TO P.G.M.

24th November, 1914. – Reference was made to an accident to the P.G.M., Bro. Lord Bruce, and a letter was sent hoping for a complete and speedy recovery. The death was reported of P.M. George Syme. He was referred to as one of the most efficient Masters the Lodge ever had and filled the chair for 15 years.

Bro. Westwater wrote that he wanted to give his honorarium as secretary to the widows of brethren belonging to Lodge Minto.

8th December, 1914. – The first member of the Lodge reported to be killed in action was Bro. Thomas Lee.

Bro. Henry Fordyce was appointed acting secretary.

20th April, 1915 – Application was received from the Kirk Session of Lochgelly Parish Church for the use of the Lodge room during the extension of that Church. This was granted on condition they be held responsible for any damage to the hall furniture or fittings.

12th October, 1915. – A levy of 1/- per year was assessed on each member of the Lodge.

14th March, 1916. – It was agreed to insure the Lodge's property against damage by aircraft.

JUTLAND

6th June, 1916. – Reference was made by the R.W.M. to the big sea fight (Jutland) with the remark: "We are indeed proud of our Navy."

7th July, 1916. – Agreed to hold a garden fete in aid of the benevolent fund and a charity concert in the Drill Hall in aid of soldiers' dependants, to be applied to those who were not connected with the Craft.

ALIENS

15th August, 1916. – Circular from Grand Lodge stated that no order existed to prevent the peace and harmony of the Craft being disturbed. It was necessary to ensure that all brethren of alien birth and nationality should not, during the continuance of the war and until Grand Lodge ordered after the

Rev. DAVID FINDLAY CLARK, B.D., D.D.

One of the best known chaplains was the Rev. David Findlay Clark, B.D., D.D. He took a great interest in the Lodge. He was then minister of Lochgelly Parish Church (now called St. Andrew's Parish). During the First World War he started and carried through a complete reconstruction of the interior of the Kirk. He left Lochgelly on his election to John Knox, Aberdeen, thence he was called to Banff Parish, his present charge. During his ministry there he received his doctorate. An Ayrshire man, he is an authority on Burns and is much in demand as a lecturer on the national poet.

"LEST WE FORGET"

The Lodge War Memorial of Brethren who fell in the 1914-1918 and 1939-1945 Wars.

Treaty of Peace was signed, attend any meetings authorised by Grand Lodge. Certain exceptions were made to the Order.

30th January, 1917. – Circulars from Grand Lodge dealt with the need for proper enquiry into all applications for admission.

GRAND LODGE ROLL OF HONOUR

1st March, 1917. – The Lodge secretary was instructed by Grand Lodge on the procedure of sending in names of the brethren serving in the Navy or the Army for compiling the Grand Lodge Roll. The entries must conform with the views of the censor with regard to brethren serving in H.M. ships. They should be described as "H.M. Navy," and if an infantry regiment, the name of the regiment only.

10th April, 1917. – A letter of thanks to the Lodge from Bro. the Rev. D. Findlay Clark, the Lodge Chaplain, thanked the Lodge for the use of the hall for Parish Church services during the past two years.

ORPHANS' FUND

9th October, 1917. – The Lodge representatives to Grand Lodge were instructed to support a Grand Lodge proposal to form an Orphans' Fund.

4th March, 1918. – The Chaplain, the Rev. D. Findlay Clark, resigned office on his election to John Knox's Church, Aberdeen. He was cordially thanked for his service to the Lodge and was given a presentation on leaving.

9th April, 1918. – the Rev W.A. McDiarmid, minister of Ballingry, was appointed Chaplain. Later in the year a service was held in Ballingry Parish Church, at which they were joined by Lodge St Fothad's, Auchterderran.

INITIATION FEE

The R.W.M. and Wardens were appointed to meet with neighbouring lodges to discuss the suggestion of raising the initiation fee.

14th August, 1918. – The Lodge agreed to invest £60 in war saving certificates on the occasion of a visit of a tank to Lochgelly.

MEMORIAL SERVICE TO THE BRAVE

22nd September, 1918. – The brethren of the Lodge attended a memorial service in Lochgelly Parish Church in memory of brethren who had laid down their lives for King and country in the recent war.

9th December, 1918. – Providing lighting restrictions permitted, it was agreed to resume the annual assembly in the Drill Hall in February.

10th August, 1919. – A Thanksgiving Service was held in the Lodge at which addresses were given by the P.G.M. Bro. Lord Elgin and the Lodge Chaplain.

18th September, 1920. – A memorial stone and roll of honour was unveiled. The P.G.M., Bro. Lord Elgin, and the past chaplain, the Rev. D. Findlay Clark, gave eloquent orations.

BRO. LORD ELGIN HONOURED

8th December, 1921. – Special reference was made by the R.W.M., Bro. David Moffatt, on the honour conferred on Bro. the Earl of Elgin, C.M.G., Prov. G.M. of Fife and Kinross, on his election as Grand Master Mason of Scotland.

12th December, 1921. – Bro. George Arrol completed 21 years in the office of Tyler and was presented with a jewel.

13th February, 1922. – It was agreed that representatives' fees for attending Grand Lodge be 12/6 per meeting and for attending Prov. Grand Lodge, train fare only.

14th February, 1922. – Intimation was received from Grand Lodge that contributions from daughter Lodges for each affiliate from another constitution be increased by 3/6.

8th May, 1922. – A series of weekly whist drives was inaugurated, the profits to be devoted to the general fund of the Lodge.

9th December, 1924. – The Prince of Wales was made an honorary member of Grand Lodge and many members of Lodge Minto attended the ceremony in the Usher Hall.

9th February, 1925. – The Lodge accepted an invitation to be represented at the laying of the foundation stone of the County Buildings, Cupar, by P.G.L., and intimating that the Earl of Elgin and Kincardine would perform the ceremony.

13th October, 1925.– The Lodge made a grant of £5 to Lodge St. Margaret's Hope No. 1184 towards the replacement of furniture which had been lost in a fire.

10th May, 1926. – The R.W.M., P.M's., Secretary and Treasurer were appointed to consider any deserving causes created through the crisis. (The 1926 strike). Power was given to disburse an amount not exceeding £25.

13th December, 1926. – A charge of five guineas was made to the County Council for the cost of electric light and heating which had been extras during the occupation of the hall by the special contingent of police brought into the burgh during the crisis.

26th November, 1929. – It was decided to record in the minutes a sense of the great loss sustained to freemasonry by the death of Bro. Lord Blythswood, Grand Master Mason. The R.W.M. referred to Lord Blythswood's visit to Lochgelly fully a year previously to install the Prov. Grand Master. All daughter Lodges were placed in mourning until 31st December.

11th November, 1930. – The R.W.M. made sympathetic reference to the death of Bro. Lieut.-Col. Peter McDuff.

9th February, 1931. – A letter was read from the secretary of Lodge Verwood, 177, Canada, showing that this Lodge had defrayed the funeral expenses of Bro. William White, of Lodge Minto and that the expenses amounted to 128 dollars. Agreed to consult P.G.L. and Grand Lodge before proceeding further in the matter.

29th February, 1931. – Bro. George Arrol, Tyler, presented to the Grand Lodge Museum a historical Masonic apron.

26th May, 1931. – Reference was made to the honour that had been conferred on Bro. Robert Bauld, a member of Lodge Minto, on being installed as Master of Lodge Maikaremona, No. 158, New Zealand. The secretary was asked to write a congratulatory letter.

8th September, 1931. – It was decided after a ballot vote, that the reading room be opened on Saturdays.

12th April, 1932 – Bro. James W. Logie, Bible Bearer, presented the Lodge with a sword to be used inside the Lodge room.

27th November, 1934. – Reference was made to the death of Bro. J Tennant Gordon, Chief Constable of Fife, and silence was observed as a mark of respect. He had long service as Provincial Grand Secretary and was well known in the Lodge.

CLUB LICENCE

9th April, 1935. – The Committee recommended that the Lodge should consider appealing for a Club licence. This was approved at the following meeting.

9th September, 1935. – It was decided to open the reading room for the session and provide evening papers. It was also decided to hold a hostess whist drive and dance on behalf of Grand Lodge Bi-Centenary Fund.

31st October, 1935. – The Lodge decided to continue fortnightly whist drives and dances and donate the proceeds from the last one to the Grand Lodge Bi-Centenary Fund.

28th January, 1936. – The brethren assembled at the East School and joined the procession to the Parish Church for a memorial service held for King George V.

5th May, 1936. – The Committee agreed to get quotations for office-bearers' aprons and collars.

4th September, 1936. – Mrs Harris Cunningham presented the Lodge with a sash and apron.

8th September, 1936. – The R.W.M. (Bro. Robert Mackay) referred to the honour that had been conferred on Bro. Charles Hornal, Depute Master, in being appointed P.G. Secretary.

23rd February, 1937. – On the suggestion of the R.W.M. (Bro. Charles Hornal) it was agreed to form an instruction class and further, that information be sought regarding the selling of liquor in the Lodge premises after 10 p.m. on special occasions.

26th October, 1937. – Bro. Prov. John Wilson, P.M., intimated that the R.W.M. (Bro. Hornal) had been elected a Scottish Grand Steward and the brethren recorded their congratulations.

26th April, 1938. – Intimation was made that Bro. the Earl of Elgin had retired as P.G.M. and had appointed Bro. Col. Philip Skene to be P.G.M. It was agreed to contribute towards a testimonial for the Earl of Elgin in acknowledgment of his great services to the Craft.

10th October, 1939. – Reference was made to the death of Bro. George Steele who had acted as secretary of the Lodge for 20 years. The R.W.M. spoke of the great service he had rendered to Lodge Minto.

7th December, 1939. – In view of the number of applications that would be made for the use of the hall for charitable purposes during the war, it was decided that the letting should be left to the secretary and a minimum donation given to the Lodge at the discretion of the Committee.

26th December, 1939. – The Lodge agreed that the sum of £3 collected at the Festival of St John for the Grand Lodge Annuity and Orphans' Fund, be made up to £10 10/-.

9th January, 1940. – The annual visit of P.G.L. was headed by Bro. Charles Hornal, S.P.G.M., a P.M. of Lodge Minto.

ACCOMMODATION OFFERED TO TROOPS

1st October, 1940. – The Lodge agreed to give facilities for recreation to any troops, who might be stationed in the district, in the Lesser Hall, and also access to the library.

It was agreed to attend a public meeting for the purpose of discussing arrangements for entertainment and hospitality to the troops.

11th March, 1941. – The administration of the licensed bar was considered and the stewards were instructed there must be due observation of regulations in accordance with the conditions of the licence.

10th April, 1941. – Appreciation was expressed of the long and faithful service of the late Bro. George Arrol, who had acted as Tyler for 41 years.

2nd April, 1941. – Under the Fire Prevention Business Premises Act, it was decided to provide fire-watchers for the Masonic Temple, and to make an appeal for volunteers through the local press.

WAR DISTRESS AND COMFORTS FUND

2nd September, 1941. – In response to a letter from the P.G. Secretary it was agreed that the Lodge members be asked to form a scheme to augment the War Distress Fund.

10th February, 1942. – The Women's Voluntary Service was granted the use of the whist tables in respect of a function that had been arranged for "Warships Week."

8th September, 1942. – The creation of a Comforts Fund for the benefit of brethren belonging to the Lodge on Service was raised and it was decided to organise special social functions towards that end. It was suggested that lists be prepared of all brethren serving in the Forces.

22nd September, 1942. – The question of saving light and heat during the emergency was considered in respect of the Ministry of Fuel and Power's recommendations. It was agreed to get an estimate from Bro. Ellis of the cost of re-arranging these services.

9th February, 1943. – A grant of £5 5/- was voted to the appeal of the Church of Scotland Hut and Canteen Committee.

5th July, 1943. – The secretary submitted the proposed new bye-laws with various recommendations by Bro. Charles Hornal, before they were sent to P.G.L. for approval. The bye-laws were later approved by G.L. and P.G.L. and formally adopted.

9th November, 1943. – It was agreed to send a donation to P.G.L. towards the testimonial to be presented to Bro. Charles Hornal, P.M.

13th December, 1943. – The hallkeeper's salary was fixed at £25 for the ensuing year.

27th February, 1945. – On the report of Bro. David R. Lyall, it was decided to accept the offer of Bro. Moffat of an organ at the price of £40, plus the old instrument.

10th April, 1945. – Two brethren of the Lodge on Service – Corporal

George Brown and A.B. Garfield Daniels – were sent letters of congratulations on being awarded the Oak Leaves.

30th October, 1945. – With regard to the fund proposed by P.G.L. to build Garden Homes to mark the Bi-Centenary celebrations, it was decided to take subscriptions and for that purpose the town was divided into districts for the collectors.

The Test Fee was raised from 3/- to 5/- and the Life Membership from £2 to £3 3/-, half of the annual Test Fee to be transferred to the Benevolent Account as at present with a corresponding amount from the Lodge Membership Fund.

4th December, 1945. – A balance of £6 3/9 in the Servicemen's Comfort Fund Account was transferred to the Benevolent Account and a donation from that fund of 20 guineas was granted to Fife and Kinross Provincial Lodge Bi-Centenary Garden Homes Fund.

TRIBUTE TO A VETERAN

Tribute was paid to Bro. David Sturrock, Lodge Thane of Fife 781, who was initiated in Lodge Minto 55 years past exactly that night.

7th February, 1946. – Mr Robert Stein, 10 Union Street, Cowdenbeath, offered to donate his father's sash and apron to Lodge Minto and was thanked for the gift. (His father was R.W.M. of Minto Lodge in 1885.)

SHRINE CHAPTER

An application for the use of the Temple for the proposed Shrine Chapter, was made by Mrs Logie, and granted.

12th February, 1946. – The R.W.M. thanked Bro. J. Owens for the gift of a mallet and stone from the stones of King Solomon's Quarries. Bro. Owens was assured the gift would be given a place of honour in the Lodge.

10th July, 1946. – On the recommendation of the Committee a kitchen was added to the offices of the building.

6th December, 1946. – It was agreed to create a Fabric Fund in place of the Redecoration Fund, and to transfer £200 from the general fund for that purpose.

26th May, 1947. – The Lodge decided to order 24 copies of the P.G.L. Bi-Centenary book at 4/- each and 12 copies at 6/- each.

The Secretary intimated the gift of apron and sash from the widow of Bro. Frank Robert Ross.

9th December, 1947. – It was decided that £100 be taken from the Benevolent Fund Account and invested on behalf of that account in 2 1/2 per cent. Defence Bonds.

Bro. David Cook, jeweller of the Lodge, was congratulated on being honoured by G.L. as Hon. Grand Jeweller.

27th January, 1948. – Bro. John Wilson headed the deputation from P.G.L. for their annual visit, deputising for Bro. Lord Elgin.

NEW GRAND SECRETARY

24th February, 1948. – Intimation was made of the appointment of Bro. Alex Buchan as Grand Secretary.

9th March, 1948. – Greetings were read from Lodge Waikaremoano No.158 New Zealand, intimating they had adopted Lodge Minto and had arranged for parcels being sent for the use of needy brethren. The thanks of Lodge were recorded and a letter of appreciation sent.

HONOURS TO BRETHREN

22nd November, 1949. – Bro. Charles Hornal, P.M., was elected Grand Master Substitute. The R.W.M. (Bro. W. Walkingshaw) suggested that in view of the high honour conferred, both on Bro. Hornal, and on Lodge Minto, a tangible token of the Lodge's appreciation be recorded. Bro. Ex-Prov. John Wilson, P.M., was asked to give an appreciation of Bro. Hornal's work in Freemasonry and in Lodge Minto in particular. Bro. Colin Morrison, P.M., also spoke on Bro. Hornal's work and incorporated the work done by Bro. Wilson himself in Grand Lodge.

23rd December. 1949. – Bro. James Hunter, P.M., was handed through the R.W.M. the Life Membership card granted by Provincial Grand Lodge. Bro. Hunter was a member for 21 years and well deserved the honour.

26th February, 1950. – A deputation attended from P.G.L. and also from Grand Lodge headed by Bro. Charles Hornal, Substitute Grand Master. Acknowledging their reception Bro. Hornal said how pleased he was to be back in Lodge Minto of which he had such happy memories.

At a later meeting Bro. Hornal was presented with an ebony writing desk.

9th January, 1951. – The Secretary, Bro. Andrew Dewar reported that the altered bye-laws of the Lodge had been passed by the P.G.L. and Grand Lodge.

WAR MEMORIAL TABLET

2nd September, 1951. – Following a church service in St. Andrew's Parish Church by Bro. the Rev F.M. Musk, the tablet which had been added to the war memorial in memory of the brethren who had fallen on service was unveiled by Bro. Ex-Prov. John Wilson, P.M.

4th December, 1951. – The rent of the hall for outside lettings was raised to 35/-.

THE BURGH DIAMOND JUBILEE

8th January, 1952. – It was agreed to accept the invitation of Lochgelly Town Council to attend the 75th anniversary dinner of the foundation of the burgh. Bro. Joseph Adams and Bro. Raeburn were appointed to attend.

13th January, 1953. – The first Provincial Visitation carried out by the P.G.M. (Bro. the Earl of Elgin) since his return from a long tour overseas took place that evening.

THE LODGE CENTENARY

The Secretary gave notice of motion that a committee should be set up to raise suitable funds for the proper celebration of the centenary of the Lodge.

DISTINGUISHED SERVICE MEMBERSHIP

The Distinguished Service Diploma was conferred on Bro. Ex-Prov. John Wilson, P.M. and Prov. Grand Depute Master, and on Bro. John Wilson, P.M., chaplain of the Lodge and Bro. Charles Hornal, P.M. and Depute Grand Master. P.G.L. was on this occasion headed by Bro. Lord Bruce, S.P.G.M.

During his speech Bro. Hornal referred to Bro. Alex Westwater, P.M., and suggested he should consider writing a history of the lodge to mark the centenary year.

DEPUTE GRAND MASTER

24th April, 1954. – A deputation from Grand Lodge of Scotland, was headed by Bro. Charles Hornal, P.M., D.G.M. He was accompanied by Bro. Lord Elgin who expressed his appreciation at being able to welcome Bro. Hornal in his capacity as D.G.M. and congratulated him on his exalted position. (Bro. Hornal, who had been Town Clerk of Lochgelly, had ten years previously been appointed County Clerk of Aberdeenshire.)

BRO. HORNAL'S SUDDEN DEATH

27th April, 1954. – The R.W.M., Bro. Kinnell, made sympathetic reference to the death of Bro. Charles Hornal who had two days previously been present in their Lodge to receive the Distinguished Service Diploma. The Dead March was played and a silence observed. The announcement of his death came as a great shock to the brethren. A letter of sympathy to Mrs Hornal and their daughter Anne was sent by the secretary.

15th November, 1954. – The Lodge donated £5 towards the cost of additional names on the Burgh War Memorial of the men and women who had fallen in the last war.

8th February, 1955. – Bro. William C. Mackay, P.M., the Lodge Almoner, was the recipient of a gift in token of his valuable work in that office. At the following meeting a presentation was made to Bro. Hugh McFarlane, Director of Ceremonies, and Bro. Robert Scott, Sen., on their emigrating to Australia.

11th September, 1956. – Bro. Mackay, R.W.M., referred to the unique event of four of his cousins being initiated that evening with their father and uncle present.

24th September, 1957.– Notice of motion was given by the treasurer to increase the initiation fee from £7 12/- to £7 17/- to cover the extra 5/- for Diploma as requested by Grand Lodge.

NAMES ON THE WAR MEMORIAL

1914-1919
Bogan, Robert
Buchan, Alexander
Cunningham, Stephen
Couper, John
Davidson, Robert
Fraser, George R.
Gillies, James
Glencross, Andrew
Henderson, James
Hugh, William B.
Logan, James
Lees, Thomas
McCallum, William
Milne, Thomas
Moyes, Andrew
Rodger, John

Spence, George
Swan, George
Thomson, James W.
Wilson, Andrew
Webster, David

1939-1945
McGregor, Charles
Smith, William
Thomson, Andrew

1950
Dixon, David E. I.

1951
McKee, Robert

R.W.M.'s 1858–1958

1858	Lord Loughborough	1913–15	John Wilson
1859-63	Andrew Galloway	1916-18	John Barclay
1864	Thomas Brand	1919-20	James Donaldson
1865-67	Andrew Galloway	1921-22	David Moffat
1868-69	William Henderson	1923-24	David Hood
1870	Dr. Robert Mungall	1925-26	James J. Rintoul
1871	William Smith	1927-28	William B. Jackson
1872-74	Andrew Galloway	1929-30	Alexander Westwater
1875	Thomas Brand	1931-32	John Wilson
1876-78	William Bethune	1933-34	George Reid
1879	Andrew Leitch	1935-36	Robert MacKay
1880-84	James Tullis	1937-38	Charles Hornal
1885	Robert Stein	1939-40	Robert Nisbet
1886	William Walker	1941-42	Martin Finnie
1887-99	George Syme	1943-44	Colin Morrison
1900	Provost John Hunter	1945-46	George B. Logie
1901	W. W. Bethune	1947-48	Robert P. Jackson
1902-03	George Syme	1949-50	William Walkingshaw
1904-06	William Greenwood	1951-52	Alfred Melville
1907-09	James Hunter	1953-54	James Kinnell
1910-12	James Kinlay	1955-56	Alexander Mackay

LORD LOUGHBOROUGH, First R.W.M.

BRO. ANDREW GALLOWAY
First Acting R.W.M.

R.W.M.'s – Biographical Notes

BRO. LORD LOUGHBOROUGH

Lord Loughborough was appointed first R.W.M. It was a complimentary and nominal position. He was unable to attend the consecration for two reasons - Grand Lodge business, and the fact that he was personally involved in a Parliamentary election for Fife County, then a single division. His opponent was another Fife man, also with a long pedigree, James Hay Erskine Wemyss, son of the Admiral. Incidentally, the latter, who stood as a Liberal, was returned.

Lord Loughborough, later Lord Rosslyn, was a scion of "the lordy line of high St. Clair," a family which guided Freemasonry for three centuries from its recognition and establishment by James I (1406). It was in the reign of the latter's son (James II) in 1437 that the St. Clairs were appointed hereditary Grand Master Masons. This honour continued till Grand Lodge was founded in 1736 when the then St. Clair voluntarily relinquished the position under the new constitution.

Lord Loughborough, who was a Master Mason of No.72 Kirkcaldie, in 1858 held commissioned rank as Substitute Provincial Grand Master. Later as Lord Rosslyn he was elected Grand Master Mason in 1872. He died in 1890 and was succeeded by his son, the fifth Earl of Rosslyn. The latter, in 1897, was appointed Provincial Grand Master of Fife and Kinross and paid a memorable visit to Lodge Minto. The present writer was present on that occasion and also at his installation in his ancestral Rosslyn Chapel on 19th June of that year. It was at his own request that the installation took place outwith the Province, an innovation, and had the authority of Grand Lodge. The event was made an Occasion by the Fife brethren who, with their lady friends, to the number of over 600, travelled by special train to Rosslyn. The brethren marched in procession to the historic chapel and witnessed an impressive service in surroundings that hallowed the event.

BRO. ANDREW GALLOWAY, 1859-63; 1865-67; 1872-74.

A member of Lodge Kirkcaldie, No. 72, he convened the initial meeting and was the promoter of Minto Lodge. He had settled in Lochgelly on being appointed factor and master of works for Lochgelly Iron Company.

Gifted with initiative and strength of character, he was a leading figure in the village. When the Fife Volunteer Battalion was formed in 1860 he was appointed a junior officer. Outside his regular work he was looked upon as the village architect. There was no doubt that through his strong personality he was instrumental in laying a solid foundation for the Lodge. He died in the early nineties.

BRO. THOMAS BRAND, 1864 AND 1875.

My recollection of Thomas Brand is that of a cautious, honest and down-right man, well informed, for which qualities he was highly esteemed. He took a great interest in the Lochgelly Workmen's Benefit Society which was formed by the prudent villagers before the institution of Friendly Societies. He was so long secretary that the Society came to be known as the "Thomas Brand's Society." A loyal churchman, he was an elder in Lochgelly Parish Church. He was first secretary of the Lodge.

BRO. WILLIAM HENDERSON, 1868-69.

During his occupancy of the chair he represented the Lodge at the Installation of H.R.H. the Prince of Wales as Patron of the Masonic Body in Scotland. He was also R.W.M. when the Lodge changed its calendar "considering the thinness of the attendance during the summer months, it was decided to have a vacation till October." When he left the chair he presented ornamental working tools - square, compass and plumb. He had a licensed grocer's business in Bank Street.

BRO. DR. ROBERT MUNGALL, 1870.

Dr. Mungall served one year, but does not seem to have given attention to his duty. All the minutes of his year are signed by the forementioned William Henderson as P.M.

As doctor for the Lumphinnans Colliery, he resided at Viewfield House adjoining that village. He had a large number of patients who resided in Lochgelly and worked in Lumphinnans pit. He was a brother of Henry Mungall, coalmaster.

BRO. WILLIAM SMITH, 1871

A publican in Main Street, he took over the Inn at Cathelmuir on the Cupar road west of Balgeddie. It became a call house for Lochgelly folks out for a long Sunday walk.

BRO. GEORGE SYME

BRO. WILLIAM BETHUNE, 1876-77-78.

A native of Largo he took over Bro. Henderson's grocery business. He was one of the first elected Police Commissioners when Lochgelly village was raised to the status of a Police Burgh in 1877. In 1877 the Lodge met in the Co-operative Hall at Knockhill Close. It was above the Society's Store and was almost destroyed by fire. Much of the Lodge property was lost, but by a fortunate circumstance the secretary, John Adam, had taken the minute books home to write up. The R.W.M. organised a successful appeal to all the daughter lodges by which fund material losses were made good.

BRO. ANDREW LEITCH, 1879.

He is best remembered for providing Lochgelly with its first gas supply. It was a primitive works in Main Street which he worked with the help of a brother. It served shops and a small number of dwelling houses and was closed down when Lochgelly Gas Company Ltd., was formed in 1884. He was owner of a public house at the West End of Main Street which went by the name of "The Black Bull." He had been an engineer in his youth.

BRO. JAMES TULLIS, 1880-84.

James Tullis was foreman in a large bakery in Bank Street. It was at one time the largest industry in the village. The proprietor, James Cook, supplied bread to three parishes by a fleet of horse-drawn vans. James Tullis went to London where he started a successful "Scotch Bakery."

BRO. ROBERT STEIN, 1885.

He was one of several Cowdenbeath men, before Thane Of Fife was formed, who became connected with either Minto or St. John, Crossgates. Robert Stein chose the former and became an enthusiastic member. So regularly did he attend the meetings that his wife nursed her wrath at his late returns. On one occasion she hid his clothes, went out and locked the door, but Bob got his attendance mark at the Lodge meeting.

BRO. WILLIAM WALKER, 1886.

Also from Cowdenbeath. He was cashier to Cowdenbeath Coal Company, Ltd., later secretary to Fife Coal Co. Ltd. In his year the Lodges of Lochgelly and Crossgates had a joint assembly in Brunton's Hall,

BRO. JOHN WILSON, P.M.

Cowdenbeath, and later in the year the Lodges held a joint procession, meeting at Cowdenbeath. After parading the streets of Cowdenbeath and Lochgelly, headed by Lochgelly Brass Band they finished at Lochgelly where the Festival of St. John was celebrated. After his term in the chair, Bro. Walker became intensely religious, spoke at open-air meetings at Cowdenbeath as a lay preacher and ceased to take interest in the craft. As secretary of the Fife Coal Co. he later proved an able administrator and figured largely in Scottish mining affairs.

BRO. GEORGE SYME, 1887-1899 AND 1902-03.

Altogether he held the chair for 15 years and initiated the scheme for a lodge room. Crippled in his youth through an accident, he held various posts in the town - Sanitary Inspector and Burgh Prosecutor. He was well read with a leaning to poetry and could quote the poets at ease. With a good memory and an eloquent delivery he was in demand for working degrees and installations in other Lodges. In addition to being R.W.M. of Minto Lodge he held for years a similar position in the Friendly Society Olive Lodge of Free Gardeners. His father was a leading citizen and one of the Lochgelly party which went to the "Gold diggings" on the Bishop Hill.

BRO. PROVOST JOHN HUNTER, 1900.

He was elected to the chair in the last year of his term as Provost. He was an active member of Auchterderran Parochial Board. Along with his brother, Andrew, also a member of the Lodge and a Magistrate, he was for long employed at Dundonald Colliery when it belonged to Alexander Naysmith.

A nephew of Professor David Page, the eminent geologist, John was keen on that science. A dogmatic controversialist, he was once countered in an argument on that subject by his opponent who, to clinch the matter, quoted from a publication by Professor Page. John refused to give up his standpoint, remarking "that he didn't care what his uncle thought; he must have been wrong."

Bro. Hunter was an elder in the Free Kirk and later acquired a grocer's licence at Glencraig.

BRO. WILLIAM GREENWOOD, 1904-06.

Bro. Greenwood was an old soldier who had seen much service in the Scots Guards in the Near East. He was R.W.M. when the Masonic building was started and finished. He took a great interest in the scheme and in the instructional meetings held on Saturday evenings.

BRO. A. WESTWATER, P.M.

BRO. JAMES HUNTER, 1907 - 09.

He is affectionately remembered by the older members of the Lodge who set a high appreciation on his loyalty to the Craft in general and his active work in his mother Lodge. In his teenage he attended the Evening Mining School, and he improved his knowledge in other directions. Gifted with an exceptional memory he could fill any office with credit both in the basic order and in the Royal Arch and Order of Knight Templars. He had an eloquent delivery. In his later years he suffered from ill health but he struggled to the Lodge to the very last.

BRO. JAMES KINLAY, 1910 - 12.

Bro. Kinlay has a very likeable disposition. He had many contacts with sister lodges and many friends among the freemasons in the country. Very competent in conferring the degrees he had also a social side which was much appreciated at gatherings. His death at a comparatively early age left a decided blank.

BRO. PROVOST JOHN WILSON, 1913 - 15.

Bro. Wilson was a distinguished Freemason and a distinguished citizen. In both these walks of life he attained to high honours. He showed initiative as R.W.M. and he had the gift of a good memory and the qualities of obvious sincerity and character which were recognised in the Lodge, in the Province, and in Grand Lodge – a kenspeckle figure in the Order. Through various offices in P.G.L. he became Depute to Bro. Lord Elgin, P.G.M., who paid a fine tribute to his long and faithful service when he died three years ago.

In public life, too, he found time to play a notable part. Provost of the Burgh throughout the anxious years of the late war he also held the position of Chief Special Constable. In the County Council, that body confirmed their confidence in him by electing him convener of the Finance Committee.

A keen bowler, he was successively president of the Lochgelly Club, the Fife Association and the Scottish Association. He was also an expert at curling and he was a generous giver.

His Lodge conferred on him the Distinguished Service Diploma. He was a member and head of the associated Orders. He also belonged to the higher degrees and had the honour of being elected by invitation to membership of the Royal Order of Scotland.

For a number of years he was District Grand Prior of the District of Fife and Kinross.

BRO. CHARLES HORNAL

BRO. JOHN BARCLAY, 1916-18.

Bro. John Barclay held the chair in part of the years of the first war. There was then an influx of servicemen. He had a busy term of office and fulfilled his heavy duties with success.

BRO. JAMES DONALDSON, 1919 - 20.

Like his predecessor he initiated many servicemen, particularly from Rosyth, before the Lodge there was established. Of a quiet and reserved nature he made a very efficient Master and was very popular with the brethren. He was an elder in the Free Kirk. While watching play on the bowling green of which he was a member, he suddenly collapsed and died.

BRO. DAVID MOFFAT, 1921 - 22.

In addition to his efficient working of degrees and handling of the business, he was an asset in a social gathering. He removed to Glasgow where he acquired a business and is now living in retirement in London. The memory of a good mason and jovial associate is still fresh in the Lodge.

BRO. DAVID HOOD, 1923-24.

Bro. Hood had two years in the chair. A native of Newburgh, he came to Lochgelly to act as an engine driver at a Lochgelly colliery. He was very precise and held strongly to his opinions. He carried through his duties well and maintained the traditions of the Lodge.

BRO. JAMES J. RINTOUL, 1925-26

Bro. Rintoul came to the town, joined the Lodge and became an active member. He was manager of a licensed grocery shop in Bank Street.

BRO. WILLIAM JACKSON, 1927-28.

Bro. Jackson was one of two brothers closely connected with the Lodge. The other, John, was for many years treasurer. Bro. Jackson made himself proficient in most of the offices and was well qualified when called to the chair. After leaving the chair he accepted the office of Chaplain. He died while yet in his prime.

BRO. ALEXANDER WESTWATER. Secretary - 1906-1914. R.W.M. - 1929 -1930.

Author of this work. Justice of the Peace for Fife; Fellow of the Institute of Journalists; Fellow of the Society of Antiquaries of Scotland; Former Magistrate of the Burgh of Lochgelly; and former member of Fife County Council and Education Committee. Lochgelly's only Honorary Burgess.

BRO. JOHN WILSON, 1931-32.

He was credited with a record of attendances, rarely missing a meeting during his 20 years' connection with the Lodge. In addition to filling the chair he acted as Chaplain for many terms. The victim of a pit accident which cost him the use of a limb, he was well-known in the other Lodges where he frequently officiated at the installation of office-bearers and at Provincial meetings. He died in the current year and a large number of the brethren showed their respect by turning out in strength to his funeral.

BRO. GEORGE REID, 1933-34.

Bro. Reid, a miner to trade, is now living in retirement. A kindly disposed man, he spends his leisure time in making toys which he sends to children's hospitals. Hundreds of these have delighted bairns all over the country and numerous acknowledgments show how highly they are valued. His reputation is national and some years ago he was invited to London by the B.B.C. and gave a television interview. This brought him many letters of congratulations on his good work which is entirely voluntary. He even pays the postage out of his meagre old age pension. George's whole life and living exudes the masonic sensibility.

BRO. ROBERT MACKAY, 1935-36.

A devotee of the bagpipes, he did more than any other to teach and popularise that music in the town and neighbourhood. Mobilised in 1914 he went to France with the 7th Batt. of the Black Watch. He was a fine type of mason and man. His other main interest was the Lodge where he was universally held in the highest esteem.

BRO. CHARLES HORNAL, 1937-38.

Bro. Charles Hornal, whose sudden and untimely death in April, 1954, was mourned by a large circle, attained high positions, both in the Masonic Order and in civil life. A native of Lockerbie, he entered a solicitor's office in

Edinburgh and attended Edinburgh University where he qualified as a solicitor. His first official appointment was as chief assistant to the Town Clerk at Burntisland and there he was initiated into Lodge Dunearn, Burntisland No. 400. He was appointed as Town Clerk of Lochgelly in 1938 and also became a County official as clerk of Lochgelly Committee of Fife County Council and Lochgelly District Council. He was also Town Clerk of Cowdenbeath during the war years. Bro. Hornal also carried on his extensive legal business; his success in these offices and his extensive knowledge of general Local Government administration was recognised and after 15 years in Lochgelly he was appointed to the responsible post of County Clerk of Aberdeenshire.

He was affiliated to Lodge Minto 385 where he was elected R.W.M., and thence to the Provincial Grand Lodge of Fife and Kinross. His interest and capacity led to his appointment as P.G. Secretary and later to the office of P.G. Depute to Bro. Lord Elgin.

In Grand Lodge he was elected to the Board of Grand Stewards in 1938 and to G.L. Finance Committee of which he became chairman. He was appointed Substitute Grand Master to Bro. Lord McDonald and was in this office when his death took place suddenly in his home at Cults. The latter event came as a great shock to his wide circle of friends. He had been to Lochgelly two days previously to receive the parchment of Distinguished Service to the Order.

In the First World War he served as a wireless operator on the Atlantic patrol. He was a keen participator in football, cricket and golf, a man of many attainments, both as a citizen and as a Freemason. His activities were dignified by character, integrity, loyalty and ability - a man who gave distinction to Freemasonry and played a notable part in public life.

BRO. ROBERT NISBET, 1939-40.

Bro. Nisbet is in the teaching profession and at present headmaster of Dunnikier School, Kirkcaldy. A native of the town, he has kinship with well known local families. For many years he was in charge of the summer school camps under Fife Education Committee.

BRO. MARTIN FINNIE, 1941-42.

Bro. Finnie came to the town to be manager of a butchery business. He now has a business in Cowdenbeath. He served faithfully during his term in the chair.

BRO. COLIN MORRISON, 1943-44.

He is a retired headmaster now living in retirement in his native island of Lewis. He came to Lochgelly as an assistant and was head of Dairsie School before being appointed to take charge of the school at Lumphinnans. A versatile man he was associated with golf and the church. He took a part in Fife golf competitions and generally was very popular in the Lodge and town.

BRO. GEORGE B. LOGIE, 1945-46.

He is a son-in-law of the late Bro. Provost Wilson. A joiner to trade he at present holds a position with the National Coal Board. He well maintained the traditions of the Lodge.

BRO. ROBERT P JACKSON, 1947-48.

A son of the former R.W.M. Like his father he carried through the duties faithfully and efficiently and continues his interest by filling a minor office.

BRO. WILLIAM WALKINGSHAW, 1949-50.

His family, too, have an old connection with Lodge Minto. His occupancy of the chair was well up to the standards of his predecessors.

BRO. ALFRED MELVILLE, 1951-52.

A very active and efficient Freemason who still takes a continuing interest in the Lodge. In his youth he was prominent in football and gained an international cap for the Scottish Schoolboys team. He is also an active member of the Bowling Club.

BRO. JAMES KINNELL, 1953-54.

Bro. Kinnell, in addition to his attention to his duties in the chair, also showed an keen interest as convener of the Entertainments Committee. A keen bowler he is prominent in competitive games in West Fife.

BRO. ALEX. MACKAY, 1955-56.

The mantle of his father, who occupied the chair twenty years previously, has fallen on his shoulders in his personal characteristics - sincerity and capability and a quiet natural dignity.

BRO. JOSEPH ADAMS, 1957.

Bro. Adams' term is a notable one. He carries an extra responsibility in this centenary year and in co-operation with the secretary, a good deal of extra attention has been called for. Bro. Adams hails from Coatbridge. He is an official in an important department of the National Coal Board.

EMINENT FIFE FREEMASON
BRO. THE EARL OF ELGIN AND KINCARDINE, K.T., C.M.G.

Bro. Lord Elgin can aptly be described as the doyen of Freemansonry in Fife; while beyond his own Province he is known and honoured wherever the Scottish rite is practised. His life work has elevated and dignified the Craft. His whole life of service is exceptional and is of special interest to the Daughter Lodges of Fife.

From his initiation in his territorial Lodge of Elgin and Bruce he became an enthusiastic adherent to the Craft in which he advanced to the highest office.

His first appointment, from the chairmanship of his Mother Lodge, was as Lord Bruce, to the chair of Provincial Grand Lodge of Fife and Kinross in 1913, rendered vacant on the resignation of Bro. Henry Hilton Brown. He succeeded his father in the Earldom in 1917, in which year he was appointed to the Army staff in France, twice mentioned in dispatches, and awarded the C.M.G.

His deep interest in the Order was recognised in his election in 1921 to be Grand Master Mason of Scotland, and in the same year he presided over the Grand Lodge of the Royal Order of Scotland; at the same time he was P.G.M. and Master of two Daughter Lodges. It must have been his vintage year for it was then he entered into a happy and successful union. The lady was Katherine Elizabeth Cochrane, daughter of Lord and Lady Cochrane of Cults.

Lord Elgin was Provincial Grand Master of Fife and Kinross for twenty-five years at a stretch. He was succeeded in 1938 by Col. Philip G.M. Skene of Pitlour, but took office again in 1945 when Col. Skene died, and retired last year when the reins of office were passed on to his son, Bro. Lord Bruce.

One of the historic schemes in Scottish Masonic history is that of the Masonic Home, Ault Wharrie, Dunblane. It was conceived on the initiative of Lord Elgin, and sponsored by his own Province. It now accommodates about 30 aged Freemasons and their dependents, and is still extending.

Lord Elgin's activities have extended beyond the Craft into numerous public services; his administrative ability has influenced almost every aspect of

BRO. EARL OF ELGIN AND KINCARDINESHIRE

our national life. In his own County of Fife, of which he is Lord Lieutenant, these qualities have been exercised in a special degree. Among the positions he has held are Convener of Fife County Council and chairman of Fife Education Authority; today he has relaxed to become Provost of the charming ancient Royal Burgh of Culross.

Tact and understanding accounts for his success as an administrator and organiser. A patriotic Scot, as befits a lineal descendant of our national libera-tor, his service has spread over many fields. Scottish affairs in the House of Lords have always found him on the alert in Scotland's best interests; the heavy job of President of the National Exhibition in Glasgow, in 1938 (with Lady Elgin as convener of the Women's Section); in organising the Scottish exhibits at British Industries Fairs; chairman of the U.K. Carnegie Trust; founder of the Scottish Development Council; the Land Settlement Association, and the National Council on Juvenile Delinquents; the Appeal Tribunal for Scotland for Further Education for ex-Servicemen.

Lord Elgin, now one of our Elder Statesmen, can look back with satis-faction on a full life of public service, generously given in the interest of his fellows. He seems indeed to have inherited that sense of duty which charac-terised his ancestors distinguished in National history in the Victorian era, and as befits a descendant of the first King of a consolidated Scottish nation.

BRO. LORD BRUCE
PROVINCIAL GRAND MASTER OF FIFE AND KINROSS.

Eldest son and heir of Lord Elgin, Lord Bruce was initiated in Lodge Elgin and Bruce, Limekilns, No. 1077 and was R.W.M. thereof in 1949-51. He showed a keen interest in the craft and as a member of Provincial Lodge served in various offices starting with Senior Deacon to become Substitute Provincial Grand Master. In 1957 he was appointed Provincial Grand Master.

Lord Bruce cut the first sod of Kincardine Bridge which opened a much needed highway connecting Fife with the south shore of the Forth. Its erec-tion, which was largely due to the enterprise of Lord Elgin, has proved a great advantage in shortening distances for vehicular traffic.

Lord Bruce was educated at Eton and Balliol College, Oxford, where he graduated Bachelor of Arts.

In the Second World War he served in the Scots Guards. Severely wounded in the Normandy fighting, his activities were restricted during a fairly long period of convalescence.

BRO. LORD BRUCE

SECRETARIES

1858	William Young	1896-99	William Duncan
1858-62	Thomas Brand	1900-02	James Wilson
1863-68	Henry Hunter	1903-04	W. Walker Bethune
1869-71	Robert Hunter	1904-06	Henry Stewart
1872	Henry Cook	1906-14	Alexander Westwater
1873	Stewart McGregor	1914-16	Henry Fordyce
1874	Henry School Braid	1916-36	George Steele
1875-77	John Adam	1937-40	John Westwater
1878	Alexander Hugh	1941	Thomas B. Ewing
1878-90	John W. Knight	1942	Andrew R. Dewar
1890-95	Robert Dick		

TREASURERS

1858-61	Thomas McKee	1894-96	David Wilson
1861-62	Robert H. Beck	1897	Robert Wilson, Jun.
1862	William Hill Clark	1898-1903	David Wilson
1863	James Angus	1904-07	Robert Wilson, Jun.
1864-66	James Cook	1908-13	John Jackson
1867	William Henderson	1914-36	Rankine Scott
1868-75	Andrew Leitch	1936-37	Robert B. Sinclair
1876-77	John Nicol	1938-41	David R. Lyall
1878	Robert Stein	1942-43	Joseph Adams
1879-80	Adam Addison	1944-45	Thomas D. Smith
1881-87	Andrew Hunter	1946	William Wilson
1888-93	James Tullis		

CHAPLAINS

Most of the Lodge Chaplains have been laymen. There were four ministerial chaplains:-

Rev. A. Houston, B.D. (later the Rev. Dr. Houston), minister of Auchterderran Parish Church.

Rev. Thomas Dewar, minister of Lochgelly Parish Church.

Rev. D. Findlay Clark, B.D. (later the Rev. Dr. Findlay Clark), former minister of Lochgelly Parish Church. Dr. Clark, who is now minister of the parish of Banff, is the only one still alive.

Rev. R. N. Paton, B.D., minister of Lochgelly Parish Church.

Treasurer and Secretary –

BROS. WILLIAM WILSON AND ANDREW DEWAR.

Bro. Andrew Dewar has held the office of secretary of the Lodge with much success for 16 years. His enthusiastic interest in the work is equalled by his efficiency, and highly appreciated by the brethren. Bro. Dewar is responsible for organising the Centenary Celebrations. He is a native of the town and at present holds the responsible position of buyer for the N.C.B., stationed at their headquarters in Edinburgh. He has been very helpful in the preparation of this book.

Another secretary, now deceased, whose memory is held in high regard, was Bro. George Steele. He held the office of secretary from 1916 - 36 (20 years) longer than any other.

Bro. Wilson has a record of excellent service in the very important office of treasurer.

On the administrative side the Lodge is fortunately placed.

THE R.W.M. AND PAST MASTERS
The present R.W.M., Bro. Adams, and Past Masters of Lodge Minto at present holding other offices, left to right, Bros. Alfred Melville, Joseph Adams, Robert Mackay and James Kinnell.

HONORARY MEMBERS OF LODGE MINTO

Bro. James Townsend Oswald of Dunnikier

Bro. Lord Loughborough

Bro. The Earl of Elgin and Kincardine

Bro. W. Ponsforth

Bro. Alfred G. Potter

Bro. Samuel Edward Jacob

Bro. Kenneth MacRae

Bro. James M. Scott

Bro. John Wilcox

Bro. John B. Irons

Bro. John Hackland

Bro. Lord Bruce

Bro. W. A. Thexton

Bro. D. S. C. McNeil

Bro. James Anderson

PARCHMENT OF MERIT – DISTINGUISHED SERVICE MEMBERSHIP

Bro. John Wilson (Ex-Provost)

Bro. Charles Hornal

Bro. John Wilson

Bro. Alexander Westwater

ADDENDUM

Roll of Members

The following is a complete roll of members of Minto Lodge throughout the hundred years. It runs to 2470 initiates.

This roll was started by the late Bro. George Steele when Secretary, assisted by the late Bro. Rankine Scott, treasurer and has been brought up to date by Bro. Andrew Dewar, the present Secretary.

1858–1931

Angus, James, Lochgelly, May 1860.
Addison, Adam, Cowdenbeath, October, 1873.
Adam, James, Lochgelly, March 1874.
Anderson, David, Lochgelly, May 1874.
Adam, John, Lochgelly, March 1875
Adam, Andrew, Lochgelly, February 1876.
Aitken, Robert, Lochgelly, June 1876.
Anderson, John, Kingseat, May 1877.
Arnott, Robert H., Glasgow, April 1878.
Adamson, Alexander, Cowdenbeath, March 1891.
Adamson, James, Lumphinnans, March 1891.
Allan, Joseph, Lumphinnans, September 1892.
Allan, Thomas B., Lochgelly, March 1893.
Anderson, John, Lochgelly, April 1894.
Arrol, George, Lochgelly, December 1897.
Anderson, John E., Lochgelly, June 1898.
Adams, Alexander, Cardenden, September 1900.
Anderson, Robert, Cardenden, January 1904.
Arnold, George, Dundonald, September 1904.
Anderson, David, Lochgelly, July 1905.
Arnott, David, Cardenden, October 1905.
Anderson, David B., Lochgelly, March 1907.
Archibald, Andrew, Lochgelly, September 1907.
Arthur, Robert,Lochgelly, February 1908.
Anderson, John, Lochgelly, February 1908.
Affleck, James A., Lochgelly, October 1909.
Arnott, Alexander F., Lochore, November 1909.
Aitken, George G., Lochgelly, March 1910.
Allan, Alexander, Lochgelly, October 1910.
Armstrong, James, Lochgelly, May 1911
Anderson, Alexander, Cowdenbeath, February 1912
Adam, John, Lochgelly, September 1912.
Arthur, Thomas B., Lochgelly, April 1913.
Armit, John, Lochgelly, April 1913
Allan, George, Lochgelly, October 1913.
Anderson, David, Glencraig, May 1914.
Anderson, Charles S.H., Lochgelly, October 1916.
Alan, David, Lochgelly, October, 1916.
Anderson, Alexander, Cardenden, November 1916

Adamson, John, Lochgelly, November 1916.
Agnew, Robert, Lochore, March 1917
Aitken, David K., Lochgelly, April 1917.
Adam, Peter, Glencraig, May 1917.
Anderson, John, Lochgelly, November 1917.
Allan, William, Glencraig, January 1918.
Adamson, William, Lochgelly, April 1919.
Anderson, Peter, Lochgelly, May 1919.
Adamson, Bruce G., Lochgelly, September 1919.
Addison, John, Lochgelly, November 1919.
Anderson, David, Cardenden, November 1919
Anderson, George, Lumphinnans, November 1919
Anderson, Andrew, Lochgelly, November 1919
Alston, John, Lochgelly, February 1922.
Adamson, George, Lochgelly, April 1922.
Anderson, David B., Lochgelly, February 1923.
Adamson, James, Lochgelly, February 1923.
Aitken, David, Lochgelly, September 1929.
Anderson, David, Lochgelly, April 1930.

Brand, Thomas, Lochgelly, December 1858,
Beck, John, Lochore, February 1859.
Brown, William, Cardenden, December 1860.
Bowman, Laurence, Cowdenbeath, November 1863.
Burt, Andrew, Lochgelly, July 1864.
Bethune, William, Lochgelly, June 1871.
Birrell, Andrew, Cowdenbeath, July 1873.
Burgess, John, Alloa, October 1874.
Brunton, John, Cowdenbeath, March 1875.
Beattie, John, Cowdenbeath, March 1875.
Beveridge, William, Cowdenbeath, March, 1875.
Bonnar, Peter, Lassodie, March 1875.
Beveridge, Alexander, Lochgelly, June 1875.
Borthwick, James, Cowdenbeath, July 1875.
Bonnar, Robert, Lassodie, August 1875.
Beveridge John, Cowdenbeath, January 1876.
Blyth, George, Lochgelly, November 1875.
Blyth, George, Loch Fitty, February 1887.
Burt, Peter, Lassodie, April 1887.

Brown, James, Lochgelly, April 1889.
Bain, Thomas, Lumphinnans, June 1890.
Bain, Andrew C., Lochgelly, August 1890.
Burton, Thomas, Lochgelly, May 1892.
Bethune, William W., Lochgelly, December 1893.
Brechin, James, Lochgelly, February 1894.
Boyd, Andrew, Lochgelly, April 1898.
Black, Francis, Auchterderran, June 1898.
Binning, Alexander, Lochgelly, September 1899.
Brown, Alexander, Lochgelly, December 1899.
Brown, Walter, Lochgelly, December 1899.
Bowman, Alexander N., Lochgelly, August 1900.
Brand, David, Auchterderran, November 1900.
Brand, John, Auchterderran, November 1900.
Butters, John, Lochore, May 1901.
Bowman, William, Lochgelly, May 1901.
Band, William, Lochgelly, May 1901.
Brown, William W., Glasgow, September 1901.
Beveridge, Alexander, Glencraig, August 1902.
Brand, Henry, Cardenden, October 1902.
Black, David, Cardenden, October 1902.
Beall, John, Cardenden, October 1902.
Brown, James, Cardenden, March 1904.
Blackwood, James, Bowhill, July 1904.
Barclay, John, Lochgelly, November 1904.
Black, Alexander, Lochgelly, February 1905.
Buchan, Walter, Lochgelly, December 1905.
Bower, Alexander, Lochgelly, June 1906.
Baxter, David, Lochgelly, September 1907.
Buchan, Alexander, Lochgelly, October 1907.
Buchan, James, Auchterderran, October 1907.
Brown, John, Lochgelly, December 1907.
Baptie, John L., Lochgelly, January 1908.
Barclay, Robert, Glencraig, February 1908.
Brown, Thomas, Glencraig, February 1908.
Bremner, John, Auchterderran, February 1908.
Bremner,William, Glencraig, April 1908.
Bonthrone, James, Bowhill, April 1903.
Barclay, Alexander S., Lochgelly, May 1908.
Beveridge, John McL, Lochgelly, August 1903.
Blair, Robert, Bowhill, September 1908.
Biggar, John R., Cardenden. October 1908.
Biggar, Alexander, Cardenden, November 1908.
Butters, Alexander, Glencraig, November 1909.
Blair, Alexander R., Lumphinnans, March 1910.
Bauld, James C., N. Glencraig, April 1910
Bauld, John, N. Glencraig, April 1910,
Baldie, William, Cowdenbeath, September 1910.
Bauld, William, N. Glencraig, December 1910.
Bain, Henry. Lochgelly, December 1910.
Baillie, Peter, Lochgelly, March 1911.
Bowman, Alexander, Crosshill, March 1911.
Beveridge, James, Lochgelly, October 1911.
Burt, Robert, Crosshill, November 1911.
Bethune, James C., Lochgelly, May 1912.
Beveridge, John W., Lochgelly, September 1912.
Bell, Frederick W.S., Lochgelly, October 1912.
Biggans, Hugh, Lochgelly, October 1912.
Baxter, Frank D., Lochgelly, December 1912.

Bauld, Thomas F., N. Glencraig, January 1913.
Bauld, James, N. Glencraig, January 1913.
Blane, David, Cardenden, February 1913.
Boyle, John, Lochgelly, February 1913.
Bartie, Hamilton, Lochore, March 1913.
Burleigh, Robert, Lochgelly, March 1913.
Baxter, John, Lochgelly, March 1913.
Bogie, David, Lochgelly, April 1913.
Beveridge, David, Lochgelly, September 1913.
Baxter, Henry, Lochgelly, September 1913.
Baxter, David, Lochgelly, September 1913.
Bogan, Robert G., Kinglassie, November 1913.
Brown, Kenneth, Lochore, November 1913.
Beveridge, John, Lochgelly, December 1913.
Butchart, George, Lumphinnans, December 1913.
Bissett, Duncan McM., Lochgelly, January 1914.
Beveridge, Thomas, Lochgelly, February 1914.
Brown, James, Lumphinnans, April 1914.
Baxter, Frank, Lochgelly, September 1914.
Beveridge, Richard, Lochgelly, September 1914.
Bell, James G., Lochore, February 1915.
Boyd, James, Cowdenbeath, October 1915.
Brown, John, Glencraig, December 1915.
Baillie, William, Cowdenbeath, April 1916
Buchan, George, N. Glencraig, November 1916.
Balloch, John, N. Glencraig, January 1917.
Brown, James, Lochgelly, April 1917.
Black, Paul, Lochgelly, May 1917.
Beveridge, Andrew D., Lochgelly, June 1917.
Brockie, James, Lochore, November 1917.
Bruce, James W., Lochgelly, January 1918.
Brown, David, Cowdenbeath, February 1918.
Black, Lochgelly, February 1918.
Bauld, Robert C., Glencraig, March 1918.
Baxter, Andrew, Lochgelly, May 1918.
Baxter, Wilfred E., N. Queensferry, September 1918.
Bain, Henry C., Lochore, October 1918.
Beattie, Henry, Lochgelly, November 1918.
Brown, David, Lochgelly, November 1918.
Brunton, William J. C., Lochgelly, November 1918.
Blair, Hugh, Lochgelly, November 1918.
Brown, John, Lochgelly, January 1919.
Barnes, Andrew, Lochgelly, January 1919.
Burt, Alexander, Lochgelly, January 1919.
Beveridge, Robert, Lochgelly, February 1919.
Baillie, Peter, Dunfermline, February 1919.
Beattie, James, Lochgelly, April 1919.
Barclay, Andrew, Kirkcaldy, April 1919.
Blamey, John, Lochgelly, April 1919.
Blamey, William, Lochgelly, April 1919.
Bell, Christopher, Lochore, April 1919.
Brown, Alexander, Kelty, April 1919,
Baxter, Andrew, Lochgelly, April 1919.
Blair, Alexander, Lochgelly, May 1919.
Burleigh, John, Jun., Lochgelly, May 1919.
Blackwood, George, Lochgelly, September 1919
Balloch, James M., N. Glencraig, September 1919.
Bell, Isaac, Lochore, September 1919.
Bennett, Robert I., Lumphinnans, September 1919.

Bauld, Thomas, Lochgelly, September 1919.
Bissett, James, Carnock, November 1919.
Baxter, James, Lochgelly, November 1919.
Brown, John, Lochgelly, November 1919.
Black, George, Lochgelly, November 1919.
Budd, Alexander, Lochgelly, February 1920.
Bird, Henry, Lochgelly, February 1920.
Boyd, John S., Lochgelly, February 1920.
Bain, John S., Lumphinnans, March 1920.
Barclay, Andrew, Lochgelly, March 1920.
Baillie, George, Lumphinnans, March 1920.
Braid, John, Lochgelly, April 1920.
Beveridge, William, Cowdenbeath, October 1920.
Beveridge, Robert, Lumphinnans, October 1920.
Bain, Thomas, Lumphinnans, November 1920.
Bell, George, Lochgelly, November 1920.
Baxter, William, Lochgelly, January 1921
Baxter, Arthur, Lochgelly, February 1921.
Bauld, Stewart S., Glencraig, March 1921.
Bauld, Christopher B., Glencraig, March 1921.
Bauld, Robert, Glencraig, March 1921.
Brown, Robert M.G., Lumphinnans, March 1921
Brown, David, Lochgelly, October 1921.
Beveridge, John, Lochgelly, October 1921.
Brown, Alexander, Cardenden, November 1921.
Brown, John, Lumphinnans, January 1922.
Brown, William S., Cowdenbeath, March 1923.
Barclay, John L., Lochgelly, September, 1924.
Brockie, James, S. Glencraig, April 1925.
Brown, Robert G., S. Glencraig, April 1925.
Barnet, Barlaw, Lochgelly, January 1927.
Bolton, Lindsay G., Lochgelly, January 1927.
Brown, Andrew B., Kinglassie, December 1927.
Brown, James H.G., Cowdenbeath, November 1928.
Banks, John, Cowdenbeath, January 1930.
Beveridge, William, Cowdenbeath, March 1930.
Brown, George G., Hythe, Kent, October 1931.

Couper, John, Lochgelly, December 1858.
Connel, John, Lochgelly, December 1858.
Cook, James, Lochgelly, June 1859.
Crawford, Robert, Cowdenbeath, June, 1859.
Campbell, Peter, Lochgelly, October 1859.
Collier, Andrew, Muirton, May 1861.
Clark, William H., Lochgelly, June 1862.
Crombie, John, Capledrae, November 1863.
Campbell, Thomas, Crossgates, July 1866.
Cook, Henry, Lochgelly, November 1866.
Crichton, Andrew McI., Crossgates, January 1867.
Cuthbertson, William, Glasgow, March 1869.
Cook, Adam, Lochgelly, February 1872.
Cowan, Andrew, Crossgates, February 1873.
Clark, William, Lochgelly, January 1874.
Christie, John, Cowdenbeath, July 1875.
Cook, William, Lochgelly, October 1875.
Cook, David, Lochgelly, February 1876.
Campbell, John, Kingseat, May 1877.
Christie, Robert, Cowdenbeath, April 1882.
Crawford, William C., Cowdenbeath, July 1885.

Clark, Richard, Auchtertool, July 1887.
Clark, William, Lochgelly, October 1889.
Clark, Andrew, Lochgelly, October 1891.
Cunningham, James, Lochgelly, February 1893.
Cunningham, John, Lochgelly, April 1894.
Clark, Thomas, Lochgelly, January 1897.
Chalmers, James, Kelty, October 1897.
Curran, William, Lochgelly, April 1898.
Christie, Robert, Lochgelly, February 1901
Chapman, James, Cowdenbeath, February 1901.
Cook, Alexander, Auchterderran, July 1901.
Clark, Andrew, Lochgelly, February 1902.
Collier, Robert, Dunfermline, January 1905.
Cook, Archibald, Auchterderran, May 1905.
Chalmers, William, Bowhill, March 1906.
Crawford, David, Lochgelly, June 1907.
Cook, David, Cowdenbeath, October 1907.
Campbell, John, Lochgelly. November 1907.
Crichton, Alexander, Lochgelly, January 1908.
Coventry, Andrew, Cardenden, March 1908.
Cant, James, Lochgelly, March 1908.
Cargill, Fletcher M., Lochgelly, May 1908.
Clark, George, Lochgelly, August 1908.
Cunningham, James, S. Glencraig, September 1908.
Campbell, Harry, Lochore, October 1908.
Currie, John, Lochgelly, March 1909.
Christie, Robert, Lochgelly, November 1909.
Chalmers, John, Glencraig, November 1909.
Couper, Robert, Cardenden, February 1910.
Campbell, Alexander, Lumphinnans, September 1910.
Couper, John, Cardenden, October 1910.
Campbell, Andrew B., Lumphinnans, October 1910.
Currie, Henry, Lochgelly, October 1911.
Crawford, Andrew, Lochore, February 1911.
Clark, John, Lochgelly, October 1911.
Campbell, George, Lumphinnans, November 1911.
Copland, David, Lochore, December 1911.
Condie, Thomas A., Lochgelly, October 1912.
Cumming, David, Cowdenbeath, December 1912.
Cunningham, Stephen B., Crosshill, December 1912.
Clark, Alexander S., Lochgelly, April 1913.
Clark, Thomas, Lochgelly, April 1913.
Christie, John H., Perth, April 1913.
Chalmers, Robert C., Glencraig, May 1913.
Campbell, William, Lumphinnans, September 1913.
Chalmers, William, Lochgelly, October 1913.
Cunningham, James, Lochgelly, October 1913.
Clark, David F., Lochgelly, October 1913.
Currie, John S., Lochgelly, October 1913.
Crawford, John, Cowdenbeath, November 1913.
Chalmers, William, J., N. Glencraig, May 1914.
Crawford, Alexander C., Lochgelly, May 1915.
Cook, Michael B., Lochgelly, January 1916.
Cuthill, Alexander F., Lochgelly, March 1917.
Chalmers, James, Cardenden, March 1917.
Chalmers, Robert, Lochgelly, April 1917.
Clark, James, Lochgelly, May 1917.
Carrick, George W.S., Lochgelly, October 1917.

Currie, Walter, Lochgelly, November 1917.
Campbell, William, Glencraig, November 1917.
Cougan, Francis, Glencraig, February 1918.
Clark, Richard, Glencraig, May 1918.
Chalmers, Robert, Lochgelly, May 1918.
Crawford, Archibald, Lochgelly, November 1918.
Crombie, William B., Lochgelly, May 1919.
Chedburn, John B., Lochgelly, May 1919.
Cairns, James, Lochgelly, May 1919.
Currie, Gilbert, Cowdenbeath, September 1919.
Cunningham, Thomas R., Lochgelly,
September 1919.
Carstairs, John D., Lochgelly, October 1919.
Craig, David P., Lochgelly, November 1919.
Campbell, Johnstone, Lochgelly, November 1919.
Clark, John M., Lochgelly, November 1919.
Chalmers, William, Lochgelly, November 1919.
Clark, John, Lochgelly, November 1919.
Cuthbert, William, Lochgelly, November 1919.
Caird, Thomas, Bowhill, November, 1919.
Crookston, James, Lochgelly, February 1920.
Campbell, Alexander F., Lumphinnans, March 1920.
Campbell, James K., Lumphinnans, March 1920.
Clark, William, Carnock, April 1920.
Currie, James, Lumphinnans, April 1920.
Clark, Michael B., Lochgelly, September 1920.
Caird, James, Lochgelly, October 1920.
Clement, William L., Falkirk, October 1921.
Cook, William, Cardenden, November 1921.
Cairns, David, Lochgelly, January 1922.
Coffin, Ernest, S. Queensferry, April 1922.
Cook, David, Lochgelly, April 1923.
Clement, Robert, Falkirk, November 1923.
Clement, Thomas C., Falkirk, February 1926.
Clement, George H., Falkirk, February 1926.
Cowan, Thomas, Lochgelly, May 1926.
Cameron, Angus, Lochgelly, November 1926.
Creighton, Adam, Kinglassie, April 1927.
Cook, Andrew, Lochgelly, October 1927.
Christie, James, Lochgelly, October 1928.
Clark, William R., Lochgelly, December 1929.
Clark, Andrew M., Lochgelly, April 1930.
Chalmers, John M., Lochgelly, April 1930.

Duff, David, Glasgow, April 1859.
Douglas, John, Lochgelly, May 1861.
Dick, William B., Lochgelly, June 1865.
Dick, Robert, Lochgelly, October 1866.
Duff, Charles, Liverpool, January 1867.
Dryburgh, Walter, Lochgelly, May 1872.
Davidson, John, Cowdenbeath, October 1873.
Dickson, Alexander, Cowdenbeath, November 1873.
Davidson, James, Lochgelly, December 1874.
Dewar, Thomas, Lochgelly, December, 1876.
Duncan, James, Cowdenbeath, December 1885.
Dunsire, Andrew, Lochgelly, February 1889.
Dunsire, Peter, Cameron Colliery, March 1890.
Dickson, Robert, Lochgelly, June 1892.
Drummond, James, Lochgelly, August, 1893.

Duncan, William, Lochgelly, February 1894.
Dawson, John, Kelty, March 1895.
Dick, John C., Lochgelly, February 1897.
Dick, Robert, Jun., Lochgelly, February 1897.
Dickson, David E., Lochgelly, December 1899.
Duncan, John, Lochgelly, July 1900.
Dewar, Thomas, Lochgelly, February 1901.
Dickson, Alexander, Lochgelly, May 1901.
Duncan, Andrew, Cardenden, November 1901.
Dickson, David, Glencraig, August 1902.
Duncan, Alexander, Lochgelly, October 1902.
Dickson, Robert, Lochgelly, March 1905.
Dall, John. N. Glencraig, February 1906.
Danskin, John, Lochgelly, September 1907.
Donaldson, James, Lochgelly, October 1907.
Duncan, John, Lochgelly, November 1907.
Dick, George W., Lochgelly, January 1908.
Dryburgh, David, Lochgelly, January 1905.
Dick, Robert, Lochgelly, May 1908.
Dall, William, Glencraig, October 1908.
Duncan, William, Cowdenbeath, November 1908.
Duncan, Wallace, Lochgelly, November 1908.
Doig, Andrew H., Lochgelly, December 1908.
Duncan, Alexander, London, September 1909.
Dempster, Thomas A., Crosshill, February 1910.
Dryden, John S., Lochgelly, April 1910.
Davidson, William C., Glencraig, December 1910.
Downie, Andrew, Crosshill, December 1912.
Dick, Thomas, Lochgelly, December 1912.
Donaldson, Robert, Ballingry, February 1913.
Drummond, Hugh, Lochgelly, February, 1913.
Davidson, James, Lochgelly, September 1913.
Davidson, Robert, Lochgelly, October 1913.
Drew, Edward M., Lochgelly, December 1913.
Donald, Neil, Lochgelly, February 1914.
Dow, Robert, Lochgelly, March 1914.
Davidson, Robert, Lochgelly, March 1914.
Duncan, John F., Lochgelly, March 1914.
Dalgleish, William J., Lochore, December 1914.
Dobson, Robert C., Glencraig, December 1915.
Duncan, Dan. H., Crosshill, May 1917.
Dawson, John, Lochgelly, May 1917.
Davidson, Alex. S., Lochgelly, October 1917.
Davidson, James, Lochgelly, May 1918.
Delop, Thomas, South Glencraig, May 1918.
Duncan, Alex. J., N. Glencraig, May 1918.
Davidson, Matthew, Lochore, September 1918.
Downie, David, N. Glencraig, November 1918.
Dall, John C., Lochgelly, January 1919.
Dewar, Andrew M., N. Glencraig, March 1919.
Dick, Robert, Lochgelly, April 1919.
Donaldson, George, Lochgelly, May 1919.
Devlin, Samuel R., Lochgelly, September 1919.
Devlin, John, Lochgelly, September 1919.
Duncan, Robert, Lochgelly, September 1919.
Dalziel, William, Lochgelly, November 1919.
Dall, Peter R.M., Crosshill, November 1919.
Dall, George, Cardenden, November 1919.
Dunsire, David, Lochgelly, November, 1919.

Dougary, John G. Mc., Cowdenbeath, September 1920.
Dawson, David, Lochgelly, September 1920.
Donaldson, William H., Lochgelly, September 1920.
Dick, Andrew, Lochgelly, February 1921.
Dunsire, Andrew B., Lochgelly, February 1921.
Dickson, Robert, Lochgelly, April 1921.
Dickson, James M., April 1921.
Davidson, James, Lochgelly, September 1921.
Dick, William D., Lochgelly, October 1921.
Davidson, Robert, Lochgelly, October 1921.
Dick, Robert, Lochgelly, November 1921.
Davidson, Peter McG., Lochgelly, January 1922.
Duncan, George, Lochgelly, October 1922.
Davidson, Andrew, Lochgelly, March 1923.
Dick, Alexander S., Lochgelly, November 1923.
Dow, Alexander, Lochgelly, January 1927.
Duncan, John G., Lochgelly, October 1927.
Davidson, Alexander C., Lochgelly, September 1929.
Dalziel, William R., Edinburgh, November 1930.

Erskine, Joseph B., Cowdenbeath, October 1873.
Erskine, George, Lochgelly, March 1874.
Ewan, John, Cowdenbeath, April 1885.
Erskine, Robert, Lochgelly, August 1892.
Erskine, James, Lochgelly, July 1894.
Erskine, George, Lochgelly, April 1896.
Erskine, George, Lochgelly, March 1907.
Erskine, John, Lochgelly, September 1907.
Erskine, James, Lochgelly, October 1911.
Easton, John, Lochgelly, April 1913.
Ewing, John, Lochgelly, September 1913.
Ewing, Samuel, Lochgelly, December 1915.
Erskine, James H., Lochgelly, February 1919.
Easton, Matthew, Lochgelly, April 1919.
Edgar, James, Lochgelly, April 1919.
Eadie, William, Lochgelly, February 1920.
Ewing, Alan S., Lochgelly, April 1923.
Ewing, David M., Lochgelly, April 1923.
Eaves, James, Lochgelly, February 1924.
Ellis, John, Lochgelly, February 1924.

Fraser, John, Lochgelly, April 1872.
Fowler, David Lochgelly, June 1873.
Ferguson, Robert, Cowdenbeath, October 1873.
Ferguson, John, Lochore, November 1881.
Forbes, William, Lochgelly, May 1881.
Fox, William, Cowdenbeath, May 1890.
Fyfe, James, Lumphinnans, November 1890.
Ford, James, Cardenden, August 1895.
Forrester, James, Lochgelly, April 1895.
Fox, John, Lumphinnans, August 1900.
Forrester, Robert, Auchterderran, March 1901.
Forrester, Andrew, Lochgelly, July 1901.
Fowler, Robert, Bowhill, May 1902.
Fox, Frank, Lumphinnans, October 1907.
Ferguson, Robert, Lochgelly, May 1908.
Fisher, Gilbert, Bowhill, June 1908.
Ferguson, Alexander, Lumphinnans, October 1908.

Ferguson, Alexander, Lochgelly, December 1908.
Ferrier, William, Lochore, January 1909.
Forrester, John C., Lochgelly, November 1909.
Forbes, William D., Lochgelly, November 1909.
Ferguson, William, Cardenden, March 1910.
Fordyce, Henry, Lochgelly, April 1910.
Ferguson, David, Dunfermline, November 1910.
Fordyce, William G.K., Edinburgh, March 1911.
Falconer, James, Lochgelly, May 1911.
Fraser, James, Lochgelly, October 1911.
Forrester, Robert C., Lochgelly, December 1911.
Frew, Thomas, Cowdenbeath, May 1913.
Falconer, William, Lochgelly, September 1913.
Fox, Francis, Lumphinnans, September 1913.
Foote, Andrew V., Lochgelly, March 1914.
Fowlis, Robert, Lumphinnans, April 1914.
Fraser, George R., Lochgelly, November 1914.
Fyfe, David B., Lochgelly, November 1914.
Falconer, Angus M., Lochgelly, October 1915.
Finlay, David, Lochgelly, April 1916.
Fenton, Arthur B., N. Glencraig, December 1916.
Fleming, Shanks, Lochgelly, April 1917.
Foote, William, Lochgelly, June 1917.
Ferguson, Richard T., Cowdenbeath, April 1918.
Fraser, James, Lochgelly, November 1918.
Fleming, George, Crosshill, January 1919.
Fraser, John, Lochgelly, April 1919.
Flockhart, David, Lochgelly, April 1919.
Foote, William, Lochgelly, April 1919.
Fleming, Andrew, Lochgelly, April 1919.
Forrester, Henry, Lochgelly, October 1919.
Fleming, Andrew, Lochgelly, November 1919.
Fraser, John, Lochgelly, November 1919.
Fleetham, William, Lochgelly, November 1919.
Fraser, Alexander B., Cardenden, February 1920.
Forrester, Robert S., Lochgelly, October 1920.
Fairlie, Andrew, Lochore, November 1920.
Finlayson, John H., Lochgelly, April 1921.
Falconer, Angus, Jun., Sholton Colliery, November 1921.
Falconer, Peter, Lochgelly, February, 1922.
Fotheringham, William, Lochgelly, May 1923.
Forrester, Henry, Lochgelly, May 1923.
Forrester, Henry J., Lochgelly, May 1923.
Fox, David, Cowdenbeath, October 1923.
Finnie, Martin, Lochgelly, December 1929.

Gillespie, George, Lochgelly, September 1859.
Gillespie, James, Cowdenbeath, November 1859.
Gibson, Henry, Blairadam, January, 1860.
Graham, Peter R., Glasgow, February 1860.
Graham, Archibald, Lochgelly, July 1862.
Geddes, George, Cowdenbeath, November 1863.
Guild, David, Lochgelly, June, 1871.
Graham, Dougald, Lochgelly, April 1872.
Geekie, Robert, Lochgelly, June 1872.
Grieg, James, Lochgelly, September 1872.
Gillespie, Robert, Lochgelly, March 1874.
Grieve, William, Lochgelly, November 1874.

Galloway, Alexander, East Wemyss, January 1875.
Gray, David, Cowdenbeath, September 1886.
Greenwood, William, Dundonald, February 1893.
Galloway, Robert, Lochgelly, March 1893.
Graham, John, Auchtertool, June 1894.
Green, John, Auchtertool, April 1896.
Garrie, Robert, Lochgelly, October 1900.
Goodall, Andrew, Lochgelly, November 1900.
Goodall, William, Lochgelly, November 1900.
Gemmell, Alexander C., Bowhill, February 1902.
Geddes, John, Lochgelly, March 1904.
Gray, John, Lochgelly, March 1905.
Guthrie, Robert, Lochgelly, August 1905.
Gold, John, Lochgelly, October 1907.
Garry, George, Lochgelly, November 1907.
Gillies, James, Lochgelly, November 1907.
Galloway, Thomas, Lochore, February 1908.
Gibb, Duncan B., Lochgelly, May 1908.
Galloway, William, Crosshill, September 1908.
Gray, James, Glencraig, October 1908.
Greig, John, Jun., Lochgelly, November 1908.
Gibson, David Lochore, January 1909.
Gray, Alexander, Lochgelly, February 1909.
Gordon, John, Lochore, March 1909.
Gowans, John, Lochgelly, November 1909.
Greig, Alexander S., Lochgelly, November 1909.
Gibson, James, Lochgelly, April 1911.
Grant, Duncan, Lumphinnans, April 1912.
Graham, William G., Crosshill, March 1913.
Gray, Robert, Lochgelly, November 1913.
Greenhorn, Andrew, Lochgelly, December 1913.
Gray, George R., Lochgelly, December 1913.
Guy, David, Lochgelly, January 1914.
Guy, John, Lochgelly, January 1914.
Greig, Ewen, Lochgelly, March 1914.
Goodall, Harry, Lochgelly, May 1914.
Garry, David H., Lochore, March 1915.
Gray, James E., Lochgelly, June 1916.
Garry, Joseph, Lochgelly November 1916.
Gillespie, John, Cardenden, November 1916.
Gillespie, George, Lochgelly, January 1917.
Gray, William, Lochgelly, June 1917.
Gray, Donaldson, Lochgelly, January 1918.
Glencross, Andrew H., Glencraig, March 1918.
Gair, Murdoch, Lochgelly, April 1918.
Goodall, Robert D., Lochgelly, May 1918.
Gibb, Lawrence T., Lochgelly, October 1919.
Graham, William, Lochgelly, February 1919.
Graham, Richard, Lochgelly, April 1919.
Gibb, George F., Lochgelly, April 1919.
Gibb, James B., Lochgelly, April 1919.
Goodwin, Robert, Lochgelly, May 1919.
Green, James McG., Lochgelly, November 1919.
Godsell, John J., Cowdenbeath, November 1919.
Gibb, George, Lochgelly, November 1919.
Gibb, George Birrell, Jun., Lochgelly, November 1919.
Gray, William, Lochgelly, November 1919.
Goodall, Thomas Penman, Lochgelly, December 1919.

Gair, David J, Lochgelly, February 1920.
Gillespie, William, Lochgelly, April 1920.
Galloway, Peter, Glencraig, April 1920.
Gray, Cuthbert Stafford, Lumphinnans, October 1920.
Gibb, Archibald, Lochgelly, October 1920.
Grier, James, Lochgelly, November 1920.
Gordon, James Skinner, Lochgelly, January 1921.
Gray, Robert, Lochgelly, March 1921.
Garstang, Colin, Cowdenbeath, September 1921.
Gair, James H., Lochgelly, September 1921.
Glennie, George, Lochgelly, January 1922.
Gray, Peter, Cowdenbeath, January 1922.
Gray, Alexander, Cowdenbeath, April 1922.
Garcia, Ivon I.G., Lumphinnans, January 1923.
Gillies, Donald, Lochgelly, March 1923.
Gray, George L., Lochgelly, April 1924.
Gibb, Alex. G., Lochgelly, April 1927.

Hugh, Thomas, Lochgelly, December 1858.
Hunter, David, On Board, Great Briton, (Steward), January 1861.
Hunter, Richard, Cowdenbeath, February 1861.
Hodge, John, Cowdenbeath, April 1861.
Hunter, Robert, Lochgelly, April 1861.
Hunter, Henry, Lochgelly, April 1861.
Henderson, William, Lochgelly, February 1867.
Henderson, Robert, Giffertown, March 1869.
Hunter, John Page, Lochgelly, December 1872.
Hugh, Angus, Cowdenbeath, February 1874.
Hodge, William, Cowdenbeath, March 1875.
Hunter, John, Cowdenbeath, July 1875.
Hunter, George, Cowdenbeath, July 1875.
Herd, Richard, Cardenden, January 1876.
Hugh, Alexander, Lochgelly, December 1876.
Hunter, James, Lochgelly, February 1877.
Hunter, Andrew, Lochgelly, February 1881.
Hugh, William, Muiredge, April 1882.
Hodge, John, Cowdenbeath, December 1884.
Houston, Archibald McN. (Rev), Auchterderran, April 1891.
Henderson, David C., Lochgelly, June, 1893.
Harvey, Edward, Lochgelly, October 1895.
Hynd, James, Lochgelly, July 1898
Herd, William, Jamphlars, Cardenden, April 1900.
Hunter, Robert H., Bowhill, Cardenden, June 1900.
Hutt, John, Cardenden, October 1900.
Hunter, James, Lochgelly, October 1900.
Hodge, John, Bowhill, Cardenden, November 1900.
Howden, William, Glencraig, February 1901.
Howden, James, Lochgelly, February 1901.
Herd, William, Westfield, February 1901.
Hunter, Hugh, Lochgelly, May 1902.
Hunter, William S., Lochgelly, January 1904.
Hynd, John, Lochgelly, February 1904.
Higgins, James, Glencraig, May 1905.
Holman, Joseph N., Lochgelly, July 1907.
Herd, Alexander, Lochgelly, June 1906.
Hunter, David, Lochgelly, September 1907.

Herd, Andrew, Cowdenbeath, February, 1908.
Hood, David, Lumphinnans, August, 1908.
Hutchison, Andrew, Bowhill, September 1908.
Hunter, William B., Bowhill, September 1908.
Hunter, R. B., Cardenden, September 1908.
Hugh, William B., Lochgelly, December 1908
Herd, Henry, Rosewell, January 1909.
Hunter, Robert, Lochgelly, October 1909.
Herd, Archibald, Lochgelly, February 1910.
Henderson, James L., Lochgelly, March 1910.
Hosie, Henry, Cowdenbeath, April 1910.
Heggie, Peter, Lochgelly, May 1910.
Hunter, Andrew, Cardenden, May 1910,
Hood, William, Glencraig, October 1910.
Hall, John, Lumphinnans, October 1911.
Hunter, Thomas, Lochore, November 1911.
Hoggan, Matthew, N. Glencraig, October 1912.
Harrison, William, Crosshill, February 1913.
Hynd, Henry, Lochgelly, February 1913.
Hodge, Alexander, Lochgelly, April 1913.
Howie, Alexander, Crosshill, May 1913.
Hay, Henry J., Glencraig, September 1913.
Hynd, John, Lochgelly, December, 1913.
Henderson, James, Lochgelly, December 1913.
Henderson, James, Lochgelly, January, 1914.
Heggie, James, Lochgelly, January 1914.
Hunter, Thomas, Lochgelly, March 1914.
Haxton, James A. W. F., Lochgelly, December 1914.
Hunter, David, Lochore, December 1914.
Hynd, David, Lochgelly, March, 1915.
Hebenton, John, Glencraig, December 1915.
Henderson, Thomas, Lochgelly, April 1916.
Hunter, Andrew, Lochgelly, November 1916.
Hynd, John, Lochgelly, January 1917.
Holmes, Donald, Lumphinnans, May 1917.
Haddow, James C., Lochgelly, November 1917.
Houston, Robert, Lochgelly, November 1917.
Hodges, Alfred, Lochgelly, January 1918.
Hynd, Charles, Lumphinnans, April 1918.
Hynd, John B., Lumphinnans, April 1918.
Hunter, John, Glencraig, May 1918.
Hunter, William V., Lochgelly, October 1918.
Hunter, Alex., Lochgelly, November 1918.
Hunter, William G., Lochgelly, January 1919.
Herd, Stewart, Cowdenbeath, January 1919.
Hosie, James, Cowdenbeath, February 1919.
Herd, William, Lochgelly, April 1919.
Hunter, Charles H., Lochgelly, May 1919.
Halfpenny, Hugh, Lochgelly, September 1919.
Henderson, Paul, Lochgelly, October 1919.
Hunter, David, Lochgelly, October 1919.
Herd, John, Lochgelly, October 1919.
Hunter, Richard, Lumphinnans, November 1919.
Herd, George, Lochgelly, November 1919.
Henderson, Thomas P., Jun., Lochgelly, November 1919.
Hunter, John, Lochgelly, November 1919.
Hodge, George E., Lochgelly, November 1919.
Herd, John Gilmour, Lochgelly, November 1919.

Hunter, James Clark, Lochgelly, November 1919.
Halfpenny, James, Lochgelly, February 1920.
Henderson, Andrew, Lochgelly, February 1920.
Halfpenny, James A., Lochgelly, February 1920.
Hunter, James, Lumphinnans, March 1920.
Hunter, Robert, Lumphinnans, March 1920.
Haldane, David Gibb, Lochgelly, April 1920.
Heelley, Thomas, Lochgelly, April, 1920.
Handyside, William, Lumphinnans, October 1920.
Hamilton, Joseph Morris, Lochore, November 1920.
Hailstones, Thomas, Lochgelly, November 1920.
Hornal, Charles, Lochgelly, November 1927.
Hunter, Henry, Lochgelly, January 1930.

Ingles, John, Lochgelly, December 1859.
Inch, John, Lochgelly, June, 1891.
Izatt, Morrison B., Lochore, January 1909.
Irving, James, Lochore, March 1912.
Irvine, Alexander, Lochgelly, December 1915.
Irvine, David, N. Glencraig, March 1919.
Irvine, Henry, Dysart, February 1920.
Inches, William, Glenfarg, May 1920.
Irvine, Simon R., Lochgelly, October 1920.
Irvine, James, Lochgelly, April 1924.

Johnstone, John, Crossgates, March 1867.
Johnstone, John, Lochgelly, May 1886.
Johnstone, Thomas, Lochgelly, April 1890.
Johnstone, William, Lochgelly, August 1892.
Johnstone, Thomas, Lochgelly, April 1897.
Johnstone, Alexander, Lochgelly, September 1897.
Johnstone, William, Lochgelly, September 1897.
Johnstone, James, Lochgelly, September, 1897.
Johnstone, David, Lochgelly, September 1897.
Johnstone, David, Lochgelly, November 1901.
Jackson, John, Lochgelly, September 1902.
Johnstone, Orr, Lochgelly, January 1904.
Johnstone, Peter, Lumphinnans, January 1906.
Johnstone, Robert, Lochgelly, November 1907.
Jack, John, Lochgelly, March 1909.
Johnstone, David, Lochgelly, March 1910.
Jardine, William, Leslie, February 1911.
Jones, Thomas, Lumphinnans, October 1912.
Johnstone, Neil S., Lochgelly, March 1913.
Johnstone, Robert, Kinglassie, April 1913.
Jackson, William B., Lochgelly, September 1913.
Johnstone, David, Lochgelly, September 1913.
Justice, William, N. Glencraig, June 1916.
Johnstone, David, Lochgelly, January 1917.
Johnstone, Peter W., Lochgelly, March 1919.
Jeffrey, James K., Cowdenbeath, May 1919.
Johnstone, Adam, Lochgelly, September 1919.
Jamieson, James S., Cowdenbeath, October 1919.
Jeffrey, David, Cowdenbeath, April 1921.
Jackson, Robert J., Birmingham, November 1923.
Johnstone, William, Lochgelly, February 1924.
Johnstone, Adam, Lochgelly, October 1927.

Kippie, Andrew T., Ballingry, October 1860.

Knight, Robert, Lochgelly, October 1884.
Kinninmonth, John, Lochgelly, March 1894.
Kinlay, James, Lochgelly, February 1901.
Kellock, George, Cardenden, January 1904.
King, John J., Cardenden, September 1906.
Kinnell, George, Lochgelly, February 1908.
Knox, William, Crosshill, May 1908.
Kinghorn, Abraham, Little Hulton, October 1909.
Keillor, James D., Lochgelly, March 1910.
King, Robert, Lochgelly, February 1911.
King, George, Lochgelly, February 1913.
King, Thomas, Lochgelly, April 1913.
Kirk, James, Lochgelly, March 1914.
Keddie, John, Lochgelly, April 1914.
Kennedy, Absolom, S. Glencraig, April 1914.
Kirk, John, Lochgelly, March 1916.
Kerr, Archibald, Lochgelly, November 1916.
King, Robert S., Glencraig, January 1917.
Kennedy, James P., Lochgelly, April 1918.
Kirke, Archibald C., Lochgelly, February 1919.
Kirk, David, Lochgelly, April 1919.
Kennedy, George, Lochgelly, October 1919.
Keddie, Alexander W., Lochgelly, November 1919.
Karswell, Courtney G., Devonport, March 1920.
Kennedy, William M., Cowdenbeath, March 1920.
Kidd, Peter, Jun., Lochgelly, April 1923.
Kinlay, David, Lochgelly, November 1923.
Kirk, Frank, Burnley, March 1926.
Kerr, James, Lochgelly, September 1927.
Kinlay, John K., Lochgelly, October 1930.
Kerr, Alexander, Lochgelly, December 1930.
Kirk, Thomas, Lochgelly, April 1931.

Low, William B., Auchterderran, December 1859.
Leitch, Andrew, Townhill, November 1865.
Laing, Thomas, Cowdenbeath, July 1873.
Leitch, John, America, August, 1874.
Leitch, John, Lochgelly, December 1876.
Laing, John, Lochgelly, December 1891.
Lonie, William, Lochgelly, August 1898.
Lindsay, Henry, Lochgelly, March 1901.
Lyle, Alexander, Lochore, May 1901.
Laird, John, Lochgelly, January 1903.
Leadbetter, David A.B., Lochgelly, September 1903.
Love, Alexander N., Lochgelly, February 1904.
Laird, Thomas, Lochgelly, October 1905.
Lowe, Henry, S. Glencraig, February 1906.
Lamb, Thomas, Cardenden, March 1906.
Lessels, Robert, Bowhill, October 1906.
Lockhart, James, Lochgelly, August 1907.
Lawrie, Charles, Glencraig, February, 1908.
Logan, William, Lochgelly, May 1908.
Lowe, Archibald McK., S. Glencraig, May 1908.
Laird, James R., Lochore, October 1908.
Laird, Thomas, Lochgelly, December 1908.
Low, Robert, Cowdenbeath, March 1911.
Logan, James, Lochgelly, March 1911.
Linn, Robert M.D., Lochgelly, October 1911.
Lind, Alexander, Glencraig, November 1911.

Linton, William, Lochgelly, January 1913.
Lister, James, Lochgelly, January 1913.
Low, John, Glencraig, February 1913.
Lumsden, George, Lochgelly, September 1913.
Laird, Robert H., Lochgelly, November 1913.
Lees, Thomas, Lochgelly, November 1913.
Lister, Peter, Glencraig, December 1913.
Leishman, James, Lochgelly, January 1914.
Lamond, David, Cardenden, January 1914.
Lees, Andrew, Lochgelly, February 1913.
Leitch, Andrew, Lochgelly, March 1914.
Lister, Alexander F., Lochgelly, March 1914.
Lees, David, Lochgelly, April 1914.
Leslie, Alexander D., Cowdenbeath, September 1914.
Laing, David, Glencraig, September 1914.
Law, John, Lochgelly, March 1916.
Livingstone, Thomas, Lochgelly, October 1916.
Lumsden, William M., Lochgelly, October 1916.
Laing, John, Lochgelly, January 1917.
Logan, Alexander, Lochgelly, January 1917.
Lawson, John, Lochgelly, October 1917.
Lister, James, Jun., Lochgelly, November 1917.
Linton, Andrew, Lochgelly, January 1918.
Lumsden, Alexander K., Lochgelly, May 1919.
Lumsden, William, Cowdenbeath, November 1919.
Leishman, Mitchell R., Lochgelly, November 1919.
Leishman, John R., Lochgelly, November 1919.
Lamond, John, Lochgelly, November 1919.
Linton, Alexander, Lochgelly, March 1920.
Lyon, Alexander F., Lumphinnans, October 1920.
Lowe, Hendrick J., Cardenden, November 1920.
Legg, William, Lochgelly, October 1921.
Logie, James W., Lochgelly, October 1922.
Logie, William M.C., Lochgelly, October 1922.
Little, Christopher, Lochgelly, November 1923.
Lyon, John, Cowdenbeath, September 1926.
Logie, George B., Lochgelly, March 1927.
Lovelock, Sidney B., Westbury-on-Trym, November 1927.
Laing, James, Lochgelly, January 1930.

Mitchell, John, Dundonald, April 1859.
Morris, William, Lochgelly, June 1859.
Mungall, Robert, Lumphinnans, December 1859.
Meikle, James, Lochgelly, January 1862.
Morton, William, Lochgelly, January 1872.
Michie, Thomas, Lochgelly, July 1872.
Muirelong, Thomas, Crossgates, December 1872.
Moodie, William, Cowdenbeath, July 1873.
Milne, John, Cowdenbeath, October 1873.
Miller, John, Cowdenbeath, June 1874.
Milne, Robert, Lochgelly, May 1877.
MacDougall, John W., Cowdenbeath, January 1878.
Moyes, Henry, Cowdenbeath, April 1892.
Millar, Hugh, Lochore, August 1892.
Martin, William, Auchterderran, June 1895.
Mitchell, William, Auchtertool, May 1896.
Mathieson, John, Lochgelly, July 1898.

Mark, George, Lochgelly, December 1898.
Morgan, Robert, Lumphinnans, October 1900.
Mathieson, Andrew, Jun., Cardenden, October 1900.
Morran, Samuel, Lochgelly, February 1901.
Mollison, Robert, Lochgelly, March 1901.
Mitchell, Alexander, Dundonald, May 1901.
Menzies, James, Lochore, June 1901.
Melville, John, Lumphinnans, September 1901.
MacDuff, Peter, Lochgelly, February 1902.
Mann, James, Bowhill, May 1902.
Martin, Hugh, Glencraig, August 1902.
Muir, Thomas, Glencraig, August 1902.
Mackay, Robert, Lochgelly, January 1904.
Menzies, Robert, Glencriag, January 1905.
Montgomery, Ernest S., Kirkcaldy, September 1906.
Milne, James, Lochgelly, September 1906.
Main, George, Cowdenbeath, December 1906.
Moffat, David, Lochgelly, February 1907.
Millar, James E., Lochgelly, February 1907.
Melville, Robert, Glencraig, February 1908.
Millar, Hugh C., Lochgelly, February 1908.
Moncur, Charles, Glencraig, March 1908.
Milne, Thomas, Lochgelly, April 1908.
Millar, George S., Cowdenbeath, May 1908.
Moncur, William, Glencraig, May 1908.
Morton, James, Lochgelly, May 1908.
Murdoch, John, N. Glencraig, September 1908.
Moyes, David, Cardenden, October 1908.
Mechesney, David G., Lochore, December 1908.
Moyes, Robert T., Lochgelly, December 1908.
Moyes, William, Crosshill, December 1908.
Muir, George T., Lochgelly, December 1908.
Mathieson, David, Lochgelly, January 1909.
Mathieson, William, Lochgelly, January, 1909.
Melville, Samuel B., Lochgelly, April 1900.
Morton, Peter, Crosshill, April 1909.
Milne, Lewis, Lochgelly, October 1909.
Marshall, Andrew, Crosshill, November 1909.
Mathieson, George, Cardenden, February 1910.
Mathieson, William, Cardenden, February 1910.
Mathieson, Thomas, Cowdenbeath, February 1910.
Marshall, David L., Lochgelly, March 1910.
Mitchell, John, Lochgelly, November 1910.
Melville, James, N. Glencraig, December 1910.
Mathewson, Robert, Lochgelly, December 1910.
Melville, David, Lumphinnans, March 1911.
Maule, John, Glencraig, October 1911.
Melville, Andrew, Cowdenbeath, October 1911.
Mann, James, Lochgelly, January 1913.
Mackie, Thomas, Lochgelly, March 1913.
Mitchell, Robert, Crosshill, May 1913.
Melville, David, Lochgelly, May 1913.
Meville, David, Lochgelly, September 1913.
Muir, Alexander, Lochgelly, September 1913.
Miller, Andrew C., Lochgelly, September 1913.
Marshall, George B., Lochgelly, September 1913.
Milne, Thomas, Lochgelly, September 1913.
Marshall, George, Cowdenbeath, September 1913.
Macdairmid, William H., Ballingry, October 1913.

Macduff, Donald, Lochgelly, November 1913.
Morrison, Colin, Lochgelly, November 1913.
Moyes, Andrew, Lochgelly, January 1914.
Muir, Thomas, Lochgelly, January 1914.
Marshall, Charles S., Lochgelly, March 1914.
Moyes, John B., Lochgelly, March 1914.
Moffat, Robert, Lumphinnans, April 1914.
Melville, William, Lochgelly, April 1914.
Methven, John, Lochgelly, May 1914.
Miller, Stewart, Lochgelly, November 1914.
Merrilees, James L., N. Glencraig, June 1916.
Moyes, John, Lochore, June 1916.
Mason, John, Lochgelly, October, 1916.
Muir, Henry C., S. Glencraig, December 1916.
Malcolm, Thomas, Lochgelly, January 1917.
Moffat, John, Lochgelly, May 1918.
Miller, Peter F., S. Glencraig. October 1918.
Mackie, David, Lochgelly, January 1919.
Muir, James R., Lochgelly, January 1919.
Muir, John, Lochgelly, February 1919.
Morgan, John, Lochgelly, April 1919.
Martin, Thomas, Lumphinnans, April 1919.
Malcolm, Andrew, Lochgelly, April 1919.
Matthew, Alexander, Lochgelly, April 1919.
Miller, James H., Cowdenbeath, May 1919.
Mathieson, James, Lochgelly, September 1919.
Mackay, Robert C., Jun., Lochgelly, September 1919.
Mitchell, Robert G., Lochgelly, October 1919.
Morris, Andrew, Lochgelly, November 1919.
Moyes, James, Lochgelly, November 1919.
Moyes, Peter, Lochgelly, November 1919.
Macfarlane, William S., Lochgelly, November 1919.
Morgan, Robert, Lochgelly, November 1919.
Muckersie, James, Lochgelly, November 1919.
Morris, Robert S., Lochgelly, November 1919.
Maxwell, John, Cardenden, November 1919.
Mathieson, Alexander, Lochgelly, November 1919.
MacNicol, Archibald, Lochgelly, November 1919.
Muir, Hugh W., Lochgelly, February 1920.
Meikle, James McK, Lochgelly, February 1920.
Miller, David, Lumphinnans, March 1920.
Michie, Adam, Lumphinnans, March 1920.
Macpherson, Lumphinnans, March 1920.
Moore, Arthur, Peterborough, April 1920.
Mechan, James, M., N. Glencraig, October 1920.
Malcolm, James G., Cowdenbeath, October 1920.
Macdonald, Archibald, Lochgelly, January 1921.
Mackay, William, Lochgelly, March 1921.
Murray, Archibald C., Lochgelly, September 1921.
Marshall, John B., Lochgelly, September 1921.
Morgan, William J., Lochgelly, February 1922.
Murray, William J., Lochgelly, February 1923.
Munnoch, Robert, Lochgelly, April 1923.
Murray, Patrick, Lochgelly, October 1923.
Mann, David, Lochgelly, October 1923.
Michie, David, Lochgelly, May 1924.
Mitchell, Alexander, Thornton, May 1924.
Muir, Mitchell, Lochgelly, May 1924.

Marnoch, James, Lochgelly, November 1924.
Mitchell, James, Edinburgh, November 1924.
Muir, David E. D., Lochgelly, February 1926.
Mitchell, George A., Glencraig, May 1926.
Mitchell, John M., Lochgelly, September 1926.
Macrae,. Roderick, Lochgelly, November 1926.
MacTaggart, William A., Lochgelly, December 1926.
MacTaggart, Ronald, Lochgelly, December 1926.
MacKinnon, James C., Glencraig, September 1929.
McColl, William, Cowdenbeath, February 1859.
McArthur, John, Cowdenbeath, November 1859.
McKenzie, William, Kelty, November 1860.
McKenzie, George, Kelty, January, 1861.
McRitchie, Michael, Craigton, July 1862.
McLean, Alexander, Cowdenbeath, November 1863.
McKinlay, Robert, Cowdenbeath, December 1873.
McArthur, Donald, Cowdenbeath, December 1874.
McKee, Robert R., Lochgelly, July 1877.
McAnuel, Gilbert, Lochgelly, May 1886.
McLean, Alexander, Lochgelly, January 1888.
McDonald, Thomas, Lochgelly, February 1890.
McLean, David, Lochgelly, August 1892.
McLean, David, Lochgelly, April 1894.
McDonald, Daniel, Lochgelly, July 1900.
McEwan, John, Lochgelly, October 1900.
McKinlay, Thomas, Lochgelly, February 1902.
McKee, Robertson, Lochgelly, September 1903.
McArthur, Donald, Lochgelly, November 1903.
McCallum, James, Lochgelly, June 1904.
McCall, James H., Lochore, December 1905.
McLean, David, Lochgelly, September 1907.
McCulloch, John, Lochgelly, November 1907.
McCaw, William, Lochgelly, January 1908.
McCaw, John, Lochgelly, April 1908.
McLuckie, Matthew, Glencraig, August 1908.
McLeod, William, Crosshill, December 1908.
McLean, William, Lochgelly, March 1909.
McCall, William, Crosshill, March 1909.
McKechnie, William, Lochgelly, March 1909.
McLeod, William, Lochgelly, April 1909.
McWilliam, John, Crosshill, September 1909.
McEwan, Robert, Crosshill, February 1910.
McLay, Finlay, Lochore, April 1911.
McLachlan, James, Lochore, May 1911.
McLean, Thomas, Lochgelly, October 1911.
McInroy, Kenneth, Lochgelly, December, 1911.
McCallum, Malcolm C., N. Glencraig, February 1912.
McFarlane, William M., Lochgelly, March 1912.
McLean, John, Lochgelly, October 1912.
McLean, James, Lochgelly, December 1912.
McQueen, James, Lochgelly, January 1913.
McCallum, William, Lochore, January 1913.
McArtney, John, Lochgelly, February 1913.
McEwan, James, Lochgelly, March 1913.
McKinlay, Archibald F., Lochgelly, March 1913.
McNeil, Henry C., Lochgelly, April 1913.
McKee, James, Lochgelly, September 1913.

McKenzie, James, Lochgelly, October 1913.
McKay, James, Lochgelly, January 1914.
McPherson, John H., Lochgelly, March 1915.
McPherson, James R., Lochgelly, May 1915.
McCathie, Henry H., Crosshill, December 1915.
McLean, Thomas, Lochgelly, October 1916.
McLean, John, Bowhill, October 1916.
McGhie, John, Lochgelly, January 1917.
McLeod, John B., N. Glencraig, March 1917.
McKenzie, James W., Lochgelly, October 1917.
McIver, Joseph, Lumphinnans, October 1917.
McCrae, Douglas, Lochgelly, November 1917.
McConnell, William, Lochgelly, April 1918.
McOwat, James, Lochore, April 1918.
McAndrew, Andrew, Lochore, April 1918.
McKay, Hugh, Lochgelly, September 1918.
McGhie, George, Lochgelly, October 1918.
McLean, William, Cowdenbeath, November, 1918.
McKinlay, Alexander H., Lochgelly, January 1919.
McLean, Thomas, Lochgelly, January 1919.
McLean, James, Lochgelly, March 1919.
McLean, John, Lochgelly, March 1919.
McEwan, David, Lochgelly, April 1919.
McLean, Robert, Lochgelly, April 1919.
McGuire, George, Lochgelly, April 1919.
McColl, Robert P., Lochgelly, September 1919.
McDougall, William, Dunfermline, September 1919.
McKinnon, Andrew, Lochgelly, September 1919.
McLean, Joseph R., Lochgelly, October 1919.
McLaren, John C., Cardenden, November 1919.
McNeil, Robert, Lochgelly, November 1919.
McPherson, Hugh, Lochgelly, November 1919.
McLean, Andrew R., Lochgelly, February 1920.
McEwan, William, Lochgelly, February 1920.
McGregor, James, Lochgelly, March 1920.
McKinlay, George, Lochgelly, March 1920.
McKenzie, Alexander, Lochgelly, September 1920.
McKenzie, William, Lochgelly, February 1921.
McLeland, Robert, Cardenden, April 1921.
McKenzie, Charles W., Uxbridge, January 1922.
McGregor, Daniel, Lumphinnans, February 1923.
McKinlay, Archibald, Lochgelly, January 1924.
McPherson, Alexander, Lochgelly, January 1925.
McLean, John, Lochgelly, February 1925.
McKenzie, James W., Kirkcaldy, April 1925.
McIntyre, Thomas, Lochgelly, September 1925.
McClelland, James, Lochgelly, November 1925.
McKerrell, Duncan, Lochgelly, November 1926.
McKee, Thomas, Lumphinnans, April 1929.
McKerron, James, Lochgelly, April 1930.
McNeil, Alexander, Lochgelly, January 1931.

Nesbit, Arthur, Cowdenbeath, December 1859.
Nicol, John, Lochgelly, February 1876.
Nicol, Andrew, Lochgelly, August 1892.
Naysmith, David, Lochgelly, September 1892.
Nicol, James, Lochgelly, November 1894.
Nicol, Thomas, Lochgelly, December 1897.
Neill, William Moodie, Lochgelly, January 1903.

Naysmith, James, Lochgelly, January 1908.
Nisbet, Alexander, Lochgelly, May 1908.
Nicholls, Andrew, Crosshill, April 1910.
Nicholls, George, Crosshill, April 1911.
Nicol, Archibald, Lochgelly, December 1912.
Naysmith, John Palmer, Lochgelly, October 1913.
Nicol, William, Lochgelly, April 1913.
Naysmith, Thomas, Lochgelly, March 1914
Nicol, Andrew, Lochgelly, January 1917
Naysmith, John, Lochgelly, April 1917.
Naysmith, Johnstone, Lochgelly, March 1919
Naysmith, David, Lochgelly, April 1919.
Naysmith, Alexander, Lochgelly, October 1919.
Nicol, Andrew, Lochgelly, November 1919.
Nutt, Thomas, Lochead, Lochgelly, November 1919.
Norton, Louis Arthur, Portsmouth, March 1920.
Naysmith, John Jun., Lochgelly, February 1921.
Naysmith, David McLean, Lochgelly,
February 1922.
Neilson, John, Lochgelly, April 1922.
Nicol, James Robertson, Lochgelly, April 1924
Nicol, James M. P., Lochgelly, May 1924.
Nisbet, Andrew, Lochgelly, October 1927.
Nisbet, Robert Thompson, Lochgelly, February 1927.
Nicol, Andrew, Lochgelly, March 1930

Oram, John, Lumphinnans, July 1864.
Oliphant, Alexander, Kelty, September 1890.
Oram, Archibald, Lochgelly, December 1907.
Oram, David, Lochgelly, November, 1911.
Oates, John Gilbert, South Glencraig, April 1917.
Oram, A. Brown, Lochgelly, July 1917
Oram, John, Lochgelly, April 1920.
Ogilvie, David, N. Glencraig, November 1925.

Paton, James, Cowdenbeath, April 1859.
Paul, John, Cowdenbeath, June 1859.
Paton, David, Lochgelly, December 1870.
Pryde, David, Lochgelly, December 1870.
Paton, John, Lochgelly, January 1874.
Penman, William, Cowdenbeath, October 1876.
Philip, John, Lochgelly, January 1877.
Paterson, William, Auchtertool, April 1882.
Paterson, John, Cowdenbeath, June 1889.
Penman, Thomas, Cowdenbeath, June 1890.
Penman, David, Lochgelly, July 1890.
Pratt, William, Kelty, September 1890.
Pierce, Frank, Cowdenbeath, October 1890.
Pratt, William, Kelty, December 1890.
Paton, William, Cowdenbeath, April 1892.
Paton, John, Lochgelly, June 1893.
Paterson, David S. A., Auchterderran,
November 1900.
Penman, William, Lochgelly, March 1901.
Penman, Richard, Lochgelly, August 1901.
Philp, Robert W., Lochgelly, February 1902.
Penman, David, Lochgelly, February 1902.
Penman, Robert, Cardenden, January, 1904.
Pearson, James, Kingsbarns, June 1904.

Philp, William, Cardenden, February 1905.
Paterson, Walter, Lochgelly, February 1905.
Paterson, George, Cowdenbeath, April 1907.
Paton, David H., Lochgelly, October 1907.
Penman, George, Lochgelly, May 1908.
Playfair, James, Lochgelly, October 1908.
Paterson, James, Lumphinnans, October 1908.
Percy, James W., Lochgelly, November 1908.
Peebles, James W., Lochgelly, November 1908.
Paul, William, Cowdenbeath, October 1909.
Page, Alexander, Lochore, November 1909.
Philp, John, Lochgelly, March 1910.
Paterson, John Jun., Auchtertool, April 1910.
Paterson, Robert, Auchtertool, April 1910.
Paterson, Thomas, Auchtertool, November 1910.
Philp, John, Dunfermline, May 1912.
Proudfoot, Adam, Lochgelly, October 1912.
Penman, William B., Lochgelly, October 1912.
Pratt, George, Lumphinnans, October 1913.
Pratt, David, Lochore, November 1913.
Paton, Alexander S., Cowdenbeath, May 1915.
Park, Robert, Lochgelly, January 1917.
Peters, Robert W., Lochgelly, January 1917.
Penman, Richard, Lochgelly, January 1917.
Prain, David D., Lochgelly, January 1917.
Patterson, Joseph A., Glencraig, March 1917.
Penman, Robert P.M., Lochgelly, May 1917.
Peattie, Andrew, Lochore, May 1917.
Paterson, John, Lochgelly, November 1917.
Petrie, John, Lochgelly, October 1918.
Paton, Robert N., Lochgelly, October 1918.
Pratt, David, Lochgelly, November 1918.
Paterson, Andrew, Cowdenbeath, January 1919.
Paterson, Robert, Cowdenbeath, January 1919.
Penman, Alexander W., Lochgelly, April 1919.
Penman, Archibald, Lochgelly, April 1919.
Penman, William, Lochgelly, April 1919.
Penman, Thomas, Lochgelly, April 1919.
Paton, William B., Lochgelly, May 1919.
Penman, Robert M., Lochgelly, October 1919.
Paton, John M., Lochgelly, November 1919.
Philips, David C., Lochgelly, November 1919.
Pollock, Hugh M., Cowdenbeath, November 1919.
Parker, James, Lochgelly, November 1919.
Paterson, Charles, Cowdenbeath, February 1920.
Petrie, Henry L., Lochgelly, February 1920.
Penman, Robert B., Lochgelly, February 1920.
Pratt, Robert, Cowdenbeath, March 1920.
Peters, John R., Lochgelly, April 1920.
Pert, William W., Cowdenbeath, April 1920.
Penman, Alexander S., Lochgelly, April 1923.
Petrie, David L., Lochgelly, May 1923.
Penman, Thomas, Edinburgh, December 1924.
Phillip, Arthur, Lochgelly, April 1925.
Parkinson, Joseph T., Glasgow, November 1925.
Penman, James, Lochgelly, December 1927.

Rattray, Thomas, Lassodie, February 1859.
Rattray, David, Kelty, November 1860.

Richardson, David, Cowdenbeath, May 1861.
Rollo, James, Cowdenbeath, January 1876.
Reid, Alexander, Lochgelly, August 1880.
Russell, William, Lochgelly, August 1884.
Russell, George, Cowdenbeath, March 1887.
Rodger, Robert, Kelty, June 1891.
Robertson, Thomas, Kelty, June, 1891.
Rae, William, Auchterderran, October 1892.
Rolland, Walter, Lochgelly, February, 1894.
Raeburn, John, Lochgelly, March 1895.
Rowan, William, Auchterderran, July 1898.
Rae, George, Cardenden, May 1899.
Ross, James, Cardenden, June 1900.
Rattray, Thomas, Kelty, March 1901.
Rattray, John R., Lochgelly, May 1901.
Rankine, John, Lochgelly, May 1901.
Rigby, Josiah E., Manchester, September 1901.
Russell, Charles, Cardenden, October 1902.
Reid, William, Lochgelly, January 1903.
Ronaldson, David, Bowhill, January 1905.
Russell, William M., Lochgelly, June 1907.
Raeburn, Robert E., Lochgelly, October 1907.
Rattray, Thomas S, Glencraig, October 1907.
Russell, John, Lochgelly, January 1908.
Robertson, Duncan, N. Glencraig, September 1908.
Russell, Alexander, Glencraig, September 1908.
Ramage, Robert, Bowhill, November 1908.
Rigg, John W., Lochgelly, November 1908.
Reid, William B., Lochgelly, December 1908.
Russell, William, Lochgelly, December 1908.
Rodger, David, Cardenden, February 1909.
Ritchie, Samuel, Lochgelly, April 1909.
Ritchie, David, Lochgelly, November 1909.
Reid, Alexander C.C., Lochgelly, April 1910.
Rodger, Malcolm McD., Lochgelly, May 19010.
Rattray, David, Lochore, May 1911.
Reid, John, Lumphinnans, October 1911.
Reid, John H., Lochgelly, October 1912.
Robertson, Alexander, Lochgelly, October 1912.
Russell, John, Lumphinnans, December 1912.
Redpath, Andrew S., Lochore, December 1912.
Ross, William, Lochgelly, January 1913.
Raeburn, George E., Lochgelly, April 1913.
Robertson, Thomas M., Dunfermline, September 1913.
Rodger, John, Lochgelly, September 1913.
Robertson, Robert, Lochgelly, October 1913.
Robertson, James E., N. Glencraig, October 1913.
Russell, James, Lochgelly, January 1914.
Russell, James, Lochgelly, April 1914.
Reid, John, Dunfermline, May 1914.
Robertson, James, Lochgelly, May 1915.
Robertson, James A., Lochgelly, September 1915.
Renton, William G., Lochgelly, March 1916.
Reid, James, Lochgelly, March 1916.
Robertson, William, Lochgelly, December 1916.
Reid, George, Glencraig, January 1917.
Reid, David, Lochgelly, May 1917.
Reid, Alexander, Lochgelly, May 1917.

Robertson, William, Lochgelly, October 1917.
Rintoul, John J., Lochgelly, October 1917.
Robertson, David B., Lochgelly, May 1918.
Rodger, John, Lochore, April 1919.
Reid, John T., Lochgelly, April 1919.
Roberts, William, Lochgelly, April 1919.
Roberts, Alexander, Lochgelly, April 1919.
Raffle, William, Lochore, September 1919.
Reith, William, Crosshill, September 1919.
Rolland, Robert B., Lochgelly, September 1919.
Rolland, William, Burntisland, October 1919.
Radar, James H., Lochgelly, October 1919.
Reid, George D., Lochgelly, October 1919.
Ritchie, Thomas, Lochgelly, November 1919.
Ross, Frank R., Lumphinnans, November 1919.
Reid, Peter W., Cowdenbeath, November 1919.
Richardson, Robert G., Lochgelly, November 1919.
Rowan, Thomas, Lochgelly, November 1919.
Rennie, James, Lochgelly, November 1919.
Reid, James F., Lochgelly, April 1920.
Ramsay, George C., Lochgelly, January 1921.
Ross, Alexander D., Lochgelly, September 1921.
Rae, William, Glencraig, December 1927.
Ross, David, Lochgelly, February 1929.
Reid, John L., Lochgelly, January 1930.

Stenhouse, James, Cowdenbeath September 1859.
Suttie, Alexander, Lochgelly, November 1858.
Steedman, James, Lochgelly, January 1860.
Stewart, John, Cowdenbeath, December 1860.
Strachan, James, Kelty, January 1861.
Smith, James, Lochgelly, June 1862.
Stewart, Robert, Cowdenbeath, December 1864.
Stewart, William, Lochgelly, October 1866.
Shepherd, William, Giffertown, April 1869.
Schoolbraid, Henry, Lochgelly, March 1872.
Speedie, Andrew, Cowdenbeath, December 1873.
Spence, Robert, Kelty, December 1873.
Stewart, John, Lochgelly, December 1873.
Stein, Robert, Cowdenbeath, February 1874.
Sharp, William, Kingseat, May 1874.
Stein, Angus, Cowdenbeath, August 1884.
Swan, George, Lochgelly, November 1884.
Speed, Andrew, Cowdenbeath, December 1884.
Syme, George, Lochgelly, June 1885.
Stein, Thomas, Cowdenbeath, September 1889.
Stein, James, Cowdenbeath, April 1890.
Stein, David, Cowdenbeath, May 1890.
Simpson, John, Lochgelly, August 1890.
Splitt, Alexander, Lochgelly, August 1890.
Sturrock, David, Cowdenbeath, December 1890.
Swinley, John, Kelty, August, 1891.
Sharp, William, Lochgelly, March 1892.
Speed, John, Cowdenbeath, April 1892.
Skeggs, Arthur E., Lochgelly, August 1892.
Shaw, John, Kelty, August 1892.
Strachan, James, Crosshill, August 1892.
Syme, Mungo, Lochgelly, August 1892.
Swan, James, Lochgelly, September 1892.

Swan, David, Lochgelly, September 1892.
Smith, Thomas, Lochgelly, January 1894.
Smellie, William, Lochgelly, April 1894.
Stevenson, William, Kelty, December 1897.
Stevenson, Alexander, Kelty, December 1897.
Small, Robert, Lochgelly, September 1898.
Sinclair, William, Lochgelly, June 1900.
Smith, David, Lochgelly, June 1900.
Shaw, William, Lumphinnans, August 1900.
Stuart, Henry, Lochgelly, October 1900.
Stewart, Archibald W., Lumphinnans,
October 1900.
Spowart, Joseph, Bowhill, December 1900.
Scott, James, Lochgelly, March 1901.
Scott, Robert, Lochgelly, March 1901.
Suttie, Robert, Lochgelly, March 1901.
Scott, Andrew, Lochgelly, March 1901.
Stark, Thomas, Ballingry, March 1901.
Smart, James, Lochgelly, May 1901.
Sinclair, George, Cardenden, February 1902.
Simpson, Andrew, Bowhill, August 1902.
Sutherland, Robert, Glencraig, August 1902.
Scott, Andrew, Cardenden, October 1902.
Smart, John, Lochgelly, April 1903.
Shaw, Hugh, Lumphinnans, August 1903.
Shaw, George, Lochgelly, August 1903.
Seath, Andrew, Lochgelly, January 1904.
Steven, Alexander, Lochgelly, April 1904.
Smart, William, Lochgelly, April 1905.
Sharp, Hugh, Lochgelly, January 1906.
Stewart, William, Lochgelly, February 1906.
Smart, George, Lochgelly, January 1907.
Simpson, Robert P., Lochgelly, May 1907.
Spence, Andrew, Cardenden, September 1907.
Steele, George L., Lochgelly, October 1907.
Smith, Robert, Lochgelly, November 1907.
Spence, Peter, Lochgelly, December 1907.
Spence, Alex. (Richmond Place),
Lochgelly, December 1907.
Spence, Alexander (Landale Street)
Lochgelly, December 1907.
Steele, Robert (Whitton Place), Lochgelly,
January 1908.
Suttie, Robert, Lochgelly, January 1908.
Strang, William, Bowhill, March 1908.
Suttie, Harry Penman, Lochgelly, May 1908.
Splitt, James, Lochgelly, August 1908.
Smith, John, North Glencraig, Lochgelly,
August 1908.
Skinner, David, Dundonald, September 1908.
Spence, James (White Street), Lochgelly,
October 1908.
Splitt, John, Lochgelly, December 1908.
Simpson, Thomas, Lochgelly, January 1909.
Swan, Thomas, Cardenden, September 1909.
Sharp, Alex. McLean, Lochgelly, November 1909.
Scott, James, Lochore, November 1909.
Sinclair, Peter Stewart, Lochgelly, February 1910.
Stahly, Charles, Lochgelly, March 1910.

Scott, Robert, Glencraig, March 1910.
Swan, Michael, Lochgelly, April 1910.
Stewart, John, Lochgelly, April 1911.
Sievwright, Colin, Lochore, April 1911.
Sharp, Andrew, Cowdenbeath, October 1910.
Smith, James, Lochgelly, October 1911.
Stuart, James, N. Glencraig, October 1911.
Stuart, Andrew, Crosshill, October 1911.
Sinclair, Fraser McEwan, Crosshill, March 1912.
Syme, Campbell, Lochgelly, April 1912.
Spence, James (North Street) Lochgelly September
1912.
Sinclair, Thomas, Lochgelly, October 1912.
Scott, Charles B., Cardenden, December 1912.
Simpson, Robert, Lochgelly, December 1912.
Sneddon, Walter, Lochgelly, January 1913.
Stewart, Alexander, Lochgelly, April 1913.
Swan, James, Lochgelly, April 1913.
Simpson, Andrew W., Lochgelly, April 1913.
Spence, Andrew, Lochgelly, September 1913.
Splitt, Thomas, Lochgelly, September 1913.
Stuart, Charles, Lochgelly, October 1913.
Swan, James, Lochgelly, October 1913.
Swan, George Jun., Lochgelly, October 1913.
Stuart, John M., Lochore, October 1913.
Salmond, James, N. Glencraig, October 1913.
Stewart, John, Lochgelly, October 1913.
Suttie, James, Lochgelly, October 1913.
Simpson, John, Lumphinnans, October 1913.
Storrar, David, Lochore, October 1913.
Seath, Andrew, Cardenden, October 1913.
Shaw, Robert D., Lochgelly, October 1913.
Spence, Robert, Cowdenbeath, October 1913.
Swan, George, Lochgelly, October 1913.
Spence, William, Lochgelly, January 1914.
Suttie, William, Lochgelly, January 1914.
Suttie, Charles, Lochgelly, March 1914.
Salmond, James, N. Glencraig, April 1914.
Simpson, George A.B., Lochgelly, April 1914.
Spence, George, Lochgelly, September 1914.
Swan, John, Lochore, April 1916.
Stewart, William McB., N. Glencraig,
December 1916.
Stirling, Robert, N. Glencraig, January 1917.
Syme, George, Lochgelly, January 1917.
Stiven, Thomas T., Lochgelly, March 1917.
Small, Joseph J., Lochgelly, March 1917.
Smith, William, Lumphinnans, May 1917.
Stewart, William C., N. Glencraig, March 1917.
Stewart, George, N. Glencraig, March 1917.
Stewart, John C., N. Glencraig, October 1917.
Simpson, John, Lochgelly, January 1918.
Stewart, Martin R., Glencraig, February 1918.
Swan, Andrew S., Lochgelly, February 1918.
Sneddon, John, Cowdenbeath, April 1918.
Steel, James, Lochgelly, May 1918.
Stewart, Andrew, Lochgelly, October 1918.
Stewart, George, N. Glencraig, November 1918.
Strachan, Andrew, Lochgelly, November 1918.

Simpson, William, Lumphinnans, January 1919.
Swan, David, Lochgelly, January 1919.
Smith, Andrew, Lochgelly, February 1919.
Shand, James, Lochgelly, February 1919.
Shaw, William, Lochgelly, February 1919.
Steele, John, S. Glencraig, March 1919.
Stiven, William, Lochgelly, March 1919.
Simpson, George G., Lochore, March 1919.
Suttie, Alexander, Lochgelly, March 1919.
Smith, James, Lochgelly, April 1919.
Simpson, Andrew, Lochgelly, April 1919.
Simpson, David, Cowdenbeath, April 1919.
Stalker, Andrew, Glencraig, April 1919.
Sharp, William, Lochgelly, May 1919.
Smith, George, Lochgelly, May 1919.
Simpson, John, Lochgelly, September 1919.
Swan, George, Lochgelly, September 1919.
Stuart, Charles E., Lochgelly, September 1919.
Shaw, George, Lochgelly, September 1919.
Simpson, Robert, Lochgelly, September 1919.
Strang, Thomas, Lochgelly, September 1919.
Straiton, Thomas, Lochgelly, October 1919.
Sibbald, George K., Cowdenbeath, October 1919.
Seath, John, Lochgelly, November 1919,
Sinclair, James, Lochgelly, November 1919.
Suttie, Alexander, Lochgelly, November 1919
Scott, Robert, Lochgelly, November 1919.
Shand, Robert, Lochgelly, December 1919.
Stewart, Christopher C., Lochgelly, March 1920.
Scott, John, Auchtertool, March 1920.
Seath, John, Auchtertool, March 1920.
Simpson, George, Fareham, April 1920,.
Spence, George, Lochgelly, February 1921.
Smith, Lawrence, Lochgelly, November 1921.
Suttie, Thomas, Blackburn, February, 1922.
Smellie, William, Lochgelly, February 1922.
Skinner, Andrew, Cowdenbeath, April 1922.
Sharpe, Archibald, Lochgelly, April 1922.
Splitt, David P., Lochgelly, November 1922.
Splitt, William, Lochgelly, February 1923.
Steele, George Jun., Lochgelly, February 1923.
Sinclair, John, Lochgelly, February 1923,
Shepherd, William A., Cardenden, April 1923.
Scott, Jesse, Port Edgar, May 1923.
Saunders, Herbert R.E., Greenwich, May 1923.
Steedman, Thomas R., Lochgelly, October 1923.
Smith, Hugh S., Cowdenbeath, October 1923,
Shearer, John, Cardenden, January 1924.
Speed, John M., Lochgelly, January 1924.
Shearer, Harry, Lochgelly, November 1924.
Speed, William, Lochgelly, April 1925.
Speed, Harold, Lochgelly, April 1925.
Skinner, Thomas G., Lochgelly, March 1925.
Stevenson, Robert, Cowdenbeath, May 1926.
Straiton, George, Lochgelly, October 1927.
Splitt, Thomas W., Lochgelly, March 1929.
Steele, James W., Lochgelly, April 1929.
Sloss, William, Lochgelly, October 1929.

Smith, A McD., Cardenden, December 1929.
Sinclair, Robert B., Lochgelly, March 1930.
Scott, Andrew, Cowdenbeath, October 1931.

Tullis, James, Lochgelly, July 1874.
Todd, Robert, Cowdenbeath, October 1876.
Thomson, David, Cowdenbeath, August 1891.
Thomson, James, Lochgelly, April 1893.
Thom, Alexander, Auchtertool, April 1895.
Thomson, John, Lochgelly, October 1897.
Thomson, James, Lochgelly, March 1904.
Torrance, Abraham, Lochgelly, September 1906.
Thomson, Alexander, Dunfermline, May 1908.
Taughnan, William, Lochgelly, May 1908.
Taylor, Thomas, Bowhill, May 1908.
Taylor, Thomas, Lochgelly, December 1908.
Taylor, Archibald, Glencraig, January 1910.
Thomson, William, Lochgelly, November 1910.
Thomson, George, Glencraig, April 1911.
Thomson, David A., Lochgelly, September 1912.
Thomson, James W., Lochore, March 1913.
Thorburn, Duncan, Lumphinnans, March 1913.
Thomson, John, Lochore, April 1913.
Thomson, Robert, Lochgelly, May 1913.
Thomson, Alexander, Lochgelly, December 1913.
Taylor, John, Ballingry, February 1914.
Torrance, Robert, Lochgelly, March 1914.
Turner, James, Lochgelly, September 1914.
Taylor, Peter, Lochgelly, September 1914.
Torrance, Robert, Lochgelly, October 1917.
Taylor, Peter, Lochgelly, November 1917.
Torrance, Andrew, Sheffield, October 1918.
Thomson, John M., Lochgelly, January 1919.
Turner, James, Lochore, February 1919.
Trail, William, Lochgelly, May 1919.
Thomson, John W., Lochore, September 1919.
Thomson, George W., Lochgelly, September 1919.
Turner, James, Lochgelly, September 1919.
Thomson, Joseph J., Lochgelly, November 1919.
Taylor, David H., Lochgelly, December 1919.
Torrance, Hugh, Edinburgh, January 1921.
Thomson, Thomas B., Lochgelly, April 1921.
Thomson, Andrew, Lochgelly, January 1925.
Thomson, James B., Lochgelly, March 1927.
Thomson, Alexander B., Lochgelly, March 1927.
Thomson, Alexander McK., Lochgelly, April 1931.

Vail, John, Barrow-in-Furness, May 1893.
Vail, Thomas, Lochgelly, June 1897.
Vail, Peter, Lochgelly, May 1908.
Vail, Michael, Lochgelly, February 1909.
Vannan, James, Glencraig, November 1916.

Whyte, Joseph, Cowdenbeath, April 1859.
Wilson, Robert, Lumphinnans, May 1859.
Watson, William, Edinburgh, January 1862.
White, George, Cowdenbeath, February, 1864.
Williamson, Alexander, Crossgates, July 1866.
Williamson, Peter, Lochgelly, February 1867.

Wilson, David, Donibristle. September 1867.
Wilson, Robert, Cowdenbeath, January 1871.
Wallace, Alexander, Cowdenbeath, November 1873.
Wilson, David, Lochgelly, December 1873.
Watson, James C., Lochgelly, March, 1875.
Welsh, Robert, Lochgelly, January 1878.
Wishart, Thomas, Bristol, August 1879.
Wilson, Robert, Lochgelly, February 1881.
Wildridge, Hugh, Lochgelly, January 1883.
Wilson, James, Lochgelly, May 1886.
Wright, William, Lochgelly, October 1886.
Wilson, Robert, Lochgelly, April 1890.
Wilson, David, Lochgelly, April 1891.
Watson, David, Cowdenbeath, April 1892.
Wildridge, James, Lochgelly, June 1892.
Westwater, Henry, Lochgelly, August 1892.
Wildridge, Peter, Kinross, June 1895.
Westwater, Alexander, Lochgelly, January 1897.
Wilson, James, Lochgelly, February 1897.
Wood, George, Kelty, February, 1897.
Wood, Charles, Lochgelly, April 1897.
Wilkie, Peter F., Lochgelly, July 1900.
Welsh, John, Cardenden, August 1900.
Watson, Alexander, Lochgelly, September 1900.
Whyte, William, Lochgelly, October 1900.
Wildridge, Alexander, Lochgelly, October 1900.
Watson, William, Cowdenbeath, February 1901.
Wood, Robert, Lochgelly, February 1901.
Wanliss, John W. S., Auchterderran, March 1901.
Walker, William, Lochgelly, May 1901.
Walker, Robert, Lochgelly, May 1901.
Wilson, John, Lochgelly, June 1901.
Wilson, William, Lochgelly, February 1902.
Walker, James, Glencraig, May 1902.
Westwater, Matthew, Lochgelly, October 1902.
Wildridge, Thomas, Lochgelly, September 1903.
Wilson, John, Lochgelly, January 1904.
Walkingshaw, William, Lochgelly, March 1904.
Wallace, William M., Cardenden, December 1904.
Williamson, Drummond, Lochgelly, April 1905.
Wilson, David, Lochgelly, June 1906.
Williamson, Finlay, Lochgelly, November 1906.
Wilson, Robert, Lochgelly, January 1907.
Wallace, Robert, Lochgelly, May 1907.
Wallace, Samuel, Cardenden, May 1907.
Wilson, John, Lumphinnans, October 1907.
Williamson, David, N. Glencraig, February 1908.
Wilson, Peter, Lochgelly, February 1908.
Watson, John, Bowhill, March 1908.
Wishart, William, Bowhill, April 1908.
Walker, James, N. Glencraig, May 1908.
Wilson, Charles C., Bowhill, May 1908.
Wilson, Daniel, Lochgelly, May 1908.
Wilson, John, Lochgelly, June 1908.
Wood, William L., Lochgelly, August 1908.
Watson, John, Lochgelly, September 1908.
Walker, Walter M., Lochgelly, December 1908.
Wilson, Alfred, Bowhill, March 1909.
Wilson, John, Lochgelly, April 1909.

Wilson, James, Cowdenbeath, October 1909.
Williamson, John P., Lochgelly, November 1909.
Watson, John, Glencraig, November 1909.
Wilson, James, Lochgelly, February 1910.
Wishart, David, Lochgelly, April 1910.
Wildridge, Thomas, Lochgelly, September 1910.
Wands, Robert, Glencraig, October 1910.
Williamson, James, Lochore, December 1910.
Wilson, Andrew C., Lochgelly, December 1910.
Wilson, William, Lumphinnans, March 1910.
Walkingshaw, Adam, Glencraig, September 1911.
Webster, Henry, Lochgelly, November 1911.
Watson, John, N. Glencraig, March 1912.
Wilson, William, D., Dunfermline, September 1912.
Wilson, John, Lochgelly, September 1912.
Whyte, Andrew D., Cowdenbeath, September 1912.
Whyte, Charles, Saline, February 1913.
Wilson, James, Lochgelly, May 1913.
Wright, Crawford, Lochgelly, October 1913.
Webster, David, Lochgelly, October 1913.
Watson, Thomas, Lochgelly, December 1913.
Wallace, Samuel, Lochgelly, January 1914.
Wood, James R., Glencraig, March 1914.
Wilson, Andrew, Lochgelly, April 1914.
Wilson, James, Donibristle, September 1914.
Wilson, Thomas, Lochgelly, March 1915.
Williamson, William C., N. Glencraig, March 1915.
Williamson, James, Lochgelly, December 1915.
White, James B., Lochgelly, January 1916.
Wilson, Robert, N. Glencraig, October 1916.
Watson, James, N. Glencraig, January 1917.
Wright, George E., Lochgelly, January 1917.
Wilkie, David, Lochgelly, May 1917.
Watson, James C., Lochgelly, October 1917.
Whyte, Andrew, Lochore, November 1917.
Whyte, David K., Cardenden, November 1917.
Wilson, Robert, Lochgelly, May 1918.
Whyte, James B., Lochgelly, July 1918.
Whiteford, William, Lochgelly, January 1919.
Whyte, James, Saline, January 1919.
Wilson, James, Lochgelly, February 1919.
Whyte, John, Saline, March 1919.
Walkingshaw, Henry R., Lochgelly, April 1919.
Wallace, James, Lochgelly, September 1919.
Wallace, Robert, Cowdenbeath, September 1919.
Wright, Crawford, Lochgelly, September 1919.
Whyte, William, S. Glencraig, November 1919.
Whyte, William, Lochgelly, November 1919.
Wilson, Robert, Lochgelly, November 1919.
Walker, David, Lochgelly, November 1919.
Wilson, James, Lochgelly, November 1919.
Walkingshaw, James, Jun., Thornton, November 1919.
Wyse, Henry, Lochgelly, November 1919.
Walker, William, Lochgelly, November 1919.
Walace, John T., Lochgelly, November 1919.
Watters, Richard, Lochgelly, February 1920.
Whyte, Robert, S. Glencraig, February 1920.
Wilson, John G., Lochgelly, April 1920.

Wilson, Robert McM., Lochgelly, April 1920.
Wilson, David L., Carnock, April 1920.
Wildridge, Alexander W., Cowdenbeath, April 1920.
Wright, James, Lochore, November 1920.
Watson, John, Lochgelly, February 1921.
Walker, Ninian, Lochgelly, October 1921.
Wilson, John M., Lochgelly, February 1922.
Wilson, Robert, Jun., Cardenden, January 1923.
Wickens, Arthur, Beckenham, October 1923.
Wilson, William, Cardenden, October 1923.
Welch, Andrew B., Lochgelly, February 1924.
Webster, James D., Glencraig, February 1925.
Wilson, David, Lochgelly, February 1925.
Wallace, Thomas, Cardenden, January 1926.
Wilson, Andrew E., Lochgelly, November 1926.
Wilson, Joseph S., Lochgelly, November 1926.
Whitehead, Robert S., Lochgelly, November 1927.
Wilson, Thomas, Cardenden, October 1927.
Wilson, John Jun., Lochgelly, October 1927.
Westwater, John, Lochgelly, October 1927.
Wilson, James, Lochgelly, December 1927.
White, Archibald M., Lochgelly, October 1929.
Wilson, William, Lochgelly, December 1929.
Whyte, William, Lochgelly, September 1920.

Younger, Thomas, Cardenden, December 1872.
Young, Henry, Cowdenbeath, October 1888.
Young, George, Ballingry, November 1903.
Young, David C., Lumphinnans, March 1919.
Young, William, Lochgelly, October 1981.
Younger, Thomas, Lochgelly, October 1918.
Young, David M., Lochgelly, May 1919.
Young, George J. T., Lochgelly, November 1919.

1931 - 1958.
Aitken, Robert, Lochgelly, January 1935.
Adamson, Thomas M., Cardenden, April 1937.
Adamson, David (Affil.), Lochgelly, April 1937.
Archibald, John, Lochgelly, September 1937.
Armstrong, James, Crosshill, March 1938.
Armstrong, Robert H., Lochgelly, March 1938.
Anderson, Thomas O., Cardenden, March 1939.
Alexander, Thomas, Lochgelly, December 1941.
Adams, Joseph, Lochgelly, April 1942.
Anderson, David B., Lochgelly, June 1942.
Anderson, Alexander, Lochgelly, March 1944.
Adamson, Andrew, Lochgelly, October 1944.
Adam, Andrew, Kinghorn, September 1945.
Alexander, Alexander, Lochgelly, December 1945.
Alexander, Hugh, Lochgelly, April 1946.
Anderson, George, Glencraig, February, 1947.
Archibald, Walter, Lochgelly, October 1947.
Allan, Thomas A.W.G., Lochgelly, October 1949.
Aitken, Robert, Lochgelly, October 1950.
Adam, John, Lochgelly, September 1951.
Allan, David, Forgandenny, April 1952.
Abbot, Richard, Lochgelly, December 1952.

Adam, William, Lochgelly, September 1954.
Archibald, Alex., Lochgelly, November 1954.
Adam, William, Lochgelly, May 1956.
Anderson, Clark, Cowdenbeath, January 1958.
Anderson, Walter, Ballingry, January 1958.

Brown, George G., Kent, October 1931.
Burden, Alexander B., Lochgelly, April 1932.
Blyth, William, Lochgelly, December 1935.
Baxter, Andrew, Lochgelly, September 1936.
Bonthrone, David B. (Affil.), Lochgelly, March 1937.
Bell, James, Cairneyhill, November 1937.
Bremner, George, Lochgelly, November 1938.
Black, John, Lochgelly, November 1939.
Brown, Thomas, Lochgelly, October 1940.
Brown, Andrew, Lochgelly, April 1941.
Barrie, William S., Lochgelly, April 1941.
Beckett, Martin, Lochgelly, September 1941.
Blair, Alexander, London, October 1941.
Barclay, W.C., Lochgelly, March 1942.
Black, Stanley, Lochgelly, June 1942.
Brunton, James K. A., Lochgelly, September 1942.
Black, William, Lochgelly, December 1942.
Beckett, Clark, Lochgelly, March 1943.
Brown, John K., Lochgelly, June 1943.
Beveridge, David, Lumphinnans, September 1943.
Bell, James, Glencraig, October 1943.
Blair, Peter, Lochgelly, December 1943.
Bathgate, John, Lochgelly, May 1944.
Bird, James, Lochgelly, March 1944.
Banks, James G., Lochgelly, March 1945.
Barrie, William, Lochgelly, April 1945.
Brown, John, Lochgelly, March 1946.
Black, James, Cowdenbeath, September 1946.
Beech, James, Lochgelly, September 1946.
Bell, David, Lochgelly, October 1946.
Bathgate, William, Glencraig, February 1947.
Barrie, John, Lochgelly, April 1947.
Bowman, James, Lochgelly, January 1948.
Blamey, Thomas, Lochgelly, March 1950.
Blane, David, Lochgelly, September 1950.
Brunton, John, Lochgelly, September 1950.
Bremner, John B., Lochgelly, October 1951.
Brodie, J. G., Cowdenbeath, November 1951.
Brown, Andrew, Lochgelly, November 1952.
Baxter, Arthur, Lochgelly, December 1952.
Brown, Robert, Lochgelly, December 1952.
Bauld, Robert, Ballingry, October 1953.
Bauld, James, Glencraig, October 1953.
Barnes, Robert, Lumphinnans, February 1954.
Burden, James L., Lochgelly, March 1954.
Black, Alexander, Cowdenbeath, December 1954.
Bennett, John, Lochgelly, February 1955.
Brown, David, Lochgelly, November 1955.
Boden, William, Lochgelly, May 1956.
Bonnar, James, Lochgelly, October 1956.
Beveridge, Archibald, Lumphinnans, December 1956.

Bowman, James, Lochgelly, March 1957.
Brown, John Bone, Lochgelly, January 1958.

Clark, Andrew M., Lochgelly, April 1930.
Chalmers, John M., Lochgelly, April 1930.
Crowe, James, Lochgelly, March 1935.
Crawford, Robert, Lochgelly, October 1935.
Clark, Robert, Lochgelly, March 1937.
Clark, David, Lochgelly, November 1937.
Curran, William J., Lochgelly, March 1938.
Curran, James A. M., Lochgelly, March 1938.
Clark, William, Lochgelly, May 1938.
Crawford, John, Lochgelly, March 1939.
Campbell, James, Lochgelly, April 1941.
Crichton, John, Lochgelly, December 1942.
Cook, James, Lochgelly, March 1944.
Clark, John, Lochgelly, April 1944.
Cairns, Robert S., Lochgelly, October 1944.
Cook, Angus H., Lochgelly, November 1944.
Cook, William, Lochgelly, November 1944.
Chalmers, William, Lochgelly, April 1945.
Cathay, John, Milnathort, April 1945.
Chalmers, Peter, Cardenden, December 1945.
Coad, R. E., Colchester, January 1946.
Carlaw, Matthew D. (Affil.), Lochgelly,
February 1946.
Conway, James, Glencraig, February 1947.
Cuthbert, John, Lochgelly, March 1947.
Cook, Robert, Glencraig, October 1947.
Cook, George, Lochgelly, January 1948.
Cairns, David, Lochgelly, September 1948.
Clelland, James, Lochgelly, October 1948.
Clark, Hugh, Lochgelly, September 1949.
Clark, Robert, Lochgelly, October 1950.
Cook, Thomas, W., St Albans, (Herts)
December 1951.
Clark, Andrew (Hall Lane), Lochgelly,
January 1952.
Clark, Andrew (Russell Street), Lochgelly,
January 1952.
Clark, James, Lochgelly, October 1952.
Courts, John, Lochgelly, March 1953.
Clark, George, Cowdenbeath, March 1955.
Charleston, James, Lochgelly, November 1955.
Craigie, Adam, Crosshill, February 1956.
Clark, Richard, Lochgelly, January 1957.
Cree, Thomas, Lochgelly, February 1957.
Clark, Charles, Ballingry, February 1957.
Clark, Thomas, Lochgelly, September 1957.
Cunningham, Robert, Lochgelly, October 1957.
Carswell, David, Lochgelly, November 1957.
Campbell, Andrew, Lochgelly, January 1958.
Carstairs, James, Lochgelly, March 1958.

Dalziel, William R., Edinburgh, April 1930.
Dryburgh, Archibald, Lumphinnans, December
1935.
Dalrymple, John, Lochgelly, January 1937.
Dewar, David, Lochgelly, November 1937.

Danskin, John, Lochgelly, November 1937.
Denew, Douglas, Lochgelly, February 1939.
Donald, Thomas, Kinglassie, November 1939.
Dawson, Andrew, Lochgelly, September 1941.
Daniel, M. J., Cornwall, September 1941.
Dow, John, Lochgelly, September 1941.
Dewar, William W., Lochgelly, October 1941.
Dick, Andrew, Cowdenbeath, January 1942.
Dawson, Joseph, Cowdenbeath, March 1943.
Dewar, Andrew R., Lochgelly, April 1940.
Douglas, James McPherson, Lochgelly, March 1943.
Deas, Joseph P., Lumphinnans, December 1943.
Dow, Robert B., Cardenden, December 1943.
Dewar, Allan, Dunfermline, March 1944.
Davidson, George, Lochgelly, December 1944.
Davidson, Adam, Lochgelly, February 1945.
Davidson, Mackenzie, Lochgelly, September 1945.
Dunsmuir, Peter, Lochgelly, October 1945.
Duncan, Alex., Kinglassie, October 1945.
Deas, Andrew, Lochgelly, April 1946.
Deas, William, Lochgelly, April 1946.
Drylie, William, Lochgelly, October 1946.
Devlin, William, Lochgelly, January 1948.
Dickson, William, Lochgelly, April 1948.
Davidson, Alexander, Lochgelly, April 1949.
Davie, Walter, Lochgelly, September 1949.
Dixon, D.E. I., Lochgelly, September 1949.
Drysdale, John, Cowdenbeath, March 1951.
Dich, James, Lochgelly, March 1951.
Dryburgh, John, Lochgelly, November 1952.
Durham, William, Lochgelly, March 1953.
Duncan, George, Cardenden, March 1953.
Dickson, George A., Lochgelly, December 1953.
Durham, Adam, Kinglassie, September 1955.
Dickie, Matthew (Affil.), Lochgelly,
November 1955.
Dewar, James, Cowdenbeath, November 1955.
Dick, Robert S., Lochgelly, January 1956.
Dick, George W., Lochgelly, January 1956.
Duncan, William, Cowdenbeath, May 1956.

English, Cecil, Lochgelly, January 1935.
Ewing, Thomas B., Lochgelly, March 1937.
Everingham, Lochore, November 1937.
Ellis, William, Lochgelly, March 1940.
Evans, Andrew S., Lochgelly, October 1944.
Ednie, James, Lochgelly, April 1945.
Eadie, John S., Milnathort, April 1945.
Erskine, George, Lochgelly, January 1950.
Evans, Scott, Lochgelly, February 1956.

Finnie, Martin, Lochgelly, December 1931.
Frisken, Peter, Lochgelly, November 1938.
Fortune, William, Lochgelly, June 1941.
Fraser, George D., Lochgelly, September 1941.
Findlay, George, Lochgelly, September 1942.
Findlay, Harry W., Dunfermline, November 1942.
Forrester, Harry, Lochgelly, September 1943.
Fleming, Ebenezer, Lochgelly, October 1943.

Ferguson, Alex., Lochgelly, October 1943.
Feeley, John, Glencraig, October 1944.
Forrester, Peter, Crossgates, November 1944.
Finnie, John A., Lochgelly, April 1945.
Forrester, James, Lochgelly, September 1945.
Forrest, George, Lochgelly, January 1946.
Finnie, William C., Glencraig, September 1946.
Fenton, John, Crosshill, January 1948.
Feeley, Fred W., Glencraig, September 1948.
Forrest, George, Lochgelly, October 1948.
Fenton, James, Lochore, March 1949.
Farrelly, James, Lochgelly, March 1951.
Ford, George, Glencraig, March 1953.
Frise, Cyril M., Lochgelly, September 1953.
Fleming, Walter, Cardenden, March 1955.
Fraser, Andrew, Lochgelly, March 1955.
Fotheringham, James, Cowdenbeath, November 1955.
Fitchet, Alexander, Lochgelly, March 1956.
Fergus, James, Lochgelly, February 1956.
Fleming, Harry, Cowdenbeath, January 1957.

Gibson, William, Lochgelly, October 1932.
Gilmour, John, Lochore, January 1933.
Glass, Samuel, Cowdenbeath, January 1937.
Guy, David, Lochgelly, March 1937.
Glass, Alfred McBain, Lochgelly, September 1937.
Gordon, John, Lochgelly, March 1938.
Gray, William, Lochgelly, January 1938.
Goodall, Henry, Lochgelly, November 1938.
Grosvenor, W.H., Lochgelly, January 1939.
Gilmour, Robert G., Lochgelly, January 1939.
Gibb, John, Glencraig, October 1940.
Gibb, Robert, Glencraig, October 1940.
Gordon, E. C., Dunfermline, April 1941.
Gibb, Alex., Lochgelly, April 1943.
Gardner, Hutton, Cowdenbeath, October 1944.
Goodall, Robert, Lochgelly, November 1944.
Grant, Peter, Lochgelly, December 1944.
Grubb, David, Lochgelly, December 1944.
Geddes, Walter, Lochgelly, February 1945.
Gray, Robert M., Lochgelly, April 1945.
Gourdie, Alex., Lochgelly, March 1946.
Gavin, John, Lochgelly, October 1946.
Gardyne, Alex. L., Lochgelly, December 1949.
Gardner, Hutton, Lochgelly, December 1949.
Gray, G. R. L. Lochgelly, February 1950.
Gibson, Alexander, Lochgelly, November 1951.
Gilbert, Chris., Cowdenbeath, November 1951.
Guthrie, Alex. W., Cowdenbeath, November 1951.
Gray, Malcolm, Lochgelly, April 1952.
Green, William, Lochgelly, September 1954.
Gow, Robert F., Lochgelly, October 1954.
Graham, Robert, Lochgelly, March 1955.
Greenhorn, William, Lochgelly, February 1956.
Galbraith, Walter, Lochgelly, January 1957.
Gow, William, Cowdenbeath, March 1957.
Grewar, James, Lochgelly, October 1957.
Graham, W. G., Lochgelly, November 1957.

Graham, Joseph, Lochgelly, March 1958.
Goodall, Andrew, Lochgelly, March 1958.
Gillespie, Andrew, Lochgelly, April 1958.

Henderson, John, Lochgelly, October 1930.
Hunter, Alexander, Lochgelly, October 1932.
Henderson, William J., Glencraig, October 1932.
Hendry, William W., Lochgelly, May 1933.
Henderson, Andrew, Lochgelly, March 1935.
Hamilton, Walter, Lochgelly, November 1937.
Harris, George, Lochgelly, March 1939.
Hetrick, James, Rosyth, November 1940.
Howard, Albert, Rosyth, January 1941.
Hutton, Ralph P., Glencraig, March 1941.
Hunter, James M., Lochgelly, October 1942.
Honeyman, Andrew, Lochgelly, October 1942.
Hamilton, Alexander, Bowhill, February 1943.
Hopton, James B., Kinglassie, September 1943.
Herd, James, Lochgelly, September 1943.
Harris, William R., Glencraig, December 1943.
Hamilton, Thomas, Kinglassie, December 1943.
Hunter, George, Lochgelly, March 1944.
Hunter, James B., Cardenden, March 1944.
Honeyman, David, Cowdenbeath, October 1944.
Hunter, George S., Cowdenbeath, October 1944.
Haxton, Robert, Rugby, November 1944.
Harrieson, William, Lochgelly, February 1945.
Hamilton, William, Lochgelly, February 1945.
Hynd, James, Cardenden, September 1945.
Henderson, Edward, Lochgelly, October 1945.
Harrower, Joseph, Lochgelly, January 1946.
Henderson, William, Kirkcaldy, March 1946.
Hunter, Peter, Lochgelly, September 1946.
Hawthorn, William, Lochgelly, October 1946.
Henderson, William H., Glasgow, April 1947.
Henderson, William, Lochgelly, September 1947.
Honeyman, Hugh Ross, Lochgelly, October 1950.
Hutton, David, Lochgelly, January 1952.
Hodge, Archibald, Lochgelly, February 1953.
Harrower, Hugh, Lochgelly, February 1954.
Harrower, James, Lochgelly, February 1954.
Harrison, Thomas, Bowhill, February 1954.
Hunter, Robert, Lumphinnans, November 1954.
Hogan, Daniel S., Cardenden, September 1955.
Hughes, Andrew, Lochgelly, October 1956.
Harrower, James, Lochgelly, March 1957.
Heigh, George, Lochgelly, March 1957.
Harrower, Joseph, Ballingry, October 1957.

Izatt, Alexander (Affil.), Rosyth, April 1937.
Inch, Andrew, Lochgelly, April 1937.
Izatt, Robert, Glencraig, November 1938.
Irvine, William, Lochgelly, March 1955.

Johnston, James H., Kelty, September 1937.
Jenkins, William C., Dunfermline, January 1938.
Johnstone, John, Lochgelly, October 1939.
Jones, J.R., Rosyth, April 1940.
Johnstone, Alexander, Lochgelly, February 1941.

Jackson, Robert P., Lochgelly, September 1941.
Jackson, Walter S., Lochgelly, September 1941.
Johnston, George, Lochore, November 1942.
Johnstone, William M., Lochore, December 1943.
Johnstone, Peter T., Lochgelly, December 1943.
Johnstone, D., Cardenden, October 1944.
Johnstone, John, Lochgelly, March 1945.
James, Leslie K., Lochgelly, January 1947.
Jackson, Henry F., Lochgelly, October 1948.
Johnstone, William, Lochgelly, December 1950.
Jackson, Thomas H., Lochgelly, October 1959.
Johnstone, John, Cowdenbeath, February 1955.
Jack, Alexander, Lochgelly, October 1955.
Johnstone, James, Lochgelly, May 1956.
Johnstone, Robert, Lochgelly, May 1956.
Jeffrey, Archibald, Lochgelly, October 1956.
Johnstone, Andrew M., Lochgelly, December 1957.
Johnstone, John I., Lochgelly, December 1957.

Kerron, James Mc., Lochgelly, April 1930.
Kerr, Alexander, Lochgelly, December 1930.
Kirk, Thomas, Lochgelly, April 1931.
Kinlay, John K., Lochgelly, October 1930.
Kirk, William D., Cardenden, October 1935.
Keay, John, Lochgelly, April 1940.
King, Robert, Rosyth, April 1940.
Kean, William T., Cowdenbeath, February 1941.
Kerr, Peter, Lochgelly, February 1941.
King, James, Kirkcaldy, January 1942.
Kirkland, William, Dunfermline, November 1942.
Kinnell, James C.R., Cardenden, April 1942.
Kerr, James L., Lochgelly, February 1943.
Kirk, David, Lochgelly, October 1944.
Kent, Robert W., Glencraig, October 1944.
Kirk, James, Glencraig, April 1945.
Kidd, George, Buckhaven, September 1945.
King, William, Dunfermline, January 1946.
Kippen, James, Lochgelly, December 1945.
Kinnel, Alexander, Cardenden, October 1946.
Kirk, Robert P., Lochgelly, January, 1947.
Kirk, James K., Lochgelly, January 1947.
Kerr, David, Lochgelly, September 1947.
Keay, Alex., Lochgelly, September 1947.
Kinlay, Peter W., Lochgelly, December 1947.
Kemp, Ronald, Dunfermline, January 1951.
Kelly, James, Lochgelly, September 1951.
Kippen, John, Lochgelly, February 1952.
Kinnear, Andrew, Lochgelly, April 1952.
Kent, Richard, Lochgelly, October 1952.
Kerr, John J., Lochgelly, February 1953.
Kinnell, James, Cardenden, February 1953.
Keddie, Robert A., Lochgelly, October 1953.
Kippen, Thomas, Lochgelly, March 1954.
Keay, James L., Lochgelly, March 1954.
Kirkwood, Alex., Cardenden, September 1955.
Kerr, James, Cardenden, September 1955.
Kerr, Robert, Lochgelly, October 1955.
Keddie, Samuel, Lochgelly, January 1957.
Kennedy, Frank, Lumphinnans, September 1957.

Kinnell, James, Lochgelly, October 1957.
Keddie, John, Lochgelly, March 1958.

Laing, James, Lochgelly, January 1931.
Lawson, Robert B., Lochgelly, December 1935.
Lyall, David R., Lochgelly, November 1936.
Leitch, John A., Lochgelly, November 1936.
Lind, Allan, Lochgelly, April 1937.
Lawson, Robert, Lochgelly, April 1937.
Lyle, John, Lochgelly, February 1938.
Lind, Harry, Lochgelly, March 1938.
Logan, David R., Lochgelly, May 1938.
Laidman, Richard, Kirkcaldy, November 1942.
Lamb, John E., Cowdenbeath, April 1943.
Lawson, Alexander S., Lochgelly, December 1943.
Lawson, Robert S., Lochgelly, December 1943.
Lamond, James, Glencraig, January 1944.
Leslie, John, Lochgelly, December 1944.
Lister, Thomas, Lochgelly, March 1945.
Low, James, Lochgelly, April 1945.
Livingstone, James, Glasgow, September 1945.
Lambert, Alex., Glencraig, February 1947.
Lister, James, Perth, October 1947.
Lindsay, George, Dunfermline, December 1947.
Lorimer, Alex., Lochgelly, March 1948.
Lumsden, William, Lochgelly, December 1948.
Lockhart, George (Affil.), Lochgelly,
September 1949.
Lamond, David, Lochgelly, February 1950.
Lindsay, John D., Perth, December 1951.
Livingstone, Malcolm, Lochgelly, October 1954.
Laird, John K., Cardenden, December 1957.

McNeil, Alexander, Lochgelly, January 1931.
Mackay, James, Lochgelly, November 1935.
Milne, George B., Dunfermline, November 1935.
McLeod, Charles W., Lochgelly, February 1935.
Mason, George, Lochgelly, January 1937.
McKean, John (Affil.), Lochgelly, April 1937.
McPherson, Neil, Lochgelly, September 1937.
Marshall, John J., Lochgelly, January 1938.
Mackay, Robert, Lochgelly, February 1938.
Miller, William, Lochgelly, February 1938.
Macdonald, William C., St Andrews, January 1938.
McLean, David, Lochgelly, September 1938.
Milne, William, Lochgelly, September 1938.
Miller, Charles, Lochgelly, September 1938.
Motion, William, Lochgelly, January 1939.
Miller, John E., Cowdenbeath, March 1939.
Melville, Andrew T., Lochgelly, March 1940.
Mason, John B., Lochgelly, September 1940.
Mackie, A.M., Lochore, November 1940.
McKinlay, George, Lochgelly, January 1940.
Mason, Charles, Lochgelly, April 1941.
McKinlay, Robert, Lochgelly, April 1941.
Moffat, John, Lochgelly, March 1941.
Mackinnon, Matthew, Lochgelly, October 1941.
Melville, Alfred, Lochgelly, December 1941.
Millar, Thomas, Lundin Links, January 1942.

Melville, Robert, Cowdenbeath, April 1942.
Melville, Thomas, Cowdenbeath, April 1942.
McGregor, Charles, Crosshill, August 1942.
Mackay, Donald, Lochgelly, September 1942.
Morrison, Andrew, Cowdenbeath, October 1942.
McConnell, Alexander, Lochgelly, October 1942.
McKinlay, James, Lochgelly, October 1942.
Marshall, Thomas, Lochgelly, October 1942.
Martin, Thomas, Lochgelly, November 1942.
McLaren, Alex., Lochgelly, November 1942.
Melville, John, Lumphinnans, December 1942.
McLean, Andrew, Lochgelly, December 1942.
Marnoch, David, Lumphinnans, March 1943.
Marnoch, William, Lochgelly, March 1943.
McVicar, David, Lochgelly, March 1943.
Mathieson, Robert E. S., Glasgow, April 1943.
Milne, Henry T. McKenzie (Affil.),
Lochgelly, September 1943.
Macdougall, Angus (Affil.), Lochgelly,
February, 1944.
McKinlay, George, Lochgelly, March 1944.
McConnell, William, Lochgelly, April 1944.
McGuire, Henry, Cardenden, April 1944.
Muir, Robert, Lochgelly, November 1944.
Millns, Kenneth, Glencraig, December 1944.
McVicar, Charles, Cowdenbeath, April 1944.
Munro, Richard, Lochgelly, December 1944.
Martin, James, Cowdenbeath, February 1945.
McPherson, James, Lumphinnans, April 1945.
McFarlane, John, Cowdenbeath, March 1945.
McPherson, William, Lochgelly, April 1945.
McGuire, James, Lochgelly, December 1945.
McIntosh, John, Lochgelly, October 1945.
McVicar, Thomas, Lochgelly, January 1946.
McCulloch, Colin, Lochgelly, March 1946.
Mitchell, John, Lochgelly, April 1946.
McLean, Thomas, Blackburn (Lancs.), April 1946.
McKinlay, Archibald, Lochgelly, May 1946.
Morrison, James, Chippenham (Wilts.), August 1946.
Murray, Peter, Lochgelly, September 1946.
Mitchell, James, Cowdenbeath, October 1946.
McKinlay, Archibald, St. Andrews, December 1946.
McKinnon, Andrew, Lochgelly, December 1946.
Martin, William, Cowdenbeath, December 1946.
Mollison, James, Lochgelly, January 1947.
Martin, Thomas, Lochgelly, September 1947.
Milne, John, Lochgelly, September 1947.
Melville, Thomas, Cowdenbeath, November 1947.
McPherson, Hugh, Lumphinnans, March 1948.
Marshall, Thomas, Lochgelly, March 1948.
More, David, Kinnesswood, March 1948.
Martin, Charles, South Queensferry, April 1948.
Morrison, Charles P., Cardenden, April 1948.
Mackie, A. D., Edinburgh, September 1948.
McGregor, Robert, Lochgelly, October 1948.
McLay, Alex, Lochgelly, December 1948.
Melville, Charles, Lochgelly, December 1948.
McKay, Andrew, Kinghorn, March 1949.
McKee, Robert, Cowdenbeath, March 1949.

McLelland, Alex., Lochgelly, April 1949.
Mitchell, Charles, Lochgelly, October 1949.
McKay, John Jun., Kinghorn, October 1949.
Mitchell, Alex., Lochgelly, January 1950.
Michie, James, Lochgelly, March 1950.
Mitchell, Andrew, Lochgelly, March 1950.
Mitchell, John M. (Affil.), Lochgelly, April 1950.
Macfarlane, Hugh, Lochgelly, September 1950.
McMurray, William, Lochgelly, October 1950.
McPherson, Andrew, Lochgelly, December 1950.
McLelland, Alex., Cardenden, January 1951.
Meldrum, Robert (Affil.), Cowdenbeath, April 1951.
McGregor, Robert, Lochgelly, October 1951.
Mew, Victor R., Lochgelly, November 1951.
Melville, Robert, Cowdenbeath, March 1952.
McLean, David, Lochgelly, October 1952.
McFadyen, John, Cowdenbeath, December 1952.
Malcolm, William, Lochgelly, September 1953.
McMillan, Charles, Lochgelly, October 1953.
Mitchell, William, Lochgelly, December 1953.
Marnoch, Alan, Lochgelly, December 1953.
Marnoch, James, Glencraig, December 1953.
McPherson, John, Lumphinnans, December 1953.
McKinlay, William, Lochgelly, February 1954.
McMoffat, Robert, Lochgelly, September 1954.
McArthur, Archibald, Lochgelly, September 1954.
McVicar, David, Lochgelly, October 1954.
McGregor, John, Lochgelly, October 1954.
McMurray, Peter, Lochgelly, November 1954.
Marshall, James, Lochgelly, December 1954.
Moyes, John, Lochgelly, December 1954.
Malcolm, William, Lochgelly, February 1955.
McEwan, Robert, Lochgelly, January 1956.
Muir, R. G., Ballingry, March 1956.
McLaren, Robert, Jun., Lochgelly, March 1956.
Mackay, Robert, Lochgelly, September 1956.
Mackay, Hugh, Lochgelly, September 1956.
Mackay, James, Lochgelly, September 1956.
Mackay, John, Lochgelly, September 1956.
McCurley, William, Lochgelly, October 1956.
Moffat, Robert, Ballingry, October 1956.
Marnoch, James A., Cowdenbeath, December 1956.
Melville, James K., Kirkcaldy, December 1956.
McPherson, Hugh, Cowdenbeath, February 1957.
McMurray, Robert, Lochgelly, March 1957.
McVicar, D., Cowdenbeath, September 1957.
McEwan, James, Lochgelly, January 1958.
McGhie, William, Lochgelly, April 1958.
Mitchell, James, Lochgelly, April 1958.

Nicol, Henry P., London, September 1932.
Nisbet, John H., Glencraig, April 1934.
Nunn, Heriot C., Glencraig, April 1934.
Nicol, John P., Lochgelly, January 1935.
Naysmith, John, Cowdenbeath, April 1937.
Nicol, George O., Cardenden, January 1940.
Newcombe, Dunfermline, December 1941.
Nelson, Robert, Lochgelly, October 1943.
Neal, Fraser, Edinburgh, December 1944.

Niven, James (Affil.), Lochgelly, March 1945.
Nisbet, David, Lochgelly, February 1947.
Nisbet, James, Lochgelly, February 1947.
Nevay, Arthur, Glencraig, January 1949.
Neilson, James, Lochgelly, April 1952.
Neilson, Andrew, Lochgelly, March 1953.
Nicolson, Robert, Cardenden, September 1955.

Pratt, Christopher, Kinglassie, March 1932.
Provan, David, Birmingham, September 1935.
Penman, John (Affil.) Dunfermline, May 1937.
Peacock, John, Lochgelly, September 1937.
Paxton, William, Lochgelly, September 1938.
Pratt, David, Lochgelly, December 1941.
Paterson, David, Dunfermline, March 1942.
Pearson, Alexander, Cluny, December 1942.
Peden, Andrew, Lochgelly, March 1943.
Paterson, John, Lochgelly, December 1943.
Pitcairn, Andrew, Cowdenbeath, April 1944.
Paton, John C., Lochgelly, May 1944.
Paton, David, Lochgelly, November 1944.
Parker, George, Kinglassie, November 1944.
Peattie, William, Lochgelly, April 1945.
Paul, William A., Lochgelly, March 1946.
Pratt, John, Lochgelly, January 1947.
Parker, David, Lochgelly, January 1947.
Primrose, Thomas, Lochgelly, April 1947.
Primrose, Robert, Lochgelly, April 1947.
Page, George, Lochgelly, April 1949.
Peel, Thomas, Lochgelly, September 1949.
Paton, Morris, Lochgelly, January 1951.
Paxton, Robert, Lochgelly, September 1951.
Primrose, David S., Lochgelly, October 1951.
Purdie, David, Lochgelly, April 1952.
Proudfoot, Andrew (Affil.), Cardenden,
September 1952.
Proudfoot, James, Cardenden, February 1953.
Potter, Thomas, Lochgelly, December 1953.
Pate, James, Lochgelly, March 1954.
Peattie, Andrew, Lochgelly, March 1955.
Penman, David, Lochgelly, October 1954.
Page, William, Lochgelly, December 1954.
Paterson, Alex., Cowdenbeath, March 1954.
Paterson, Thomas, Lochgelly, March 1955.
Primrose, Robert D., Lochgelly, March 1956.
Penman, Andrew F., Lochgelly, March 1956.
Peebles, Robert, Lochgelly, February 1957.
Playfair, John, Lochgelly, March 1958.

Ritchie, William H., Lochgelly, March 1937.
Ramage, Thomas H., Lochgelly, September 1937.
Ritchie, Peter, Lochgelly, February 1938.
Reid, James F., Lochgelly, June 1941.
Reid, William, Lochgelly, October 1943.
Russell, Robert, Lochgelly, January 1944.
Ramsay, William R., Cowdenbeath, April 1944.
Raeburn, John, Lochgelly, May 1944.
Robb, William, Cowdenbeath, March 1945.
Rolland, Andrew, Lochgelly, March 1945.

Ramsay, James, Lochgelly, October 1945.
Riddell, Robert, Kirkcaldy, March 1946.
Richard, J., London, August 1946.
Robertson, William, Lochgelly, September 1946.
Robertson, Abraham, Lochgelly, October 1946.
Raeburn, Archibald, Lochgelly, December 1946.
Reid, Robert, Bowhill, December 1946.
Ritchie, Andrew, Lochgelly, September 1947.
Reid, James R., Lochgelly, October 1947.
Riding, Arthur, Cowdenbeath, April 1948.
Robertson, Alex., Lochgelly, September 1949.
Robertson, Robert, Lochgelly, September 1950.
Robertson, Edwin, Cowdenbeath, March 1952.
Russell, Thomas, Lochgelly, November 1952.
Russell, Andrew, Kelty, September 1953.
Rogers, Edward J., Kinghorn, October 1953.
Rhind, Andrew, Lochgelly, March 1955.
Robertson, Thomas L. (Affil.), Lochgelly,
November 1955.
Reid, William H., Lochgelly, January 1956.
Raeburn, John, Lochgelly, February 1956.
Riddock, William, Ballingry, February 1957.
Robertson, Andrew, Lochgelly, September 1957.

Scott, Andrew, Cowdenbeath, October 1931.
Seath, Andrew B., Cardenden, March 1933.
Spence, Thomas, Lochgelly, October 1934.
Stewart, James E., Lochgelly, September 1935.
Stewart, Walter, Lochgelly, November 1936.
Steele, John S., Kirkcaldy, March 1937.
Stahly, George, Lochgelly, April 1937.
Shand, John B., Lochgelly, January 1938,
Smith, Alexander, Cowdenbeath, January 1938.
Swan, George, Cardenden, March 1938.
Scott, Edward, Lochgelly, September 1938.
Scott, Maurice, Lochore, September 1938.
Stiven, Harry D., Lochgelly, September 1938.
Smillie, William H., Cowdenbeath, February 1940.
Smith, Thomas D., Lochgelly, January 1942.
Scott, Andrew, Lochgelly, March 1942.
Summers, James, Lochgelly, March 1942.
Smith, William, Lochgelly, June 1942.
Shaw, Hugh, Crosshill, April 1942.
Smart, Robert, Lochgelly, September 1942.
Sharp, Alexander, Lochgelly, October 1942.
Stiven, James, Lochgelly, February 1943.
Seath, William, Lumphinnans, September 1943.
Searle, Roy, Lochgelly, December 1943.
Steedman, John, Lochgelly, December 1943.
Stephen, James, Lochgelly, February 1944.
Scott, John, Lochgelly, February 1944.
Scott, John, Lochgelly, May 1944.
Squirrell, George E., Tain, October 1944.
Scott, John, Lochgelly, March 1945.
Sime, Andrew, Milnathort, April 1945.
Soutar, John, Lochgelly, September 1945.
Scott, John, Lochgelly, December 1945.
Steele, George L., Lochgelly, February 1946.
Smillie, William, Lochgelly, March 1948.

Shanks, Robert, Lochgelly, April 1946.
Stewart, Samuel G., Lochgelly, April 1946.
Seath, Andrew, Lochgelly, December 1946.
Soutar, Andrew, Lochgelly, December 1946
Small, Archibald, Hill Of Beath, February 1947.
Shand, Charles, Lochgelly, December 1947.
Seath, Alex., Lochgelly, December 1947.
Simpson, William, Lochgelly, September 1948.
Sharp, William, Lochgelly, January 1949.
Stewart, David, Lochgelly, January 1949.
Salmond, James, Lochgelly, April 1949.
Scott, Robert, Lochgelly, October 1949.
Swan, Alex. D., Lochgelly, December 1950.
Salmond, John, Ballingry, December 1950.
Shaw, Hugh, Lochgelly, December 1951.
Simpson, Peter, Cowdenbeath, January 1952.
Simpson, Alex., Cowdenbeath, January 1952.
Shaw, Frank, Lochgelly, February 1952.
Spence, Gavin W., Lochgelly, November 1952.
Simpson, Archie, Cowdenbeath, December 1952.
Simpson, John, Cowdenbeath, February 1953.
Stewart, Samuel, Lochgelly, December 1953.
Sharp, Samuel, Lochgelly, December 1953.
Syme, Mungo R., Lochgelly, February 1955.
Sutherland, David, Lochgelly, September 1955.
Shand, Andrew, Lochgelly, October 1955.
Shand, David, Dunfermline, October 1955.
Simpkins, George, Lochgelly, November 1955.
Steedman, Thomas, Lochgelly, January 1956.
Speed, William A., Lochore, December 1956.
Stuart, Peter, Lochgelly, January 1957.
Swan, H. B., Lochgelly, November 1957.

Thomson, Alexander, Lochgelly, April 1931.
Thorburn, John W., Glencraig, February 1932.
Taylor, William, Lochgelly, October 1935.
Taylor, Hugh, Lochgelly, March 1937.
Thomson, Robert C., Lochgelly, February 1940.
Thomson, Andrew, Lochgelly, September 1940.
Thomson, James, Lochgelly, October 1940.
Turnbull, William M. B., Glencraig,
September 1941.
Taylor, John, Kelty, January 1942.
Taylor, Alexander, Lochgelly, January 1946.
Thomson, John, Edinburgh, April 1947.
Thomson, Andrew, Lochgelly, September 1947.
Thomson, Andrew, Lochgelly, December 1948.
Thomson, Robert, Cowdenbeath, December 1948.
Taylor, John D., Lochgelly, March 1949.
Tandy, Francis A., Lochgelly, October 1950.
Thomson, James, Cowdenbeath, March 1952.
Taylor, George, Glencraig, September 1953.
Thomson, James, Lochgelly, April 1958.

Vickery, H.J.J., Dunfermline, November 1940.

Whyte, Hugh M., Lochgelly, September 1930.
Whyte, William G., Scotland Wells, October 1932.

Wilkie, James McKenzie, Lochgelly, December 1933.
Walkingshaw, Adam, Lochgelly, September 1936.
Walkingshaw, William B., Lochgelly, March 1937.
Walker, William, Lochgelly, September 1937.
Williamson, James (Affil.), Lochore, October 1937.
Webster, Peter, Lochgelly, February 1938.
Wilson, George, Lochgelly, September 1938.
Wylie, Hunter, Lochgelly, January 1939.
Watson, Andrew J., Lochgelly, October 1938.
Watson, Peter, New Zealand, September 1940.
Whyte, William, Lochgelly, April 1941.
Wildridge, Laurence, Lochgelly, June 1941.
Wallace, William B., Lochgelly, January 1942.
Willan, Thomas S., Lundin Links, January 1942.
Wilson, Robert, Lochgelly, January 1942.
Walkingshaw, William, Lochgelly, April 1942.
Wyse, Robert, Lochgelly, September 1942.
Walker, David, Lochgelly, March 1944.
Wilson, Robert, Lochgelly, May 1942.
Wilson, William H., Lochgelly, April 1945.
Wllson, James S., Lochgelly, September 1946.
Walker, William, Lochgelly, April 1947.
Wildridge, Alex C., Lochgelly, December 1947.
Wilson, John, Lochgelly, January 1948.
Whyte, Andrew, Lochgelly, January 1949.
Whyte, Archie, Lochgelly, January 1949.
Walker, William (Affil.), Lochgelly, January 1949.
Wilson, George, Cowdenbeath, March 1949.
Wilson, Thomas, Lochgelly, January 1950.
Watson, George, Lochgelly, March 1950.
Wilson, James M., Lochgelly, March 1950.
Walker, James, Lochgelly, December 1951.
Whyte, Hugh, Cardenden, January 1951.
Whyte, David, Cardenden, January 1951.
Wilkie, Andrew, Cowdenbeath, March 1951.
Webster, William, Glencraig, October 1951.
Wilson, John, Lumphinnans, October 1951.
Wilson, Hugh, Lochgelly, November 1952.
Whyte, John M., Lochgelly, December 1953.
Wilkie, William, Cowdenbeath, December 1953.
Wilson, John P., Lochgelly, February 1955.
Wilson, Thomas, Lochgelly, October 1955.
Wills, Ronald, Lochgelly, October 1955.
Whitehead, Allan, Lochgelly, December 1956.
Watson, George, Glenrothes, September 1957.
Wilson, John, Alloa, October 1957.
Wyse, Henry, Lochgelly, December 1957.
Wilson, George R., Buckhaven, December 1957.

Young, Robert R., Lochgelly, February 1943.
Yumon, Robert W., Lochgelly, April 1949.
Young, William, Lochgelly, January 1950.
Young, Andrew, Lochgelly, January 1950.
Yeoman, John A., Lochgelly, February 1952.

LODGE MINTO, NO 385, LOCHGELLY

Centenary, 1958
Programme of Events

Sunday, 21st September-

CHURCH SERVICE in St. Andrews Church.

The Brethren will witness the Dedication of the new Lodge Aprons and Sashes by the Provincial Grand Master before leaving the Lodge Room for the Church.

The preacher is Rev. Bro. F. M. Musk, B.A., and the lessons will be read by the Pro. Grand Master and the R.W.M.

Solos will be rendered by Bro. Matthew Nisbet, Lodge The Gael, No. 609.

Saturday, 27th September -

The Lodge will meet at 4 p.m. for the **RE-DEDICATION of LODGE MINTO** by the Grand Lodge Office-bearers headed by Bro. Sir George Graham, O.B.E., D.L., J.P., Depute Grand Master.

The Lodge will adjourn to the Town Hall for a **DINNER.** Tickets, 7/6 each for Lodge Minto Members, and 10/- for other Brethren.

Friday, 3rd October -

A DINNER DANCE will be held in the Town Hall, when the Brethren will pay 10/- and their Partners will be free. Visiting Brethren will be welcome, but they will pay 10/-.

Saturday, 11th October -

The old members of the Lodge over 65 will be the guests of the Lodge at a **SUPPER and CONCERT** in the Masonic Hall.

Sunday, 12th October -

CHURCH SERVICE in the Churchmount Church, where the preacher will be Rev. Dr. W. E. K. Rankine, Pro. Grand Senior Chaplain.

LOCHGELLY EQUITABLE CO-OPERATIVE SOCIETY, LTD.

Co-operative Week

8th to 15th SEPTEMBER, 1951

Notes on the Early History of the Society

Programme of Week's Events

LOCHGELLY CO-OPERATIVE SOCIETY, LTD.

"A Business Romance"

It is said that life is a matter of "ups and downs." In the case of Lochgelly Equitable Co-operative Society Ltd. it has been a case of "ups" all the time. The only "downs" were brought about by three disastrous fires (to which reference is made later in this article) but they proved a very temporary setback.

The expansion of the Society down its 86 years of trading is something in the nature of a business romance. That is not an overstatement when we consider that it started without capital, in a shop rented at £9 a year, and one employee, and with a stock of £10 of groceries, with a few dozen members, to a membership of 9,257, members' share capital of over £319,000, a turnover of a little under a million and a half pounds and 530 employees.

Lochgelly Society is among the oldest in Fife and, indeed, in Scotland. While it started from scratch in the financial aspect, it had the great asset of being founded by hard-headed, independent, responsible men, who believed in its principles. That sure foundation has been its mainstay in the years of the great growth of the district. The tradition of the Society inspired confidence.

The idea of Co-operative Trading orginated a little before the middle of the last century. Its basis was economic, the underlying principles of providing cheaper goods by saving the middleman's profit. It has been expanded, of course, since that time, and now manufactures many of the goods that sell retail. From the principle of selling at the minimum profit to cover expenses came the necessity for some "plough-back" for capital for expansion. The policy of paying dividends on purchases and investing these dividends where desired, enabled share capital to be built up for expansion. The dividend also served the purpose of saving against a rainy day. It has been said that the greatest incentive to save money is to possess a little. So it has proved in the Co-operative movement, as borne out by the enormous capital invested by wholesale and retail Societies in the country.

The Co-operative movement was born in an eventful political and economic era. It was contemporary with the struggle for the legality of Trade Unionism; indeed, it was not until six years after the start of Lochgelly Society that Trades Unions obtained legislative protection for their funds and were given the legal right to combine.

In the political field was the struggle for the franchise. When Lochgelly Store was started very few people in Lochgelly had a vote and there was no compulsory education.

It may be interesting to recall that in the same period, Lochgelly played a big part in starting the Fife Miners' Union. The then village was the centre round which the new Union was built up. Alexander Macdonald (later to be the first T.U. Member of Parliament), the spearhead of the movement, spent much of his time in Lochgelly; while the village furnished the Union's first secretary in the person of Henry Cook, a product of Auld Launcherhead.

It is unfortunate that early records of Lochgelly Society were all lost in the second fire. It was, in a way, a fortunate circumstance that exactly 50 years ago, the writer of the present article, on the occasion of the opening of the new branch premises, got the opportunity of a search through the first minute book for the purpose of an article for the "Lochgelly Times." That remains the only source of its original history and it is from that and what is personally known by the writer that this article is compiled. The late John Mitchell, so long manager, made three attempts to save that minute book but was thrice driven back by flames and smoke.

Previous to the Society being formed, the requirements of the employees of Lochgelly Iron and Coal Coy. Ltd. were supplied at a store run by the Company. It was situated in one of the houses at the corner of the old row at Auchterderran Road, connected with Grainger Street. Goods were got on a fortnight's credit (fortnightly pays then) and the amount deducted from the pay line. That was before the passing of the Truck Act which affected the system of such contracts by the employer. Incidentally, the most of the old Coal Company stores were licensed to sell liquor. Before the Truck Acts, workers were more or less thirled to the Company store.

In 1864 the move was made to form a Co-operative Society by a handful of leading villagers, not by any means confined to miners. Indeed, with the Company Store in the background, the miners found it more judicious to remain at first in the background. It was then decided to form a Society but much had to be done and it was not till April 24, 1865, that the first regular meeting was held in the village hall which has been known by several titles, but which was termed in the minute, "the Iron Company's Hall" and the "Society's Hall." The building (two storey) is still at the top of Hall Street and bears the date "1839."

At the meeting, rules were drawn out and approved and a committee was formed as follows, on the motion of Henry Cook seconded by George Erskine, father of the last ex-Provost Erskine:—President, Wm. Arnott; secretary, Wm. Smith; treasurer, George Westwater; committee—Alex Thomson, Wm. Penman, And. Galloway, John Westwater, Robt. Fairful, Edward McCormack, Robt. Mathieson, Robt. Hunter, Thomas Anderson, Henry Penman, Andrew

Connelly and Wm. Grant. The older residenters generally will be able to identify all the foregoing as then leading men in the village.

As a matter of interest it may give some of our readers a mental exercise in identifying the following other names of the early members. They are names to conjure with. It will be found that in most cases their descendents are still connected with the Society:—

Alex. Naysmith, Robt. Dick, Laurence Anderson, Alex. Westwater, George Westwater, Henry Brown, Wm. Herd, And. Galloway, Wm. Penman, Thos. Anderson, Angus Hugh, Wm. Rolland, Robt. Gillespie, And. Reekie, James Webster, Geo. Shand, Thos. Brand, Robt. Fowler, Thos. Splitt, Henry Morris, James Dewar, Peter Lindsay, Wm. Brown, David Sharp, John Gilbert, Henry Sneddon, Michael Vail, Henry Fisher, Peter Guthrie, Henry Hynd, Geo. Swan, James Beattie, Arch. Cook, James Greig, A. McKinlay, A. Suttie and Robt. Wilson.

A knowledge of these men leaves the impression that no organisation could have been founded on a more stable foundation.

The committee appointed was authorised "to treat with Mr Thos. Hugh and Mrs Littlejohn (both spirit merchants with shops adjoining) on what conditions their premises could be let." Thos. Hugh's shop in High Street (next door to his public house), which was then occupied as a provision shop, was chosen at an annual rental of £9 and Wm. Hill was appointed salesman. For some months previously, in the latter half of 1864, a few pioneers laid in a stock (the value of the first stock was £10) and opened the shop in the evenings. It was supervised by Alex. Westwater, then retired (he died three years later) and the serving was done by enthusiastic potential members. All the work was unpaid.

Wm. Hill was the sole employee when the shop was opened daily in 1865. A "very carefully prepared list of goods had been drawn up by And. Galloway and a sub-committee was appointed to purchase them. With regard to potatoes, Thos. Anderson and Alex. Thomson were instructed to buy these at the cheapest rate possible to the extent of £10."

The first quarterly meeting was held in the Iron Company's Hall. On that occasion, the minutes inform us, the president gave "a spirited address on the benefits of co-operation and urged all the members to patronise the Store."

By the end of the year (1865) business had increased to such an extent that the committee were forced to advertise for an apprentice to assist the salesman and James Lindsay was appointed "on six weeks trial." About the same time we find Thos. Hugh making a claim for interest on a deposit due to him on the shop rent. The committee thought it an unusual charge, but agreed to offer half the sum, which was accepted.

Early in 1866, Robt. Mathieson, who had been appointed the second president, resigned from that office and And. Galloway was appointed. The latter, who was also R.W.M. of Minto Lodge, was a master of works for the Coal Company and a leading man in the village.

The first dividend was 1/9 per £ of purchases to members and 10-$\frac{1}{2}$d to non-members. The secretary was instructed "to report to the committee of all members not purchasing at the Store." This measure seems to have had some effect as the sales for the next quarter were reported to show a considerable increase.

Business continued to increase and another apprentice was appointed (Robt. Swinton) and so, within a year, the number of employees had increased to three. At the same time, the committee decided to no longer sell bran. The reason is not given.

Reference has been made to the Lochgelly Iron and Coal Company's store. It had been removed from its original position in Auchterderran Road to the corner of Bank Street and Berry Street. There had evidently been business transactions between that store and the Co-op. Store for we find in the minutes the Society "protesting to the Company against the latter being paid a non-member's dividend." The democratic co-operators were evidently in no mood to deal softly with the opposition store for in a minute dated February, 1866, a proposal was made by Henry Cook "that the dividend be paid this time as it had been paid last quarter, but to discontinue paying the Company Store any dividend in times to come."

In May, 1866, William Hill, the first employee, resigned and was thanked for his exertions on behalf of the Society and James Meikle was appointed.

Ten years after the start, larger premises were acquired and an old single storey property at the top of Bank Street was purchased and rebuilt as a double storey. Unfortunately, after two years (James Hunter, manager), it was almost destroyed by fire. That was in 1877. Though practically nothing was saved, after a short interval trading was resumed. The damage was covered by insurance. In the hall above, the Masonic Lodge 385 and Friendly Societies also suffered loss in their equipment. Speedily the work of rebuilding the premises, which included a bakery, a business taken over some years previously from Lochgelly Baking Society, went ahead.

The next development in the extension of business took place in 1884 when a fleshing shop was opened in Bank Street, almost opposite the main building, and in 1887 a feu was taken on the north side of the Minto Hotel and a large bakery erected. It consisted of four ovens and a front sales shop.

Further extension of premises led to the erection in 1893 of another fine and solid building on the north side of the bakery for grocery and drapery departments. The latter department had been started in the old premises which were now converted into Reading and Recreation rooms and a Library was started. Later, in the recreation room, the first billiard table in Lochgelly (three-quarter length) was installed.

An Educational Committee also ran lectures during the winter months. At that period there was little in the way of counter attractions and for many years these lectures proved highly popular. The chairman was the late John Rolland.

With the development of the coalfield around Lochgelly district and the consequent great increase in population, an important change of policy was brought about—since greatly extended—the opening of branches away from the Central premises. Glencraig came first and Auchterderran followed shortly after, and the process of extension has gone on ever since. About the same time, twenty dwellinghouses were built, bringing about the opening up of Dundas Street.

Bonuses seem to have been a practice at this time, such as the manager being voted "£1 for services and 10/- for extra trouble." Another extra item was 10/- awarded for measuring cloth voted to a gentleman who had a tailor's business.

The first year's trading showed the turnover to be £963; members' share capital £104 and the membership 323.

To-day, the branches and distribution centres number 43 with five extra productive services.

It was intended in this article to deal with the second and third disastrous fires but they will have to be kept for a later time.

Sufficient, however, has been said to give an indication of the early years and the development of an organisation which has had a profound influence on the economic life of the village and burgh of Lochgelly and of the landward parts of the parishes of Auchterderran and Ballingry.

A.W.

LOCHGELLY CO-OPERATIVE SOCIETY, LTD.

Fife Co-operative Week

8th to 15th SEPTEMBER, 1951

International Co-operative Day, Saturday, September 8

Programme of Events

SUNDAY, 9th SEPTEMBER, at 3 p.m.

GRAND RALLY

In ALHAMBRA PICTURE HOUSE, DUNFERMLINE

(Organised by Fife Co-operative Association and District
Council)

Speaker—Mr Jack Bailey, General Secretary of
Co-operative Party

Admission Tickets, together with Bus Tickets, may be had
on application to District Offices.

TUESDAY, 11th SEPTEMBER, at 7 p.m.

MUSICAL EVENING

By DYSART CO-OPERATIVE JUNIOR CHOIR
In CO-OPERATIVE HALL, CHAPEL STREET

THURSDAY, 13th SEPTEMBER, at 7 p.m.

LOCAL RALLY

In CO-OPERATIVE HALL, CHAPEL STREET

Speaker—Councillor William Thomson, Cowdenbeath
Musical Items by Members of Lochgelly Senior Choir
Solos, Duets and Quartettes

SATURDAY, 15th SEPTEMBER

GRAND PARADE

GRAND PARADE OF SOCIETY'S VEHICLES DECORATED BY
AUXILIARY BODIES AND TRADING DEPARTMENTS, AND
FANCY DRESS PARADE FOR ADULTS AND JUVENILES.

Parade will leave Melgund Place at 2 p.m. accompanied by Lochgelly
Ladies' Pipe Band, Lochgelly Brass Band, Bowhill Colliery Silver Band
and Lochore and District Pipe Band and parade through the town to
West End Playing Field.

Competitors for Fancy Dress Parade are requested to report at
Society's Garage, David Street, at 1.30 p.m.

At the Field there will be Displays by Country Dancing Teams and
Keep Fit Class, and Musical Items by the Choirs and Bands.

In the event of Inclement Weather, a Concert will be held in Town
Hall, commencing at 2.30 p.m.

ESSAY COMPETITION
(LOCAL)

Children between the ages of 12 and 15 years are invited to enter for this Competition. Entrants should in not more than 200 words state what they consider the "Need for Co-operative Education." Entries should be addressed to Managing Secretary, 30 Bank Street, Lochgelly, to arrive not later than Monday, 10th September.

ESSAY COMPETITIONS
(FIFE COUNTY)

Essay Competitions for all ages are being promoted by Fife Co-operative Association and District Council.

For Particulars, see Separate Hand Bills

THE LATE JOHN MITCHELL
Outstanding Figure in the Society's History

The most outstanding personality in the history of the Society, John Mitchell, Managing Secretary, retired in 1938 after a service of sixty years.

COMMITTEE OF MANAGEMENT

Front Row—Thomas Leitch, Thomas McLean, Charles McEwan (Managing Secretary), David Arthur (President, Mrs. Jean Shaw, Alex. Page.

Back Row (left to right)—Alex. Geddes, Robt. Whitehead, Samuel Miles, William Adamson, James Dryburgh, Robt. Gilfillan, John Butler, William Cook.

Danders Round Lochgelly

Alex Westwater often spoke at meetings of various local societies and institutions, most frequently at meetings held under the auspices of St Andrews Church of Scotland – he first spoke there shortly after World War I, and his last talks were delivered in the 1950s.

Among his papers are the manuscripts of four talks, three from the 1930s, the other from 1957. In these, he took the Church as his starting point, and "dandered" north, south, east or west, for about five miles, pausing in his stroll to reminisce, and to comment on buildings, personalities, and traditions. This chapter consists of excerpts from these talks; some of the anecdotes appear in other historical sketches, and have been omitted here; and, as is almost inevitable with speaker's manuscripts, there are handwritten marginal notes which would have been expanded on delivery – but exactly how cannot be said now.

When we set out on a dander we have always a starting point and we'll choose the centre of our radius as the Auld Kirk. In olden days all roads led to the Auld Kirk and they also radiated from it. It's in the heart of our town, and in very close proximity we have the most important of our town activities. Round about it are the Town House, the hotel, the Town Hall, the Bank, the local newspaper office, the Co-operative store, the Masonic Lodge and the largest and oldest and most important school. When this church was built none of these existed. What is the Times Office was one of the only two other buildings in the whole of Bank Street.

Where the Church stands was a small sparsely wooded plantation stretching across to the Old Lochgelly Moor, the scene of the fairs and markets and formerly the camping ground of the gypsies.

The foundation stone of the church was laid in 1855 while the Crimean War was raging. My father witnessed the ceremony sitting on the stair leading to the platform and he has told me of the great crowd that assembled and of the big event it was reckoned to be. Originally it was intended to build both the church and manse in the school plantation but on representation to the Earl of Minto to have it nearer the centre of the population, he granted the site we now stand on. It cost £1180. Previous to then there was the United Presbyterian Church in Mid Street, latterly the music hall and now dwelling houses. Of the three church buildings now in the town this is the oldest.

There must however have been a meeting house in Lochgelly connected with Auchterderran Parish Church, for as far back as the 1600s we have religious services at Lochgelly meeting house recorded in the minutes of the Kirkcaldy presbytery. These too had been going on during the years of persecution. One date given is 1688, the year that marked the end of the killing time, for four months later William of Orange had landed and the long years of struggle for religious freedom were over.

Shortly after the church was built, Lochgelly Iron Company built a store opposite the church. It is still a Grocery Shop. That was before the days of the Truck Act, when the miners got their provisions from the Company and the cost was deducted from their pay. Previous to then the Company store was in Auchterderran Road.

The Manager was John Coupar who came here in 1853 and continued in the new building. When the Truck Act was passed he wanted to rent or buy the premises but failed to come to terms with the Coal Company. He thereupon started to build premises for himself on the North side of the church. Before this building was finished a big fire took place in the shop opposite the church and as he was not insured he lost everything. He had to give up the new place that was being erected and it was taken over by the Morris family and became the Minto Hotel. This John Coupar, by the way, conducted the psalmody in this church for six years gratis to help the church clear off its debt.

The Union Bank was built three years after the church, transferred from a house on the Main Street where it had been since it was opened in 1853. This place was the Parochial Office and later when the burgh was formed in 1877 it became the first office of Lochgelly Police Commissioners. It was when this bank was erected that Bank Street got its name, its name started through my grandfather using "Bank Street" as his business address.

Further on is the East or Higher Grade school. By the older generation it was known as the Iron Company's school, for it was they who built it 85 years ago. The Company did much for education. As showing how advanced they were more than sixty years ago, they had cooking and sewing classes, and the school attained a very high reputation in the educational world.

Leaving Bank Street we enter Station Road. The Manse was the first house built there. That was before the cutting was made to the Railway Station hence the high wall. It used to be reckoned a joke to tell visitors that the top of the manse wall was built before the bottom. The depth of the cutting at that point can be gauged by the height of the wall. This cutting was made in 1868 not long after the manse was finished. On the east side of the

road stood old Cooperha' and further on Launcherhead. The former comprised four single houses and two double. There the miners resided, the
weavers, for Lochgelly fully a century ago was more a weaving than a mining
village, being domiciled in the top part of the village. Cooperha' has long disappeared and old Launcherhead is a mass of rubble. They were the oldest
houses in the town, except for a few in old Lochgelly, and they belonged to
the Minto estate. Some of the houses in Stationhead were erected when the
Railway was made and I think, though I am not yet positive, that they were
built by the Railway Company.

In 1848, the Railway was made between Thornton and Dunfermline.
Lochgelly at first was only a passenger station, all the goods being taken into
Cowdenbeath and carted back. After the cutting was made through Station
Road (it formerly consisted of three distinct steep braes) Lochgelly was made
a goods station, and Lochgelly goods were no longer carried on to
Cowdenbeath. The Station buildings consisted of a wooden hut which some
will remember as standing on the west side of the present Station House.

We now reach the hub of Lochgelly's industry, the Coal Company headquarters. Much local history has been made there.

It is mere speculation to discuss when coal was first worked in Lochgelly –
probably as far back as the time of the monks. At first coal was more or less
quarried, and it was not till near the end of the 18th century that it came to be
regularly mined. There are traditions regarding Lochgelly which may be
accepted as fairly reliable. The best account, and I have searched in many
quarters for data, is from a manuscript left by the late Archibald (Bauldie)
Cook. He had first hand information handed down three generations and
particularly from his Granny, Hannah Hodge, who would be born about the
middle of the 18th century and worked in the mines almost up to the time
when female labour below ground was prohibited by Act of Parliament.
Bauldie tells us in his interesting reminiscences that a man named John Keeler
held a contract to work minerals on Lochgelly estate and that he was forced to
give up through his seam taking fire. The heat was so strong on the surface
that when snow fell it melted as soon as it touched the ground. In 1775 Sir
Gilbert Elliot, brother of the authoress of the "Flowers of the Forest", who had
acquired Lochgelly Estate through marrying an heiress, restarted coal mining.

What we are certain of is that the first mine of any consequence was sunk
on the west side of the road opposite the Coal Company's office. That was
about the turn of the century and its inception was due to the enterprise of the
first Earl Of Minto. He employed a grieve whose remuneration was 5/- a
week and two acres of land. The workers got 9/- a week. In an account book

we find that the total number of workmen in the mine in 1806 was 13. The names of the hewers are still represented in our oldest families, Henry Baxter, Charles Baxter, Hannah Hodge, James Hunter, George Erskine and James and Robert Chisholm. The highest wage was that of George Erskine who received £1:3:2½d and the lowest Charles Baxter 8/9d. Some weeks the proprietor had a loss and sometimes a gain. The coal was carried up on the backs of the bearers but in 1808 a gin or windlass was erected at the pit head. It was propelled by horse power. Eight years later other excavations for coal were made and a manager was appointed, and in 1812 the Earl of Minto granted the first coal lease to two partners named Chisholm and Brown. They soon improved matters for we find a year later that a condensing steam engine had been fitted up by Mr Scott, Inverkeithing. The partnership however was not a success, said to be through too heavy an expenditure. In 1827 they became bankrupt and the coal at the pit bank was sold by auction to satisfy the creditors. Minto again carried on the work but soon gave another lease to one Nicol Thomson, who continued till 1831 when they came into the hands of John Henderson. This was really the beginning of Lochgelly's coal development. Under him the Colliery extended. Just a hundred years ago the number of employees had risen to 51, of whom 12 were women and 39 men. Ten years later there was a further development when he took into partnership Messrs Grainger, Kennard and Russell and the partnership assumed the name of Lochgelly Iron Company.

This brings us to the Iron Works which for a number of years held a more important place in our local economy than coal. Two blast furnaces were erected in 1848 (the same year as the railway) and another two eight years later. I have heard old residenters speak of the lurid flames that used to shoot out of these furnaces lighting up the whole district for miles around. Most of the ironstone was raised from two pits situated near East Colquhally farm and therefore convenient to the Iron works.

The furnaces were finally closed down in the seventies. Shortly before then a fatal explosion occurred at one of the latest type which had only recently been erected. Grainger Square was built to house the workers at the furnaces.

An Oil work and a Brick work were established shortly after mid century. All this shows considerable enterprise. I hear mention that crude oil was also manufactured at Lochore and Westfield. Who knows but under the hydrogenation or other process we may see the oil industry re-established in our midst.

The full story of Lochgelly's coal industry is too exhaustive to deal with in the compass of this paper and we will have to cross the burgh boundary if our dander is not to come to an abrupt end.

Proceeding north on our left is the estate of Cartmore, once the property of a family named Syme, who also for a short period owned Lochore. A scion of this family, Professor Syme born in 1799, was a notable man. Dr John Brown, the famous author of "Rab and His Friends," was a pupil of his and he describes him as the greatest surgeon Scotland ever produced. Refusing an appointment at Edinburgh Infirmary Professor Syme established the Minto House hospital in Edinburgh at his own expense. The Cartmore property latterly passed into the hands of the Earl of Minto whose broad Lochgelly Estate is made up of a number of little ones acquired during the last 150 years.

Minto's land stretches down to the burn at Glencraig. The Contal Row, now no more, was on the South side in Lochgelly quoad sacra Parish.

A fairly large stream, variously known as the Clune burn and the Contal burn and the Fitty burn, separates the parishes of Ballingry and Auchterderran.

The north side of that stream lands us into territory with a story of great historic value but unfortunately much of it cannot be proved. The Parish of Ballingry was undoubtedly the scene of important human activities long before the dawn of written history. Its ancient history however can only be estimated by inference and deduction but the evidences which have been traced over its rocky and waterlogged surface disclose to the antiquarian the existence of Pictish townships, of the presence of the Romans, far off forgotten things, and battles long ago.

We come to the Clune. The earliest mention of the Clune I have been able to get goes back a good bit. I possess a history of Inchcolm written by a minister of Aberdour. He states, from a chartulary in Fordel House, that a little hill called Clon and sometimes Clon-Vane was feued by the Monastery of Inchcolm in 1244 from Constantine de Lochore, the then owner of Lochore Castle, and Constantine got 15 years prepayment because he frankly stated he was hard up. Landowners even in these days had their financial difficulties. The feu duty for the Clon was half a mark yearly (equivalent to $1\frac{1}{2}$d of sterling money).

The name Glencraig was the subject of correspondence in the "Times" thirteen years ago. I wrote to the late George Constable who was proprietor of Glencraig before it was acquired by the Wilson and Clyde Coal Coy, to adjudicate on the matter, and he confirmed the opinion given by the Rev David Jamie in his Church history of Ballingry. It had been surmised by a local antiquarian that the original name of Glencraig was Clunecraig. The facts are that Glencraig is a new name and was given when four little estates came to be united. They were the Contal, the Clune, Inchgall and Templeland. It may be interesting to relate how they all became one estate.

The Contal for 150 years belonged to a family named Betson or Beatson, the last member of which built the present Glencraig House, a little to the south of an older house. The Clune also belonged to the Betsons. It came to them through marriage. This family also acquired the estate of Templeland. This still leaves the estate of Inchgall which belonged to a Mr Henderson. Henderson and the last of the Betsons were bachelors and great friends and they made their wills that whichever lived the longest would succeed to all that both possessed. Henderson died first and thus Betson secured the four estates and the title Glencraig came into being. That was just over a hundred years ago. There was an anticlimax however for when Betson died it was found that he had not destroyed the will he made in Henderson's favour or made another one. The consequence was that the Hendersons stepped in and in turn claimed the whole. In 1872 the property came into the hands of the Constables.

There is an assumption that the Templeland was one of the possessions of the Knights of the Order of the Temple, a body which had persisted in Scotland alone from the time of the Crusades up till the Reformation, when along with the Roman Catholic Church, they were despoiled of all their property.

A little to the northeast of Glencraig is the Shirram Brae surmounted by the Harelaw. Here in 1891 an antiquarian discovery was made which amplified other evidence and traditions that the district had an importance away back in prehistoric times. Mr George W. Constable, the then proprietor of Glencraig, and his friend Mr R. Burns Begg, Sheriff clerk of Kinross-shire, were keen antiquarians and they decided to institute a search on the cairn at Harelaw which they reckoned might be a tumulus or burial ground. The cairn was composed of 700 to 800 loads of stones. As it turned out their deductions were confirmed. On a Saturday forenoon in August 1891 they started the excavations and at a distance of 21 feet in a depth of 3 feet from the surface a stone cist was discovered. In this chest was found a cinerary urn of baked clay. It was covered with rude attempts at ornamentation. Within the urn were decayed bones and ashes indicating a prehistoric burial. All the articles found were sent to Edinburgh for expert antiquarian examination and are now in the Museum there. The general conclusion was that the remains were Pictish. Whether Roman or Pictish they were considered to confirm that a battle was fought in this area and that the cairn covered the remains of a person of distinction.

Following these discoveries several antiquarians came to visit Mr

Constable and they had a look at the forts on the Clune hill. A detailed description of these forts was made in a survey by a well informed local antiquarian, Mr Charles Brown. The opinion of Mr Constable and his fellows forty years ago was that these Clune forts had been either outposts in connection with the camp at Lochore or built by the natives who were opposed to or in conflict with the Romans. I have gone over the area with Mr Brown twice. One would however require the antiquarian sense and knowledge to be impressed.

Away to the south west of the Clune in the Heather Park of Lumphinnans Farm is an old road still clearly defined. It is a wide road with its boundaries well founded with whinstone blocks. It can be taken as fairly certain that this was part of the old north road leading from Pettycur ferry to Perth. With various breaks it can still be traced to the south over by Lochhead and northwards it fords the Fitty burn, and continues on to Parenwell, thence skirting Benarty. I have met those who had it direct from their grandparents that it was the Coach Road and that the ruined building which we know as Shepherd Mary was a coaching inn or change house. On old maps the road can be clearly traced. It is very likely that Mary Queen of Scots was brought this way from Leith to her imprisonment in Loch Leven Castle after her arrest following the battle of Carberry Hill. The route after her escape was of course through Blairadam to the south west.

Returning to the highway we proceed by North Glencraig up the brae to the Spail Inn. I have until recently not been able to find out whether this was a regular inn or not. No one living can remember it being a licensed house but in the First Statistical Account which was written in the1790s it is stated that there are two lawful liquor houses in the Parish of Ballingry. The Shank of Navity would be one and it is tolerably certain that the second could only be the Spail Inn. The term used "two lawful houses" seems to presume that unlawful public houses existed in the parish. In his Church Life of the Parish the Rev David Jamie says that there was a joiner's shop there and that the word spail might be derived from the planks of wood built up crosswise looking from the distance as spails or splinters of wood. Rev Jamie does not mention it was an inn. I do know that the wine of our country could be had there less than a hundred years ago. I had it from an old Ballingry curler, Mr William Steedman, that when the club played on its first pond at Lochgelly the curlers used to send over to the Spail inn for their refreshments. It may of course have been a shebeen. These were very common before, and after, the Forbes-Mackenzie act was passed in the 1850's.

Previous to then the licence laws were loose. The legal houses could supply for the whole 24 hours if they chose.

We now approach the oldest monument of ancient times in our whole district. Of Lochore Castle not much is known in detail but there is no doubt that its several territorial families played a very important part in Scottish history. For authorities we have Sibbald, the first historian of Fife; Grosse the antiquarian for whose entertainment Burns is said to have written Tam O' Shanter and who visited Lochore in his antiquarian quest in Scotland; Ross deals with it in his Scottish antiquities and early information is given in a chartulary of Inchcolm published by a former minister of Aberdour. The existing ruin is not likely to be that of the first building, which would probably be of wood with stone foundations. What we now see is likely to have been built in the fifteenth century, perhaps a hundred years before Falkland Palace.

Round about the second half of the twelfth century, shortly after the period when Queen Margaret become the wife of Malcolm Canmore, one Duncan built a castle at the east end of the lake which up till its draining about a hundred and fifty years ago covered an area of several acres. There were no surnames then and he was known as Duncan de Lochore. This Lochore family played a leading part in early Scottish history up till about the death of Robert the Bruce. Some were patriots and some were not. One at least was not for the name David de Lochore appears on the Ragman's Roll which you will recall was a list of those of the Scottish nobility doing homage to Edward I at Berwick and declaring him overlord of Scotland. Later however we hear of him fighting alongside Wallace. He was taken prisoner at Dunbar and later returned to service with the English King. Another brother Hugh was confined in Chester castle. Their sympathies, or should I rather say their interests, as a whole seemed to lean to the English side. It is more satisfactory to know that another of the family, Thomas de Lochore, was one of the Scottish Parliament which met at Ayr and declared Robert the Bruce King of Scotland and his heirs for ever. This was a year after Bannockburn and we may infer that Lochore and the vassals of his estate which then extended over Lochgelly to Auchtertool would take part in the famous fight. Other members of the family were sheriffs or thanes of Fife. One of them must have been almost in direct succession to MacDuff, the most famous of all the Fife thanes.

The estate, a large one, as I have indicated, eventually fell to a sister who married a Fife landowner, Adam de Valloines. He was also a supporter of the English side. The Valloines (Vallance) family, as was common in these warlike times, also terminated in an heiress. This lady married Sir Andrew Wardlaw of Torrie. With this family we have a further connection with Scottish history. The brother of Andrew was Cardinal bishop of Glasgow and his son, Archbishop Henry Wardlaw, founded in 1411 the University of St. Andrews, the first University in Scotland. Other members of the Wardlaws of Lochore filled important appointments under the Scottish Crown, including the sheriffship of Fife. The Wardlaws either rebuilt or greatly improved the castle. Old writers state that the name "Robertus Wardlaw" was carved above the entrance to the tower.

In the reign of Charles I another family, the Malcolms, came into the possession of Lochore, by which time the estate had decreased in size. I have mentioned that it was known in early times as Lochore-shire and comprised the whole of Ballingry and the most of Aucherderran parish southwards as far as Lochhead. When the Malcolms got it, the estate comprised Lochore (or Inchgall), half of Capledrae, Ballingry, Benarty, Navity and a portion of Balbedie. The Boswells of Balmuto also held land in the parish, and Balbedie and Capledrae were once owned by James Hamilton, a favourite of James V, who was the architect of Falkland Palace. The Malcolms parted with their Lochore land in 1790 to Captain Park but continued in possession of Balbedie. They were long the principal heritors in Bingry Kirk and several are buried there. One of them was out in the Fifteen rebellion under the Earl of Mar along with a number of other Fife lairds but he hedged when it came to fighting and did not take part in the battle of Sheriffmuir.

Captain Park came into possession of Lochore in 1790. It was he who had the loch drained hoping thereby to reclaim the land and utilize it for purposes of husbandry. A good deal of cutting was necessary through whinstone, but the task was finished in 1798 and the waters of Loch Ore emptied into the river. The scheme however did not prove the success anticipated for the soil was not found suitable for crops and it was utilised for the growing of meadow hay. Even that proved unprofitable, for it was no uncommon occurrence for the hay to be washed away in the flooding that took place over the reclaimed acres.

There seems no trace of the burgh of Crosshill of five hundred years ago. Some very old houses however were in existence about Crosshill a generation ago. Even now one or two are standing which must be very old. The markets would be held probably on the moor, which is now Ballingry Golf Course and there would doubtless be the Mercat Cross. Close by an old drove road can be easily traced. It is shown on old maps as Torres Loan and connected with the road that leads to Bingry Kirk.

The big Mary Pit has taken the place of the numerous old mines and pits which were scattered over Crosshill, Rosewell, Lochore and Capledrae. The latter raised a good class of cannel coal which was supplied to gas works. At that time it was believed gas could be made only from this type of coal.

Nowadays gas can be made from almost any kind of coal. Over to the north west, just beside Chapel farm, you would have found less than a generation ago, the remains of a Roman camp. As such it is still marked in the maps. You are all, I daresay, familiar with the almost unquestioned fact that an important battle was fought in this vicinity between the Roman invaders and the native Picts in 83 AD. It was the battle of Orrea, and it will be found referred to in translations of Roman historians. Briefly, the Roman General Agricola, after consolidating the territory from the Forth and Clyde line, was forced by the continuous surprise attacks of the natives north of that line to try and subdue them. Accordingly he sent the Ninth Legion across the Forth. At Lochore it was attacked by the Fife Pictish tribe, known as Horresti, and nearly defeated. Some historians even go the length of claiming that this was the site of the famous battle of "Mons Grampius" which resulted in a decisive defeat of the Caledonians. It is common knowledge that the Romans never could settle beyond the great wall which stretched from the Forth to the Clyde, and that is why in Fife there have been few discoveries which can be attributed to Roman occupation. Fife never was conquered and so the old poet writes of "the Kingdom": "with truth, thou didst scorn Rome's capture for to be, and kept thyself from Roman legions free."

The Roman camp was 2020 feet in circumference and Sibbald the first historian of Fife writing in 1690 says that "to the east of Lochore may be seen Cairns of stones such as were raised where there were fights by our ancestors. In the bogs adjoining, there was, not above a hundred years ago, found swords of brass and brass heads of lances, some of which were kept in Sir Andrew Balfour's cabinet of rarities, and other ancient implements and arms have been found at Bogside Farm."

On part of the Roman camp a chapel was built called the Chapel of Inchgall, the old name for Loch Ore. You have that fact preserved in the name of Chapel Farm. Under the soil where the Loch was drained was found a stone cannon ball, a silver spoon and a marble slab.

☆ ☆ ☆

Going south, I propose to start from here because this kirk (St. Andrews) is not only the physical centre of modern Lochgelly, but it was here that much of the business that affected the public services of the village was transacted, as also the deliberations that led up to the transformation of the village into a police burgh in 1877. Many of the leaders too in these movements and in the development of Lochgelly were the founders of this kirk. It was here that the old Parochial Board met. From it was formed what was known as the Lochgelly Local Authority (really a local Committee of the Parochial Board), and out of it in turn originated the Police Burgh. This local Authority was something in the nature of the present District Councils and they had the administration of roads, drainage and water subject to the Board of Supervision.

As we dander south, we move through the whole of old Lochgelly: that is the village of say three generations ago with its population of under 700. The old village was bounded on the south as it still is by South Street and on the north by Main Street. Less than 100 years ago there was only one house between Main Street and the old houses of Launcherhead, now demolished.

Old Lochgelly was a weaving village. Let us visualise that village. It must have appeared a picturesque place viewed from the north or west or east, whitewashed houses clustered on a hillside, many of them with thatched roofs and scattered about with little resemblance of regular streets; looking indeed as if they had been scattered from a pepper box. It was before the days of a town council and town planning did not apply.

A century ago practically no miners lived in the village of Lochgelly. There were less than fifty persons then engaged in coal mining, all resided at Cooperha' and the old Launcherhead I referred to. As time went on and mining developed the weavers and their families took to the pits. As you walked past the doors of the village you would have heard the clatter of the shuttle. In that old village some men were born who gained a national distinction.

We have therefore not far to dander from here to get into the old village. Bank Street is comparatively modern. There is Knockhill, a two storey house which belonged to one Francis Berry, who had a small estate bounded by his house on the east and by what is now Francis Street on the south, and North Street on the north. This house dates back to 1744.

Not much is left in the Main Street of the old village. There are those here who however will remember a number of white washed houses, many with thatched roofs. In east Main Street is a building that holds considerable interest. Now a ladies shop, it was at one time the centre of all Lochgelly's public affairs. It was a but and ben in which the Union Bank opened a branch here in 1853. On the erection of the present Bank, this office was taken over by the Parochial Board and there the routine work of the parish was done. When the first Education Act was passed in 1872 it was utilised as the headquarters of the School Board. On the foundation of the Police Burgh in 1877 it also became the Town House and was also the first office of Lochgelly Gas Company. All these concerns used it at the one time, till in the late eighties the Police Commissioners bought, after long negotiations, an old almost derelict building on the site now occupied by the Town House, which had been the subscription school.

The first election of Police Commissioners took place in January 1877, and the following were returned – Robert Dick, David Wilson, Andrew Landale, George Williamson, George Gillespie, Thomas Dick, James Cook, Thomas Hugh and William Bethune. The unsuccessful were – James Bethune, Andrew Leitch, Alex Thomson, Andrew Galloway. Andrew Landale was appointed chief magistrate and Robert Dick and David Wilson junior magistrates and George Gillespie as treasurer.

One of the first of the many duties of new Police Commissioners was to fix the names of the streets and numbering houses. In the particular district under notice at the moment the following names were made official – Bank Street, from corner of Gillespie's shop to East School; Knockhill Close at the back of the Co-operative store; side streets off Bank Street to be named respectively, Francis Street, Berry Street, North Street; Knowledge Street to be changed to Plantation Street; High Street as at present; Hall Street to be that street from the old village school eastwards to Haggis-haugh Park; Church Street as at present; South Street as at present; Music Hall Street to be changed to Mid Street, Trotters Row to Park Street (East), Rotten Row to be changed to Gardiner Street; property off High Street to be named Brewery Court. The cost of painting the names was 1/3d each.

Branching to the east off High Street is Plantation Street, formerly known as we have seen, as Knowledge Street. This name was given to it partly because it was the birth place of Professor David Page, and partly because it was occupied mostly by the weavers, who were the best informed of the village population. The last loom by the way was worked in this street.

The Professor Page referred to became one of the most distinguished geologists of his age. He was a delicate youth and probably this may have led to him being more studious than his fellows. His schooling was mostly got at Auchterderran Parish School and later he went to St Andrews University. There was the inevitable struggle of his poor parents to put him through. I have heard it said that his granny walked periodically from Lochgelly to St. Andrews carrying his meal pock on her back and walked home again. At one time Page was editor of the Fife News. Page, who was one of the greatest Scottish geologists till Geikie and Millar, was a fellow of the Royal Geographical Society and had literary tastes. He wrote numerous books of collected verse. Shortly after this church was built Page preached in it. He was so feeble that he had to be carried into the pulpit. He was a distinguished scholar in an age of greatness. The hundred years from the middle of the 18th to the middle of the 19th century were the most prolific in our history, when Scotland rose to the highest peak of literary and philosophical fame. That was an epic age for Scotland, when as Sydney Smith said in the Edinburgh Review, "Scotsmen were able to cultivate literature on a little oatmeal". It was something to be a distinguished man in that age and Lochgelly may well be proud of her son.

Further up the High Street on the right hand side is, or was, Brewery Court. There a brewery was carried on for many years. No one living can remember it as such, but it certainly was working in the fore part of the last century. The feu charter was dated 1760, granted to a David Thomson, described as a maltsman and brewer in easter Lochgelly, so that an earlier brewery may have been in existence. It was not uncommon in these days for villages to possess breweries or brew houses. Beer of course was then the principal beverage, for tea in the eighteenth century and whisky too was practically unknown among common people. Whisky didn't come into common use in the Lowlands till the middle of the 18th century, and I venture to say the Scottish ale produced a more vigorous, virile race than will be the outcome of generations of tea drinking. The ale was known as "tuppenny" and there was very little duty on it. One Scots pint equalled four English quarts.

When the brewery ceased to operate, the buildings were converted into dwelling houses and they latterly had the appearance of city slums. The property got into the hands of Kirkcaldy lawyers and the last owner, Mr Dewar, left it for behoof of the poor of Lochgelly with the magistrates as trustees. A number of years ago the whole of the Brewery Court was demolished and a housing scheme built on the site. The trust brings in about £90 a year and this is annually distributed to old Lochgelly people who are not in receipt of Public Assistance.

Turning into Mid Street, known at one time as Music Hall Street, we find a whitewashed building formerly a model lodging house. It was known by the name of Castle Rags. I don't know its age but would judge it to be well over 200 years. It too will soon be disappearing. I know how it came to be called Castle Rags. There is, or was, a Castle Rags in Edinburgh. Probably the name to it through the class of people living there (it had long been a common lodging house), mostly of the vagrant type or lowest labouring class.

Further along the street is the old United Presbyterian Church with a manse adjoining, latterly the music hall, and long turned into dwelling houses. This congregation is by far the oldest in the town. It was formed almost a century before the others, in 1741.

In that year a number of people in Ballingry, Beath and Auchterderran petitioned the Burgher presbytery of Dunfermline for a supply of sermon. There had been a dispute in Auchterderran Parish Kirk, over the appointment of a minister, and this swelled the number of dissenters. Two of the nearest ministers, Swanston of Kinross, and Shirra the eccentric minister of Kirkcaldy, were ordered to take up that duty.

Behind the church was a park or loan where tent preachings were held. These tent preachings drew enormous crowds and were generally taken part in by several ministers. The Communions were known as the "Occasions". At the time of the church's ter jubilee, the late Miss Steedman gave me an interesting article on the Kirk. She recalled through her grandmother who was born in 1780, the great tent preachings and how she had been told that Mr Shirra would announce to the assembled crowds that he "had ladlefuls of the gospel" for them. The people came from long distances, the women walking barefoot with traditional Scottish thrift, carrying their footgear in a napkin and putting them on just before reaching the village.

That old kirk in Mid Street was seated for 500. Exactly a hundred years after the old kirk was built, the new one was erected in the Tent Park and a manse was furnished two years later. The second minister of the Lochgelly U.P. Church was a notable divine, the Rev David Greig who had sat under Swanston of Kinross. He was minister of the Lochgelly Kirk for 50 years – 1773 – 1823.

Another of the ministers, the Rev Wm. Reid, was of the real old school. This Mr Reid greatly disapproved of vanity or display. He refused to be driven in a cab to a wedding, calling such a butterfly wedding. When the masonic lodge started here in 1858 they had a torchlight procession and he was very incensed at the regalia expressing his opinion in the words of St Paul – "When I was a child I spoke as a child but when I became a man I put away childish things". It's exactly a hundred years, by the way, since this Mr Reid was ordained at Lochgelly. The U.P. Church was then of course in the centre of the village which had 650 inhabitants.

Just opposite in Church Street was a school kept by one John Ewing, mentioned in a poem by James Halfpenny "Where mony a scholar guid cam' oot – and aiblins mony a fule" and round the corner is East Park Street, formerly known as Johnny Trotter's Raw. The term "Raw" for a street seems to be peculiar to this district. Edinburgh has its closes, bows, its courts, its gaits: Kirkcaldy its wynds; St. Andrews and Dunfermline their lanes or loans, but Lochgelly had its raws. You will find raws in all the villages round about – the Contle Raw, the Milton Raw, the Caravan Raw in Lochore, and you get them also in Kelty and Cowdenbeath. In our town all these raws became streets when the burgh was formed in 1878. The other raw in this area was the Rotten Raw (Gardiner Street). The origin of its name is not certain but the term is not uncommon. London has its famous Rotten Row and you find the term also in Glasgow and Aberdeen. In these cases it means the route taken by the ecclesiastics, but in our case its more likely to have some association with the species associated with Pied Piper of Hamelin.

Up in South Street still stands the but and ben where the brothers Gray, who both won great distinction in science, were born. These Grays were stone masons but they had ambition, and exceptional talent. The elder, Thomas, led the party which laid the first electric cable in Japan, just then emerging from feudalism and he died professor of an American University. The other, Andrew, was one of the famous scientists of his age. He was assistant to Lord Kelvin in Glasgow University and when Kelvin died he succeeded him in the chair of natural philosophy there. I have once or twice published references to the Grays which most of you will have read. Andrew, by the way, married a Lochgelly woman by name Anne Gordon who resided in Berry Street. There again you had literature cultivated on a little oatmeal.

The Well Road, I believe it was once the Well Raw, takes its name from a common well at the corner of the Birnie Braes. These braes, now covered with houses, were a common, and there the travelling circuses used to set up after the Moor Common was built over. Feuars had the right to take sand and turf from the braes. The prospect looking from the braes was a very fine one looking over the the Lomonds, the Cleish Hills and the Ochils beyond. A very nice poem was written by the late James Halfpenny entitled the Birnie Braes. I shall quote one verse in this connection

> "I've read about Loch Lomond's Banks
> And Ben Lomond Towerin' high
> The Beauty of Killarney's lakes
> And Italy's cloudless sky
> They may be grand, I dinna ken,
> But I think it's just a craze,
> Tae me they ne'er could look sae weel
> As oor ain Birnie Braes".

That sentiment will find an echo with many here.

Lochgelly at one time drew its water supply from numerous wells in and around the village. As the population grew, and standards of hygiene rose, engineers were commissioned to report how a better supply of water could be obtained. The first scheme proposed was to form a small reservoir at the Birnie Braes, but this was soon dropped for the reason that water could not be delivered to the high part of the town, and because there was not a sufficient amount of gathering ground. Other schemes were investigated, six or seven in all, including one based on Benarty, and some involving co-operation with other communities. On 4th February 1878, after ten years of consideration, the question was finally settled when Lochornie was decided on. The amount of water deemed necessary for Lochgelly was fifteen gallons per head per day, but, looking to the future, it was decided to set the capacity at 20 gallons per head. The reservoir was filling in April 1881, and the water was turned on shortly afterwards.

We now pass to the ridge of Lochgelly just under 600 feet above sea level, to the domain of the lord of the manor. The lands of Lochgelly are mentioned in documents many centuries back. They are referred to as the tafts of Lochgelly easter and wester. What was easter Lochgelly is not easily defined; for wester we have the westertoon. When exactly the two estates were joined I cannot at present say but before the middle of the eighteenth century they came into the possession of the present owners, the family of Lord Minto. The family name is Elliot Murray Kinninmonth, and it was the son of the union of Gilbert Elliot and Agnes Murray Kinninmonth the heiress of Lochgelly, who was the first Earl of Minto.

The earliest owners of the lands of Lochgelly, as far as can be traced, were the Lochore family, followed by the Wardlaws, both of which families played a very prominent part in Scottish History from the time of Malcolm Canmore till after the period of the Reformation. The Parishes of Ballingry, Auchtertool, and a part of Auchterderran were comprised in the estate known as Lochoreshire. The term shire did not then mean the same as it does today. We had six or seven shires in what is now the Sheriffdom of Fife and Kinross, and the only one left is the Bishopshire. The term shire came into use with the feudal system and is older than the term parish, though in many cases the extent of territory was sometimes not much larger. Shire of course is civil and parish was for ecclesiastical purposes.

Sir Gilbert Elliot, who secured the estate by marrying the heiress, was a notable figure in contemporary Scottish history. He was a prominent politician and held the office of Lord of the Admiralty. He was also the author of the song "My sheep I neglected" which Sir Walter Scott declared was one of the finest pastoral songs. It was his sister, Jane Elliot, who wrote "The Floors of The Forest" and as the two were close friends she would doubtless be a frequent visitor at Lochgelly. It was the brother of these two that was the famous General Elliot who conducted the siege of Gibraltar, one of the great epics in world history. Doubtless he too would be a visitor at his brother's house. Sir

Gilbert took a great interest in the villagers and it has been handed down to us that he frequently had them at the big hoose, danced with them on the green and supplied them with ale brought doubtless from the Lochgelly Brew House. As showing his popularity the villagers had a song -

"O bring tae me Sir Gilbert
For he's a bonnie man".

He was locally known as "Gibbie o' the gowden garters". It was this same Sir Gilbert who really started coal mining in Lochgelly, the story of which I dealt fully with in my last talk here. The second earl started the Lochgelly Curling Club, at the centenary of which I had the honour to preside four years ago when the present Lord Minto was present and presented a centenary cup.

Up till a generation ago the Minto family resided frequently at Lochgelly. I can personally recall the Hon. Hugh Elliot who was Editor of the Edinburgh Review giving entertainment in the old music hall to adults and children. He handed out presents to the bairns. Being an editor he was interested in printing and frequently he would drop in to my father's little printing shop for a crack and at times tried his hand at setting type.

At the bottom of the ridge on the south side lies our loch which is roughly 2 ½ miles in circumference. During the old fashioned winters we used to have, there was great sport there for curlers and skaters. It belongs to four proprietors – Minto, Wemyss, Novar and Lochend. It was at one time believed that there was coal underneath it and a project was underfoot 30 to 40 years ago to drain it. The four owners could not however all agree. I believe it was the little estate of Lochend that held out.

Two theories are advanced for the name of Loch Gellie. One is that it is from the Gaelic and means the bright or clear lake; the other is that it got its name from the prolific shoal of leeches or gellies that it contained. At one time the gathering of leeches was quite an industry here. They were used largely in earlier days by the medical profession and Lochgelly leeches were said to be of a specially good quality. They were taken to Kirkcaldy and sold there for distribution.

On the south side of the Loch is the estate of Wemyss of Wemyss. It has been in that family longer than Lochgelly has been owned by the Elliots, as far back indeed as the fifteenth century. In the year 1583 it is recorded that a dispute arose between the laird of Wemyss and the laird of Balmuto (that is the Boswell who owned Boswell Knowe). The difference was over the fishings of the loch. So bitter was the feeling that the laird of Wemyss sent his eldest son with six score men to defend his rights. They built a fort on their own (the south side) of the loch, dug a moat round it, stored it with food and munitions and put a boat on the loch. This incident is recorded in the Chartulary of Wemyss. The dispute was eventually settled by the intervention of the King, that would be James VI, the "wisest fool in Christendom". He was well known as a mediator.

On the east side of our dander is the Spittal farm. It has been assumed from the name that a hospice or religious hospital once existed there but that is mere surmise. There is said to have been a religious building in the farm of Lochhead, where, it is recorded by an old historian, St. Finnan planted a monastery. Several stone coffins were found there a considerable time ago. From St Finnan it is suggested we get that name Lumphinnans.

Many years ago a cist (an old tomb) was found on the farm of Powguild and antiquarian finds have also been unearthed to the south of our loch. Indeed between Lochgelly and the sea much life must have existed in the early times. Over this ground roamed the Romans on their march to Benarty and later the Danes. The last battle fought by Danes in Scotland, according to Sibbald, was north of Kinghorn. Later on the area figured in the Wars of Independence, the invasion of Cromwell and in the Fifteen Jacobite Rebellion.

On the next ridge – Fife is a county of ridges – is Little Raith and Lochhead belonging, as I have said, to the Wemyss of Wemyss. Coal was worked on that estate by the second Earl of Wemyss. He has the following entry in his diary – "John, Earle of Wemyss 1643, did work a levell to four colles in his lands of Louchhead nire Lochgellie, first meeting in ye mine with a good colle of 3 fitts thick, another four fitts thick, 3 of five fitts thick and also one of 8 fitts all good burning colles".

On the east side of Little Raith is Gleniston which at one time belonged to a family named Glen – Glen's toon. Round from Gleniston and down the path we come to the ruin of a castle which must at one time have been of considerable dimensions and strength. It is known as Hallyards, sometimes called Camilla, and round these now ruined walls much history was made, some of it of national significance. The earliest record we have of it is as a hunting lodge of Malcolm Canmore whose royal house was of course at Dunfermline. In 1127 his son David 1, the "sair saint for the croon", who gave so much of the royal possessions to the church, granted the lands to the newly erected bishopric of Dunkeld and it was made an episcopal residence. Fifty years later the endowment was given to the Priory of Inchcolm.

One of the bishops who occupied Hallyards was the hero of a notable deed here a few years after the battle of Bannockburn. He was Bishop St. Clair. I shall quote his heroic action direct from Sibbald – "Robert the Bruce was absent in Ireland supporting his brother Edward for the crown of that

country when a party of maurading English anchored in the Forth. The Earl
of Fife and the Sheriff having 500 men under their command attempted to
oppose the landing; but intimidated by the number of the English they made a
precipitate retreat. Bishop Sinclair, then staying at Hallyards, happened to
meet the fugitives. "Whither are you going?" he said to the commanders,
"you deserve to have your gilt spurs knocked off." Then throwing aside his
ecclesiastical vestments he seized a spear and cried "Who loves Scotland,
follow me." He led the Fifers again to the charge and impetuously attacked
the enemy. The English gave way and were driven to their ships with considerable loss. When the king heard of it he said "Sinclair shall be my bishop."
And as the "King's Bishop" and sometimes the "fechtin' bishop" he was long
known to his countrymen. Gavin Douglas, who was also Bishop of Dunkeld
1514 – 1522, would also likely be a frequent visitor at this episcopal residence of Hallyards. He won his honours in a different sphere, as a great
Scottish makar or poet. He came to be known as the "Scottish Virgil"
through his translation of the "Aeneid".

The castle and lands came into lay hands a little before the Reformation.
The Roman Church foresaw the storm and they tried to secure their immense
property by a system of "feu farm". They thus hoped to retain actual ownership with a view to getting it back when the storm blew past. And so the great
family of Kirkcaldy of Grange comes within our purview. It was Sir James
Kirkcaldy to whom Hallyards was given over and he removed there with his
family shortly after. It must have been a more important place than Grange.

While the Kirkcaldys were in possession (father and son James and
William – two great names in Scottish history) two important affairs
happened. The first was the visit of James V, distracted from the rout of
Solway Moss, making his way to his Palace of Falkland. Knox related the
matter thus "the king made inventories of all his jewels and other substances,
and ashamed to look any man in the face, secretly dispatched to Fife, and
coming to Hallyards was humanely received by the lady of the house. With
him was William Kirkcaldy. The lady at the supper, perceiving him pensive,
began to comfort him and willed him to take the work of God in good part.
"My portion of this world" replied the King "is short, for I will not be with
you 15 days". His servants asked him where he would hold his Yule which
then approached. He answered with a disdainful smirk "I cannot tell; choose
ye the place; but this I can tell you, ere Yule day ye will be masterless and the
realm without a King." "Because of his displeasure" adds Knox "no man dare
make contradictions to him". The King left Hallyards next day accompanied
by its young laird. Both Sir James and William were with him when he died

at Falkland and doubtless heard his prophetic utterance with reference to the crown of Scotland – "It cam wis a lass and it'll gang wi' a lass".

Not long after, another affair of importance happened at Hallyards. It was there that the plot was hatched to dispose of Cardinal Beaton. The story of the seizure of St Andrews Castle and the murder of the Cardinal is familiar. It was lairds from round about here that carried it through. Kirkcaldy was one, the Laird of Raith, Melville a brother in law was another and Norman Leslie of Leslie another. Of the 35 summoned at the Cross of Cupar for the Cardinal's death no fewer than twelve were of the connected families of Raith and Hallyards.

In the next century Cromwell's forces over-ran this district. After the battle of Pitreavie, he marched north from his headquarters at Burntisland and lay with his army for a time at the base of the Bishop Hill. It was in our district that a story is recorded which shows his sense of justice and his stern discipline. His army at that time was evidently not in its usual state of subordination. One of his soldiers had been making a practice of forcibly taking milk at a cottar house. He went the length of milking the cow and drinking the milk. The cow belonged to a woman. She suffered patiently for a time but one day she followed him and made the serious complaint to headquarters. Cromwell asked her if she was positive as to the man and she declared she was. He made his men form into line and asked her to fix on the guilty one. Cromwell several times reminded her she would need to be perfectly certain because if she caused an innocent man to suffer her life would be forfeit. He called the man out to be hung forthwith and his body opened. This was done and the milk was found curdled in his stomach. This, of course, proved his guilt and at the same time saved the woman's life. (This incident is related in Small's Antiquities of Fife.)

We pass on to the next century to find Hallyards again in the news. This was the first Jacobite rebellion. Fife folks, at least the gentle folks, were closely involved in this affair though they took little or nothing to do with the later one in '45. By that time Hallyards had passed into the well known Fife and Aberdeen family of Skene, and John Skene, then owner of Hallyards, played a prominent part in the rising. It was on the topmost turret of Hallyards that the Fife lairds raised the standard of revolt. Skene was taken prisoner at Preston and condemned to death but was later pardoned but he was again in the thick of it at Glenshiel. It is said he died of grief at the failure of the Stuart cause.

The district had two visits from troops connected with the 1715 rising. The first was while the Earl of Mar had his headquarters at Perth before the battle of Sheriffmuir. His staff got information that a ship with stores and arms for the royal forces had been forced to take shelter at Burntisland harbour and he sent the Master of Sinclair, who commanded the Fife lairds, with a body of mounted men and baggage horses to capture the ship and carry back its stores. This force was followed by 500 highlanders who advanced as far as Auchtertool to protect the return of the raiders. Both contingents came by the way of Kinnesswood and would pass through or near by Lochgelly. The vessel was captured but the return was marked by insubordination by the highlanders. Sinclair's diary has a longish story in which he says when he got back to Auchtertool only forty men were left out of the 500. The rest were roaming over the country roundabout thieving and plundering. They threatened to shoot Sinclair for interfering with them and it was only by a ruse that he got them to clear out and return north. He told them the Duke of Argyll (the commander of the Hanoverian forces) was only three miles off. This had the desired effect for he records they then left diligently.

At this period we had also a visit from the bold Rob Roy and his caterans. After the battle of Sheriffmuir, when Rob played rather a doubtful part, he withdrew to Falkland and from there harried the country right to the sea. It may be taken that our village and neighbourhood would be a subject to his deprivations.

✩ ✩ ✩

Just opposite the Kirk is a grocery shop still with the name Fraser above the door. It was built by one John Coupar who had been in charge of the Iron Company's store in Auchterderran Road. This was a shop run by the Iron and Coal Coy where the workers traded and had the value of their purchases deducted from their fortnightly pay. Such stores were common in all mining villages. The practice was stopped by the passing of the Truck Act. John Coupar built that property and had started to build the hotel on the north side of the church. His property was destroyed by fire. He had not kept up his insurance premium and the loss was such that he could not carry on and had to sell what had been built as the hotel. The building was completed by James Cook.

At the rear of the church was a large kitchen garden for which John Fraser, the grocer opposite, paid a small sum in rent and sold the produce in his shop. I was told that when of very tender years I disappeared for a long time. My mother got anxious and searched round the streets. Eventually the truant was found in the Kirk garden chasing birds with a pickle salt in his little kneive, trying, of course to catch a bird by the well known method. I am more sophisticated today!

On the opposite side of Berry Street my father and my uncle over 100 years ago took a feu off the Berry Bequest and each built a room and kitchen house. Later they each added an attic and then two rooms to the north and south. The house where I was brought up consisted of half of the present stationery shop, the other part was the kitchen in which my father started a small printing business. There was a lean-to wash house which my mother used as a kitchen, a front room and bedroom and an attic room with a large window from which I saw much of Lochgelly's pageant. I looked out on the Lochgelly Volunteer Coy marching off to the Queen's historic Wet Review in 1881. I recall one Sunday when I was not at Kirk – I must have been ill – seeing a handful of elders leaving after the bell had ceased and adjourning to Willie Bethune's licensed grocer's shop – he was one of them – and remaining there during most of the service. It was then a well known howff for a dram.

The feu is on the Berry Trust estate. When the foundations were being laid a bunch of copper coins was uncovered which my father told me were French pennies. The ground had been the orchard for Knockhill House.

Next to my uncle's house was a butcher's shop kept by Hughie Scott. He was the local pig killer and on the vacant ground he was kept busy. The bairns on their way to school looked through the barred gate watching him sticking the pigs – no humane killing then – and then we saw him throw the carcase into a big tub of boiling water. Hughie was married to a sister of Bailie Dick, known as was the custom then by her own name Eassie Dick. She kept the purse (wisely) for Hughie was very found of a dram. When he went to her for a sixpence she refused him at first with the exclamation – "Oh the monster." Then she would relent and out of her apron pocket hand over the 6d with which he went to Henry Penman's in Church St, his favourite pub. Hughie always looked dirty and untidy. He minced his beef with a small mixer which he called a mincer, and with his dirty paws handed it over to the customer. There was little in the way of hygiene when I was a boy. Pig styes and cow byres were generally within a few yards of the back doors.

Knockhill was a little estate and belonged to Francis Berry, a farmer in Beath Parish. He had an only son who died when coming out as a minister and he left Knockhill lands to the Parochial Board of Beath to be applied to the education of Beath natives up to the University. The house bears the date and the initials. It was an old Scottish custom when a pair got married and a house of their own to carve their initials on the lintel of the door.

The square known as Knockhill Close used to contain a large whin stone with a flat top. It was used as a soap box by speakers of all shades of subject, candidates for Parliament, showmen, medical quacks selling medicine to cure all ills and pulling teeth without pain (no anaesthetics were then used for tooth extraction). The stone, from which a Prime Minister spoke – Ramsay MacDonald – acquired a certain veneration and there was much indignation when it disappeared, broken up to be used as road bottoming. I have asked very old inhabitants about it but all they could say was that it was there a long time. It had no marks. Perhaps it was a boundary stone or a moot stone in earlier times where our rude forefathers of the hamlet met to discuss affairs; something in the nature of a Village Cross.

The site of the present Store building at The Cross, the second Store (the first shop was in High Street) was previously occupied by a low storey building which included a cobbler's shop. The Society cleared the site and erected the building as it stands today. It had a large grocery shop where almost everything was sold from a cradle to an anchor – clothes, boots, kitchenware etc. That building was seriously damaged by fire in 1879. I was four years old then and I remember my father carrying me out in the middle of the night wrapped in a blanket to see the blaze.

Harking back to the east side at the top of Bank St there was a large garden ground cultivated by the tenants in the property opposite the church. One morning I saw from the attic window a huge hole 12 – 15ft in diameter and as much in depth. It had caved in during the night, due to subsidence of an early coal working. It was later filled up. Part of the Cinema is on that site.

Then we came to a range of single storey buildings which contained a licenced grocer's shop and two dwelling houses. It was a property of John Addison who had a smiddy down the Cinema close. He and his wife – no family – lived in a cottage house with a retaining garden wall, now a baker's shop, and the shop at the corner was the first Store butchery. The butcher was one named Kirk and the killing house or slaughter house was in North Street. It later became a smiddy and for years has been used as a garage by the Railway Coy.

This John Addison owned a good deal of property. He could be seen each morning at the mouth of the Close. He was gazing westwards and was always ready to tell when the day would be rainy or fine. His eyes were on a particular tree on the Hill of Beath. If he could see it, the weather would be fine; if not visible then it meant rain. South of his property was vacant ground built on about 70 years ago by David Wilson, joiner. It has two shops and dwellings above. Then the joiner's shop of the Wilsons, David and Joseph, cousins. It is a moot point whether the Wilsons or the Westwaters are the oldest family in business in the town. David Wilson, the principal partner, was a responsible type. He was an elder in the U.P. Kirk and his wife, who had been a teacher, took a great interest in Education and social work. He also owned property in both east and west Main street.

On the west side of Knockhill Close was Robert Knight's smiddy. He was succeeded by his son John and two maiden daughters, one of whom was the village postman. It was said that Maggie Knight could always announce the news on a postcard before she delivered it. Their brother John was gie fond of a dram and the sisters kept a careful eye on him. When the noise of the hammer on the anvil ceased they were round to see about it. So John circumvented them by getting a boy to whom he gave a penny to clang on the anvil while he popped round to Davie Paton's back door. I know a boy who, when off school for a time ill, was ever on the watch for a call from the smiddy.

David Paton's public house was a single storey building with an attic. Later a storey was added and it now belongs to the Public House Society and is known as the Queen's Arms hotel. There was a stable and coach house behind the house. On the occasion of a wedding or a ball this pub was in great demand. It was "the thing" to drive to these functions. Probably the awful conditions of the footpaths accounted for that. I have known mothers bring their daughters to a ball wrapped in a shawl so that the ball shoes would not get dirty. The public house was the howff of the Free Masons when they held their meetings in the Co-op Hall. After their meetings, no matter how late the hour, they crossed the close to the side door and carried on often till midnight. The police turned a blind eye, though I remember a number of prominent Lochgelly men were caught. Their influence however got the breach healed and I don't remember a prosecution. With three shops, houses above were built by the Patons. They are now owned by the Goth. The first tenants were a bootmaker named Boswell; a chemist named Alex. Graham and a tailor, Geo. Millar.

West of Paton's was the Well Green, site of the Miners Welfare Institute. The well on the green was the main one for that part of the town. The water was pumped to a street hand well situated in a half circular recess, and on the kerb was a water trough for horses. The green was the subject for a dispute with the Town Council when about fifty years ago they started laying granolithic pavements. It was on Lord Minto's land and the Council wanted him to pay the cost of the footpath. He objected on the ground that it was a grant to feuars on his estate to take water and bleach their clothes. The feuars were approached and they refused liability. Finally the Town Council paid the bill.

Adjoining the Well Green was a two storey building. It was built by Thos. Dick, a worthy elder in the Free Kirk. It was the first house to have a lightning conductor and I think the only one in the town. Single storey houses next to it are scheduled for demolition and they include a shop famous for its tripe kept by an old wife called Jean Stalker.

In an attic lived and died our soldier poet, John Pindar. His only income was a pension of 1/- which he collected each month. It was soon blown for Pindar was very fond of a dram. In the interval he existed on tick from the public houses. A niece told me one day when up with his dinner he was gie fu', and angry. He had been refused a drink on credit and vented his rage on a time piece which stood on the mantle shelf. Reaching for it he dashed it to the floor with the remark "If there's nae tick for me there's gaun to be nane for you".

Pindar was gie fond of the lassies and most of his songs sung their praises. I remember a bevy of fine looking young girls from Dunfermline starting what was called a Temperance Society. They held a meeting at the Cross and then walked in procession with their followers to the hall where the meeting was continued. Pindar was attracted to the astonishment of onlookers and joined in the procession. He had a limp as the result of an accident in the pit. It was said it was the good looking girls who had attracted him into following them. His conversion did not last long.

At the rear of the shop Andrew Leitch set up the first Lochgelly gasworks. It was a primitive affair and when the Lochgelly Gas Coy was formed in 1886 Andrew offered them his place. They valued it at £10 which was refused. Relics of the wee gasworks remained for years. Andrew Leitch had previously been in the public house at the extreme west end, known as the Black Bull.

This point takes us to the boundary between the parishes of Auchterderran and Ballingry. On the opposite (south) side of the Cross at the corner of Church Street (now being reconstructed by the Co-op) was a shop kept by a pair of maiden ladies named Lumsden who had a drapery business. Next door was Charlie Wilkie's boot shop but he removed to a new building in Bank Street. Further west was the first chemist's shop occupied by Alex. Graham and later by a cousin of mine. The first occupier of it was named Erskine, and later Andrew Dunsire. Next was a row of small houses, still extant but doomed for demolition, and then the Free Kirk which was opened in 1857. At the west side of the Free Kirk was a right of way called the dykeside which was a shortcut from the tap o' the toon to the main street. From that point, within my time, there was not a single building on the south side of the road to the north end of Cowdenbeath.

Again to the north side was a public house opposite the Kirk owned by one named McLean, and David Henderson's cabinetmaker's shop and works. Further on was a tinsmith, James Melville, who was Lochgelly's second provost. He was an amateur astronomer and could be seen at night with a telescope studying the heavens. By the way, he was a descendant of a

Kirkcaldy man who was involved in the famous Mutiny of the Bounty. A shop next to James Melville's was occupied by a shoemaker named Hardie. He succeeded his father-in law.

The Opera Picture House was built by ex-Provost Reid over 50 years ago. It was extended for variety entertainments, then it became popular for roller skating and was eventually turned into a picture house.

The Cross was widened a little in 1902 when the Town Council asked the Co-op Society to sell the butcher's shop. They agreed only to take down the east gable and round the corner to Bank Street and rebuild it in a straight line with the buildings on the other side. That would give five feet more of a footpath at the south end corner and one foot at the north corner. The Town Council were to pay all expenses which an architect estimated at about £75. The Town Council agreed to ask the County Council to help in the cost.

☆ ☆ ☆

Eastwards from the church (St Andrews), there were practically no houses a hundred years ago. Where St Andrews church now stands was a triangular wood surrounded by pasture land stretching northwards and moor land to the east.

Beyond the church was the old quoiting ground, a favourite rendezvous for the miners in their leisure time. A number of outstanding players were associated with the ground, including two national champions. The first was Robert Gillespie who later emigrated to Salt Lake City, and a generation later another product of the Lochgelly Club, William Watters, won the championship of Scotland. Another, Robert Suttie, is credited with the quoiting championship of England. Just over the wall from the quoiting ground was laid the first bowling green. It was connected with the Minto Hotel and its membership consisted mostly of professional and business men with a few miners who because of their association with this club were known as the aristocratic colliers. I'm not sure in what year the green was laid but it was certainly over 60 years ago. The Lochgelly Club was one of seven in Fife which met in 1879 to form the Fifeshire Bowling Association. This green was closed when the present one was made in 1896.

Adjoining the quoiting ground on the south side stood the subscription school. It was run by feuars and others in the village not connected with the Iron Company, who subscribed to maintain a teacher. The last master there was one Johnstone by name. He went by the nickname (nicknames used to be common in Lochgelly) of sugar fit Johnstone, doubtless because of a deformed foot. This building stood derelict shortly after 1872, when the first Scottish Education Act was passed. It was purchased by the Lochgelly Police Commissioners in the early eighties and reconstructed to provide a public office and courtroom as well as the Headquarters of the burgh parochial board, school board, Gas Company etc. Twenty five years ago the present Town House was erected on the site.

Beyond this point to the north there were no houses till the development of coal mining when a number of streets were made in the moor area. There is one exception, the clachan of Cooperhall, the home, along with old Launcherhead, of the earliest Lochgelly miners. The buildings at Cooperhall were razed about 30 years ago. Cooperhall field was the centre of sport for a generation. Before the advent of football, which came comparatively late to Lochgelly, a strong cricket club played there. Our cricket club had a good county reputation. More than half a century ago they had fixtures with Cupar, Dunfermline, Kirkcaldy and Burntisland, all still prominent clubs, and later they won the Fife Junior Championship three times in four years. When football was introduced it gradually pushed out the fine game and today there is not a cricket pitch in the town.

Across the square from the Town House is Hall Street. It took its name from the Friendly Society's hall which has a date stone denoting that it was erected in 1839. The hall was on the top flat and this hall was the centre of village life for many years.

There the penny weddings took place. In it the friendly societies met. It was the lodge room too of the Free Masons. It was here that the Free Church (now Macainsh) congregation had its inception a few years after the Disruption. It was also, up to the erection of the Drill (Town) Hall in 1892, the headquarters of the local company of volunteers.

The other houses in Hall Street (north side) were built by Lochgelly Iron Company in 1854. They are still occupied but unless reconstructed will doubtless soon be scheduled for demolition. Within my recollection there was a house near the bottom of the street on the south side which came to be known as the Auld Hoose. It had a thatched roof and it was commemorated by a local blend of whisky, the label of the bottle bearing a picture of what must have been one of the oldest houses in the town. I haven't seen that particular blend for many years though I can answer for its good quality. This house was occupied by the Chisholm family, who came from England and were involved in the management of the Lochgelly Pits.

We are now on the site of the old Lochgelly Moor or Common, for long associated with the Lochgelly tribe of gypsies and the Lochgelly Markets.

The Lochgelly band or gang as they were sometimes termed was well known over the north and east of Scotland. Lochgelly Moor was one of the four recognised settlements in Scotland of that peculiar people and indeed for a period Lochgelly ranked only second to Yetholm. Part of the Lochgelly band had a smaller settlement at Pattiesmuir down about Limekilns. These gypsies should not of course be confused with the modern tinker for they still retained the characteristics and breed of the race which first came to Scotland in the sixteenth century. They were real gypsies, a race apart. They had their own language though in the course of time they would also speak the vernacular. Robert Chambers calculated that they entered Scotland about the year 1540 and that they were of Hindu origin, driven from their homes by foreign invaders and wandering right across Europe. Their speech, features and complexion lend colour to this theory. They called themselves Romain and styled their leaders "Lords and Dukes of Little Egypt". They roved above in bands, "swapping" horses, telling fortunes by palmistry (a speciality of their women folk), besides robbing henroosts and practising tinkering, making horn spoons, so much in vogue in auld Scotland. (I remember as a boy supping my porridge with a bone spoon out of a luggie.) Towards the end of the reign of James V the gypsies entered Scotland from England and John Faa, their leader, obtained a writ from the King, which recognised his jurisdiction within his own band, thus saving the gypsies from the grip of Scottish law. James accepted them at first as noble refugees, but in time they were discovered to be mere rogues and vagabonds for later the Privy Council declared that "the commonwealth of this realm was greatly damnified and harmit through certain idle, vagabond and counterfeit people of divers nations falsely named Egyptians, living on stowth (theft) and unlawful means".

Many laws were passed in the course of time against them and many of the barbarous punishments of the time inflicted on them but they continued to carry on their horse stealing and other offences with impunity. Coal masters were authorised to put them to labour at the time when the colliers were still in serfdom.

When the band settled in Lochgelly is not known but certain it is that this place was their headquarters in Fife.

They held such interest at the beginning of last century as to attract the attention of Walter Scott. Scott was interested in gypsies and introduced them into his romance of Guy Mannering. As this was written after his visit to Lochgelly he may have made use of the information he gained at Lochgelly in describing the gypsy traits and characters in that novel. Scott states that he went to Lochgelly where he met a man (1816) who was able to furnish many particulars of the tribe. He gives a list of common surnames which include Gordon, Shaw, Brown, Kennedy, Young, Blyth, Allan, Johnstone and Marshall, and he also states that descendants of these gypsies settled down in the village. Comparing them with the border tribes, Scott comments on the similarity of manners and speech. "They have certain signs," he says, "by which a gypsy of Lochgellie in Fife could in a moment, and at considerable distance, recognise one of his own fraternity."

Sir Walter proceeds to give some stories of what he terms "that celebrated band that resided in the west of Fife called the Lochgellie Band."

"I have been at considerable pains" he writes, "in scrutinising some of the traditions relating to those Lochgellie gypsies and the following traditional facts which I believe myself to be true relate to that horde who were dreaded for their depredations and at one time well known to the country people all over the shires of Fife, Kinross, Perth, Angus, Mearns and Aberdeen by the name of the Lochgellie band."

"That I might be fully satisfied" he continues "with the truths related of this desperate band I went to Lochgellie on purpose where I heard from the mouth of _____ (he leaves the name blank) a great many particulars." He quotes from the statistical account of Auchterderran where they are referred to as tinkers or horners, half resident and half itinerant, who are feared and suspected by the community.

The gypsies however observed that usual policy of keeping their ain holes clean but sometimes messengers from as far off as Perthshire were seen searching their tents or houses for stolen articles but they never found anything and it is actually stated that since the gypsies left Lochgellie, petty thefts have become more common in the village. Such was the number of gypsies assembled at Lochgelly that it was difficult to say who were residents and who were not. Some of them in time got feus from the proprietors of the estate of Lochgellie and built houses.

"Old Charlie Graham about 30 years ago (30 years before Scott paid our village the honour of a visit) was considered their chief, but when I put the question to _____ he said – 'They were a' chiefs when drunk but Charlie was the auldest.' I have however," continues Scott, "received certain information that the Grahams were the principal family and transacted the principal business of the horde. Graham was an uncommon stout fine looking fellow and was banished from the Kingdom for his many crimes."

On one occasion when he appeared in Court, the judge in a surly manner demanded of him what had brought him there. "The auld thing again, my lord, but nae proof" answered Charlie.

Ann Brown, one of his wives and chief female of the band was also sentenced to be banished for 14 years. She was nine years at Botany Bay, married a gypsy there and returned to Scotland with more than £100 in cash. With this she started to hawk earthenware. Asked why she left Botany Bay when making so much money there she said "It was jist tae lat them see I could come hame again."

Young Charlie Graham, son and successor of the chief of the Lochgellie band, was hanged at Perth about 1790 for horse stealing. The anecdotes told of this wonderful man are numerous. When he was apprehended a number of persons assembled to look at him as an object of wonder, it having been considered almost impossible to catch him. He became infuriated at their curiosity and called out with great bitterness to the officers "Let me free and gie me a stick three feet lang and I'll clear the knowe o' them".

It was his faithful dog which proved his undoing for it disclosed to the pursuers his place of concealment. Knowing that a picket of soldiers was pursuing him, Charlie took flight to the north. In the vicinity of Perth he found the soldiers again on his track. Escaping, he ran to the Kinnoull hill, then a wild upland, and with characteristic stratagem secreted himself in a thicket of whins and bushes. Then the incident of touching pathos occurred. The faithful dog, whose fidelity had overcome its sagacity, sprang forward in a clamour of threats on hearing the footsteps of the soldiers and thus made known his whereabouts. He was thereupon apprehended. His feet and hands were so small and handsome in proportion to the other parts of his athletic body that neither irons nor handcuffs could be kept on his ankles or wrists. They were always slipping over his joints. He had a prepossessing countenance, an elegant figure, had much generosity of heart, and was, not withstanding his tricks, an extraordinary favourite with the public. But by habit and repute a thief the scales of justice eventually brought down this unfortunate gypsy. He was first married to a native of Fife but he abandoned this woman because she could not travel about with him.

He once, unobserved of course, converted a young colt into a gelding. He allowed the animal to remain in the same field for a short time and then stole it. He was immediately suspected but the owner of the horse swore to one type of horse whereas the horse Charlie was caught with was a gelding by which stratagem he got off clear. He sold the same horse to a third person, again stole it, and at last replaced the beast in the park of the original owner.

He seemed to take great delight in stealing in this ingenious way trying how dexterously he could carry off the property. He sometimes stole from wealthy individuals and gave the booty to the poorer people. So accustomed were the people to his robberies that some only put spurs to their horses as they passed with the remark "Aha, Charlie, you've missed your mark the nicht."

The widow of a large family at whose house he frequently stayed was in great distress for want of cash to pay her rent. Graham lent her the money required, but as the factor was returning home with the cash in his pocket, he robbed him and gave the woman a full discharge for the sum she had borrowed. When asked immediately before his execution if he had ever performed any good actions during his life to recommend him to the mercy of his offended God, this incident of giving the widow and fatherless children the rent of which he had robbed the factor is the only instance he adduced in his favour, thinking thereby he had performed a virtuous deed.

On the morning of the day he was to suffer he sent a message to the magistrates of Perth requesting a razor to take off his beard, at the same time in a calm and cool manner desiring the messenger to tell the magistrates "that unless his beard was shorn he could neither appear before God nor man." This extraordinary expression, observes Scott, warrants the opinion that at this moment of his life he imagined he would appear in his mortal frame before the great judge of the universe. These dreadful words further made one think that he believed that God Almighty was a being composed of flesh and blood like an ordinary earthly judge.

A short while before he was taken to the gallows he was observed very pensive and thoughtful leaning upon a seat. He started up all at once and exclaimed in a mournful tone of voice "Oh, can ony o' ye read sirs; will some o' ye read a psalm to me", at the same time regretting much that he had not been taught to read. The 51st psalm was accordingly read to him by a gentleman present which soothed his feelings exceedingly and gave him much ease and comfort of mind. He was greatly agitated when he ascended the platform, his knees were knocking against each other but just before he was cast off his inveterate gypsy feelings returned upon him with redoubled violence. He kicked from his feet both his shoes in sight of the spectators and it was understood by all present this was to set at naught some prophecy that he would die with his shoes on.

A number of his Lochgellie band attended his execution and when his body was returned to them they all kissed it with great affection and held the usual "late-wake" over it. His sweetheart or gypsy wife – I am not sure which, says Scott – of the name of Wilson, put his corpse into hot lime, then buried the remains and sat on the grave in a state of intoxication till the body was rendered unfit for the use of the medical gentlemen for dissection, it having been reported that the body was to be taken out of the grave for that purpose.

So passed away the most famous of the Lochgellie gypsies.

Another chief of the Lochgellie tribe was Geordie Drummond. Scott says he died a natural death within 16 years of his visit to Lochgelly, so that Drummond must have been living less than 140 years ago. He consoled himself in his last moments with the satisfaction of never having been guilty of murder but acknowledged with the greatest indifference, even indeed boasted, that he had committed almost every other crime.

We find however, adds Scott, that there had been numberless murders committed by gypsies in their internal quarrels among their own tribe, but they all appear to have great reluctance in taking the lives of the natives among whom they resided.

From another source than Scott, I came across a reference to another Lochgellie gypsy by name Sandy Brown, a noted member of the band. He sustained sometimes the part of the strolling gypsy and sometimes that of the gentleman highwayman somewhat after the style of Blande Duval. In the latter capacity he wore, when in full dress, a hat richly ornamented and trimmed with beautiful gold lace which was then the fashion among the highest ranks in Scotland. His coat was made of superfine cloth of a light green colour, long in the tails and having one row of buttons at the breast. His shirt, of the finest quality, was ruffled at the neck and bands and he had a stock and buckle round his neck. He also wore a pair of fashionable boots with silver plated spurs, all in the fashion of the day. Below his garments he carried a large knife and in the haft or butt-end a small spear or dagger was concealed. His brother-in-law, a gypsy called Wilson, wore a similar garb and both rode the finest horses in the county. Both were said to have been favourites with the country people.

In his capacity as a mere gypsy thief, Brown was as expert as he was dashing in his other capacity as a highwayman. Once being in need of butcher meat for his tribe he resolved to steal a bullock which he had observed grazing in a field in the country of Linlithgow and which by some accident had lost about three fourths of its tail. He purchased from a tanner the tail of a skin the same colour as the bullock and in an ingenious manner made it fast to the remaining part of the tail of the living animal. He then drove off the booty for his Fife encampment. But as he was shipping the beast at the Queensferry on his way home a servant who had been dispatched in quest of the depredator overtook him. An altercation immediately commenced; the servant said he could swear to the ox in Brown's possession were it not for its long tail, and was accordingly proceeding to examine it closely to satisfy himself in this particular when the ready witted gypsy took a knife out of his pocket, and in view of all present, cut the false tail from the animal, taking a part of the real tail along with it, which instantly drew blood. "Swear to the ox now you scoundrel" said he, throwing the tail into the sea.

In the end, after many hairbreadth escapes, Brown and his brother-in-law came within the sweep of the law. They were hanged together in Edinburgh, and horrible to relate, "while these wretches were shivering in the wind, in the throes of death, Martha, the mother of the former and mother-in-law of the latter, was apprehended on the spot on the act of stealing a pair of sheets that were to be used to wrap the bodies of the two poor unfortunate men."

The gypsies did a good deal of kidnapping. One of the exploits charged against the Lochgellie tribe was the stealing of the great Scottish philosopher economist Adam Smith when a child. Smith of course was a native of Kirkcaldy and was taken for a change to stay with friends named Douglas, then occupying Strathendene House a little beyond Auchmuir bridge on the north road to Leslie. The gypsies were chased and the child recaptured. One can hardly refrain, says a writer, from putting the query, where the modern science of political economy would have been had Adam Smith become a gypsy.

The Charlie Graham already referred to as chief of the tribe once entertained a prominent English gypsy. This man had entered Scotland disguised as a gentleman. Graham while out scouting in Fife recognised by signal this ambassador who was well dressed and mounted. They were exceedingly happy at meeting with one another. This stranger was taken to Lochgellie and there feasted and entertained with all the hospitality and kindness peculiar to the tribe. Female gypsies from England are also reported to have been seen in this district.

It is wearing on to a hundred and fifty years since the Lochgellie tribe was dispersed and they are now rarely referred to. I can recall however when they were, and the phrase often used – "watch or the gypsies'll tak ye awa." Tradition has it that several settled in the village and married with Lochgelly folks. In this they broke from their own custom of only marrying within their own circle – A Romany lass for a Romany lad. I have heard the names of old Lochgelly families mentioned as having gypsy blood but perhaps it would not be expedient to mention these names.

Lochgelly Muir, which has such a close connection with the gypsies, was in a general sense of considerable extent, but in a more particular sense confined only to a portion of the area which today is known as the Moor and includes Haggis Ha.' It is on Haggis Ha' and not on the moor proper that the Happy Land is built. Lochgelly Moor however covered a big area stretching south and south-westwards from Auchterderran Road. Right along to Cowdenbeath the land has been described as a vast area of heather and whins which was all but impassable in the summer months. Along that moor of the wayside encampments, says a writer, could be seen the blazing fire with pot suspended over it; the panniered ass and the little dark-eyed tawny-faced children slung in baskets, the sun-burnt swarthy men and equally swarthy women lounging lazily under their canvas shade.

The moor proper which was the Lochgelly Common, extended to ten acres. It was on this common or moor that the Lochgelly fairs and markets were held. They were established by act of parliament in 1705 when Murray of Melgund, who had married a Kinninmonth, owned Lochgelly estate. He was granted an order to hold two fairs at the town of Lochgelly, one on the third Tuesday of May and the other on the third Tuesday of September. They were mainly cattle fairs but horses and all sorts of merchandise was brought there for sale. Lochgelly markets came to an end about the middle of last century but at the old dates stalls continued to be set up round about the present Town House for years after.

In Oliver and Boyd's Almanack for 1869 the Lochgelly fairs are still mentioned, one on the first Thursday of April (old style) and the other on the third Wednesday of July. Two cattle markets are also in the Scottish list, one on the third Wednesday of September and the other on the first Thursday of November. Lochgelly in earlier days was an important centre and the fairs were an event for the country folk for miles around.

The cattle sales were however finished when Lord Minto appropriated, or alternatively reclaimed, the common land which had been granted for the markets by an ancestor and thus paved the way for the building of Grainger Street and the other streets adjoining.

The first houses erected by the Iron Company were built in 1848. Incidentally, the Police Station was built in 1875.

The streets used to have different names to now. What was Kennard Street was formerly School Raw (due doubtless to its proximity to the Iron Company's School); Grainger Street was then the Store Raw on account of the Iron Company store there; and Minto Street was the Plantin' Raw, for the present Public Park (the Berry plantin') at one time stretched down to near Auchterderran Road.

When the superior took over the moor there was great indignation in the village. It had, they claimed, been used for certain prescriptive rights, such as taking sand and pasturing cattle. There also the Lochgelly weavers steeped their lint in the water holes. There was a lot of talk, I have been told, of the villagers contesting the right of the superior to take possession of the common but eventually Lord Minto confirmed his claim to it by legal process.

After being ejected from the moor, fairs continued to be held in the open space on the east side of the Town House which then stretched further north.

Alexander Brown, the poet, was a pupil at the old Subscription School where the Town House now stands, and which he speaks of as being just outside the village, referred to these markets in his reminiscences of old Victorian days. When the stalls were being set up, he says, in front of the school, there were many furtive glances of the youngsters out of the windows. They never considered the market to be fully constituted till Rabbie Salmond's big gingerbread van appeared on the scene and his stand was fitted up. Rabbie Salmond was the very picture of pleasantness and politeness and had a nice word for everybody without saying too much. Rabbie Salmond came from Kirkcaldy and was for long a household word in the village.

The moor, continues Mr Brown, was the village playground. When he first went to school (which would be about 1840 or 41) and his attention was called to two circus rings, he was told that one was Checkers ring and the other Ord's. Thomas Ord, who was the son of a border clergyman, was the most famous of Scottish circus performers. He was a regular visitor to Lochgelly and created great delight to old and young. He was a man who was highly respected and there was a belief current that he went to church every Sunday wherever he was and that he always put a £1 in the collection plate.

In my young days the Square was still used for shows. Among my earliest recollection is being taken to a menagerie there and seeing wild animals for the first time. Later the circuses put up at the Birnie Braes and were run by one called Delaney who is said to be a son-in-law of the famous Ord.

The present names of the streets in the moor area were given when the burgh was formed in 1877. They perpetuate the partners of Lochgelly Iron Company formed in 1846 – Henderson, Grainger, Kennard and Russell. The other streets in that part are named after the second and third provosts of the town – James Melville and John Hunter, and the two together are known as the Happy Land. The latter were erected when Minto (Brighills) Colliery was started early in the present century. I recall seeing the plans. They showed the ground between the backs of the streets as laid out for gardens and drying greens but unfortunately this idea was not carried through.

The burgh boundary terminates on the east on the road that leads to the old brickwork sawmill. On the right of the road is the Newton farm better known as Boswell Knowe. This name recalls that the lands of Easter Lochgelly at one time belonged to that famous family which produced the biographer of Dr Johnson and the Fife branch of which had been centred for centuries in the Auchtertool district. I had a considerable search in this connection when I wrote a retrospect of Lochgelly for a book for this church on the occasion of a big bazaar 24 years ago. I found that originally it was church land included in the extensive possessions of the Monastery of Inchcolm. Later it came into possession of the Boswells.

This farm of Boswell Knowe is the only evidence left of the Boswell superiorship. It is now of course in the estate of Lord Minto to whom it came through the Kinninmonth of that ilk. Along what was once a fine avenue the road leads to the cemetery. The older part was laid out in the sixties of last century. Previous to then all burials were at Auchterderran Kirkyard. The latter was closed to new interments many years ago and there are only one or two persons now living for whom interment there can be claimed. About thirty years ago Lochgelly cemetery was extended westwards and the two are now known as the old and the new cemeteries. They are better known locally as Shakemdud. I have tried without success to get at a derivation of that word. In his history of the parish of Auchterderran the late Dr Houston gives an explanation of the origin of the name Shakemdud. He says "it is really shaking your duds (clothes) in token of having passed through the gypsy camps around the moor without becoming a victim of their crimes." The word "shake," he adds, is a symbol of "liberty". This is a somewhat ingenious explanation but personally I don't attach much value to it.

At Brighills we cross the river Ore. Across the water we enter a district in which formerly were many small estates. Dr Blair of Dunblane (a distinguished native of the parish) in a short essay on the district declared that in the course of fifteen minutes walk from Dundonald to Silvertoon he counted twelve lairds' lands in regular succession. These lairds were known as Bonnet Lairds, the bonnet showing their social status. It was of course the custom in earlier days that one's social grade was known by the apparel one wore. At one time indeed this was regulated by several acts of the Scottish Parliament.

One of these estates just beyond Brighills was known as "Hunger 'im oot." I think that might be identified as the present Ingleshall. I have seen the name "Hunger 'im oot" on an old map. Dr Blair says the name might have an allusion to an experiment practised on a herd laddie a long time ago but in stopping there he only excites curiosity. We would have liked to have heard something of the experiment. The old map also very properly spells Brighills "Bridgehills", the farm having apparently got its name from a conjunction of the bridge and its undulating natural features.

Another peculiar name a little further on beyond the Knabbs is Jamphlars. It is supposed to be the French Champfleur, place of flowers. Dr Blair also relates a story of an old laird of this estate. He rented his land to a farmer and did nothing but draw the rent. When weary of the indolence of his couch he betook himself to a tree near his house from which was suspended a luxurious

swing. Twisting his large corporation through the chains he swung and vibrat-
ed as if he were the pendulum of the parish, to the infinite delight of the young
laird and ladyship.

Away to the right is the farm of Spittal. This is supposed to have been the
site of a hospital or hospice but the only reason for that supposition is its
name. It may however have had some connection with the religious settlement
of St Finnan.

On the opposite side of the Lochgelly burn which runs through Carden
Den, locally the Den, is the ruin of Carden Tower. There is now little of it left,
due, it is said, to the act of a farmer named Smith who pulled down a portion
of the walls a hundred years ago to fill up drains. It is reckoned to have been a
structure of large dimensions, a baronial castle. There was once a barony of
Carden, for long in the possession of a family of the name of Betson. A
recluse named Rodney is said to have lived in a cave in the den not far from
the castle, who was so agile of foot that on one occasion he sat his kail pot on
the fire and went to Kirkcaldy and returned with the ingredients for his dinner
before it came to the boil. The den was the scene of the last duel fought in
Scotland, between two men from Kirkcaldy, one George Morgan a banker, and
the other Landale, a merchant. Landale had overdrawn his bank account to the
extent of £2,000, and he blamed the banker for telling others. They fought
with pistols (which can be seen in Kirkcaldy Art Gallery and Museum.)
Morgan was mortally wounded, and Landale was tried and acquitted.

The Burgh of Lochgelly

(Written for the Third Statistical Account of Scotland)

Lochgelly is the pivotal centre of the eastern part of the West Fife coal-field, as comprised by the parishes of Auchterderran, Ballingry and Beath. Within a perimeter of eight miles are Dunfermline, Kirkcaldy, Burntisland, Leslie, Thornton and Kinross. In earlier times, its position gave it a special importance, and, up to the middle of last century it was a market town for the three parishes mentioned. Its name is taken from Loch Gelly, a stretch of water on the south side of the town, and, like many Fife placenames, it has a Gaelic origin and means "the bright water". At one time, it was well known for its leeches, when these formed an important item of pharmacopoeia. For a time, large quantities of eels were trapped locally and sent to the London market. Trout, too, abounded, but this species of fish has long disappeared, the victims of the voracious pike.

A community termed Lochgelly can be found in records of the 16th century, and it is probably much older. Starting from a hamlet of "tafts", it progressed in the 18th and 19th centuries to a village of growing proportions, and 70 years ago was raised to the status of a police burgh. The town is built on the northern side of a gently sloping hill, with a ridge some 600 feet above sea level dividing it from the loch. The principal superior is the Earl of Minto. A part of the town on the west side actually lies in the parish of Ballingry, and, there the land is owned by the Earl of Zetland, apart from a small portion which is the property of the Berry Trust. This small estate was bequeathed to the parish of Beath for educational purposes, and is now administered by the County Council. It is almost wholly feued by miners, who have built small brick houses for their own use. In the O.S.A., Dr Murray describes Lochgelly as the only village in the parish with a population estimated at 400. It increased gradually for a time but later at a very accelerated pace, the population doubling itself between 1881 and 1901, and, for a second time, between that date and 1921. Since then, it had declined somewhat, and in 1947 there were 9,405 inhabitants. Following the strikes of 1921 and 1926, a large number of miners emigrated to Commonwealth countries and to the United States.

THE LOCAL ECONOMY

The town's development during the last hundred years, from a weaving and agricultural village, was occasioned first of all by the production of ironstone, and later by the exploitation of a large field of bituminous coal. Coal mining started in Lochgelly towards the end of the 18th century, and, by 1836 about 100 tons per day were being produced, and 50 persons were employed. Shortly after that time, a lease of the minerals on the Lochgelly estate was granted to a partnership, which eventually became, in 1851, the Lochgelly Iron Company. The mining of ironstone and the manufacture of iron had been taken up some years previously. Blast furnaces were built in 1847, and between then and 1865 a great number of shallow pits were sunk to what proved to be a profitable deposit of blackband ironstone. In 1872, the name of the Lochgelly Iron and Coal Company Ltd, was adopted, and, from then on, efforts were mainly concentrated on the mining of coal. The importation of Spanish ore was making it increasingly uneconomical to continue the iron industry, and the furnaces were damped down in 1875.

In the middle of the 1890s a big development took place, both in Lochgelly and in the surrounding district. The annual output of coal at that time was nearly half a million tons, and came from the Mary, Melgund, Jenny Gray and Arthur pits, on the Lochgelly estate, and the Dora and Lady on the Little Raith leasehold. Under the development scheme, two pits were sunk at Brighills (the Minto Colliery), the Nellie pit was re-opened and deepened, and the Mary pit was sunk to a lower level to enable a level crosscut to reach the lowest workable seams. In 1910, the Dundonald Colliery was purchased and modernised, and, by 1913, coal output had risen to over 1 1/4 million tons. From 1893, when records were first kept, up to and including 1946, the pits in the Lochgelly area have produced 44 million tons of coal.

Mechanisation started early and continued at a rapid pace. The 75 horses used underground in 1910 had all disappeared by 1932. The first coal cutting machine and conveyor were installed in 1905, and by 1914 more than a quarter of all the coal produced was cut by machinery. In 1939 it accounted for the whole output, while all but a small fraction was transported by mechanical conveyors.

The lack of employment opportunities outside of mining has been severely felt in the town, and this is particularly true in the case of women. A generation ago they were employed in large numbers in the linen factories of Dunfermline, travelling daily in a special train. Their day lasted from five in the morning till home was reached at seven o'clock at night. A minority entered domestic service in the cities. Nowadays, both of these outlets seem to have lost their attraction, and the inclination is more towards jobs as shop assistants, typists and so on. Very badly needed locally is some industrial development of the kind that will provide work suitable for women, and alternatives for men who do not wish to become miners.

Apart from coal mining, the principal agency in the economic life of the town is the Co-operative Society. Established in 1865, in a small shop on the High Street, it has now extensive central and branch premises, within the town and in the villages of Lochore, Glencraig, Bowhill and Dundonald. The following comparative figures show the growth of the Society:-

	1865	1948
Membership	323	8,204
Trade	£936	£224,710
Share Capital	£184	£322,929
Annual Valuation of Property	£9	£3,275
Number of Employees	1	388

The one-man type of business has greatly decreased, circumscribed by the Co-operative Society and the several multiple shops that have come to the town. The decline is particularly noticeable in craft trades, like tailors, shoemakers and dressmakers, but also applies to provision and drapery businesses. Two kinds of shop that have become more numerous are those selling fish and chips, and ice-cream.

LOCAL GOVERNMENT, SERVICES AND HOUSING

The rapid growth of the village and the need for urban, communal amenities, led to the desire for municipal authority, and Lochgelly was formed into a Police Burgh in 1877. In 1892, the Police Commission became a Town Council, which, today, has twelve members from whom a Provost, four Bailies and a Dean of Guild are chosen. The Council seats are now contested on party political lines, and with one exception the present members represent the Labour point of view. It is difficult to get experienced men to stand for election. Generally, almost the entire council is composed of miners. Lochgelly was formerly the centre of parish administration for many services. Auchterderran Parochial Board met here, and, later the Public Assistance Committee, but these have now been merged into larger organisations, and the centre for such services is Cowdenbeath.

One of the first acts of the new Police Commission, after its establishment, was to provide a gravitation water supply. Hitherto the only supply had come from wells, of which there were over twenty in the town. Most of these were found, on analysis, to be contaminated. Lochornie, in the County of Kinross, was decided upon as the site for a reservoir, and gravitation water was turned on in 1881. Previously, gas lighting had been introduced in 1860, when a small works was set up in Main Street. The growth of population brought the need for a larger concern, and, in 1886, a Limited Liability Company was formed, sponsored by the managing director of the Coal Company, and supported by a number of local business men. The Company developed into a very large undertaking which, at present, manufactures just under 100 million cubic feet of gas per year. Electricity was introduced into the town in 1909.

Up till little more than a century ago, the local miners did not live in the village, but in "rows" half a mile away known as Launcherhead, The Square, Stationhead, and Cooper ha'. The village itself comprised 300 houses eighty years ago, but few of these original houses are now extant. Most of them were of the "but and ben" type, built of stone and with a large garden, and initially they belonged to the occupiers – cottars, who worked on the land and engaged in weaving and handicrafts. As mining developed, the village lost its rural aspect and gained a new environment. The Coal Company, who had owned some of the old houses, added greatly to their property in the coal boom years between about 1890 and 1914. In the same period, business premises were extended, and many small brick dwellings were erected by the miners themselves. Even so, there was insufficient accommodation, and three "model" lodging houses were always filled, mostly by unskilled labourers. Now there is still a shortage of houses, despite the programmes of the Town Council, who have pulled down many of the old "rows", and who, between the wars, built houses. Few old houses in the burgh have been reconstructed, and there has been little private building for the past two decades.

It should be noted that no coal has been worked under the old village, where the feus are "protected". In the older feu charters there is no reservation of the minerals by the landowner, who could consequently, be held for compensation for damage that might be done to property by underground workings. The coal wrought by the Company was also outside the village perimeter. That, however, does not apply to the much extended Burgh boundaries, and that a risk exists there is evidenced by the precautions that are taken against subsidence in the new housing schemes. Their foundations have been strengthened by concrete " floats", but, so far, and contrary to the experience of most mining communities, no damage to property by subsidence has yet occurred within the Burgh. Immediately beyond it, however, much water covers land where the level has fallen; and, in parts, the rivers Ore and Fitty have overflown, more or less permanently, into miniature lakes. At present, flooded land covers many acres.

EDUCATION AND RELIGION

A separate quoad sacra parish was disjoined from Auchterderran in 1856,and, as Lochgelly parish, it functioned for religious and educational services. Before Lochgelly School Board was constituted in 1872, education was well catered for in the village by a school established by Lochgelly Iron Company (and known as the Iron Company School), and by a Subscription School, administered by the feuars. The former eventually became the East School, and a new building, to replace one at "Number Four", set up by the Earl of Zetland for the benefit of miners on his property, was built at the west end of the town. Some fifty years ago a small school for Roman Catholics was built near Lumphinnans. This was the first denominational school in the district, and there are now six existing in the area which this one formerly served alone. As the school population grew, extensions were made to the Schools mentioned above, and a third was erected in High Street. Today these three together with a large school for Roman Catholics in Station Road meet the educational requirements of the Burgh, apart from higher secondary education which is got in Cowdenbeath.

When the Old Statistical Account was written Lochgelly had one Church – a Burgher congregation, later to become the U.P. There are now three Presbyterian Congregations in the burgh, all with churches built within eight years of each other, round about 1860. A Catholic Chapel was erected in 1877, and has now been replaced by a large iron church; there are Scottish Episcopal and Baptist Churches; the Salvation Army possess their own Hall; and other smaller religious denominations, like the Church of Christ, have their meeting places. There is also a Spiritualist Circle. It is noteworthy that, when the Presbyterian Churches were first erected and for long afterwards, all three were much better attended than they are now, with a population four or five times as great. The best attendances are now to be seen at St Patrick's (Roman Catholic) Church.

RECREATIONAL AND SOCIAL LIFE

Social and cultural organisations kept pace with the growth of the town.

For a long time Friendly Societies were of the first importance. Before the introduction of workmen's compensation, health insurance, etc., they proved of immense value to the miners in their hazardous occupation. The earliest, known as the Lochgelly Benefit Society, was started in 1830, but, with the inauguration of the national Friendly Societies, this pioneer became a Funeral Society, and disbursed its surplus funds annually to its members. Still carrying on in the town are the Foresters, Ancient Order of Free Gardeners, and British Order of Free Gardeners. No longer existing are the Shepherds, Rechabites, Oddfellows and Buffaloes. At one time, the Good Templars had a strong lodge, but it, too, has ceased to function.

The Lochgelly Floral and Horticultural Society was started in 1866, and was the only society of its kind in the three parishes. Its annual Show was once a red letter day, but the Society has now been defunct for many years. A seed and root show was also held in Lochgelly, run by the farmers of Auchterderran and Ballingry, but it ceased after the 1914-18 war. Much else of value has gone – the village library, and the Choral Union, both rooted in the enterprising days of the latter half of the 19th century. Lately, a Musical Society has been started. It produces musical comedy, and has so far been very successful, while instrumental music, organised in the form of bands, has always held its own. It is a form of recreation that has never failed to hold a strong appeal for the miner. The first records are of a flute band, followed by a brass band, which, 45 years ago, won the championship of Scotland, and later became junior champions of Great Britain. It still exists though its popularity fluctuates. A pipe band has had its being during the past three decades, and has won honours in the County and at Cowal, while a ladies' pipe band, of several years standing, has proved an attractive asset to the town, and is in much demand over a wide area.

An old-established annual event – the "Gymnastic" Games – became defunct soon after the 1914-18 war. In the days when the miners had only two or three holidays, and before the arrival of easy travel facilities, the Games provided the main event of the summer. The youth of the town eagerly looked forward to them, and trained to compete. With their demise, interest in field athletics declined, though individual athletes still figure in the prize lists of many a Highland Gathering. For the Games gave Lochgelly an athletic complex, which, in some measure, still survives. The town has produced more athletes and sportsmen who have represented their country than probably any other community of comparable size, as the following list shows:-

Sport	No. of Internationalists
Football (Senior)	6
Football (Junior)	5
Football (Juvenile)	1
Football (Schoolboy)	5
Football (Amateur)	1
Rugby	1
Hockey	3
Angling	3
Boxing	3
Bowling	7
Chess	1
Quoiting	2

While football has predominated for the past 60 years, it was a comparatively late arrival. Cricket, quoiting and field sports had retained a firm hold up to then. Once established, however, football gradually ousted cricket, and there is no club today, while both the former quoiting grounds have gone. For long, the town had a team of senior status, but, when the neighbouring Cowdenbeath club passed into the First Division, it proved too strong a rival. Golf was started in 1896, when a 9-hole course was laid out on the Spittal Farm. Since Cowdenbeath and Ballingry lost their courses, players from these places have joined Lochgelly, which, including the ladies' section, has over 200 members. The game of bowls began with the formation of a private club in 1874. Later, in 1896, a town club was formed, which has won all the County trophies and has a membership of 140. Tennis has been played intermittently, but the last court was taken over as part of a housing site, and the game has not been resumed. The oldest game of all associated with the town is curling, for the club was instituted in 1831, and holds the Centenary Medal of the Royal Caledonian Club. Play took place on the Loch, and, from the finding of old stones, it may be conjectured that the game is older than the Club. The modern, indoor game has almost eliminated play on the Loch.

Indoor games have become increasingly popular. Favourites are whist, bridge and billiards, unknown in the town two generations ago. Draughts also has spells of popularity, and there is talk presently of forming a Chess Club. The Miners' Welfare Institute is extensively used for all recreations of this kind. A notable development that has taken place in the past two decades is the formation of social clubs, principally for women and young people. Of the former, the oldest is the Co-operative Women's Guild, while others are the Institute Women's Guild, Black Watch Women's Guild, Brown Memorial

Women's Guild, British Legion Women's Section, and a Catholic Women's Guild. In addition, each of the three Presbyterian churches, and the Baptists, have similar organisations.

GENERAL

Over the long period, a great change has taken place in the town' s social life. The churches have lost their influence to a considerable extent, an old established Y.M.C.A has been defunct for many years, and gone, too are the Literary and Mutual Improvement Societies that exercised such a profound moral and educational influence. The bias is now towards spectating rather than active participation – towards easy entertainment like the pictures, dancing and attendance at ice hockey matches in Kirkcaldy and Dunfermline. The general impression is that modern generations are more superficial than those of an earlier day, and that a fall from traditional standards has taken place in almost every direction. Figures for juvenile delinquency reflect that general impression.